HOW TO DRAW MANGA

BISHOUJO Around the World

HOW TO DRAW MANGA: BISHOUJO Around the World
by Hikaru Hayashi, Go Office

This English edition was published in 2001 by © Graphic-sha Publishing Co., Ltd.
1-9-12 Kudan-kita, Chiyoda-ku, Tokyo, 102-0073 Japan

Planning & Production: Yasuo Matsumoto, Jun Matsubara, Kento Shimazaki, Riho Yagizawa, Takehiko Matsumoto, Kimiko Morimoto, Tomo Otomo, Kiyoe Yokoyama, Yuu Manabe
Cover drawing: Keiko Shiono
Cover Coloring: Takashi Nakagawa
Reference work: Minoru Aki, Kimiko Morimoto, Keiko Shiono, Takashi Nakagawa, Yuu Fujio
Composition & Scenario: Akira Hayashi (Go Office)
English cover logo: Hideyuki Amemura
English cover design: Shinichi Ishioka
English edition layout: Shinichi Ishioka
English translation: Christian Storms
English translation management: Língua fránca, Inc. (an3y-skmt@asahi-net.or.jp)
Japanese edition editor: Motofumi Nakanishi (Graphic-sha Publishing Co., Ltd.)
Foreign language edition project coordinator: Kumiko Sakamoto (Graphic-sha Publishing Co., Ltd.)

Distributed by
NIPPAN IPS CO., LTD
11-6, 3chome, Iidabashi, Chiyoda-ku, Tokyo
102-0072 Japan
Tel : +81(0)3-3238-0676
Fax: +81(0)3-3238-0996
E-mail: ips03@nippan-ips.co.jp

First printing: March 2001

ISBN: 4-7661-1149-4
Printed and bound in China by Everbest Printing Co., Ltd.

HOW TO DRAW MANGA

BISHOUJO Around the World

Table of Contents

How to Use This Book

Chapter 1 - Bishoujo Around the World Character Drawing Theory

Manga characters were previously divided by the differences in their hair. Presently, the differences in the face are also becoming important. The key points are: eyes and nose, the size of the mouth and the shape of the face. The expression of the hairstyles and qualities are also important in differentiating bishoujo around the world. Through anthropology, people of the world based on their looks can be simply divided into three types: Caucasoid, Negroid and Mongoloid. Studying the differences in the necessary facial features is an easy way to tell the difference. They make good reference not only for drawing people from various countries but also for increasing ordinary character variations.

Chapter 2 - How to Draw Bishoujo From Different Countries and Regions

Representative traditional clothing and fashions that can be applied to manga were selected. When drawing only one illustration, the structure of the clothing is not really necessary; however, in manga, since drawing the same piece of clothing from a variety of angles is necessary, if you don't understand the structure of the clothing and how it is worn, you can't draw it properly. In addition, by understanding the logic behind even a simple waist wrap, you can create your own fashion designs.

Chapter 3 - Ancient and Prehistoric Bishoujo

Fantasy and out-of-this-world apparel design are often based on fashion from ancient civilizations. Characters dressed in male attire, as the name suggests, follow the male fashion of these times.

Tones Mentioned in This Book

SE-61: Dotted, Delita tone (amitoons) of the number 61
TH: Design tone
IC: I. C Screen
Max: Maxon
Letra: Letraset
Sand tone
Gradation

Terms Used

Native American - The term Indian is what Columbus called the original settlers of America when he discovered the country thinking that he had landed in India. Native American is the preferred term for these people.

Eskimo - The term was once erroneously thought to mean "eaters of meat." The Arctic peoples of Canada and Greenland in general prefer the term Inuit, while those of Alaska still generally favor the term Eskimo. The term 'Eskimo' has been used throughout this book.

Supplemental Information

In addition to Mongoloid, Caucasoid and Negroid, the three body types found in anthropology, the term Australoid (for native of Papua New Guinea and Australian aboriginals) has been advocated. However, this term does not seem to be generally known. Since the frequency of use of these characters and their appearance in manga is relatively low, coverage of this term was left out in this book.

Chapter 1

Bishoujo Around the World Character Drawing Theory

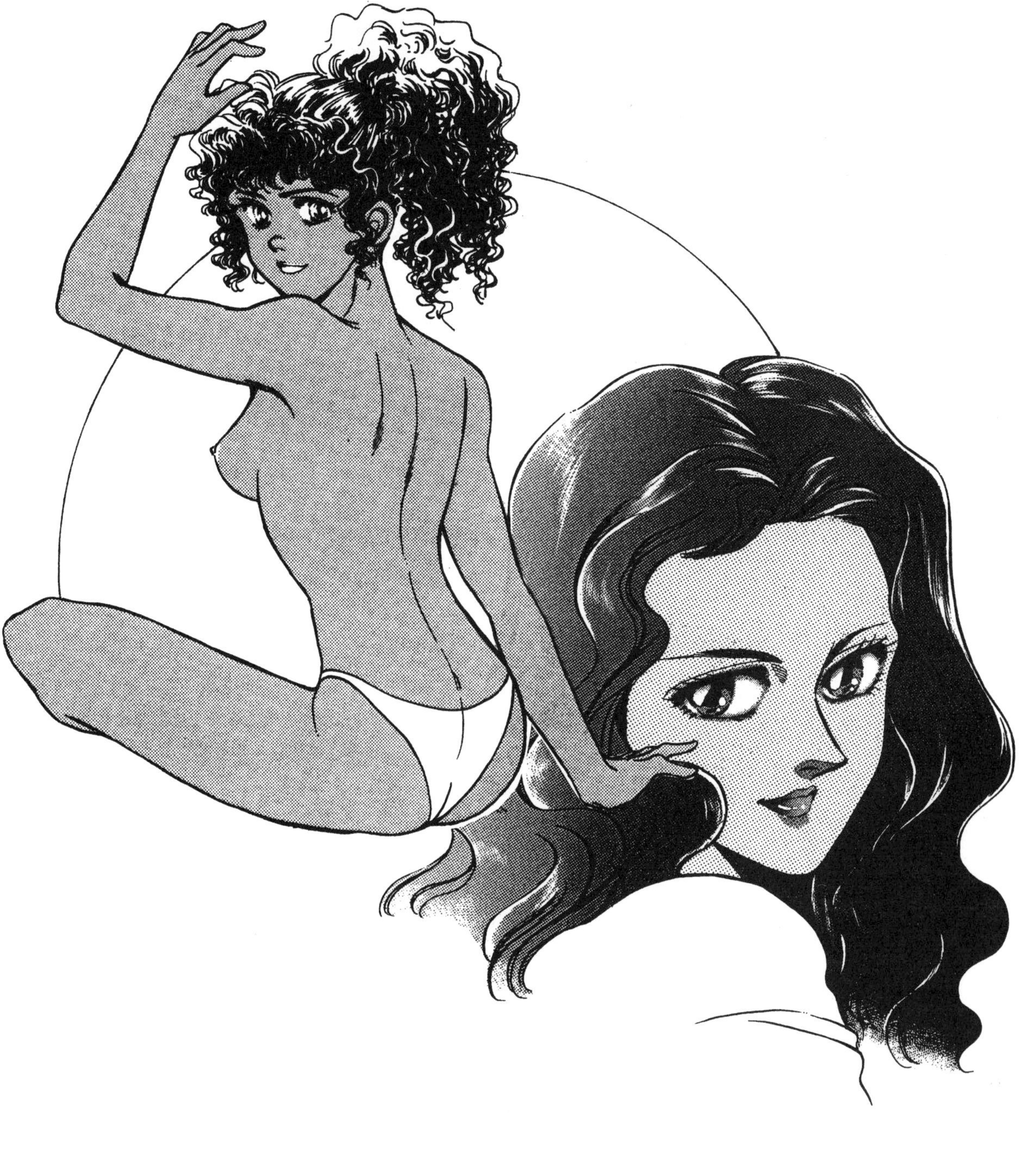

Three Types Found in Anthropology

The human race can visually be divided into three main types: Mongoloid, Caucasoid and Negroid.

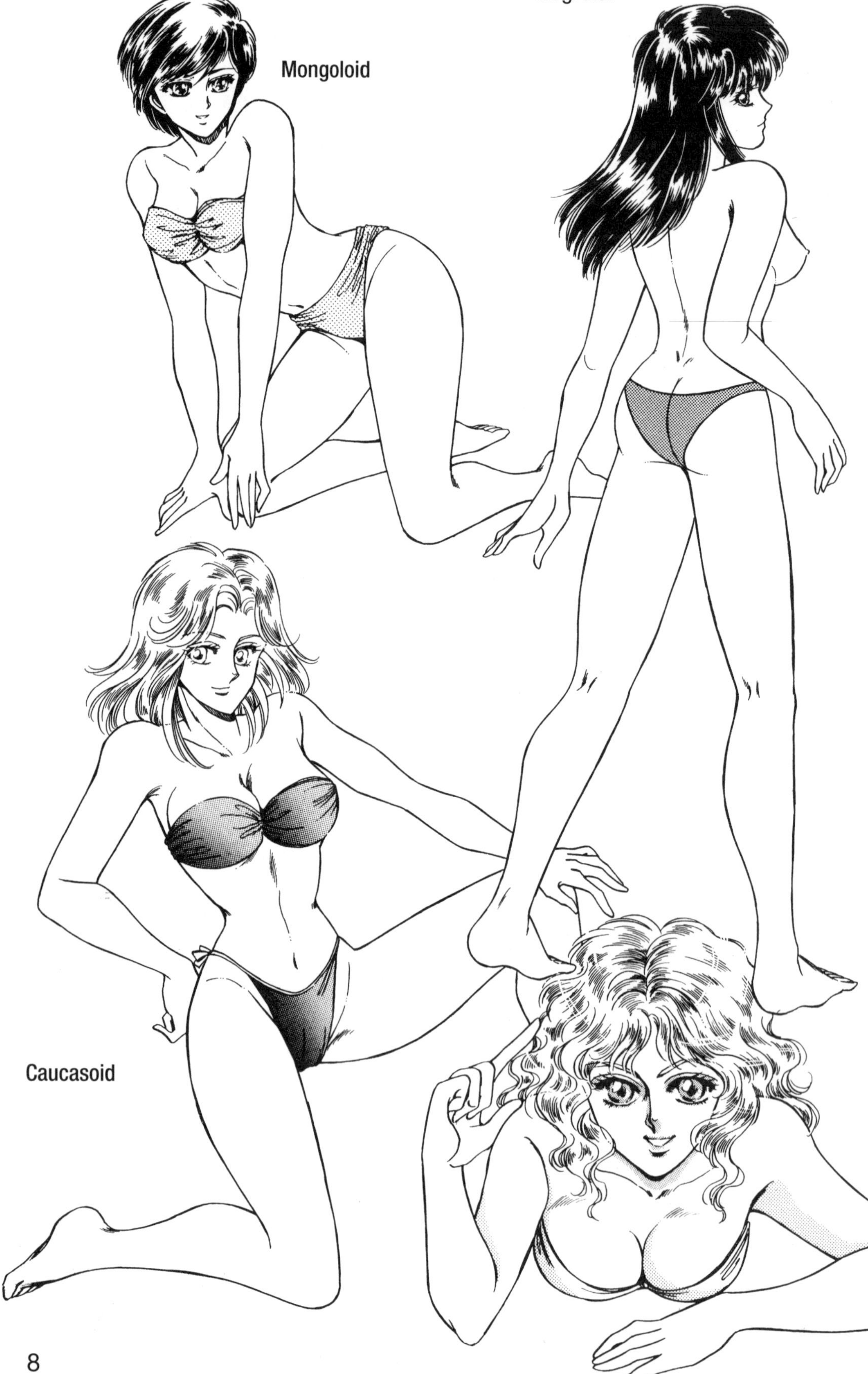

One

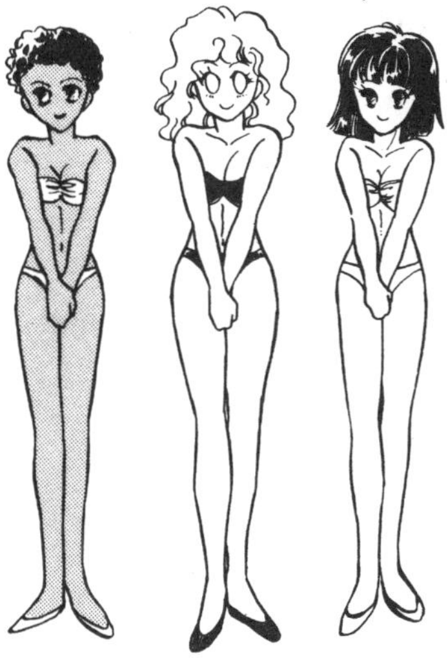

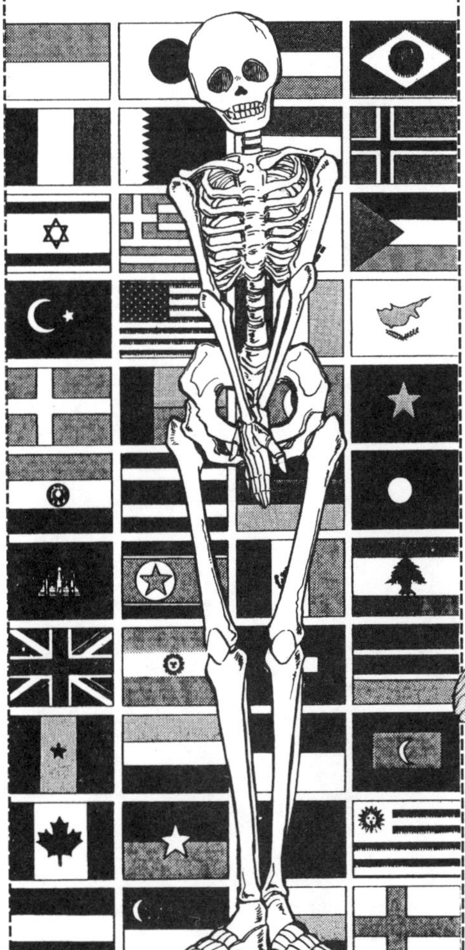

Everyone has the same skeletal structure.

Negroid

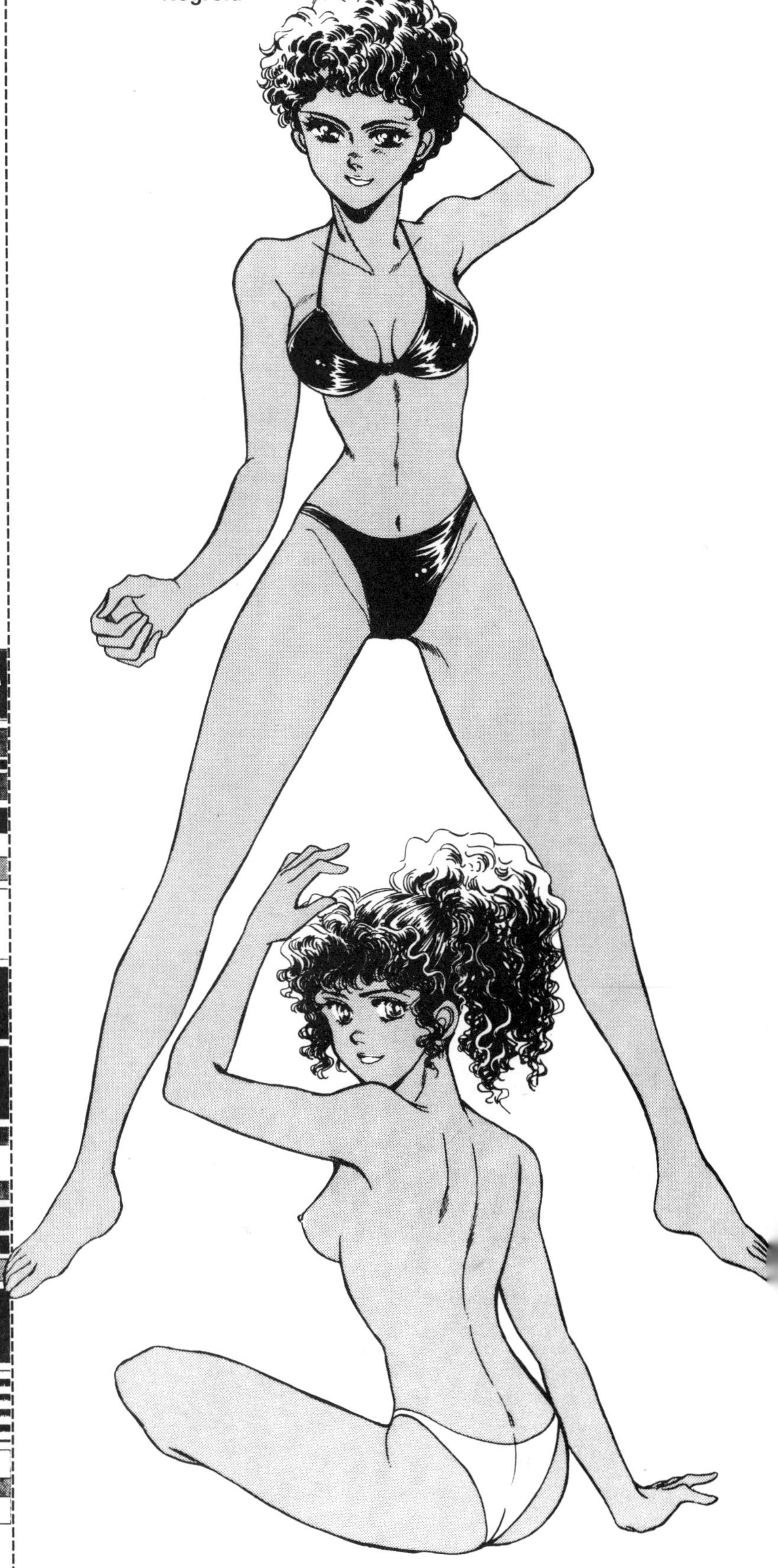

Key Differences

Facial Characteristics

Mongoloid

For Bishoujo from Japan, China, Korea and Southeast Asian

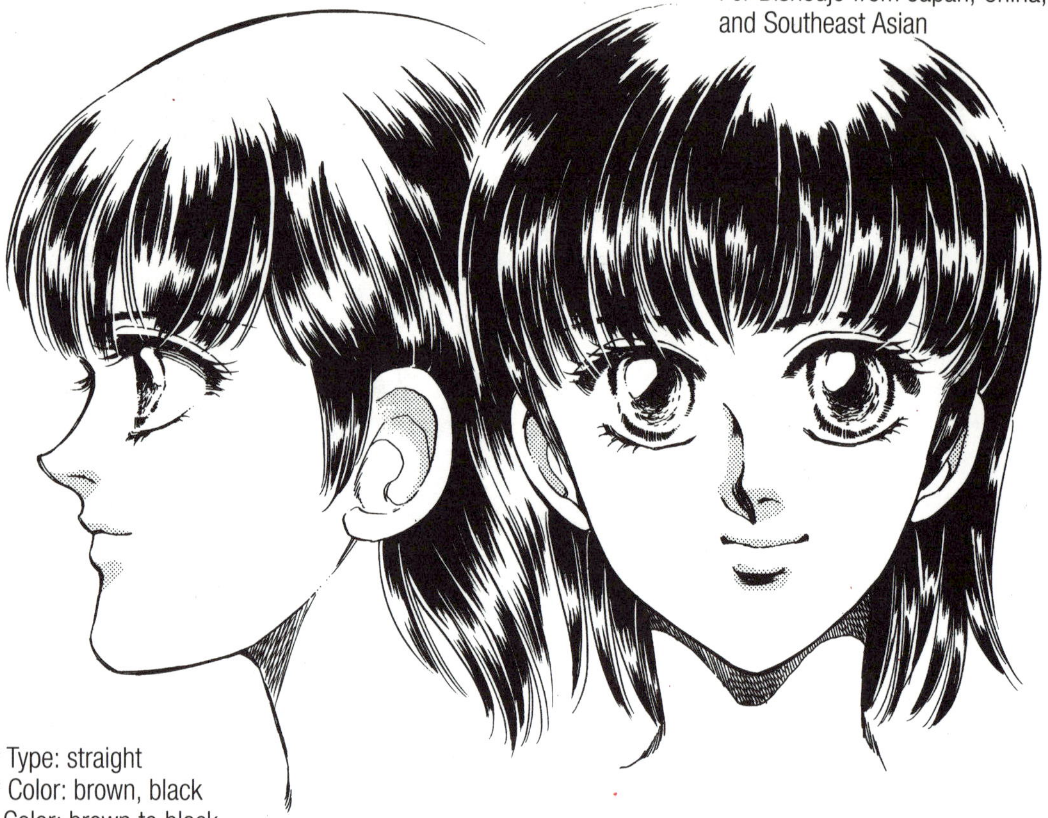

Hair Type: straight
Hair Color: brown, black
Eye Color: brown to black
Size of Nose/Mouth: small

Caucasoid

For Bishoujo from Europe, Scandinavia, the Mediterranean and the Middle East

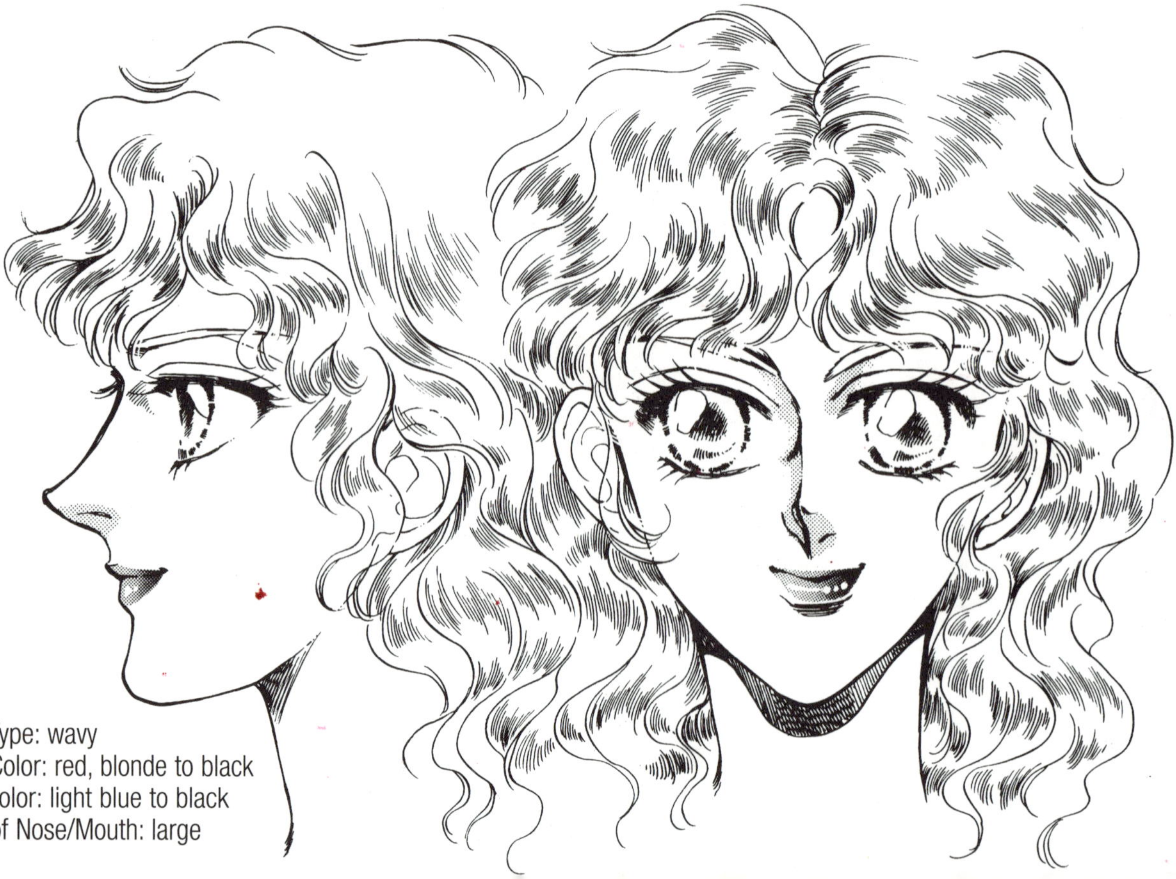

Hair Type: wavy
Hair Color: red, blonde to black
Eye Color: light blue to black
Size of Nose/Mouth: large

Negroid

For Bishoujo from Ethiopia and other African Nationalities

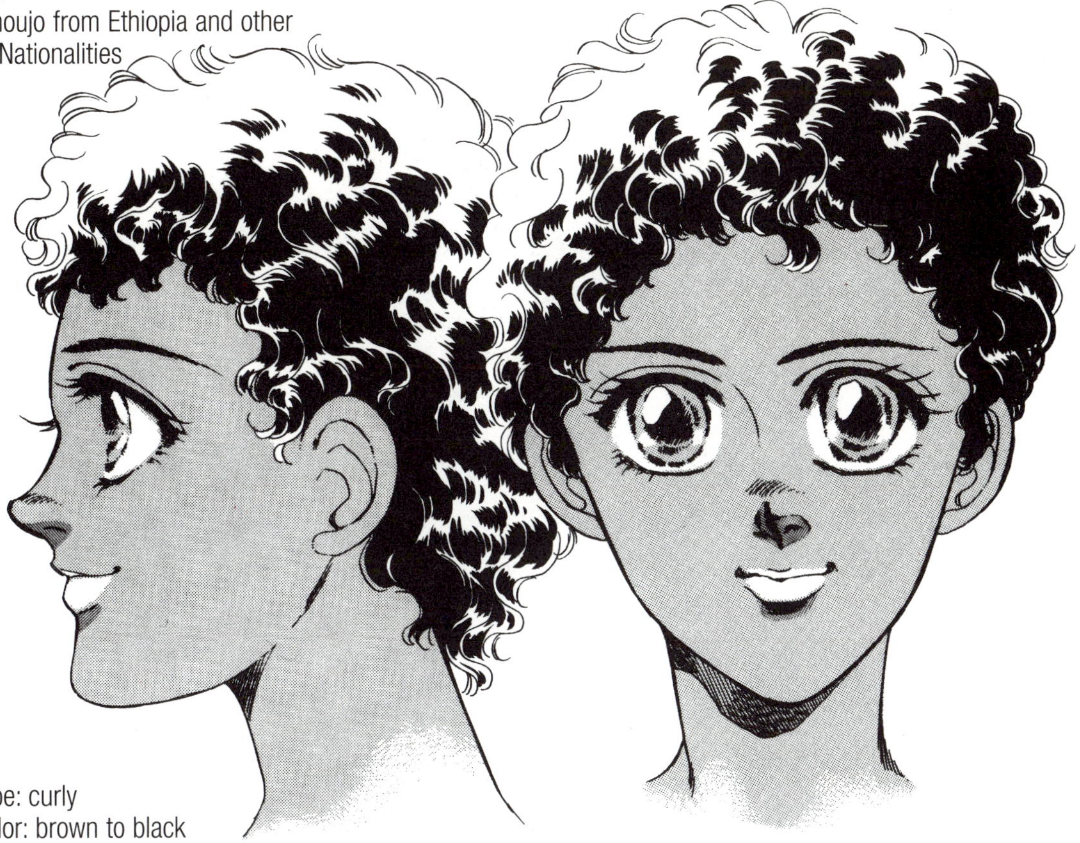

Hair Type: curly
Hair Color: brown to black
Eye Color: brown to black
Size of Nose/Mouth: compared to other types the nose is smaller and the mouth is larger.

Glossy Negroid Skin

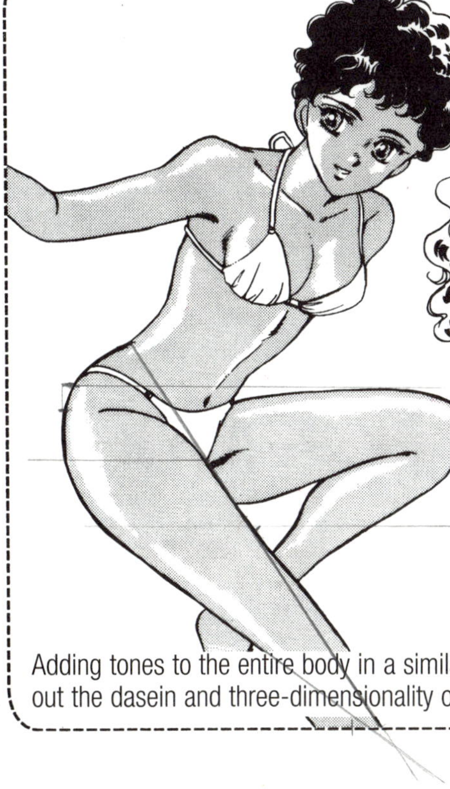

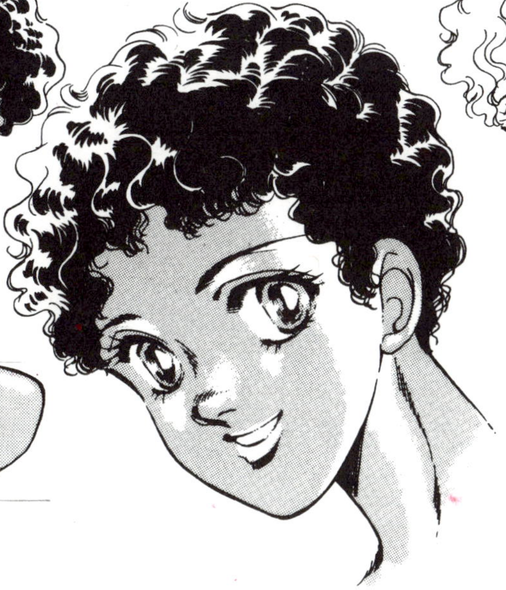

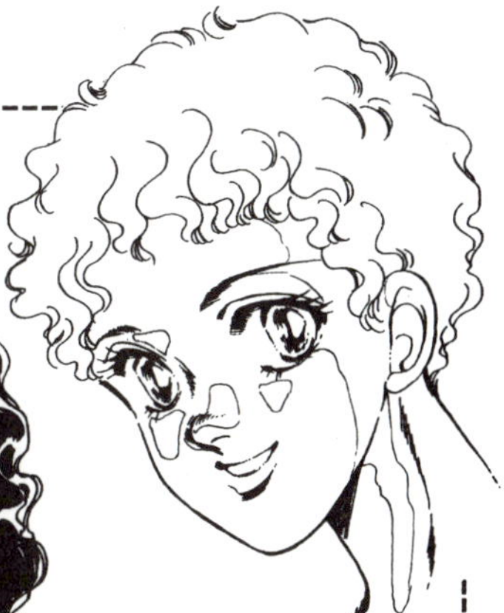

Negroid characters have glowing skin. Etching tones and adding shine makes these characters attractive.

Adding tones to the entire body in a similar manner brings out the dasein and three-dimensionality of the physique.

Use 10% to 30% tones. Finely dotted tones (amitoons) are easy to use with both close-ups and long shots.

Physical Characteristics

Caucasoid | Negroid | Mongoloid

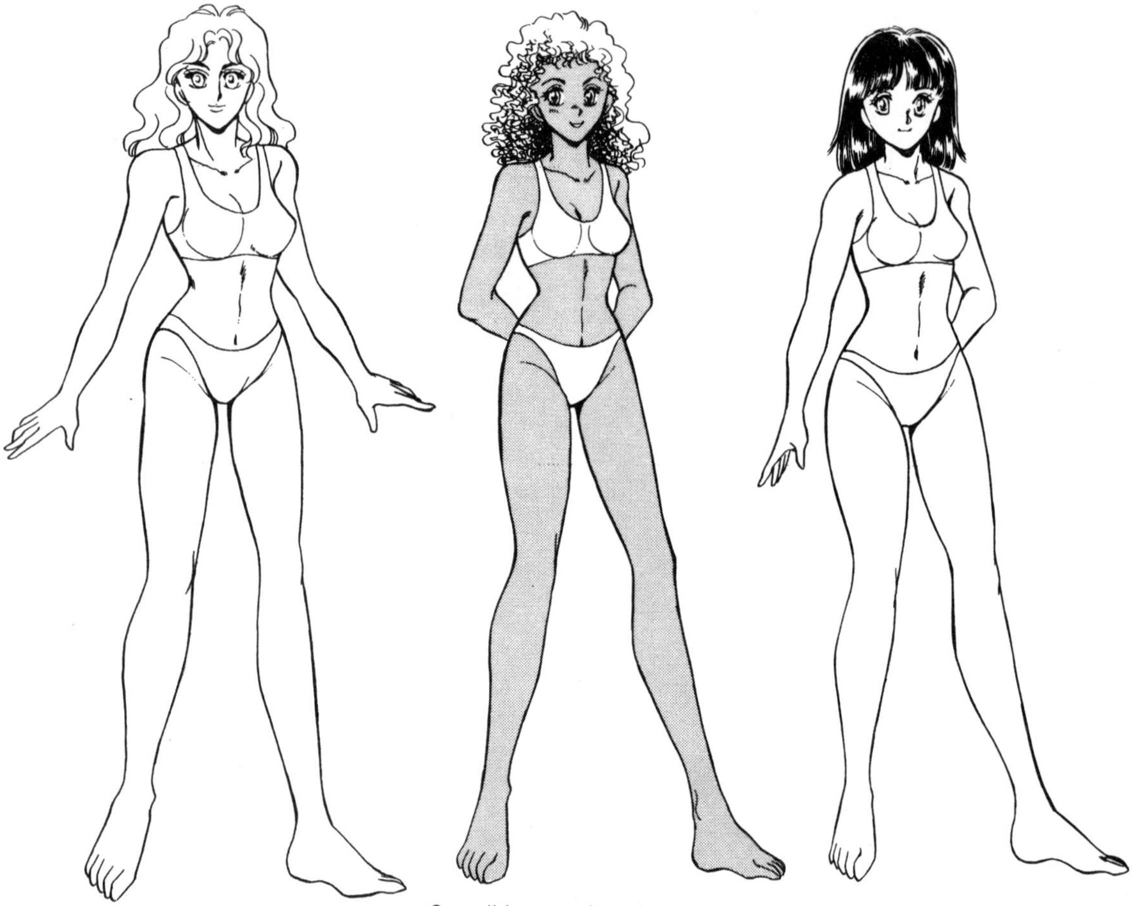

Overall Image: strongly built
Shoulders: wide
Make the width of the shoulders and buttocks larger.

Overall Image: dauntlessness, sharp
Shoulders: sturdy
Draw the buttocks on the small side and position the waist on the high side.

Overall Image: round
Shoulders: narrow
Try drawing the buttocks on the large side.

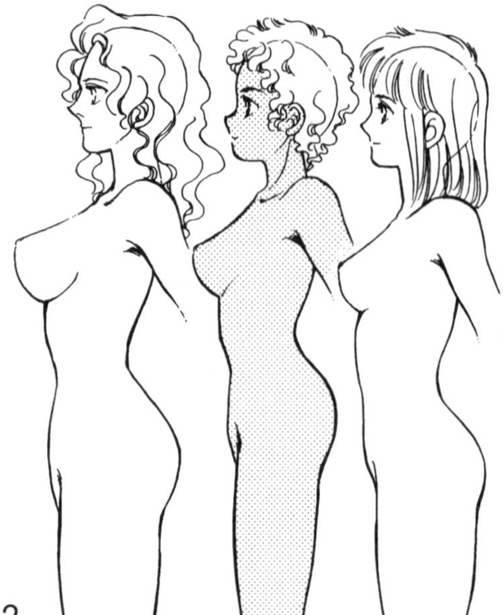

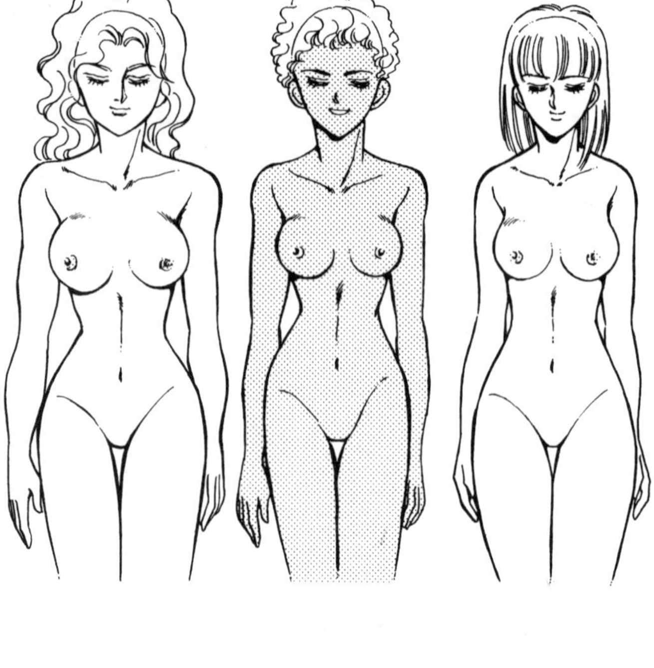

Emphasize the relative differences when drawing. The key is to choose one as a standard so that you can draw the other two by making changes here and there.

Sharpen the tip of the shoulder.

Firmly broaden the shoulder.

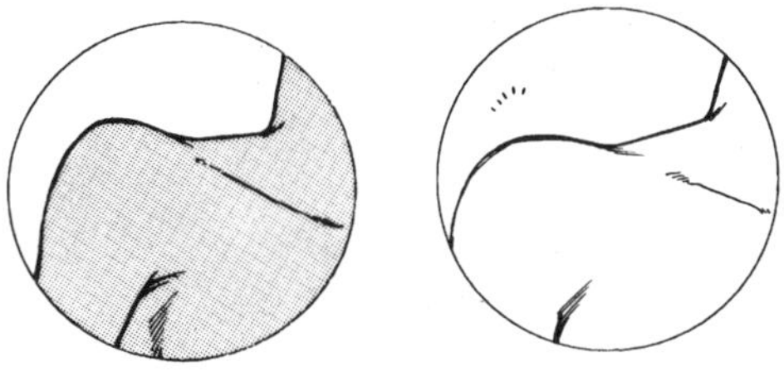

The arms and legs are slightly longer with these two types than that of a Mongoloid bishoujo.

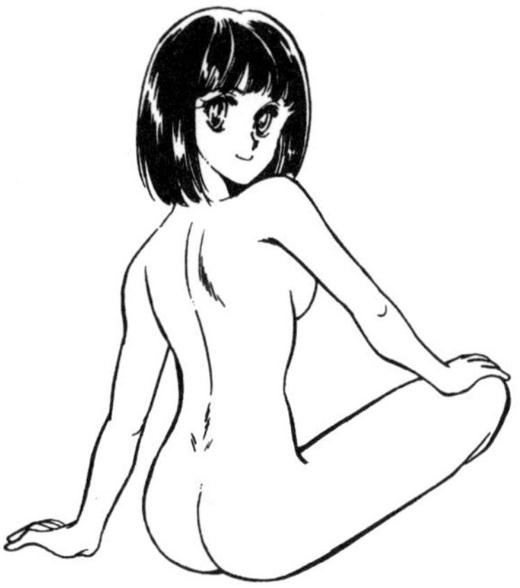

If you draw a Mongoloid bishoujo, then...

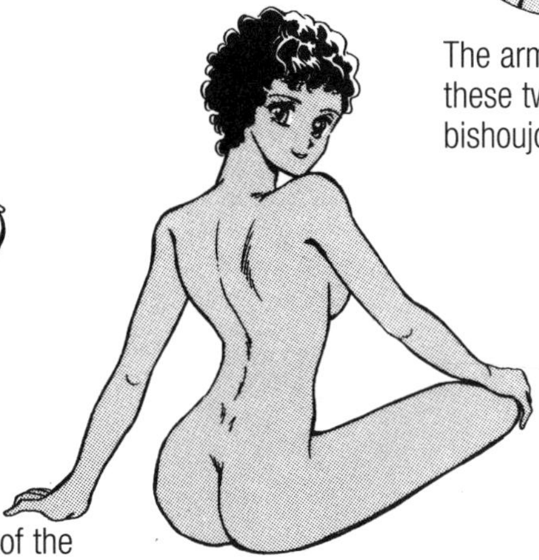

change the lines of the arms and thighs rendering sharp muscles.

Emphasize the bay of the waist and buttocks.

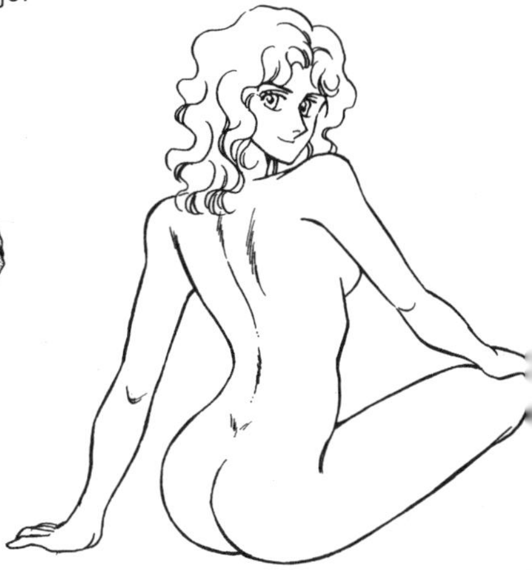

Expand the width of the side of the buttocks.

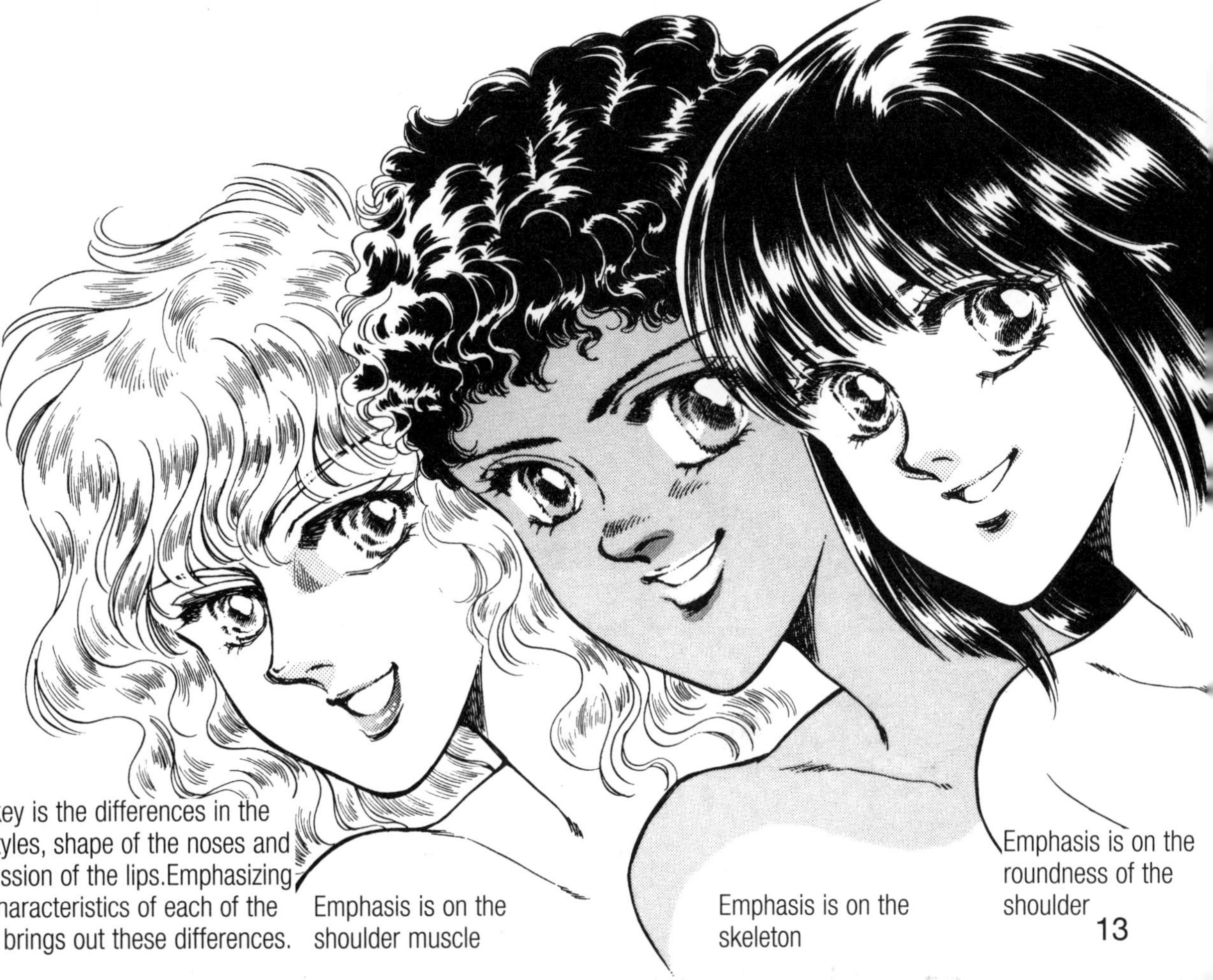

The key is the differences in the hairstyles, shape of the noses and expression of the lips.Emphasizing the characteristics of each of the parts brings out these differences.

Emphasis is on the shoulder muscle

Emphasis is on the skeleton

Emphasis is on the roundness of the shoulder

Mongoloid Bishoujo

Drawing East Asian, Southeast Asian and Central South American Girls

The hair is fundamentally straight and colors range from brown to black.

Making the eyes black brings out the Asian look.

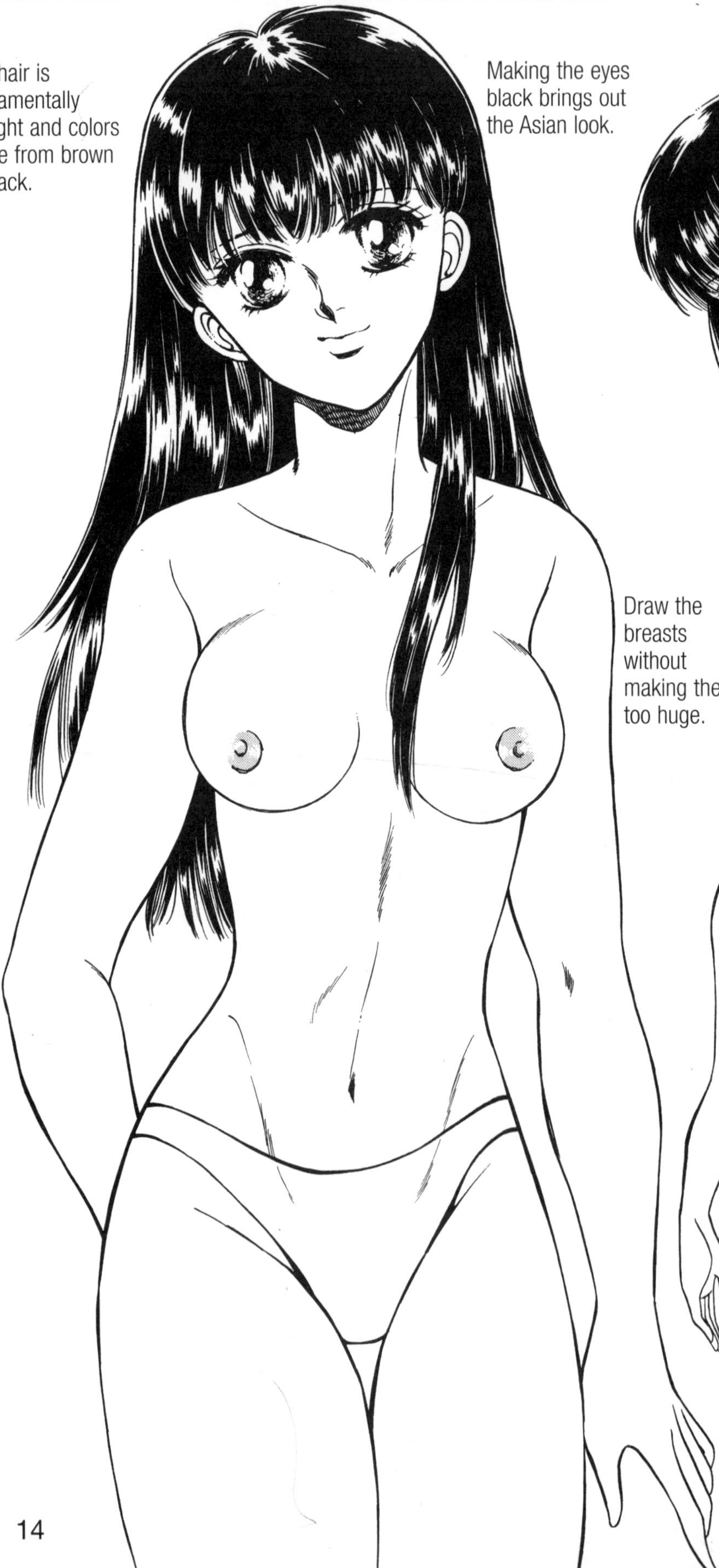

Draw the breasts without making them too huge.

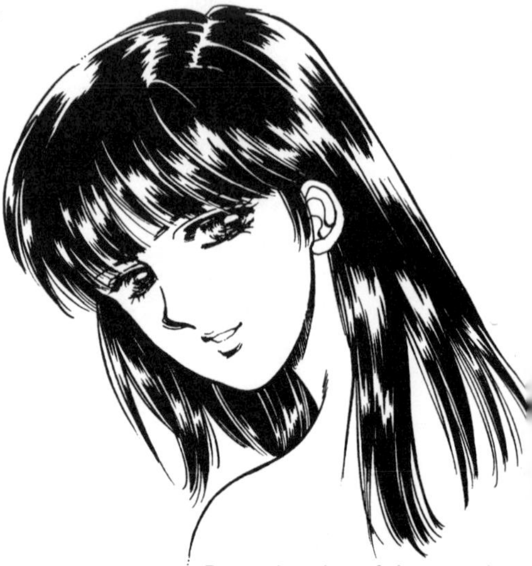

Draw the size of the mouth and lips with moderation. Pursed-up lips are mainly used.

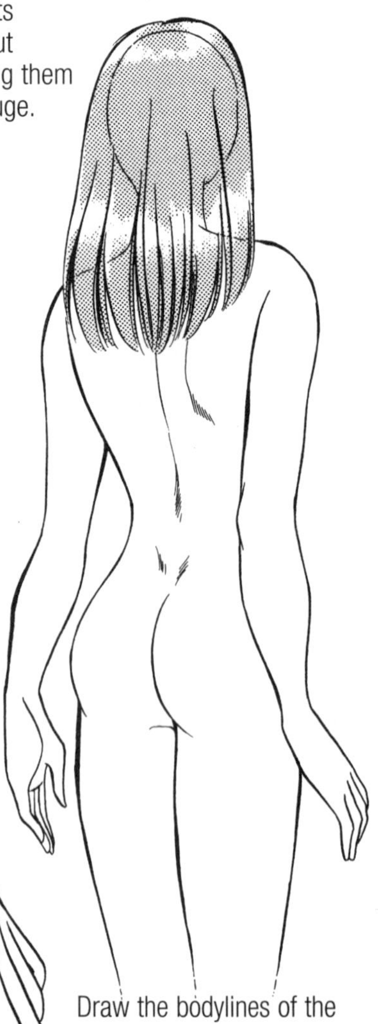

Draw the bodylines of the shoulder, back and buttocks lithely.

Graceful Asian types exist among Mongoloid characters.It is a good idea to depict this generally accepted idea.

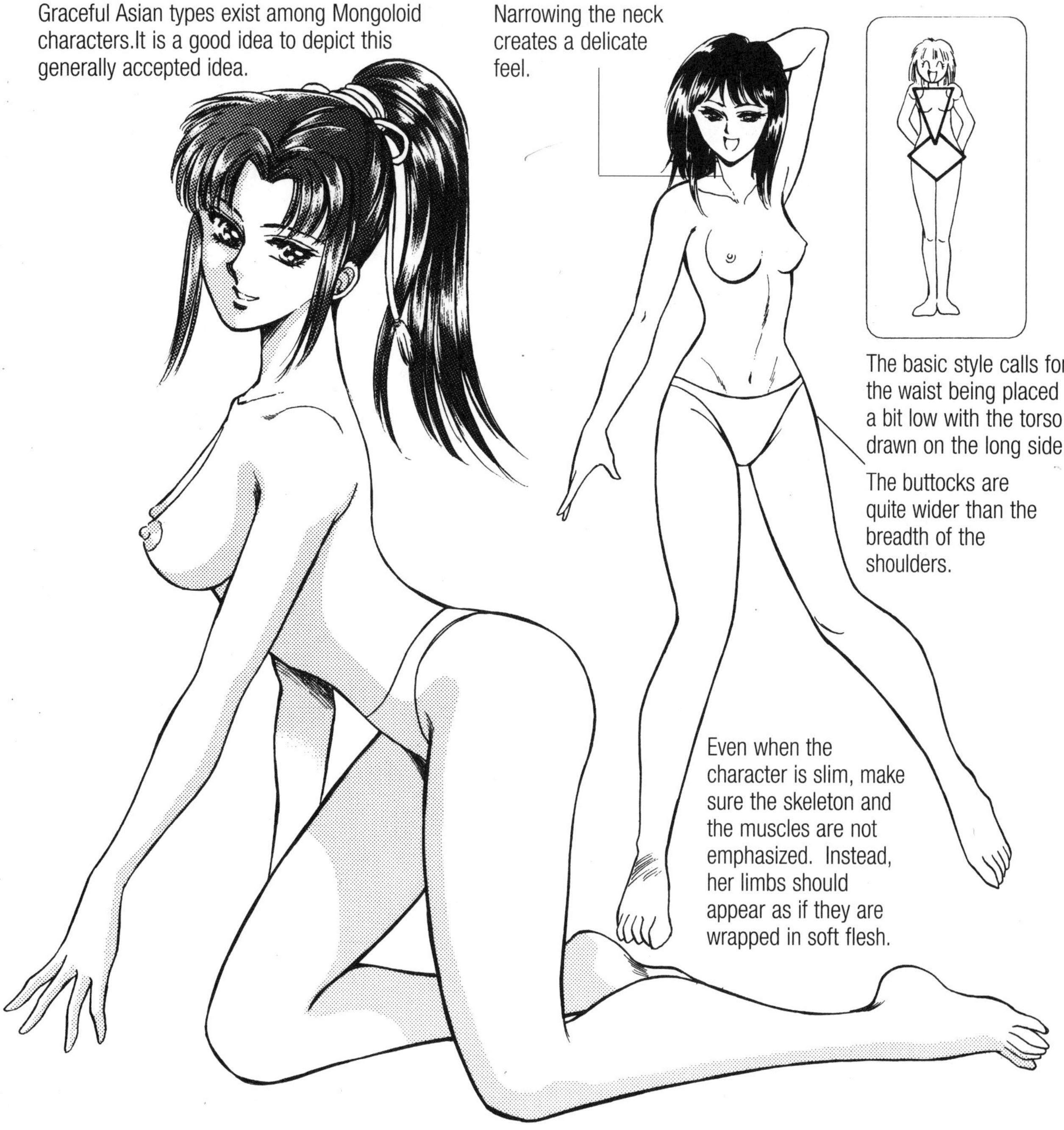

Narrowing the neck creates a delicate feel.

The basic style calls for the waist being placed a bit low with the torso drawn on the long side.

The buttocks are quite wider than the breadth of the shoulders.

Even when the character is slim, make sure the skeleton and the muscles are not emphasized. Instead, her limbs should appear as if they are wrapped in soft flesh.

Make distinctions in your drawings by differentiating the line from the back that approaches the waist into three types.

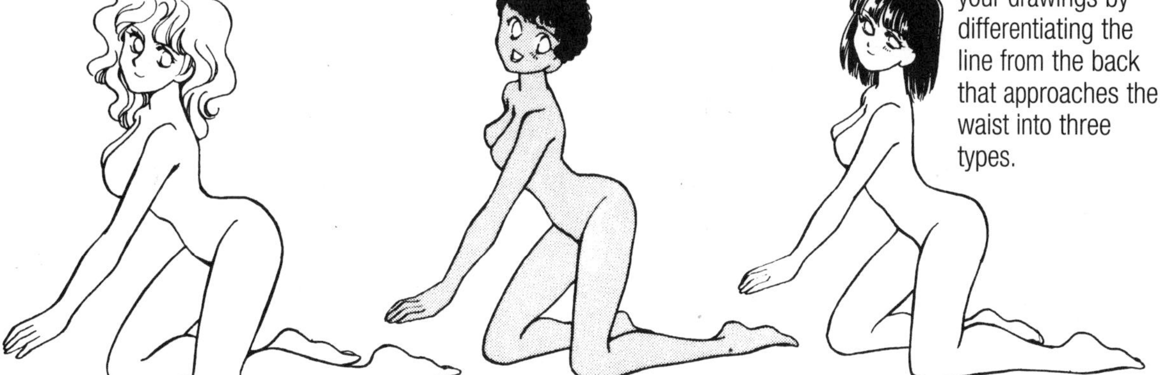

Expressing Black Hair

Give shape to the drawing.

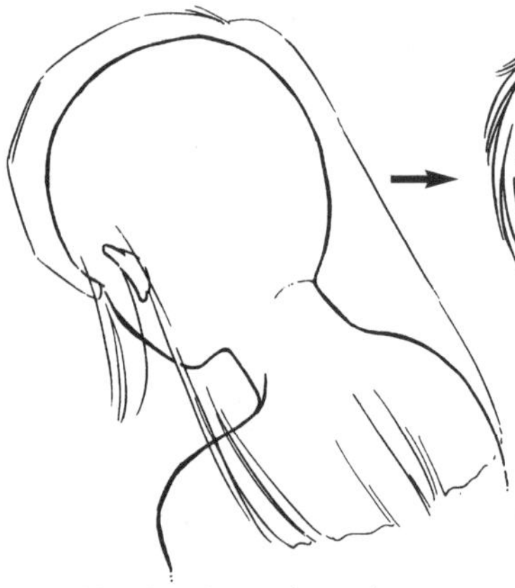

The key is to draw the hairline along the roundness of the skull.

Mark the areas that reflect light

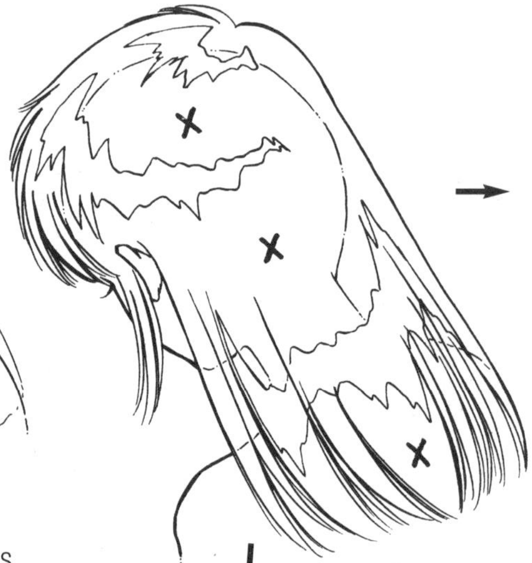

Blacken the areas where light does not reflect.

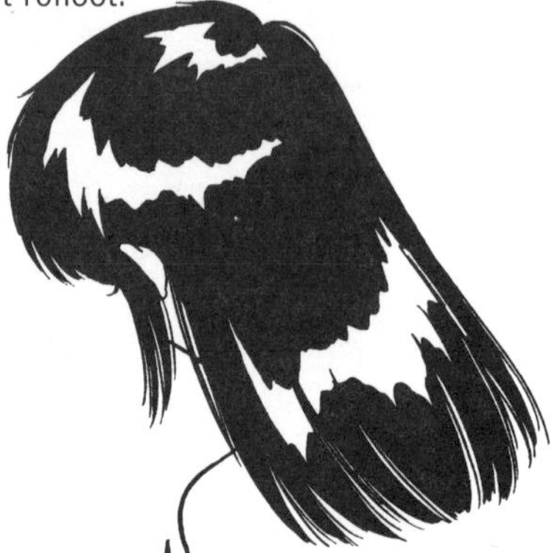

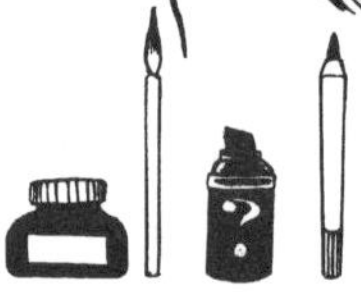

Inking with brushes and brush pens or even magic markers will do fine.

Matted and Jet Black Hair

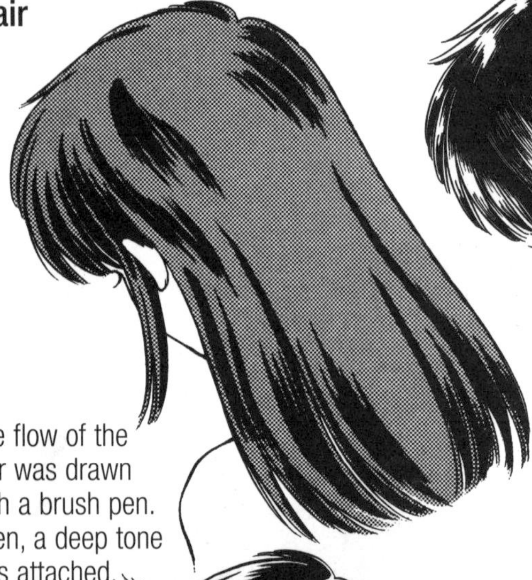

The flow of the hair was drawn with a brush pen. Then, a deep tone was attached.

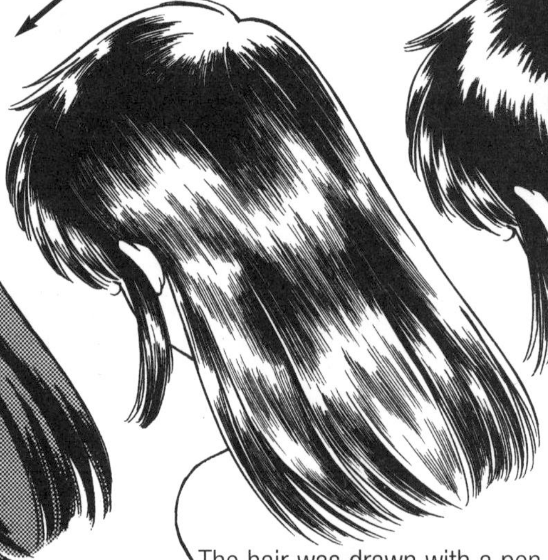

The hair was drawn with a pen. Dryness and wetness can be expressed according to the touches and strength of the strokes.

Lustrous Hair

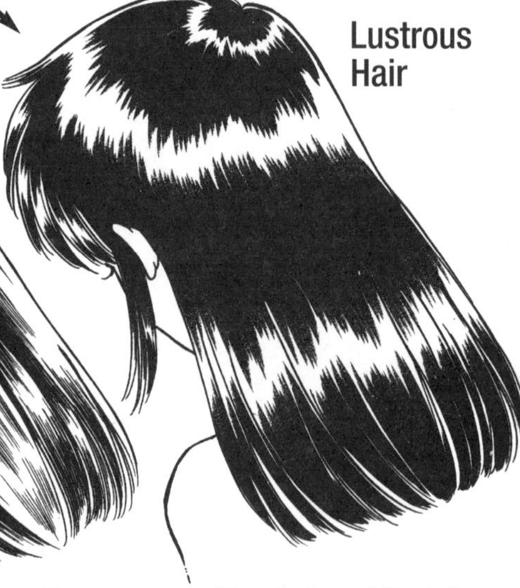

The strokes of the hair were drawn with a brush pen.

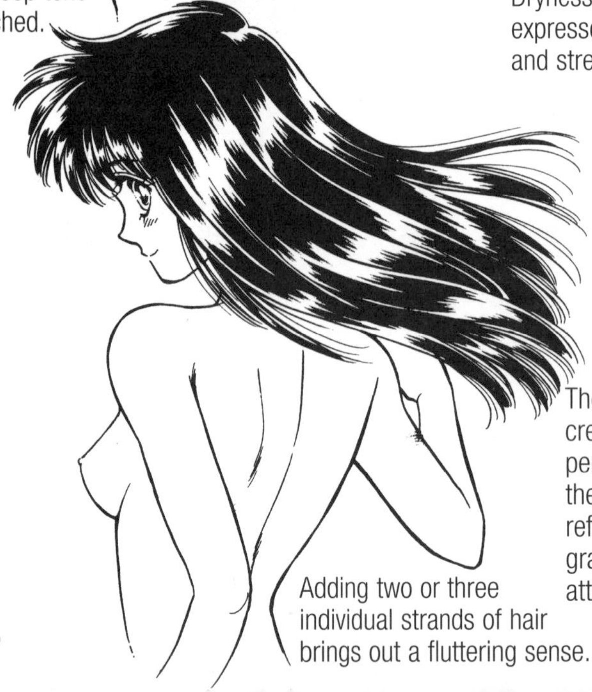

Adding two or three individual strands of hair brings out a fluttering sense.

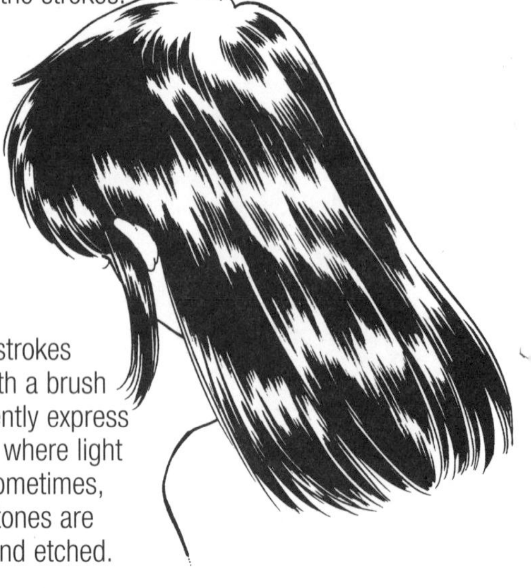

The short strokes created with a brush pen frequently express the places where light reflects. Sometimes, gradation tones are attached and etched.

Various Mongoloid Characters

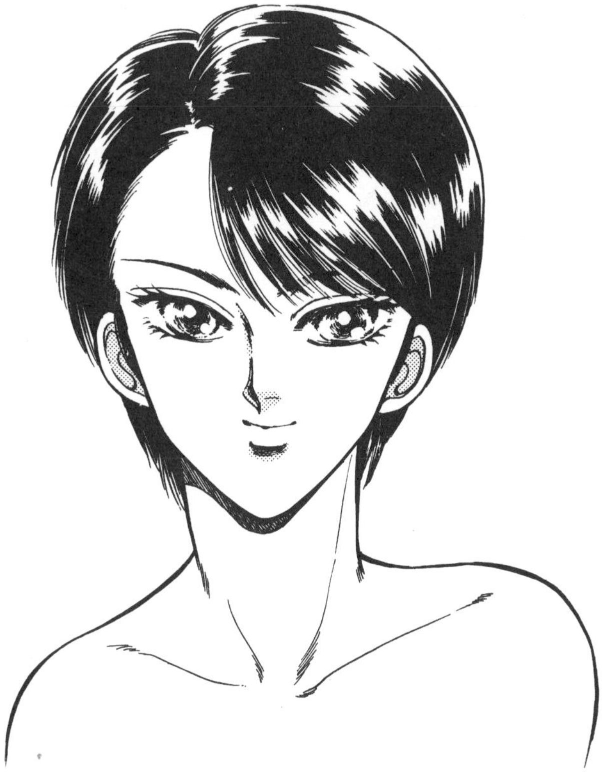

Chinese/Korean Look

Slanted eyes are often selected. Do the face a bit on the small side to bring out the sharp features. The breadth of the shoulders should be a little narrow despite the strongly built skeletal frames.

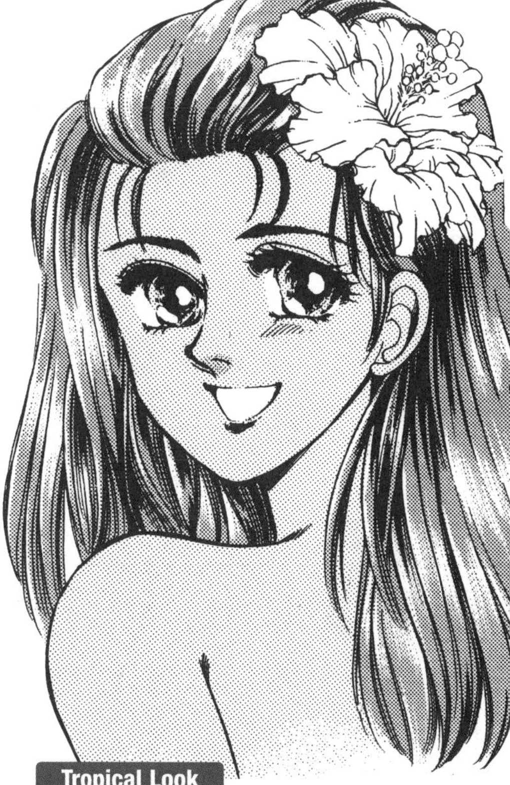

Tropical Look

Emphasize the line of the nose a bit. Draw the mouth a bit on the large side bringing out a mood of openness. Separate the hair into fluttering sections to make the girl look like she was raised near the ocean. Also, attach a light tone to visually direct a suntan (light-brown).

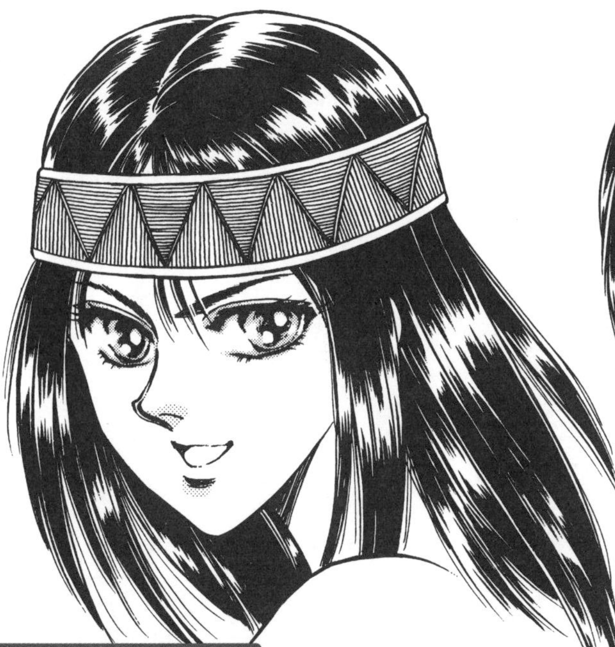

Native American Look

She is sharp-eyed. Emphasize the line of the nose to bring out the clear-cut facial features. Add small props like a bandana for visual direction.

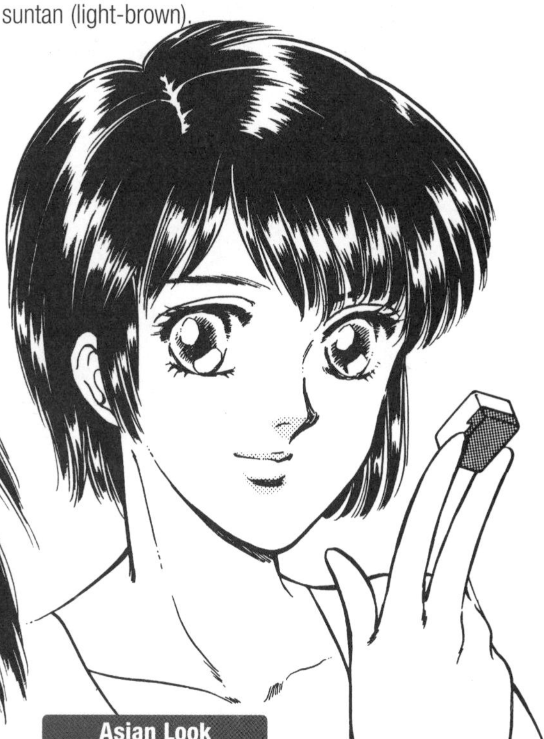

Asian Look

Do not emphasize the line of the nose. The key is to bring out smoothness.

Negroid Bishoujo

Drawing African and Oceanian Girls

Every strand of hair is curled. Hair colors range from brown to black.

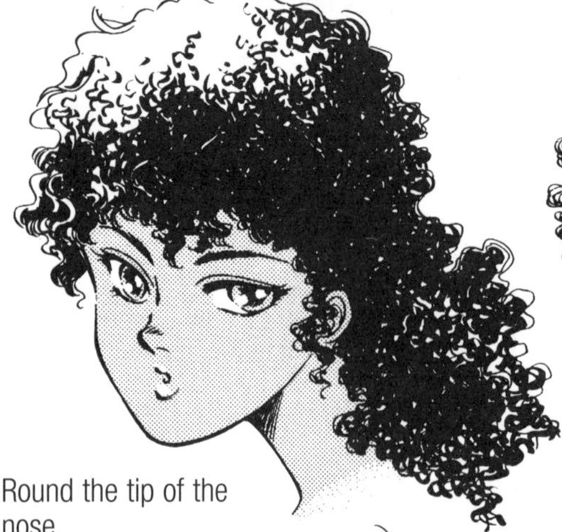

Round the tip of the nose.

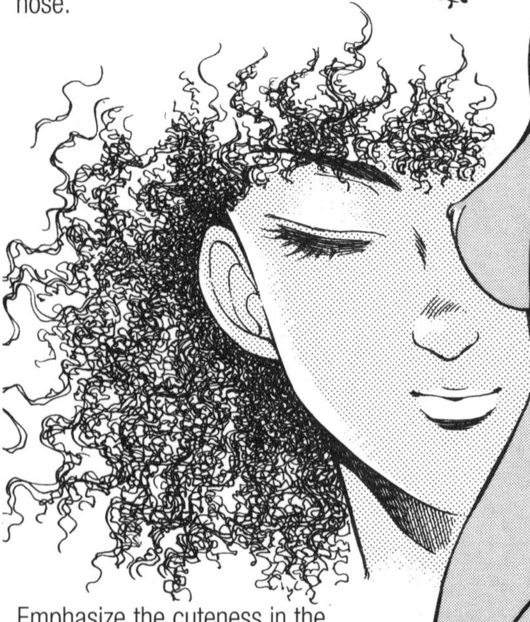

Emphasize the cuteness in the lower lip.

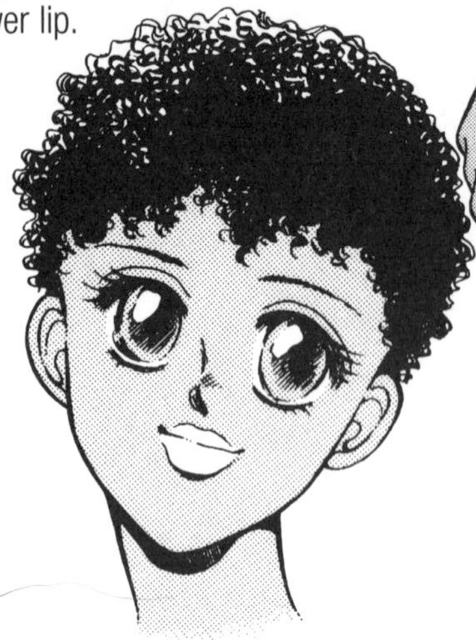

By drawing her eyes wide and keeping her mouth small, her lips will appear cute.

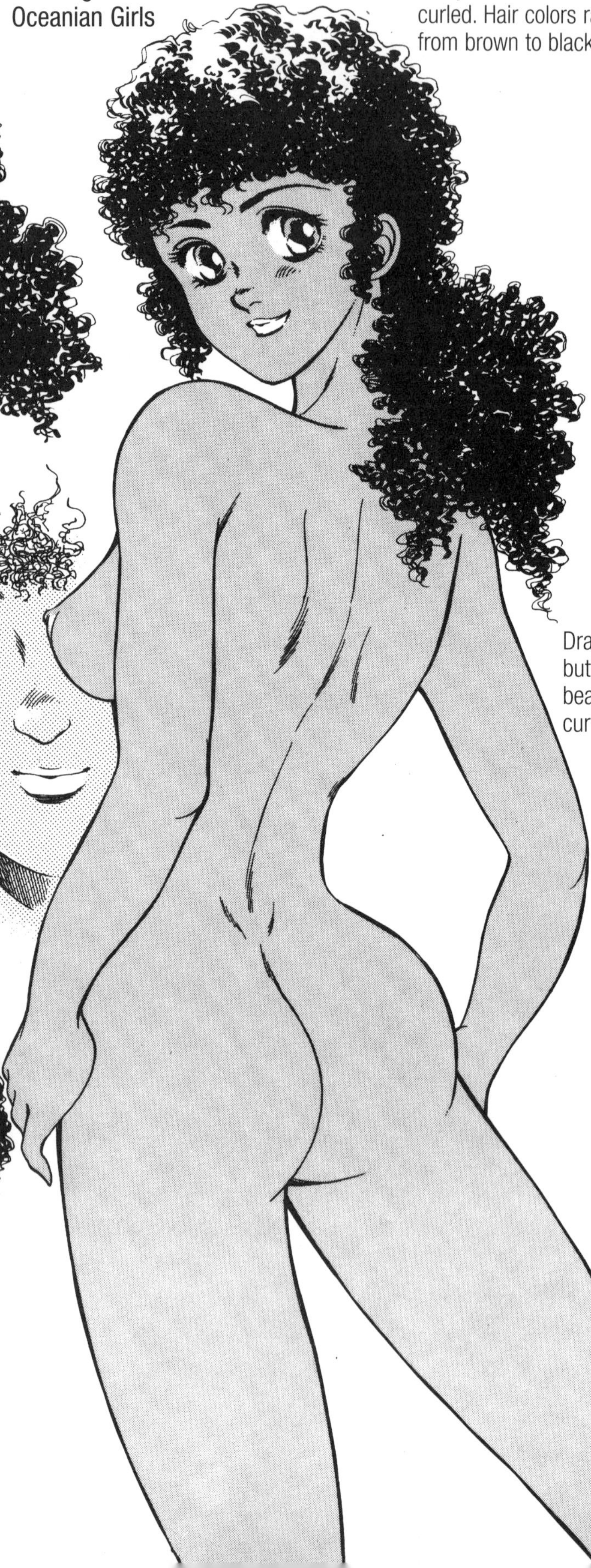

Draw the buttocks with beautiful, round curves.

The tint is melanin in nature and may differ across various nationalities.

The face is drawn a bit on the small side.

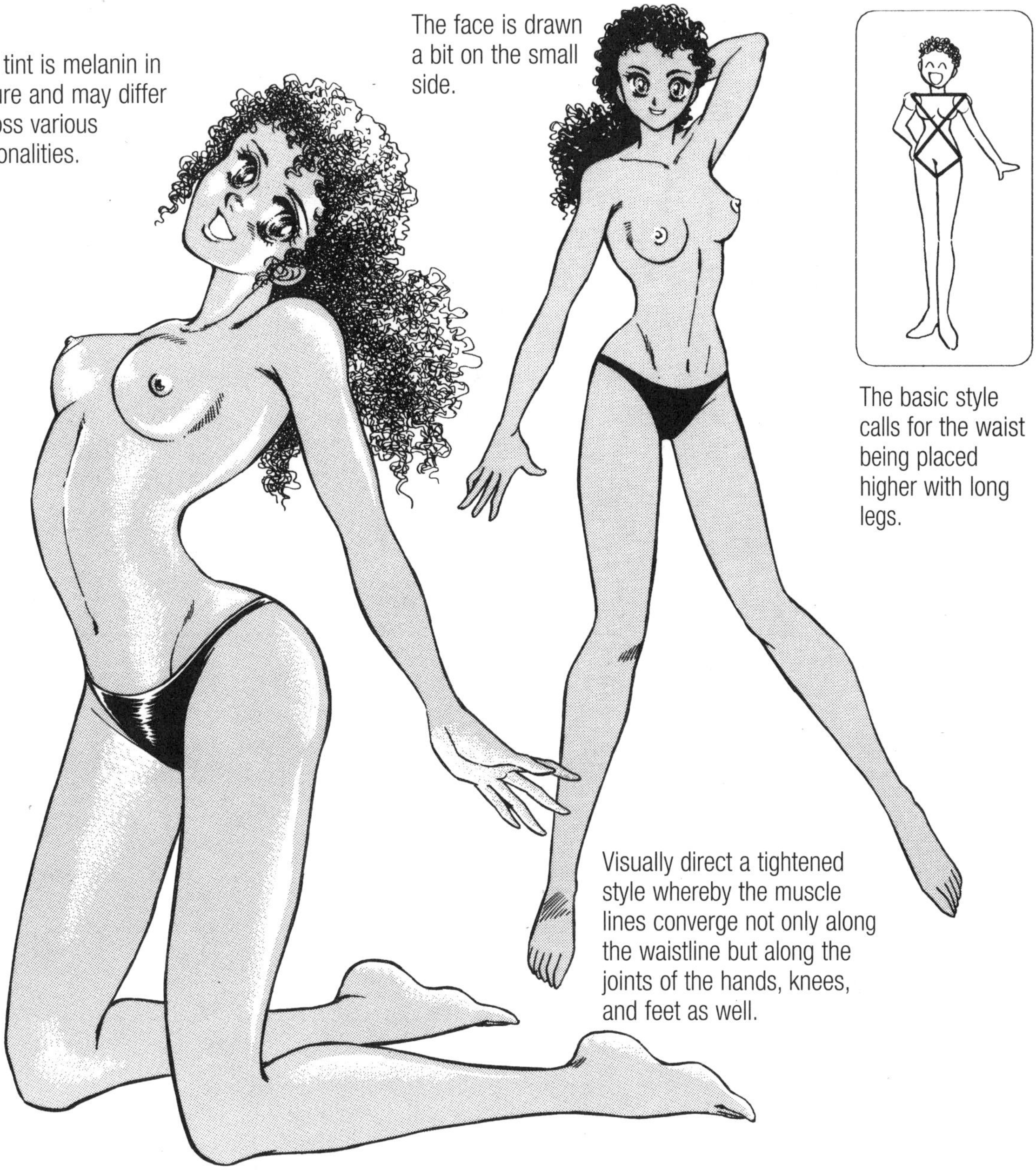

The basic style calls for the waist being placed higher with long legs.

Visually direct a tightened style whereby the muscle lines converge not only along the waistline but along the joints of the hands, knees, and feet as well.

Distinguish her from the Caucasoid type with the position and size of the breasts as well as the line from chest approaching the lower back.

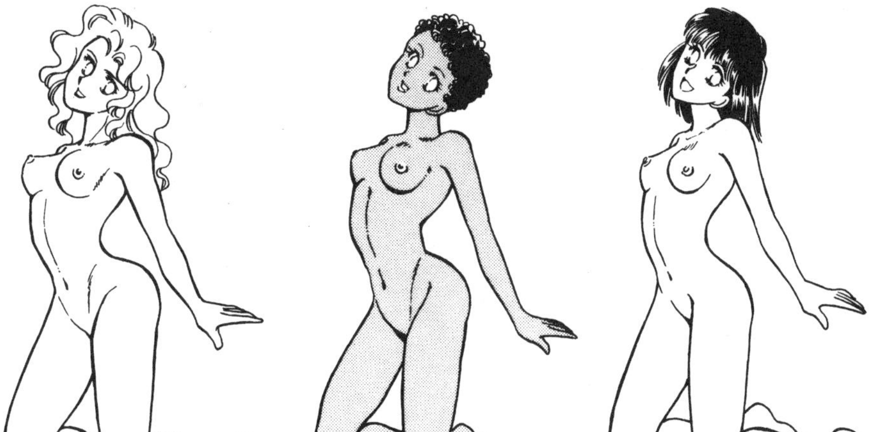

Expressing Curly Hair

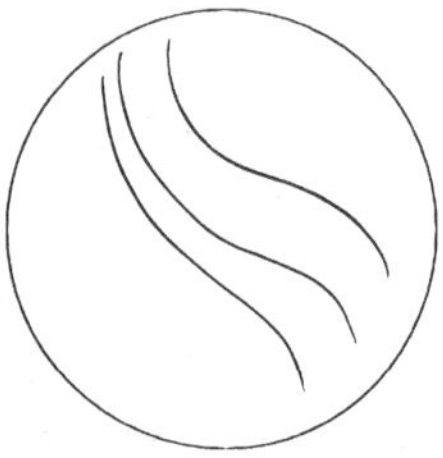

With ordinary wavy hair, each strand of hair is smooth.

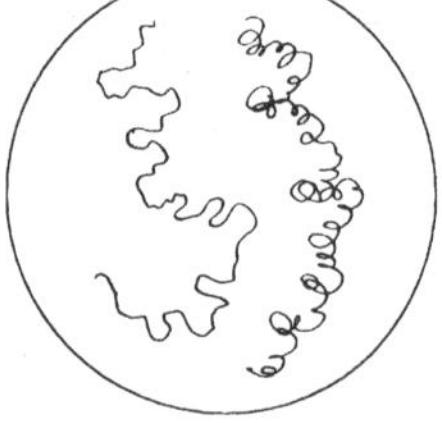

Each strand of hair is curled.

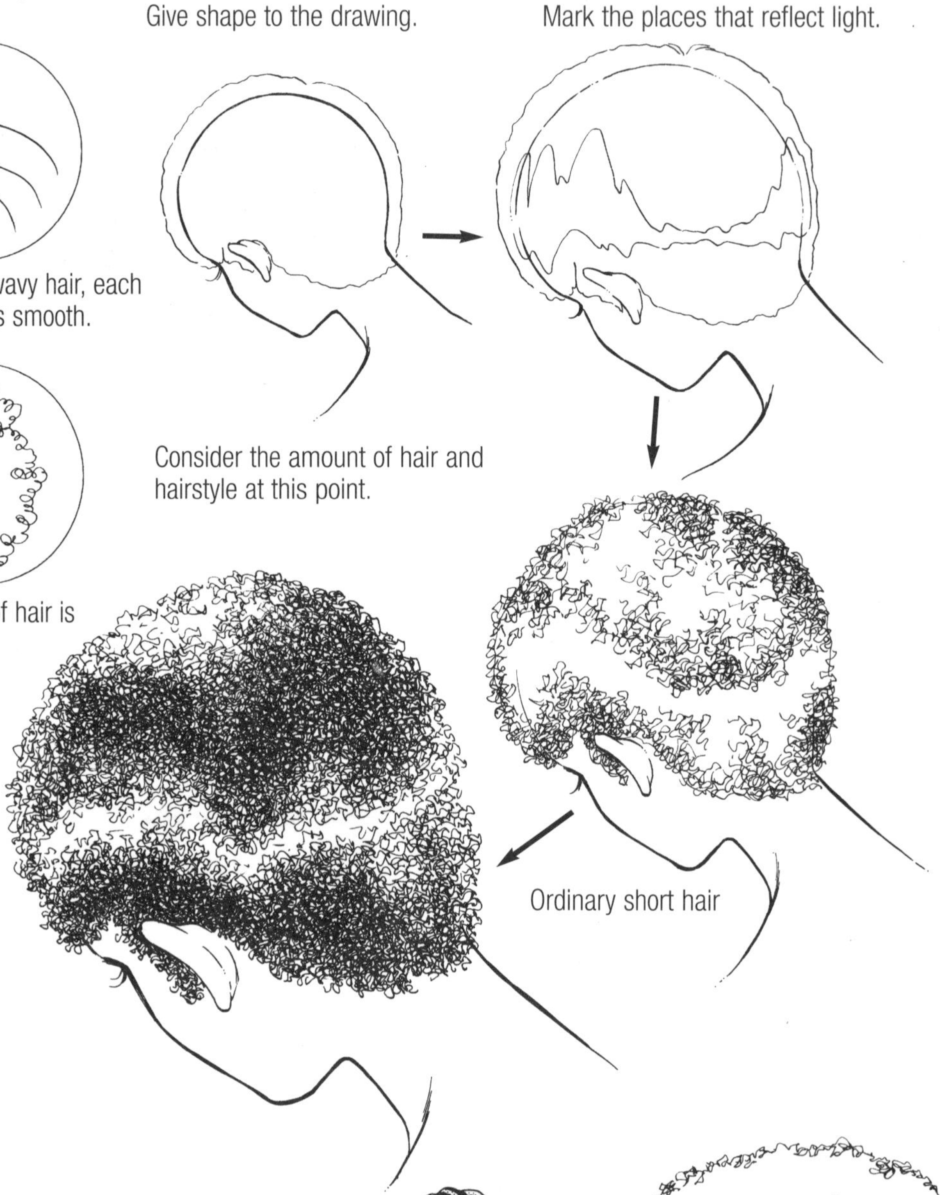

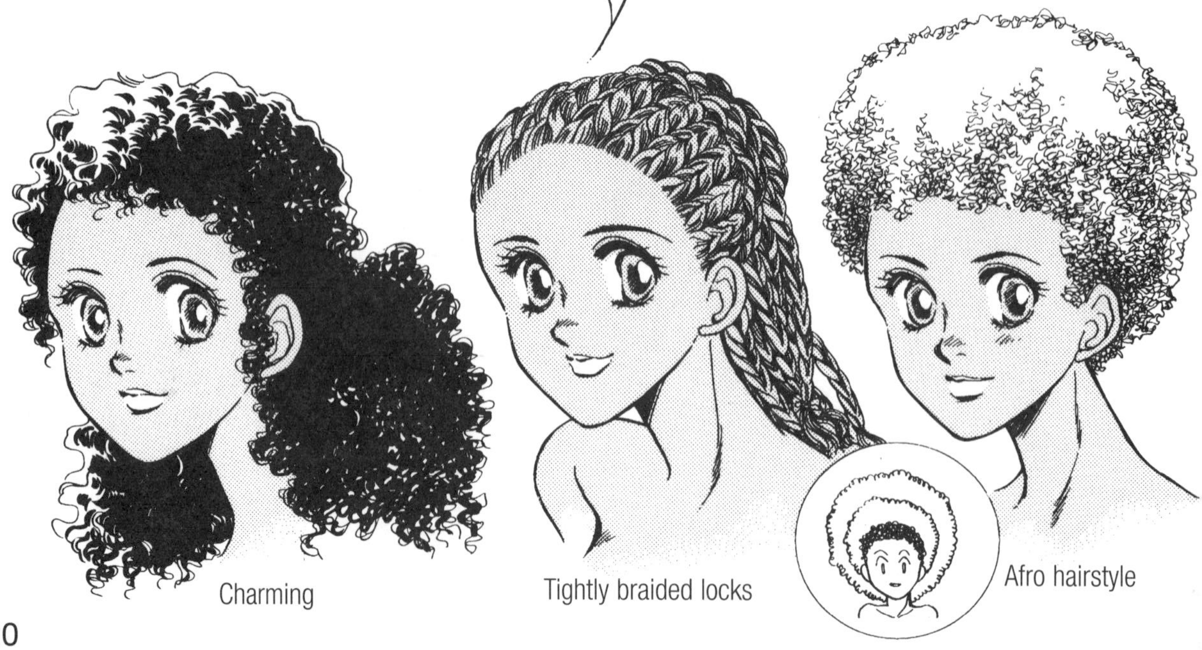

Various Negroid Bishoujo

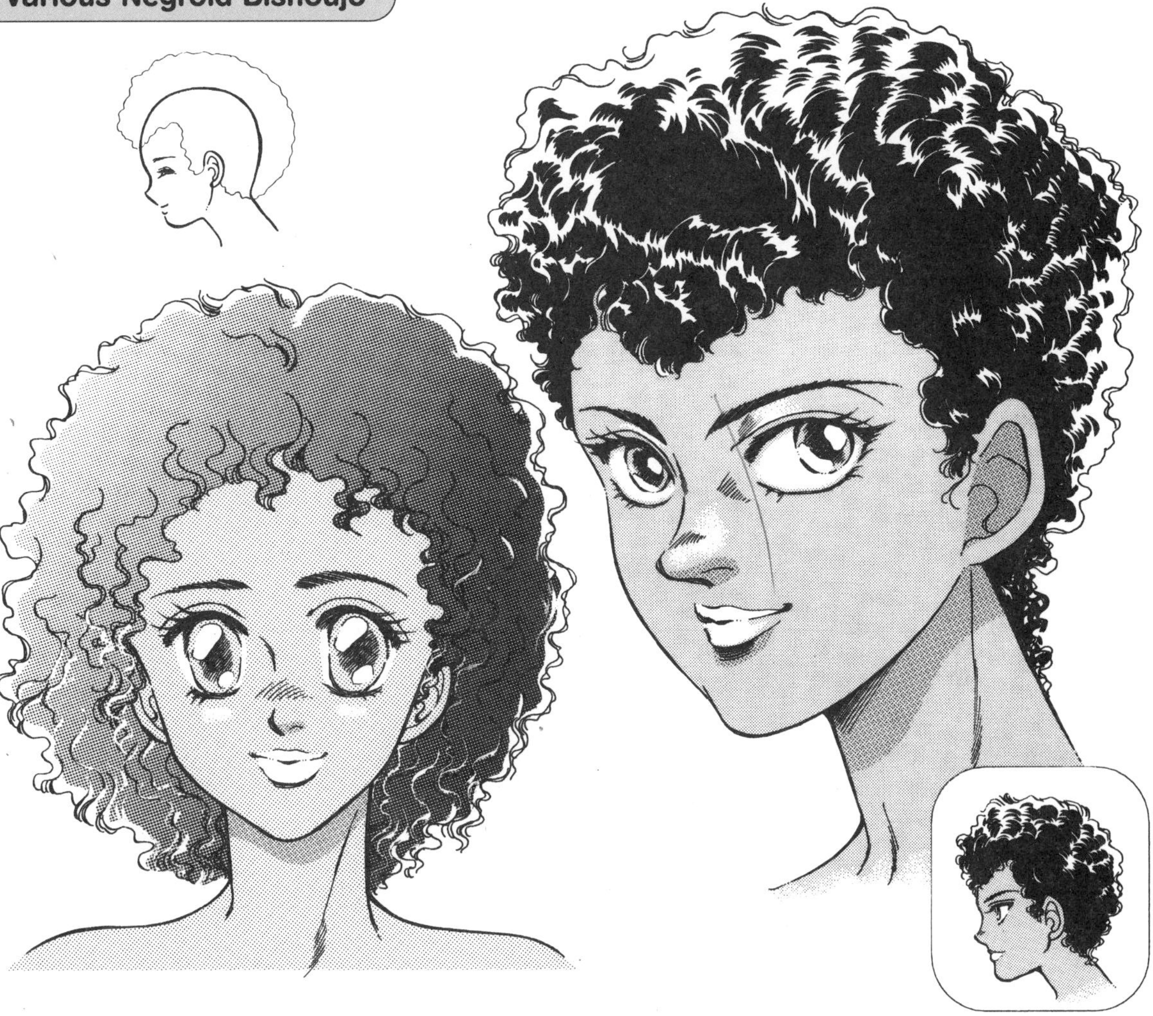

Marine Look

In contrast to the example to the right, she has large vertically long eyes which bring out a sense of serenity. A flowing sauvage type hairstyle and a thicker lower lip can give a gentle, carefree impression.

Wild Look

Large slit eyes a bit harsh, long eyelashes and a slightly overhanging chin gives the character an air of strength and wildness. Also, dropping a shadow above the eyes creates clear-cut facial features that can be used to visually direct a strong-willed expression.

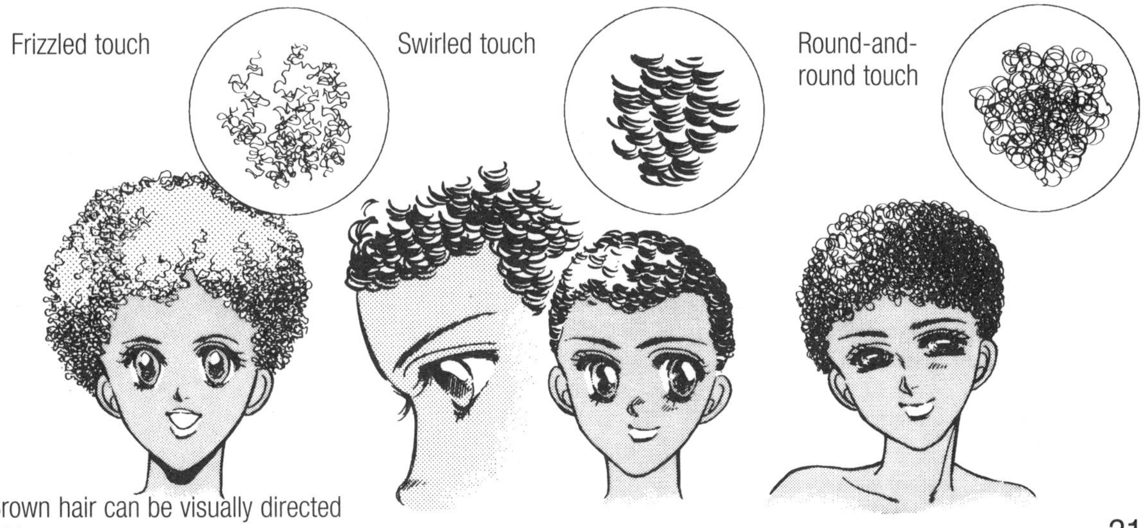

Brown hair can be visually directed with coarse tones.

Caucasoid Bishoujo

Drawing North American, Mediterranean, European and Middle Eastern Girls

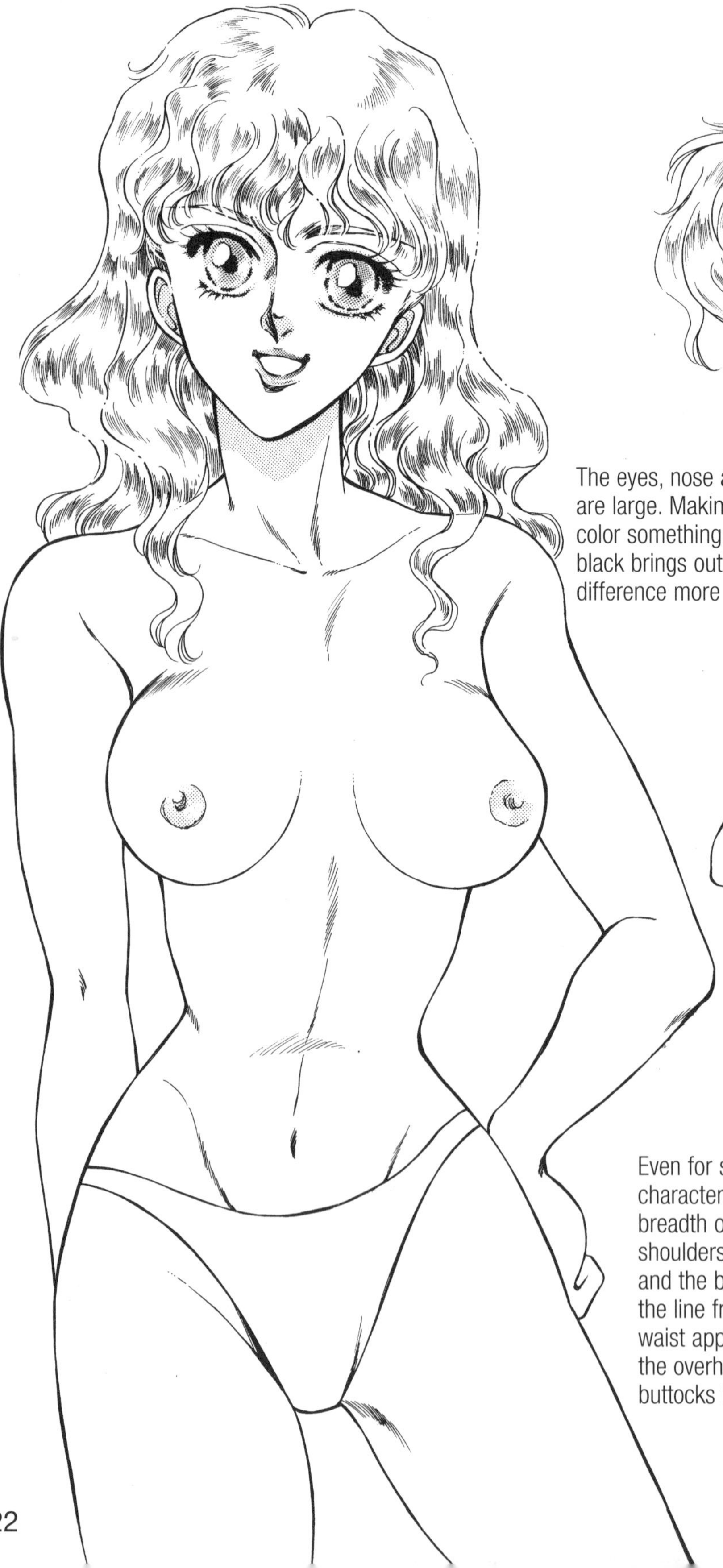

Wavy hair and clear-cut facial features are the distinctive characteristics. There are a wide variety of hair colors ranging from red to blonde to black.

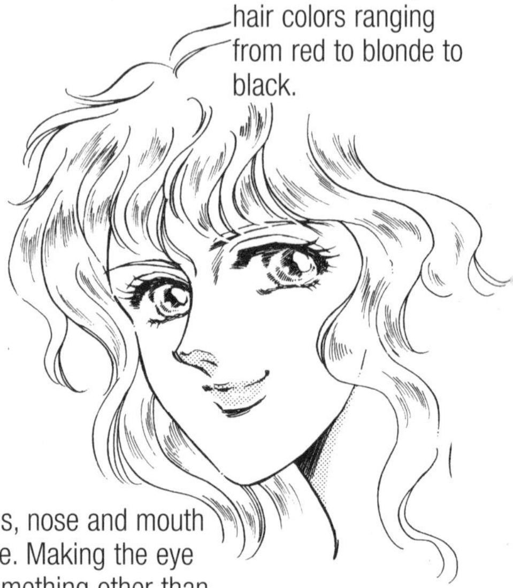

The eyes, nose and mouth are large. Making the eye color something other than black brings out the difference more easily.

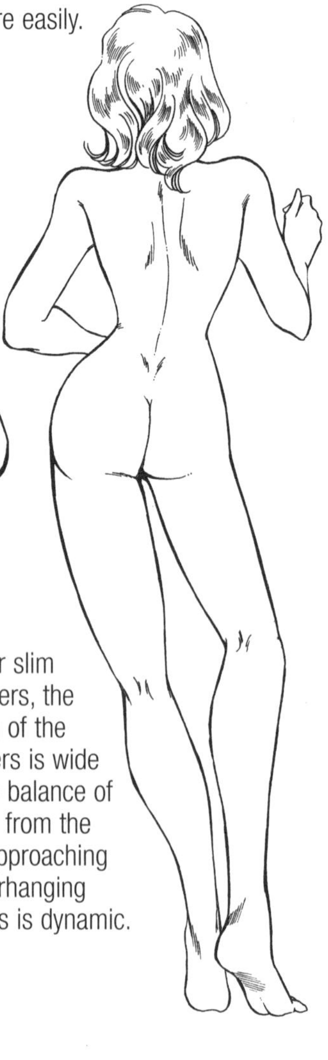

Even for slim characters, the breadth of the shoulders is wide and the balance of the line from the waist approaching the overhanging buttocks is dynamic.

Draw developed breasts and hips to emphasize the sturdy build of the character thereby making her look healthy.

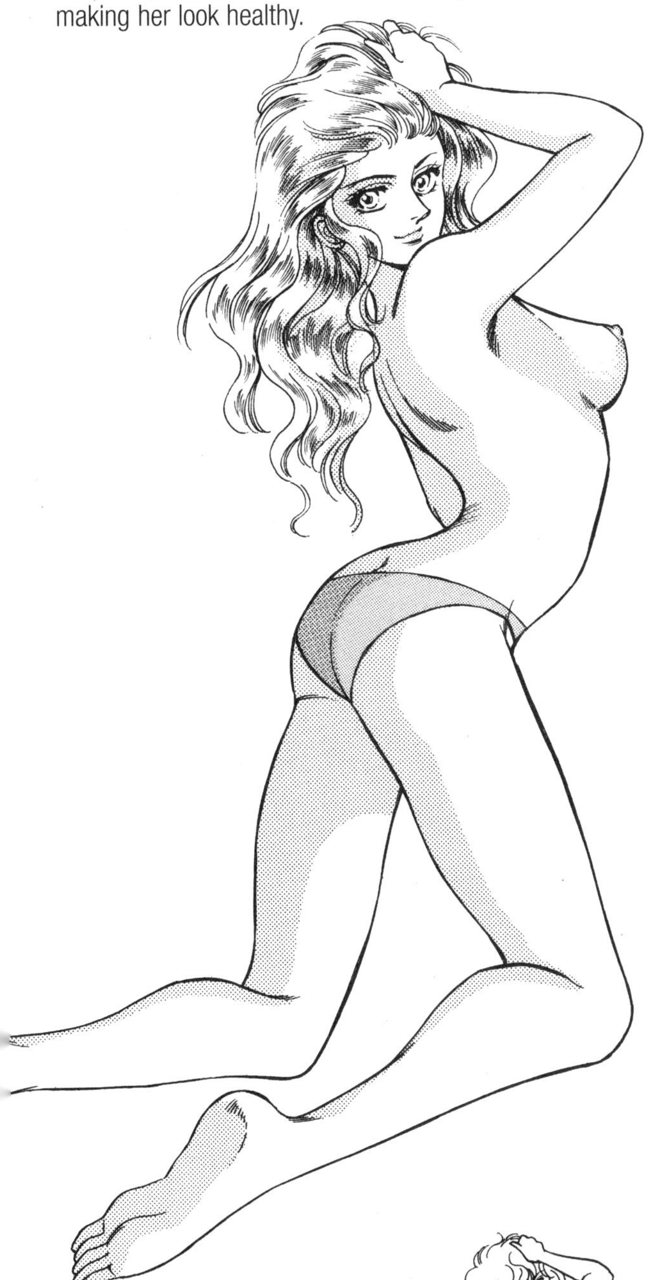

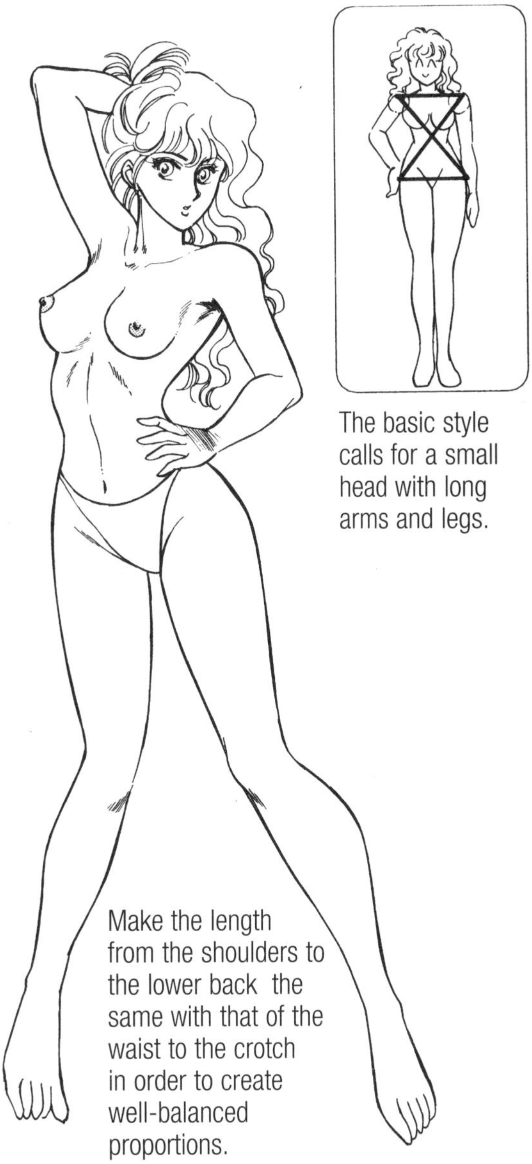

The basic style calls for a small head with long arms and legs.

Make the length from the shoulders to the lower back the same with that of the waist to the crotch in order to create well-balanced proportions.

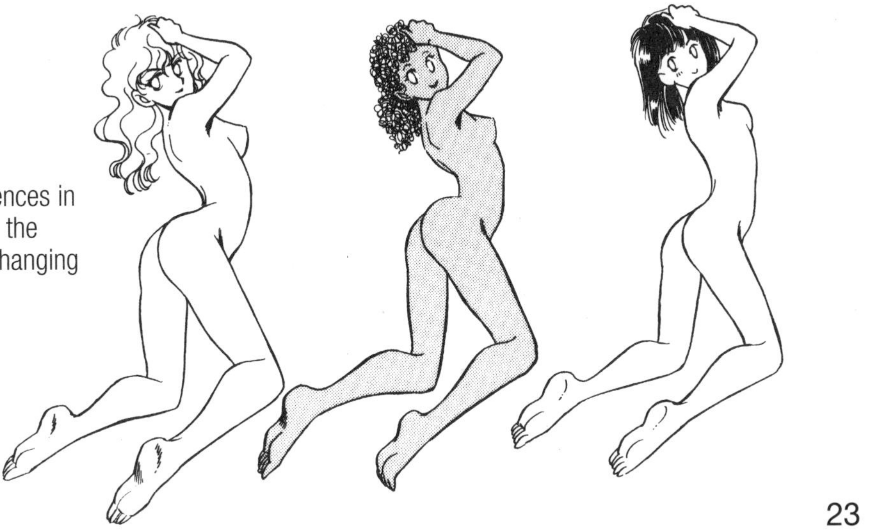

Bring out the differences in the narrow areas of the waists and the overhanging of the buttocks.

Expressing Wavy Hair

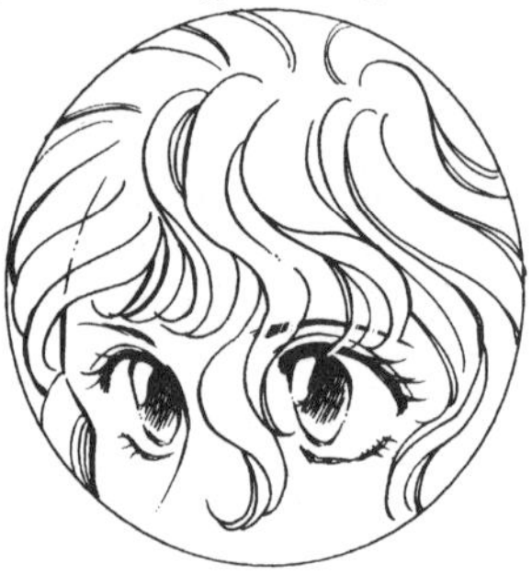

"S-shaped" curves
highlight wavy hair.

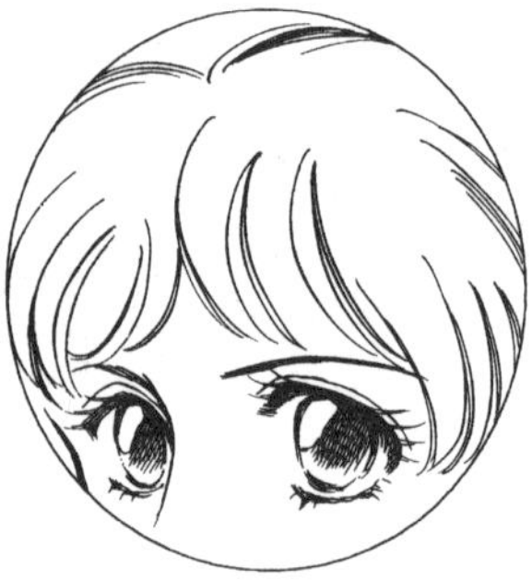

For short hairstyles, there are types that only have gentle curves.

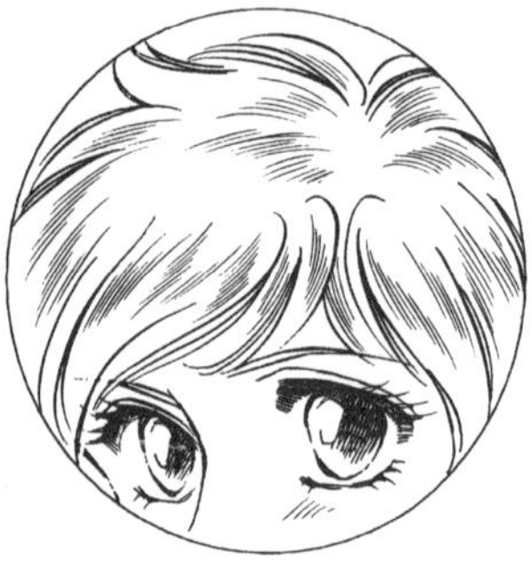

Add touches to make it look like light is reflecting.

Give shape to the drawing.

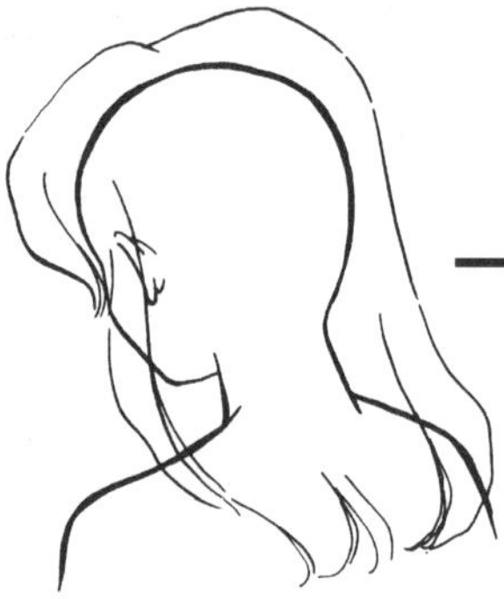

Decide how the hair grows out and divide large flowing areas into blocks.

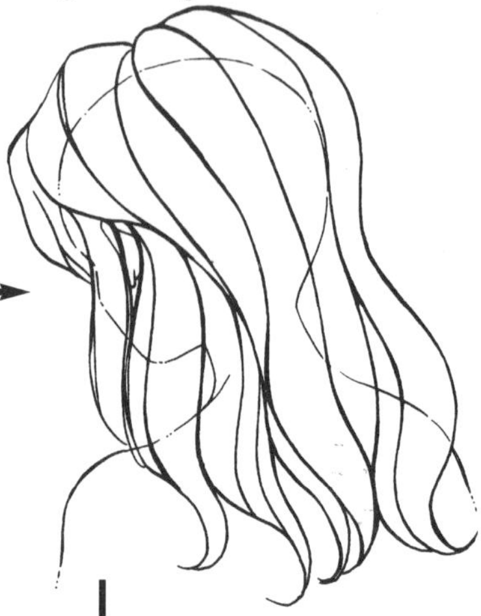

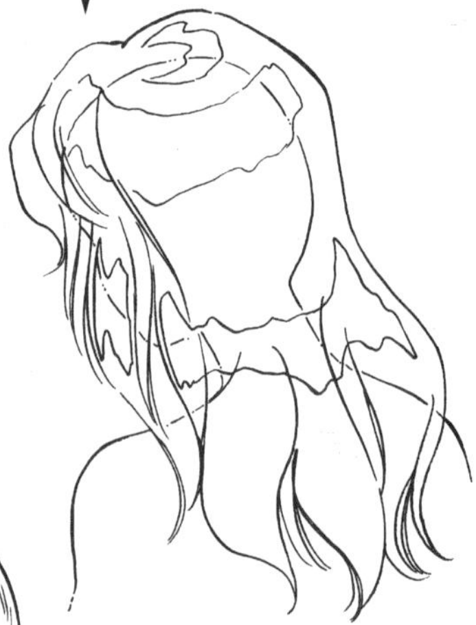

Mark the areas that reflect light.

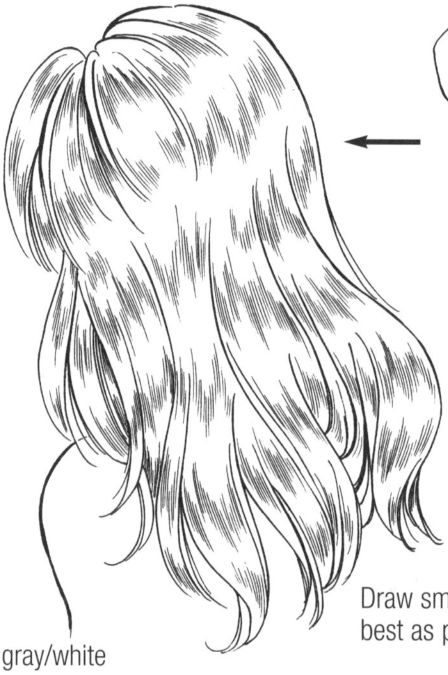

Draw smooth lines as best as possible.

The expression of blonde, silver and gray/white hair in manga is almost the same.

Gray / White Hair

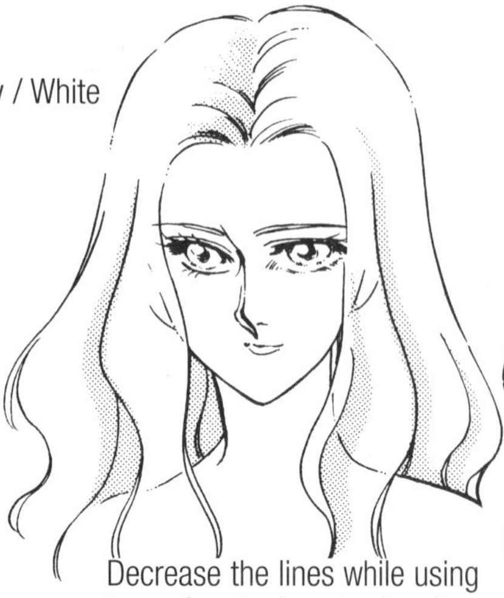

Decrease the lines while using tones for shadows to visually direct three-dimensionality.

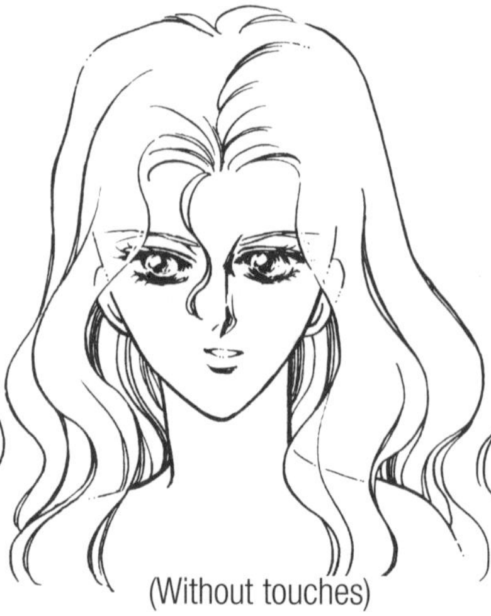

(Without touches)

Silver Hair

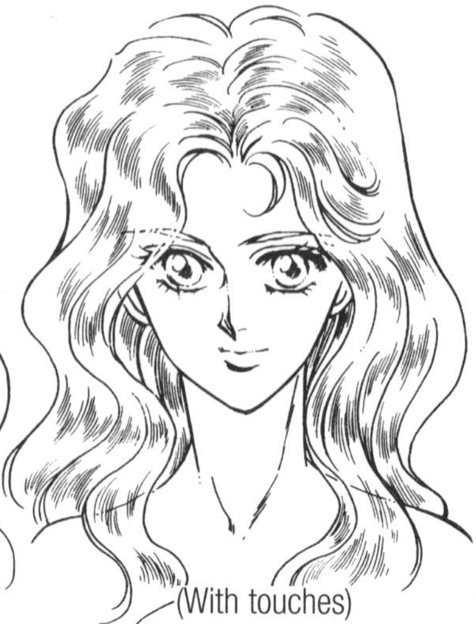

(With touches)

Blonde Hair

Various Caucasoid Bishoujo

Arabian Look

Black Hair: Use gradation with wavy hair and attach dark tones.
Black Eyes: Attach deep tones in the eyes too.
Arabian Makeup: Strengthen the impact of the eyes by making the outline of the eyes dark.
Red Lips: Use gradation for deep parts.

Use coarse 10% tones for the face. This will result in a different, deeper and darker look that distinguishes her from the standard Negroid bishoujo.

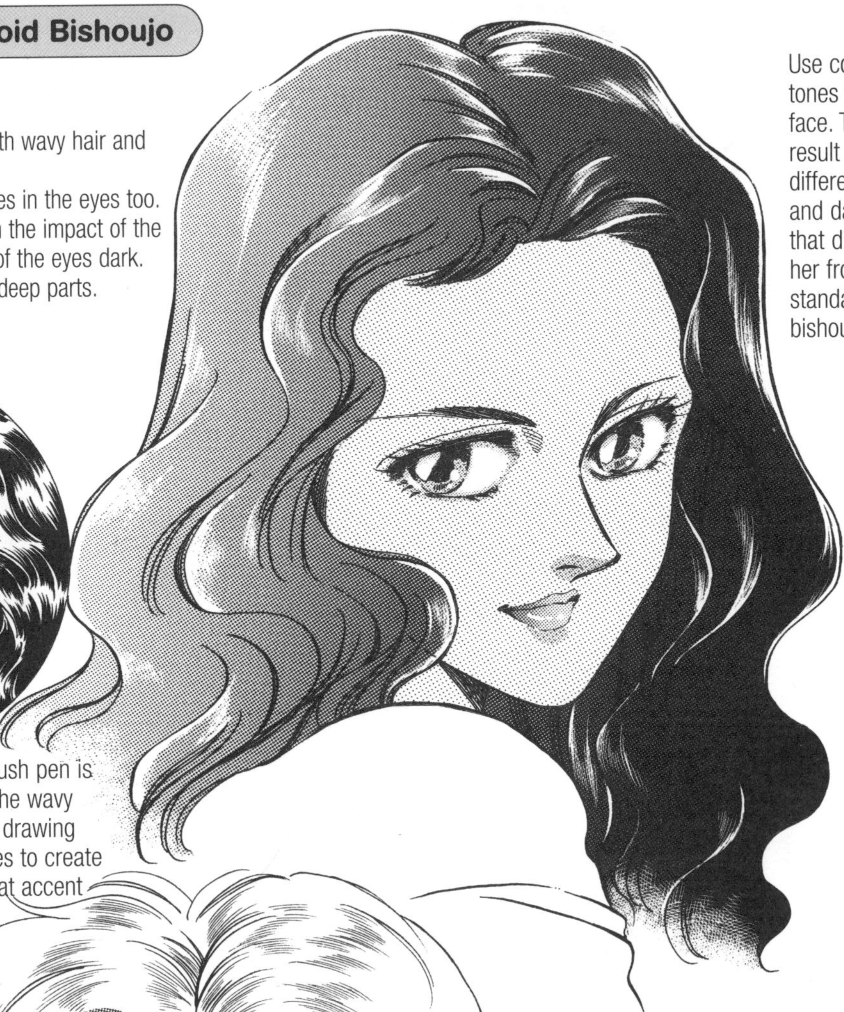

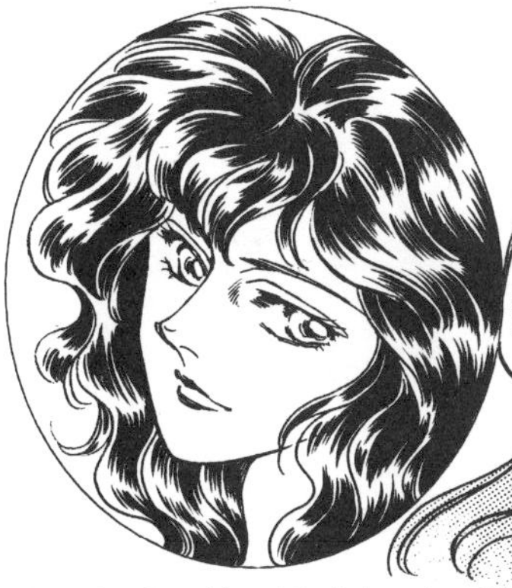

Coloring in with a black brush pen is also useful way to create the wavy hair. In this case, by firmly drawing the eyes and nose, it serves to create clear-cut facial features that accent the Caucasoid nature.

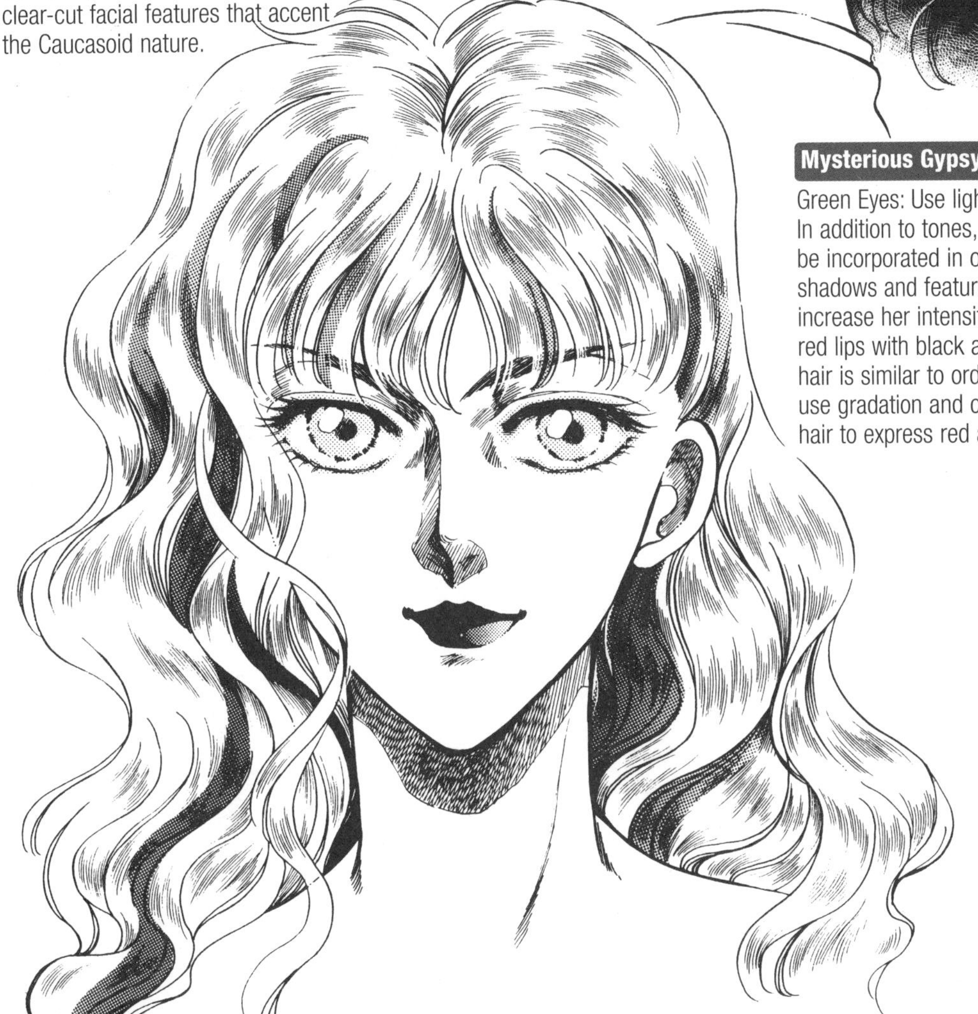

Mysterious Gypsy Look

Green Eyes: Use light tones.
In addition to tones, pen touches may also be incorporated in order to express facial shadows and features. This in turn will increase her intensity. Color in the deep red lips with black and add lit areas. The hair is similar to ordinary blonde; however, use gradation and coarse tones for the hair to express red and yellow highlights.

Expressing Eye Colors

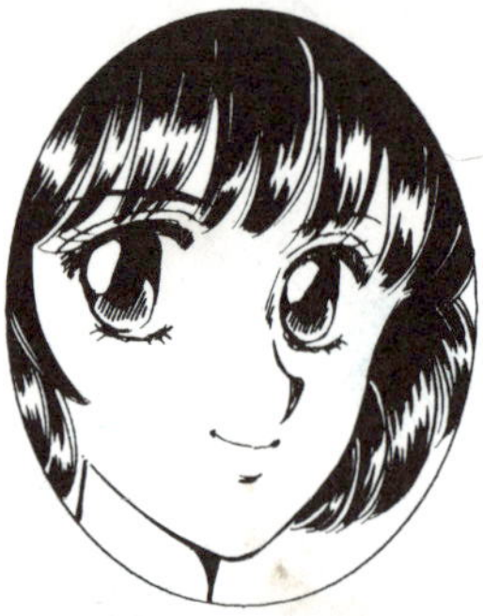

Mongoloid
Eye Color: black to brown

Black Eyes

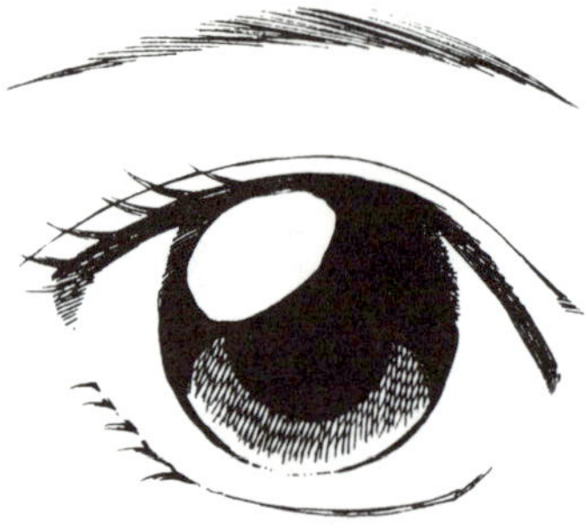

Black and oblique lines are used.

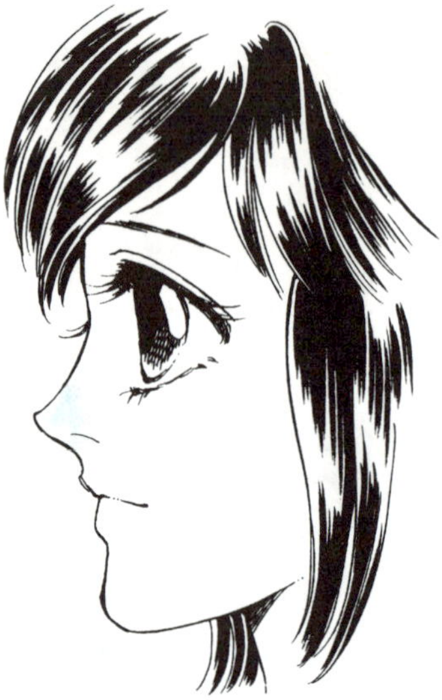

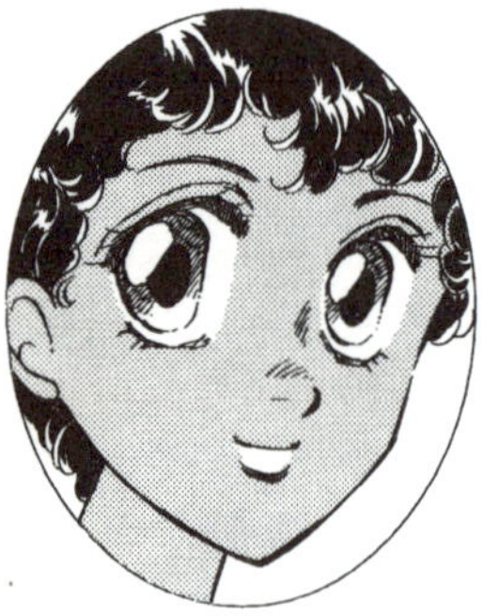

Negroid
Eye Color: black to brown

Brown Eyes

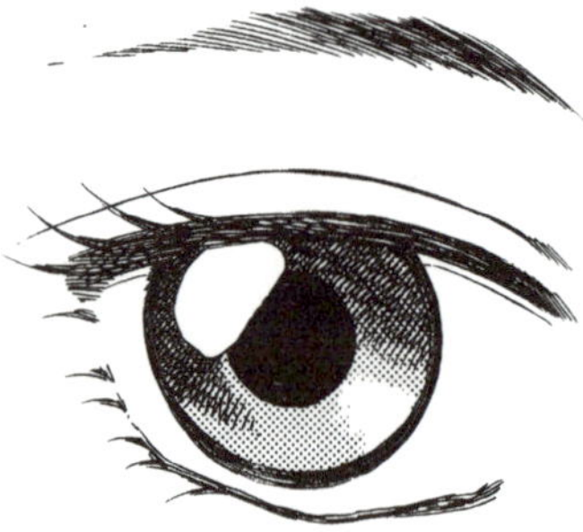

Black and tones are used in the same proportion. Use half tones with the black.

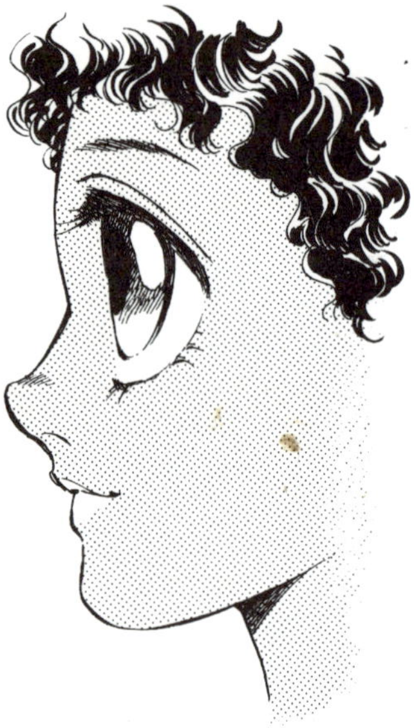

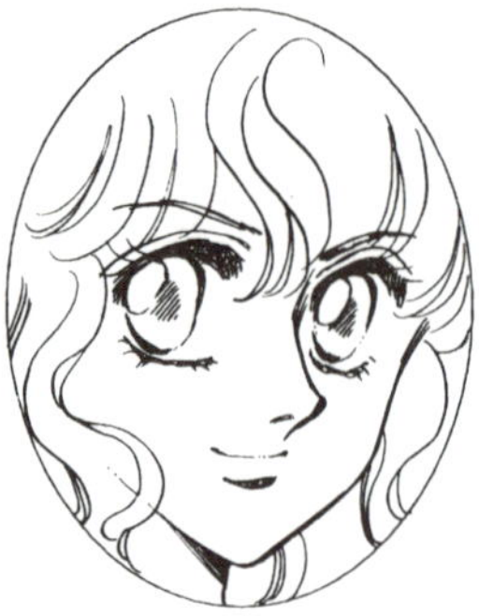

Caucasoid
Eye Color: light blue to black

Blue and Green Eyes

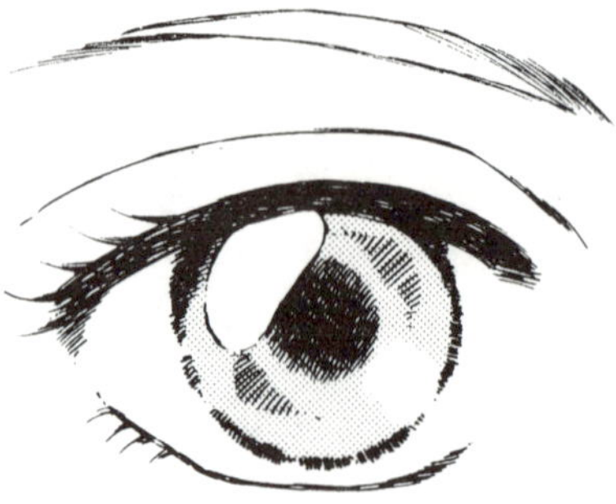

Black is hardly ever used. Tones dominate while pen marks are used every now and then for light and shape.

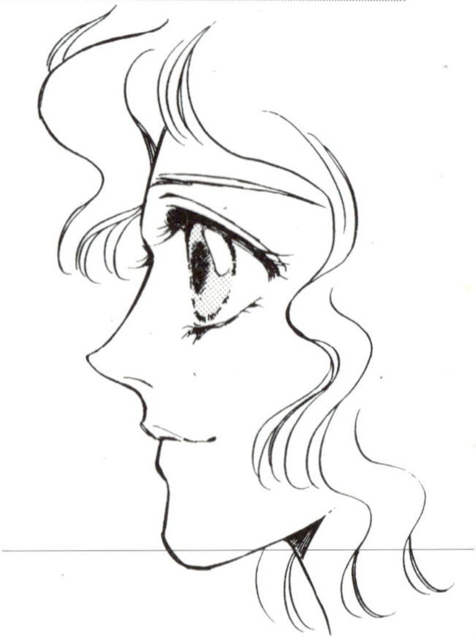

Black Eyes

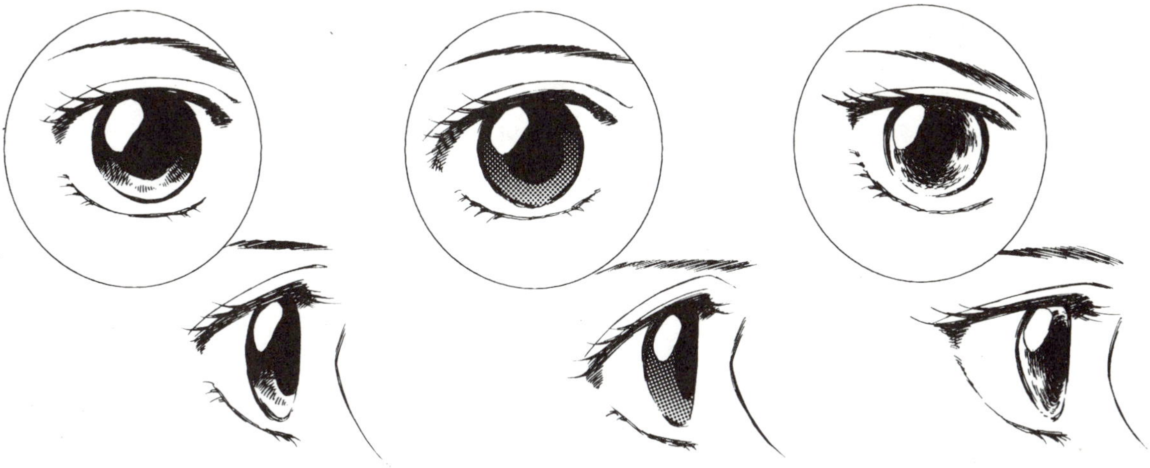

Brown Eyes

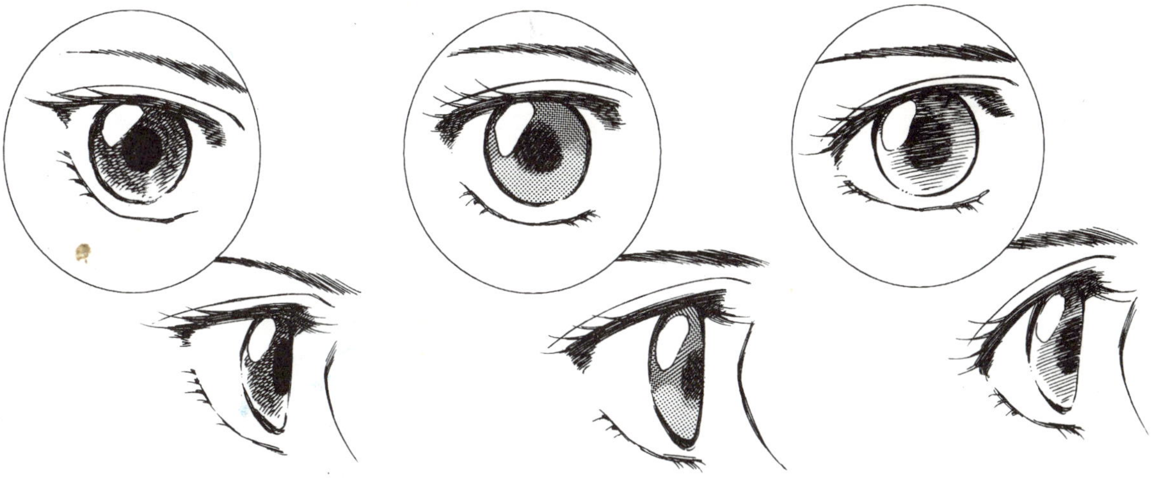

Blue and Green Eyes

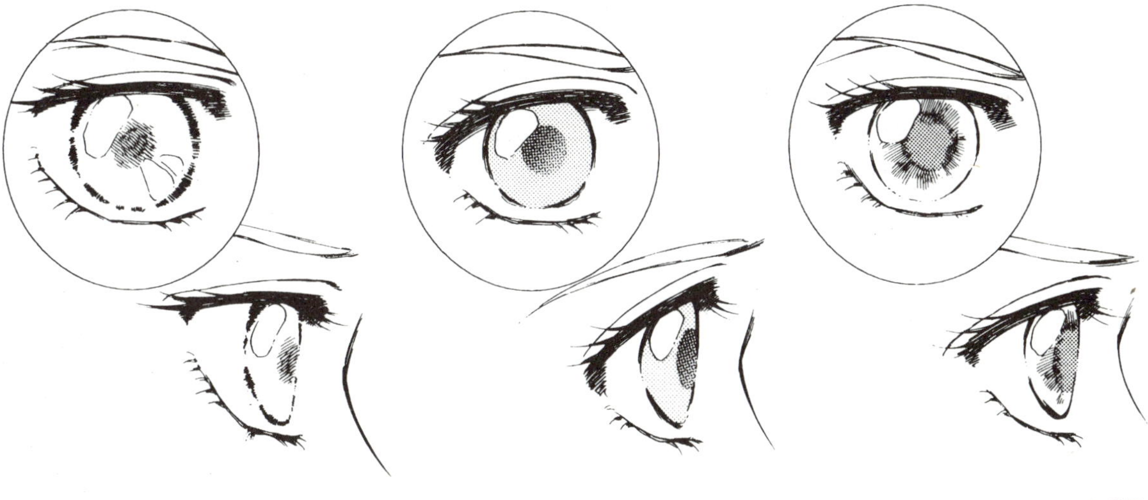

Expressing Noses and Lips

Mongoloid

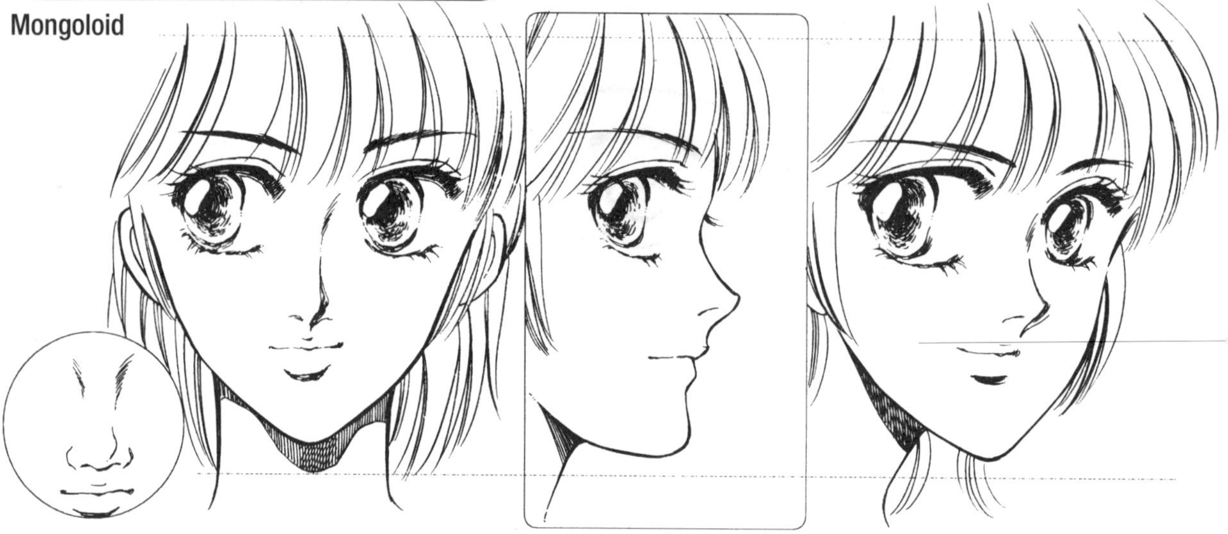

Negroid

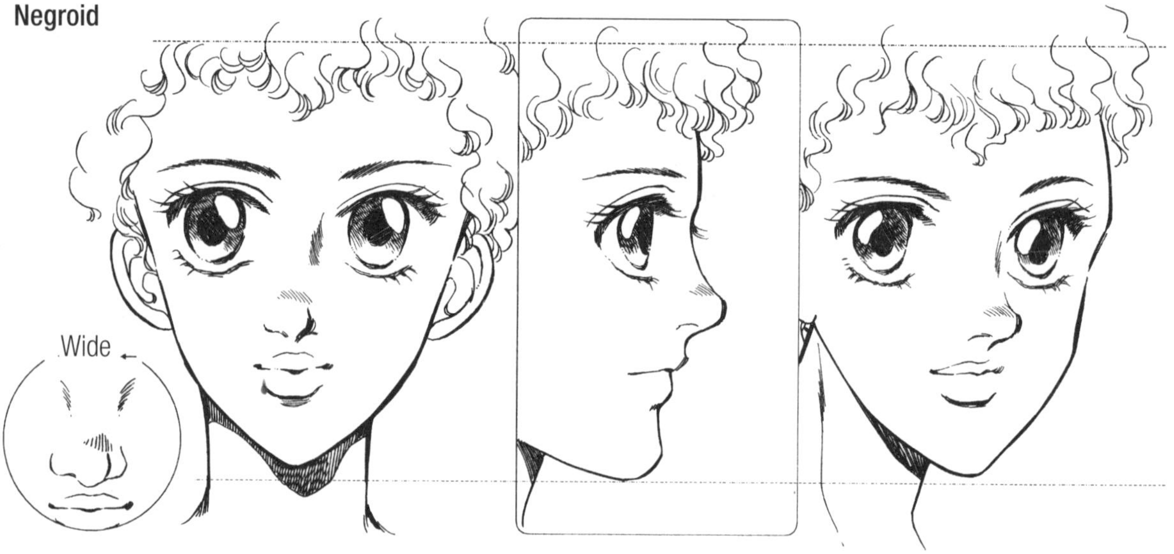

Caucasoid

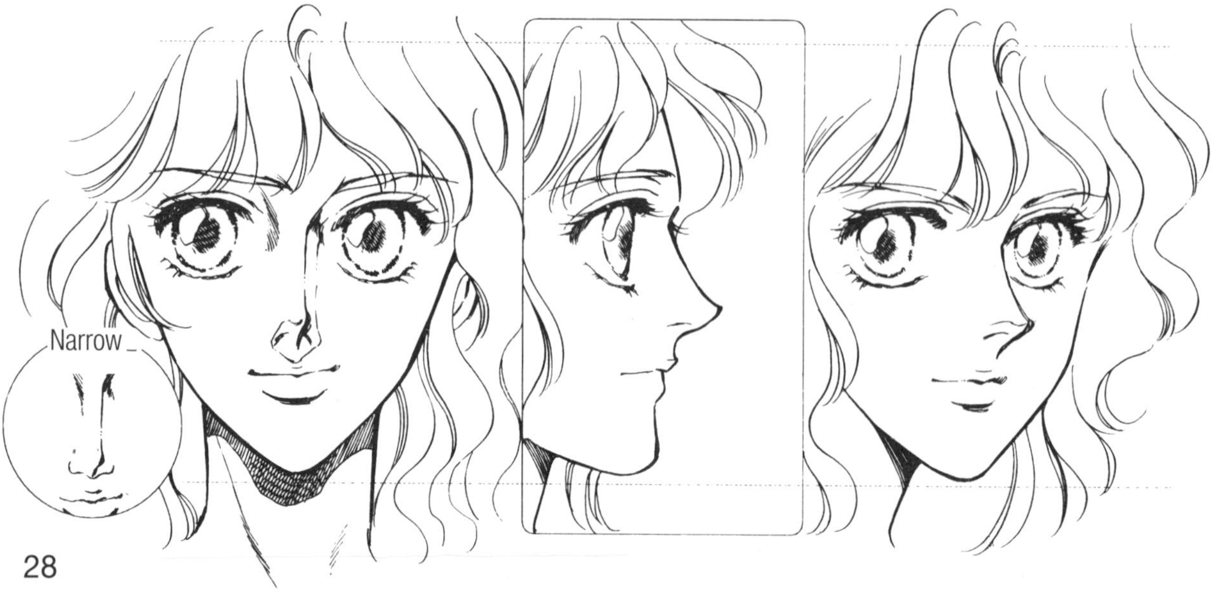

Simplified version

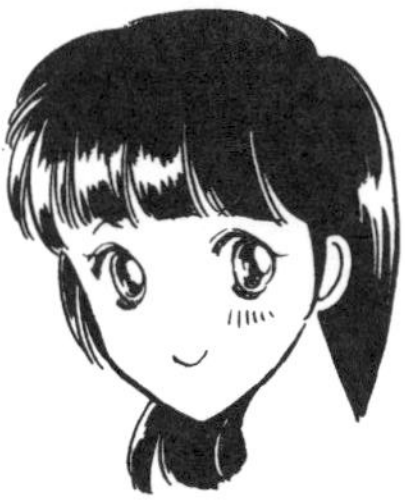

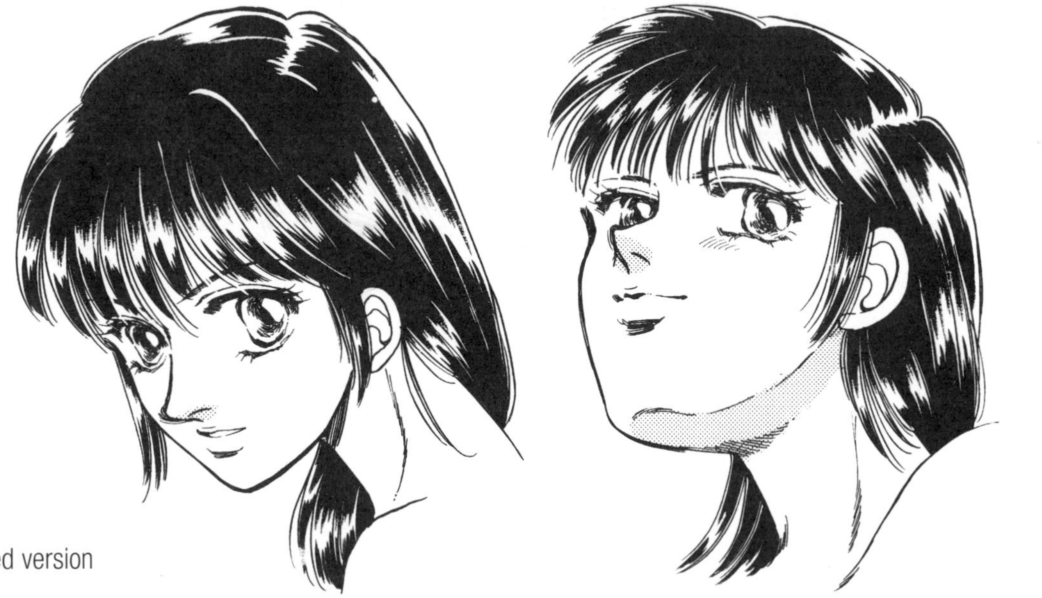

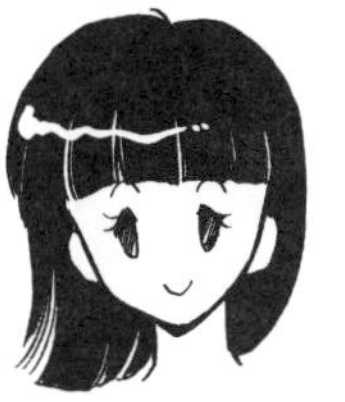

Extremely simplified version

Simplified version

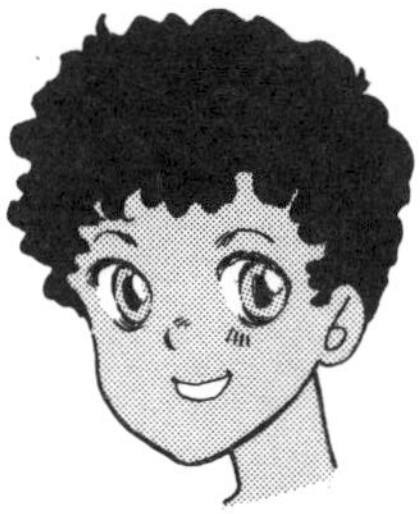

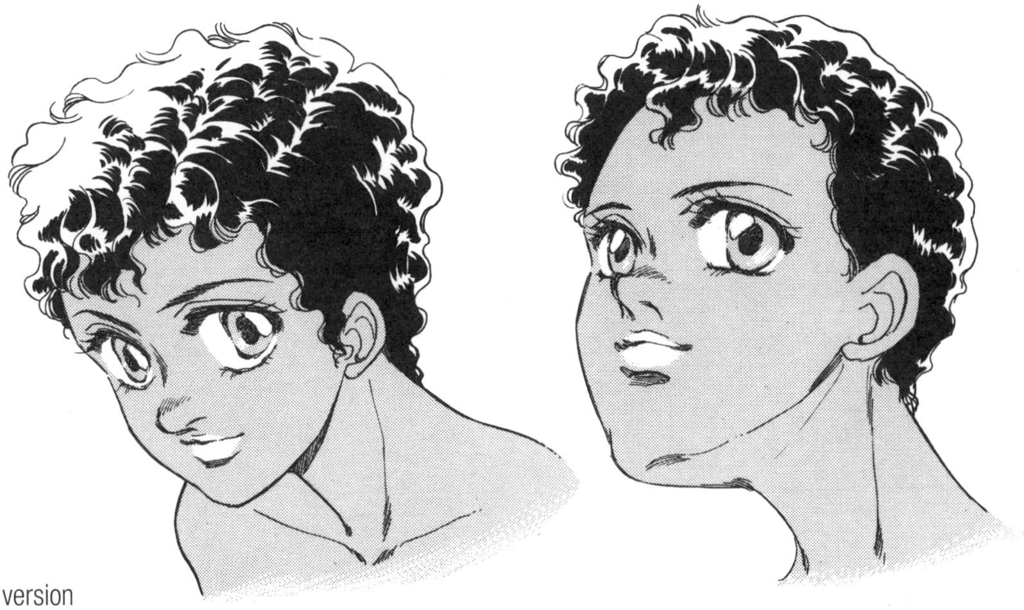

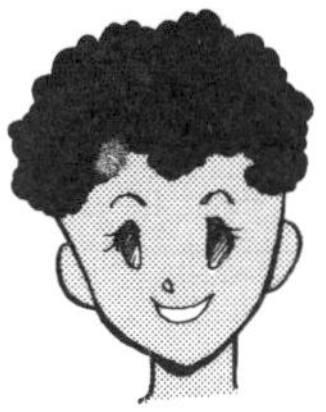

Extremely simplified version

Simplified version

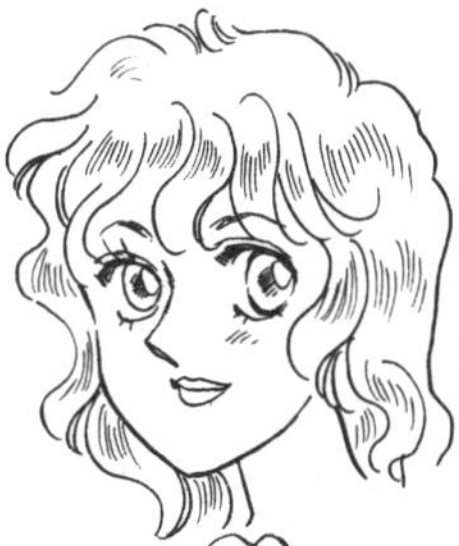

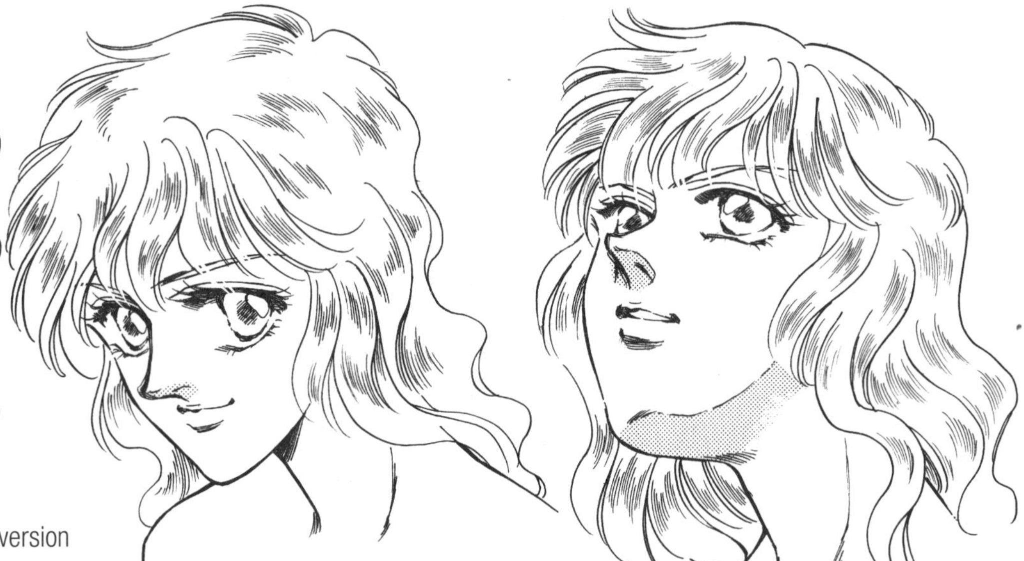

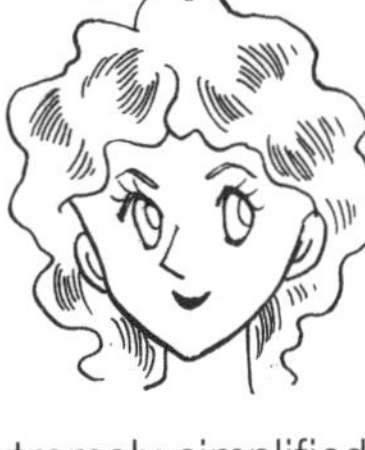

Extremely simplified version

Expressing the Definition of Facial Features

Variations on the three types can be increased further with the definition of facial features.

Face with less-defined features

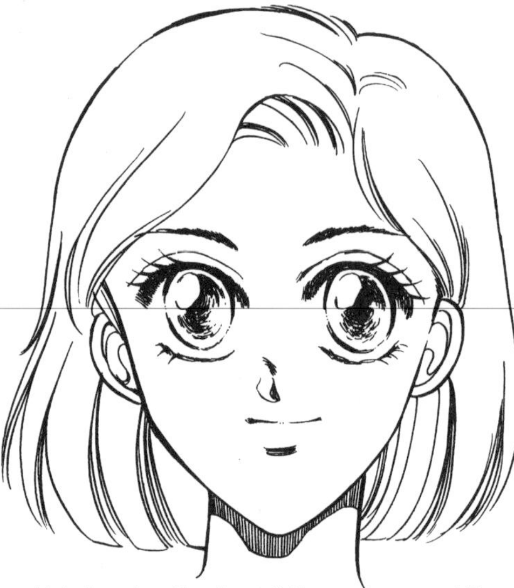

Not drawing the line of the nose nor adding shadows renders a smooth, child-like face.

Face with well-defined features

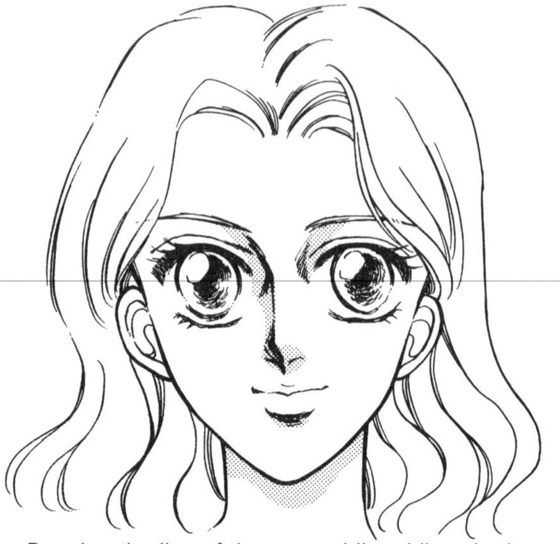

Drawing the line of the nose while adding shadows renders a clear-cut face. On one hand, the looks become well defined, however, the cuteness fades away resulting in a more adult-like face.

Cute foreheads are drawn wide.

For sharply defined foreheads, the curve is gentle.

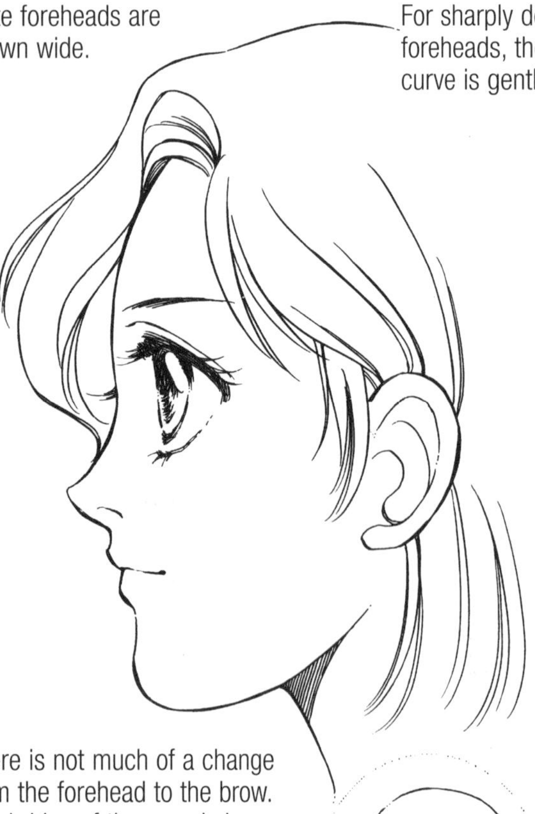

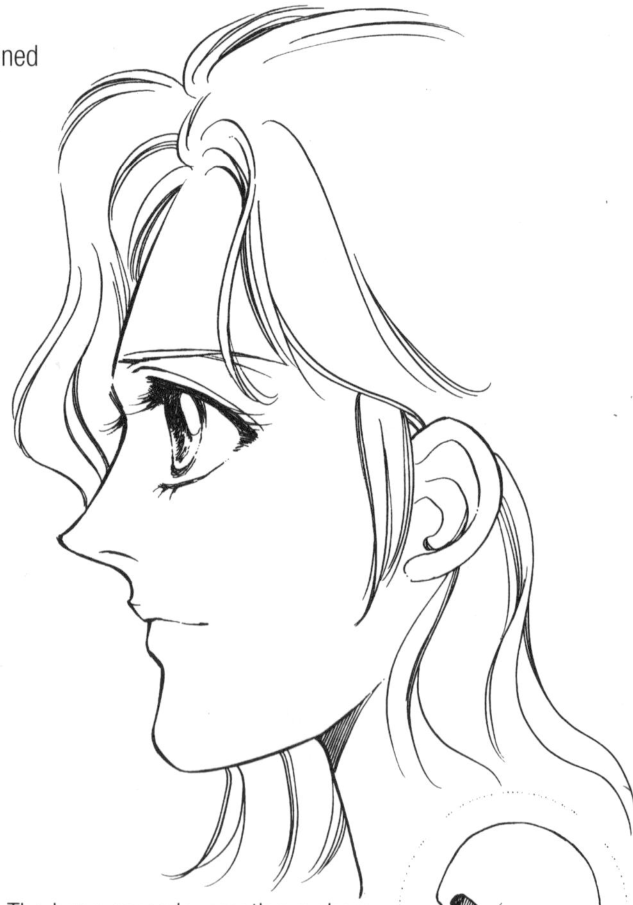

There is not much of a change from the forehead to the brow. The bridge of the nose is lower, and the nose itself is small-sized. Combined with the soft jaw-line, it gives a delicate impression.

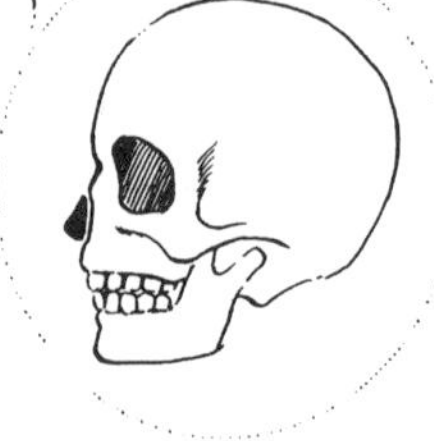

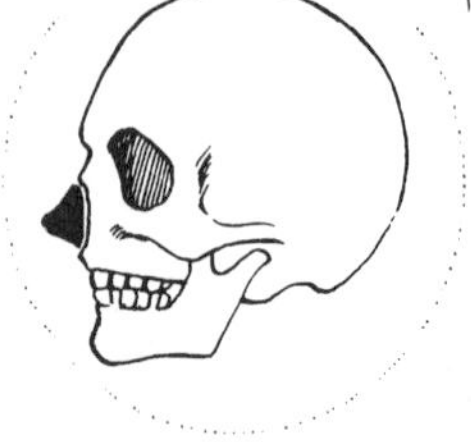

The brow caves in, creating a sharp contrast with the protuberance of the forehead. The bridge of the nose is higher while the nose is larger. Also, the jaw is often stout.

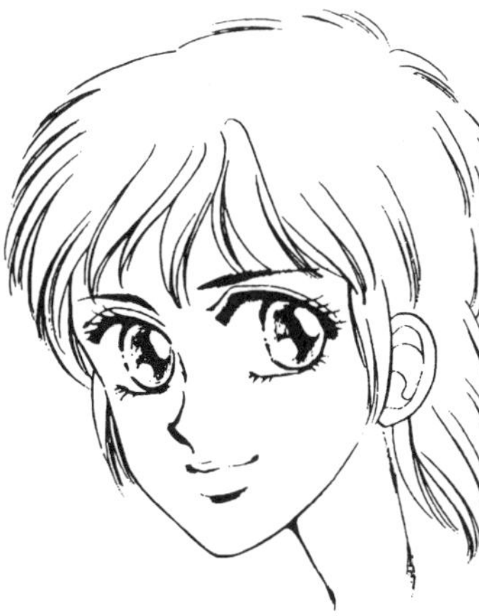

If you choose not to connect the line of the eyebrow with the nose, the result will be a cute face with less-defined features.

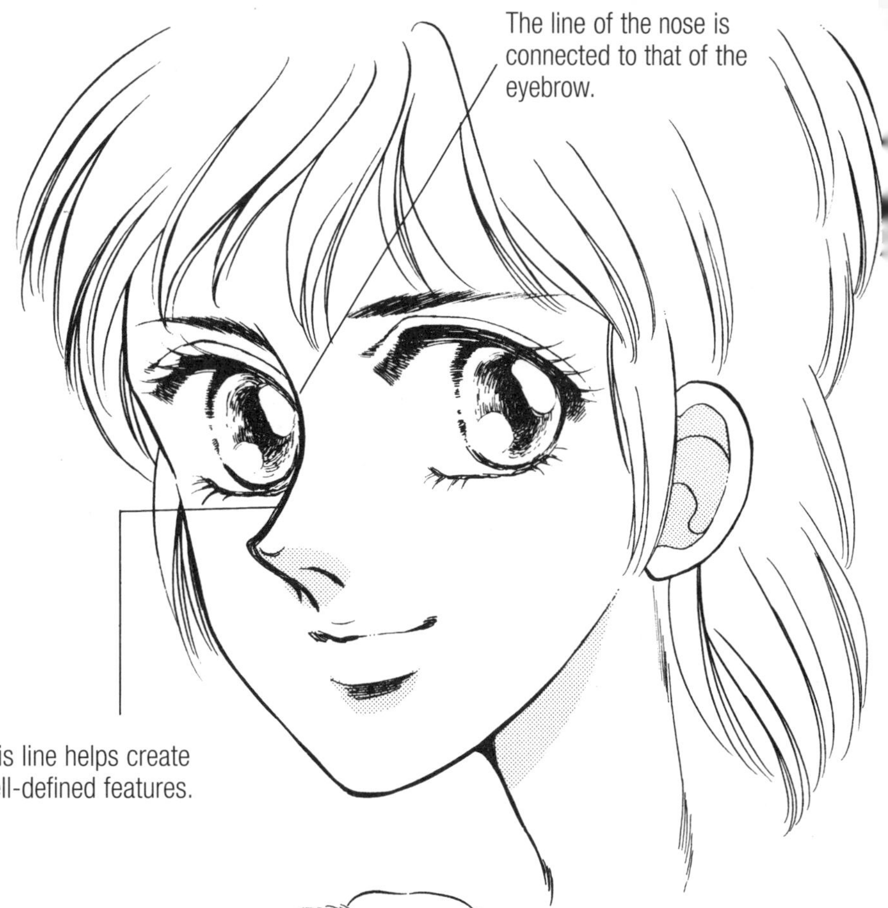

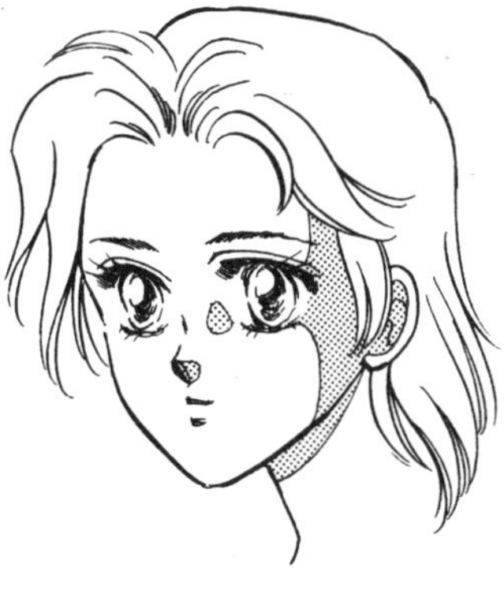

In this case, not much of a shadow results from strong light at a slanted angle. It looks simple rather than flat.

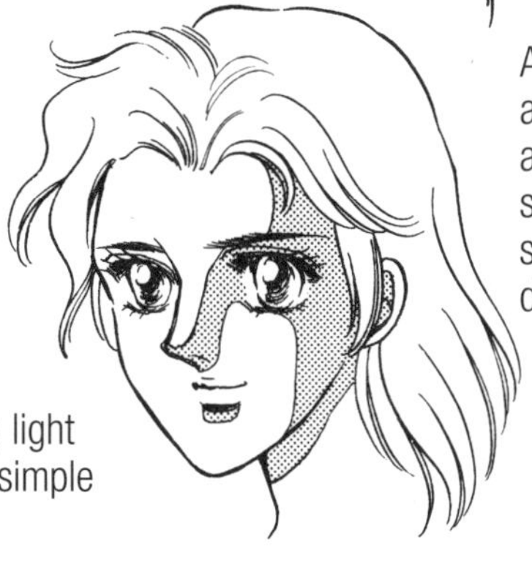

A strong light directed at a slanted angle from above casts a full shadow and drastically shows the three-dimensionality.

Mongoloid and Negroid Bishoujo with Clear-Cut Facial Features

Clear-cut facial features and the nose line are distinctive traits of Caucasoid characters. However, these traits can be applied to both Mongoloid and Negroid characters as well.

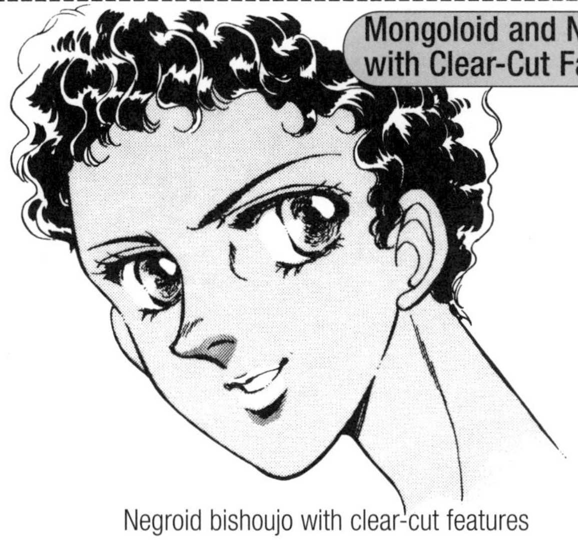

Negroid bishoujo with clear-cut features

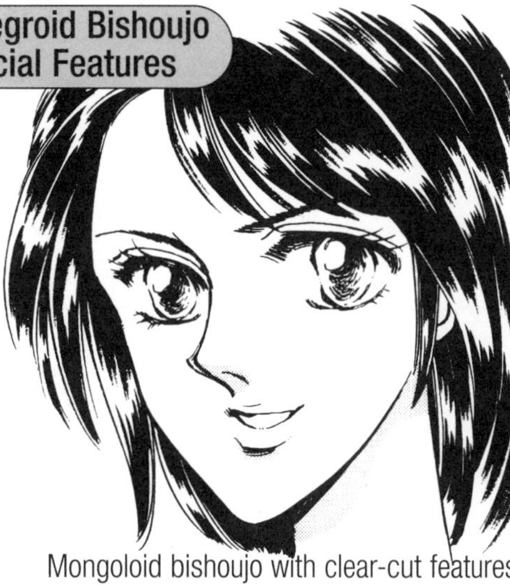

Mongoloid bishoujo with clear-cut features

Expressing Variations

There is a variety of individual styles and balance among the three types.

Proportions

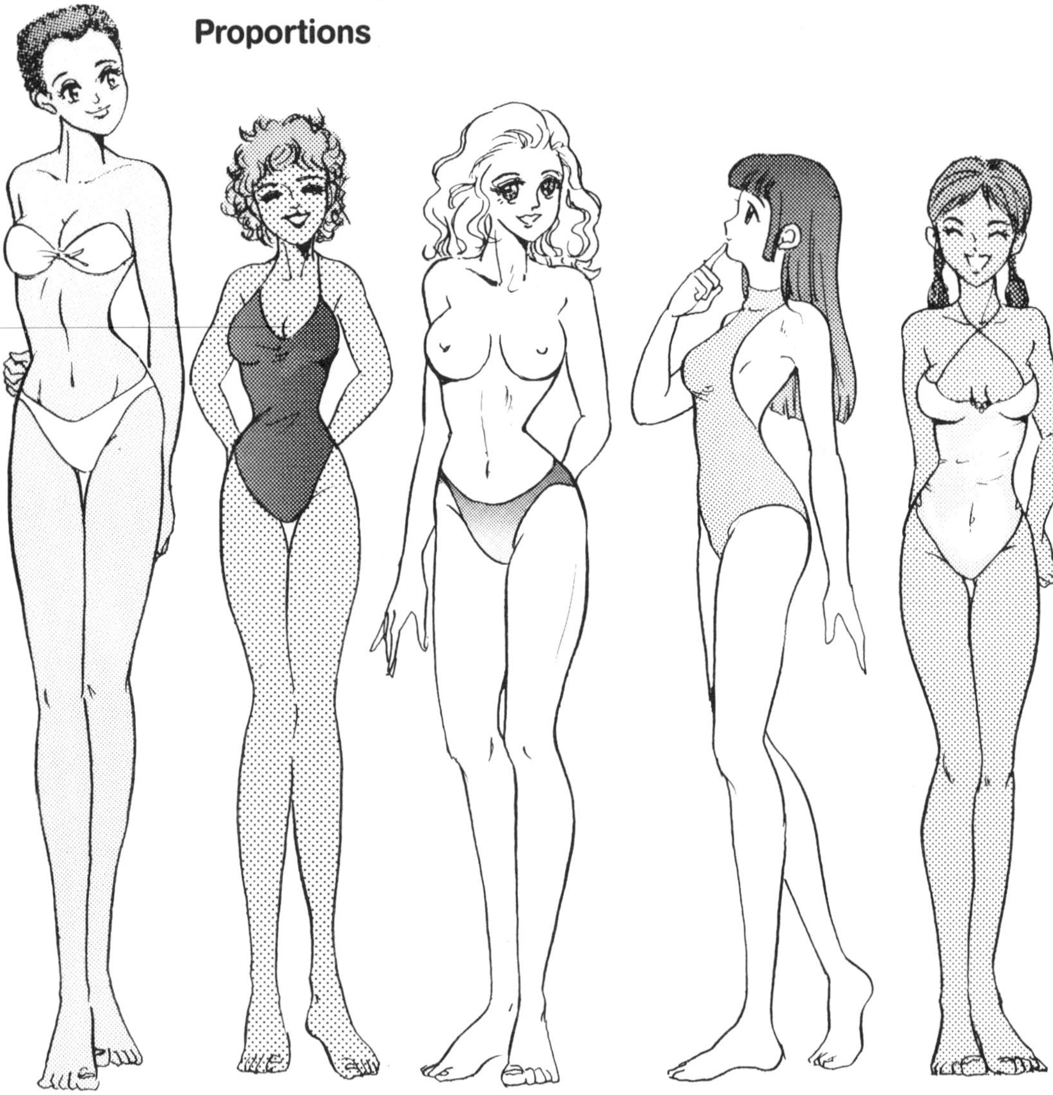

Negroid **Caucasoid** **Mongoloid**

Even Mongoloids of the same height have individual differences in the height of the breast and crotch areas.

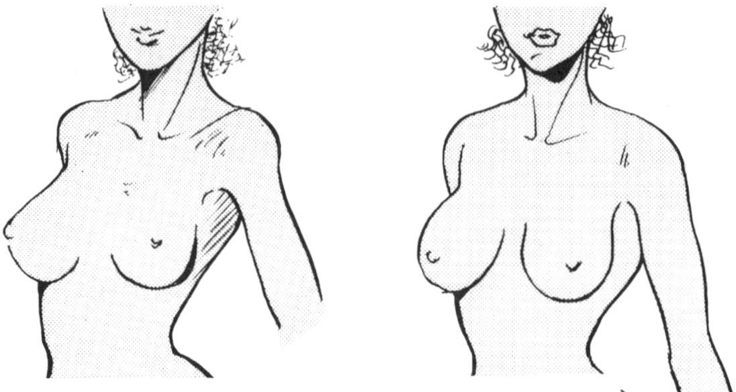

While both represent Negroid type breasts, by making minor changes in details, you can expand the range of your characters.

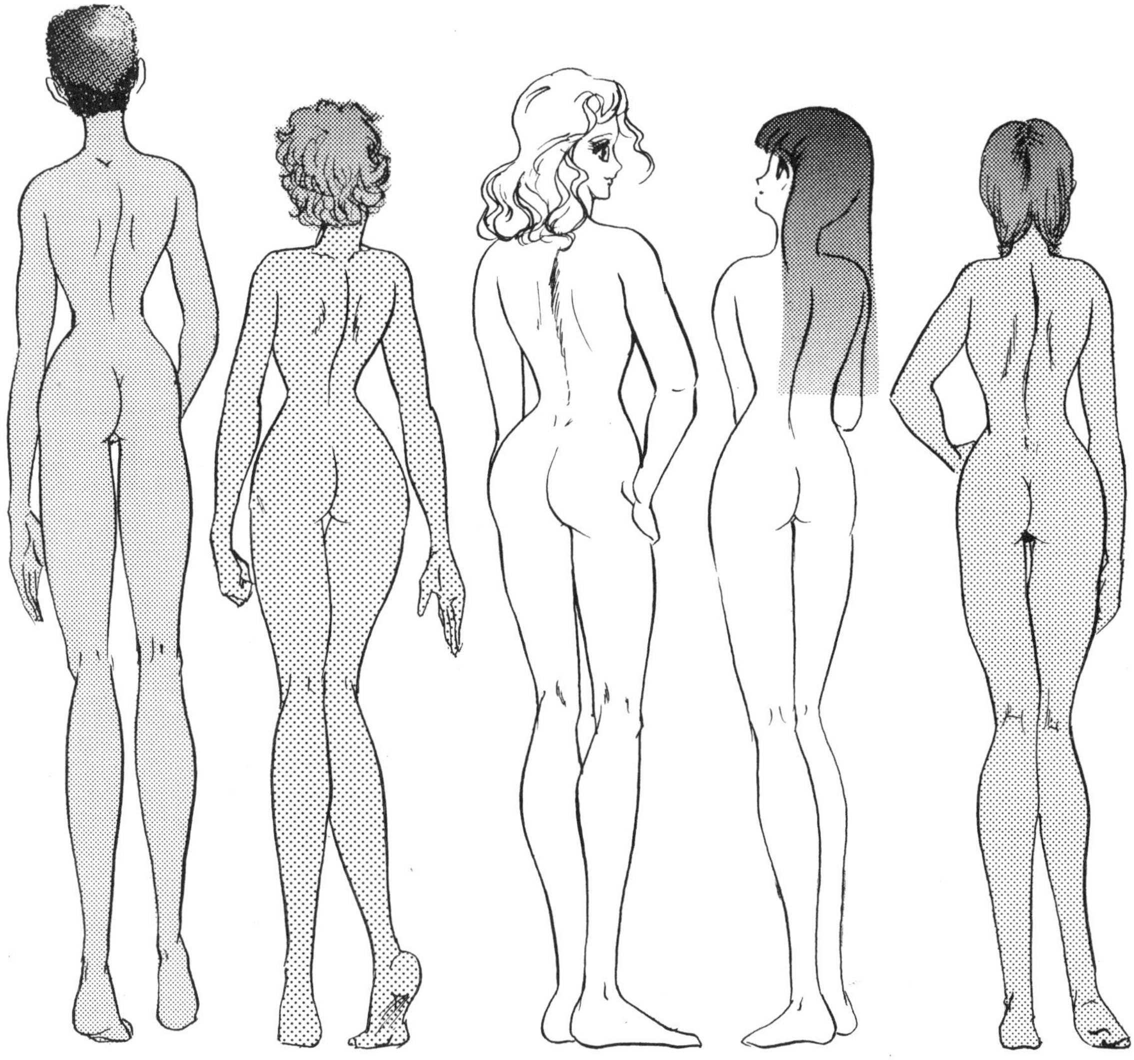

Negroid Caucasoid Mongoloid

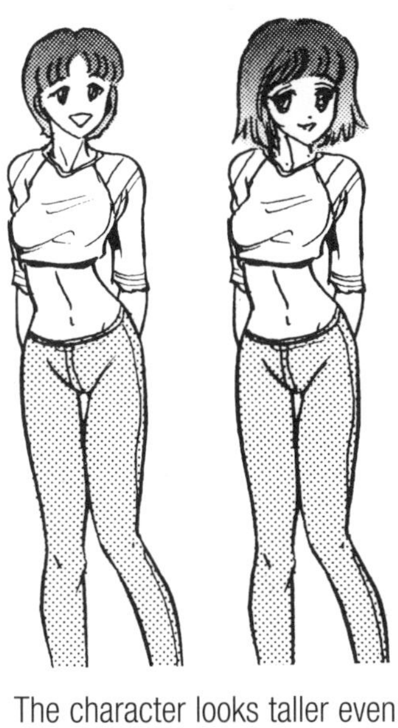

The character looks taller even with the same height and figure when the head is small.

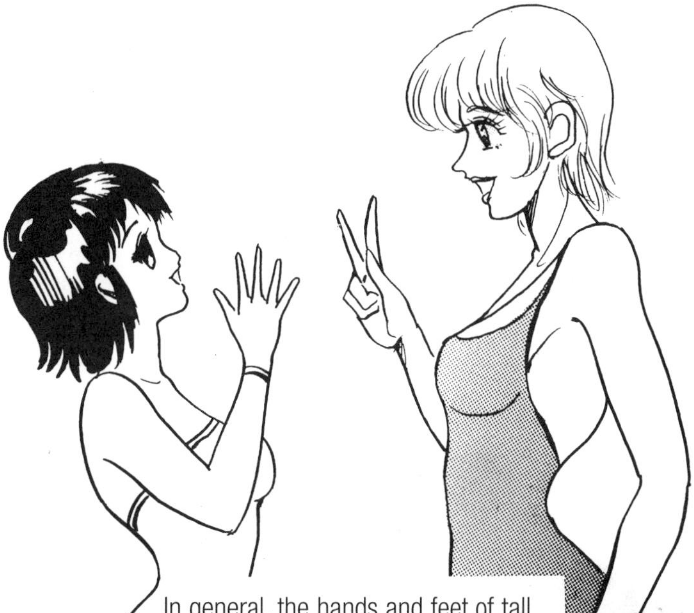

In general, the hands and feet of tall characters are larger than those of shorter characters.

Bringing Out The Dasein and Three-Dimensionality

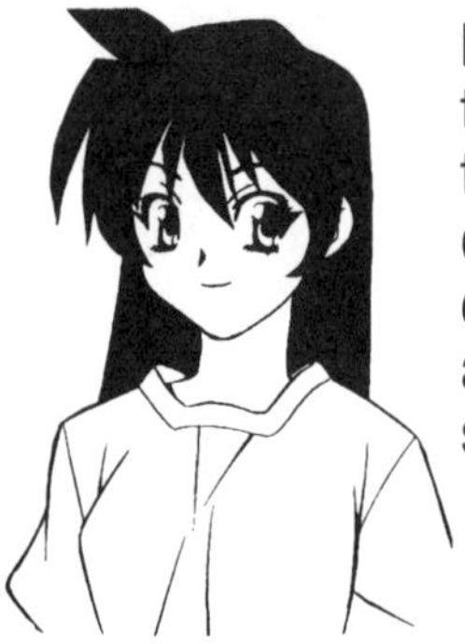

By expressing shadows on the body with tones and the like, the three-dimensionality of the character becomes distinct and the dasein grows stronger.

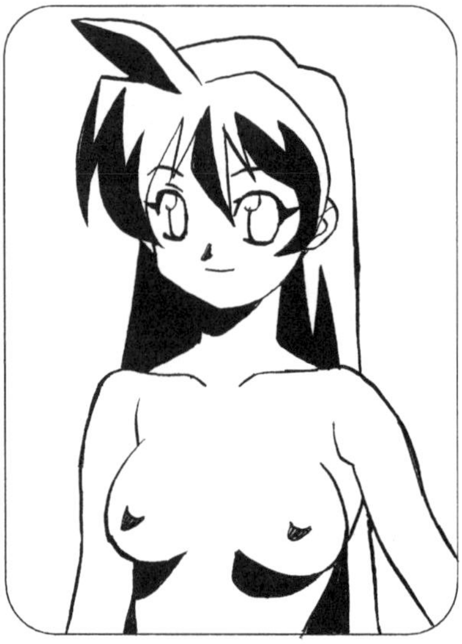

When a bright light is shown on the subject, the shadows become darker.

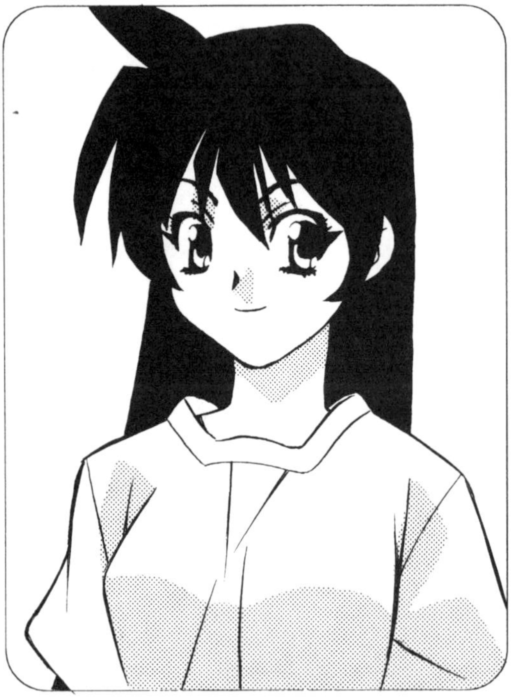

Ordinary indoor light represented with a 10% to 20% tone.

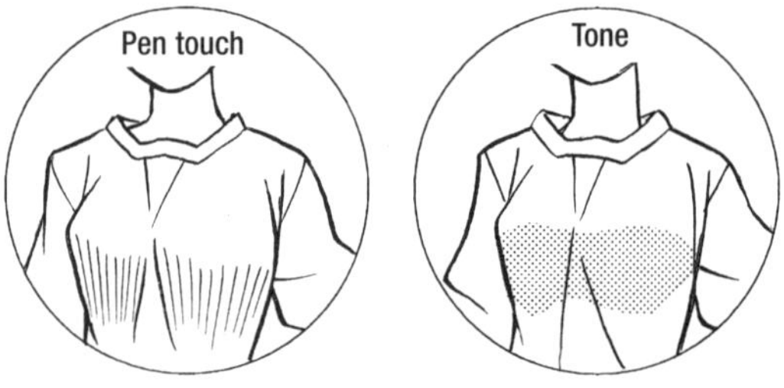

The expression of the wrinkles in the shirt and the swelling of the chest are some of the ways to express shadows.

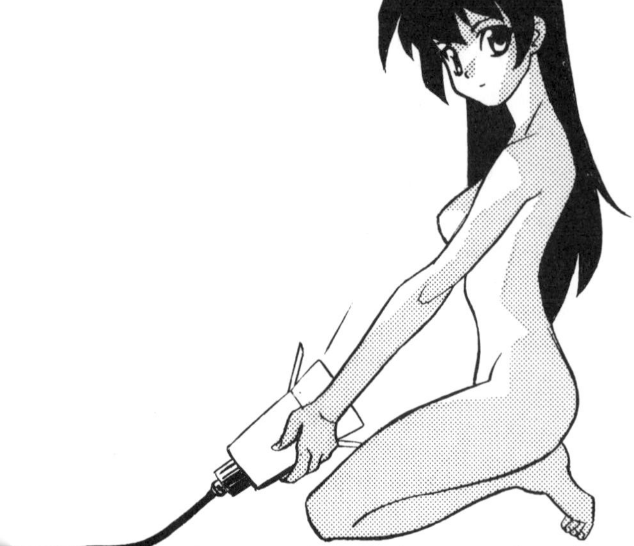

The edge of the shadows runs along the curved areas of the body.

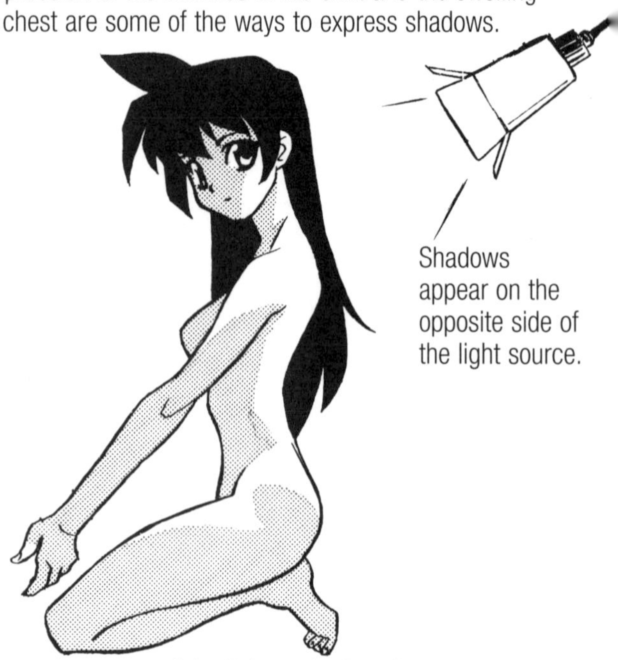

Shadows appear on the opposite side of the light source.

Areas that are stuck by light and reflect light are white.

Even with the light source in the same position, depending on the pose taken, the shape of the shadows will change.

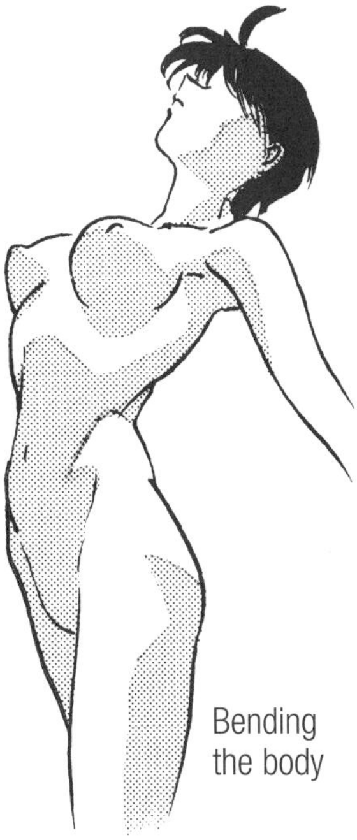

Bending the body

Light directly from above

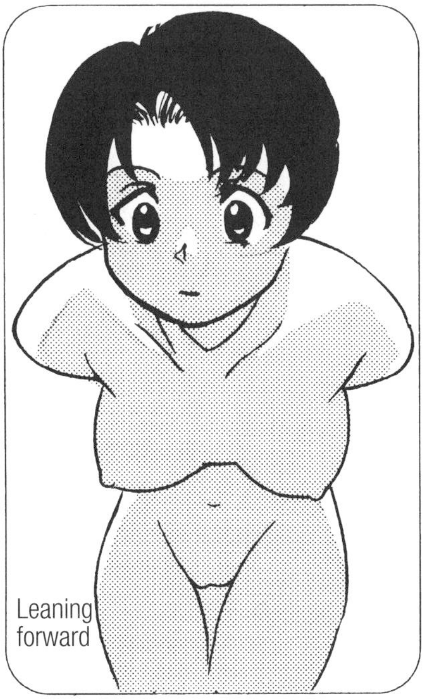

Leaning forward

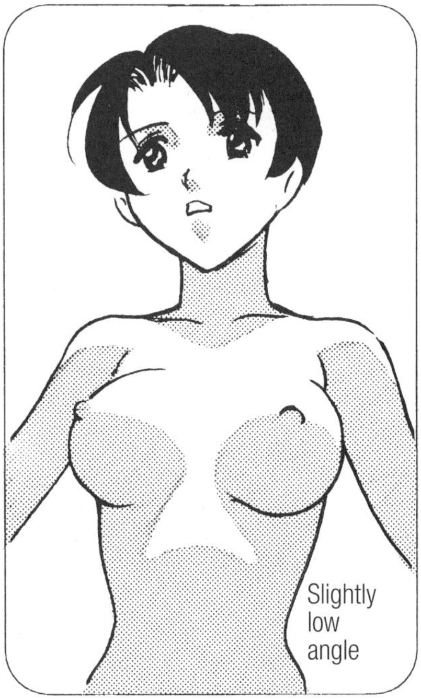

Slightly low angle

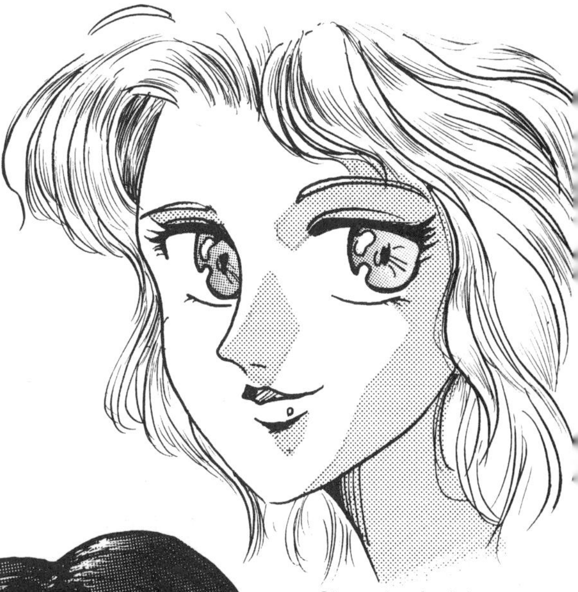

Since the facial features in Caucasoid bishoujo are clear-cut, shadows easily appear.

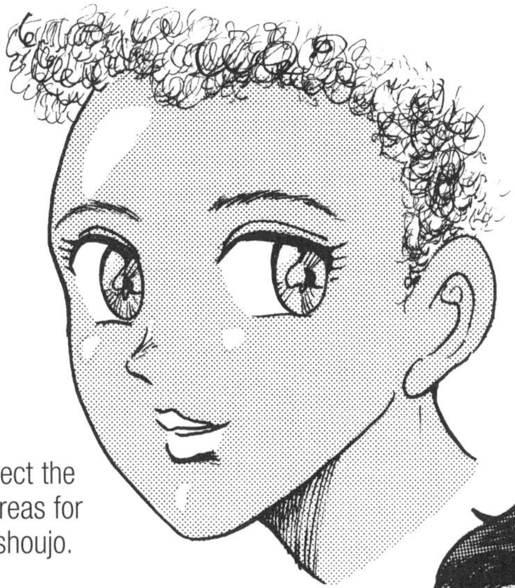

Visually direct the reflected areas for Negroid bishoujo.

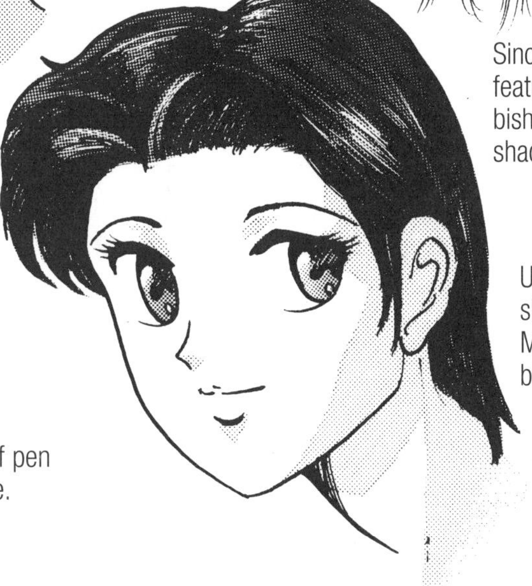

Use light shadows for Mongoloid bishoujo.

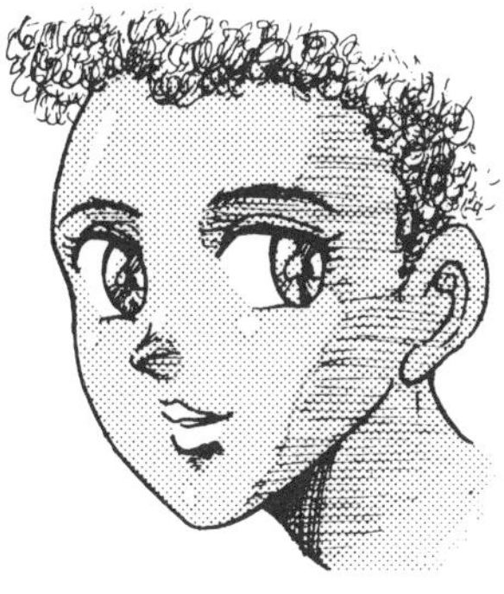

Combination of pen touch and tone.

Light Source Positioning

Shadows are created by light along the peaks and valleys of the body. Choose the location of the light source before drawing the shadows.

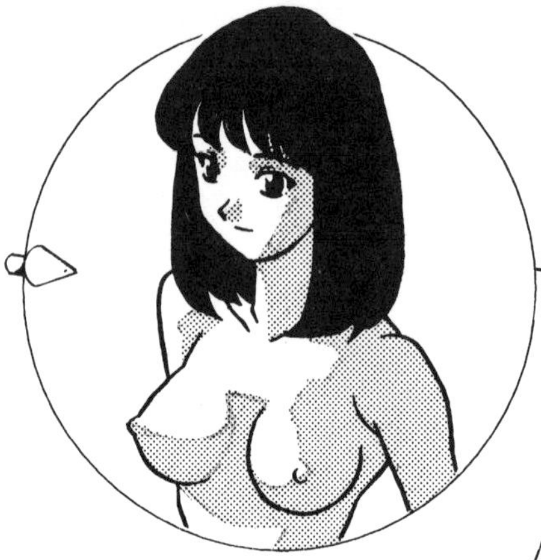

Light from the left

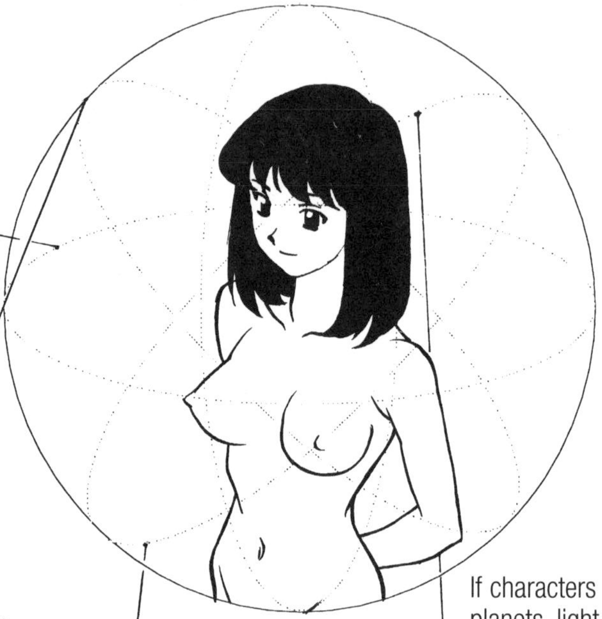

If characters were planets, light sources can be imagined as orbiting satellites.

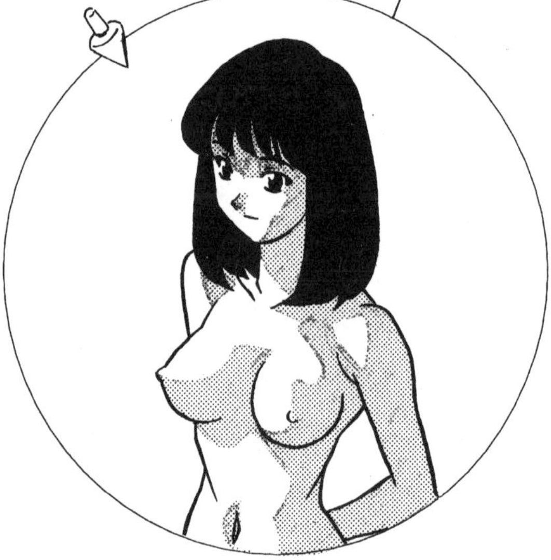

Light from the front left

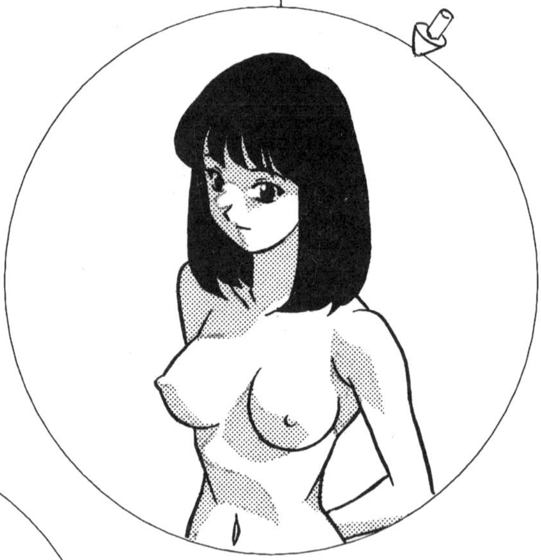

Light from the right and above

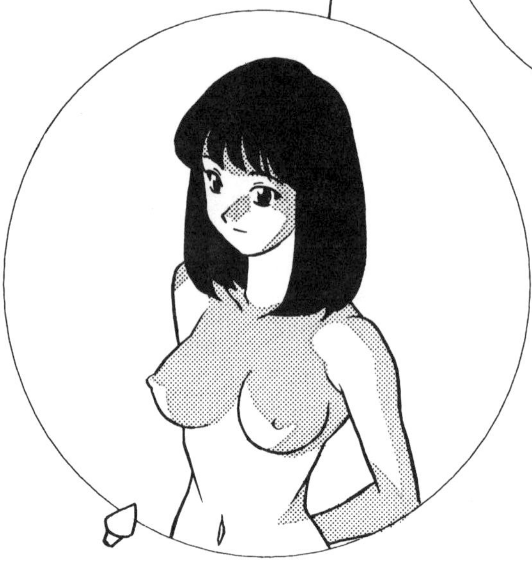

Light from the left and below

Lines of the Muscles

The lines of the muscles and bones (i.e. clavicle) that are drawn on the body, arms and legs are actually expressions of shadows. Using shadows is one method of expressing the qualities of the muscles.

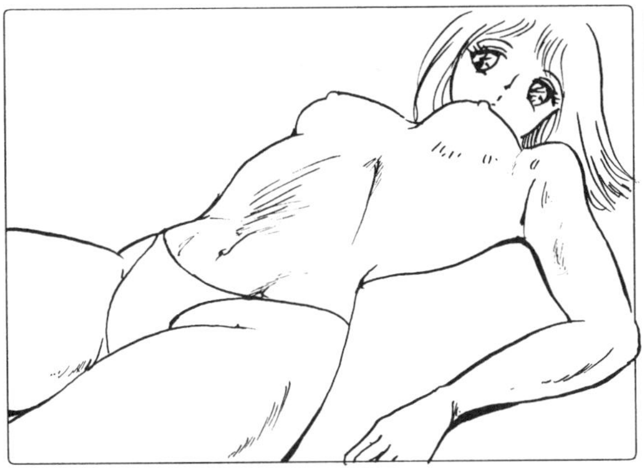

Slanted lines emphasize the muscularity.

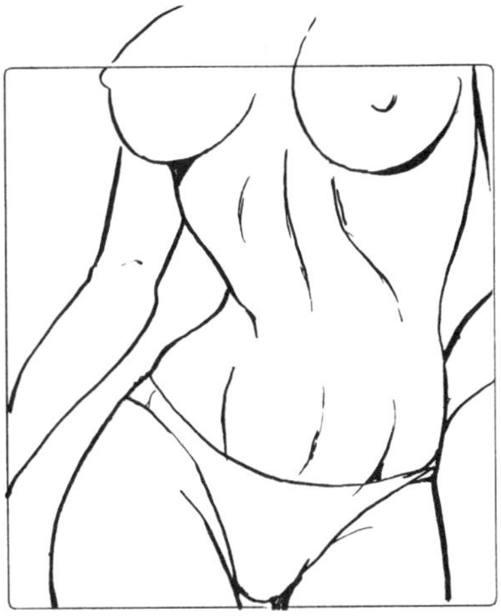

An example of the undulating lines of this ordinary body. Curved lines help express its limberness and softness.

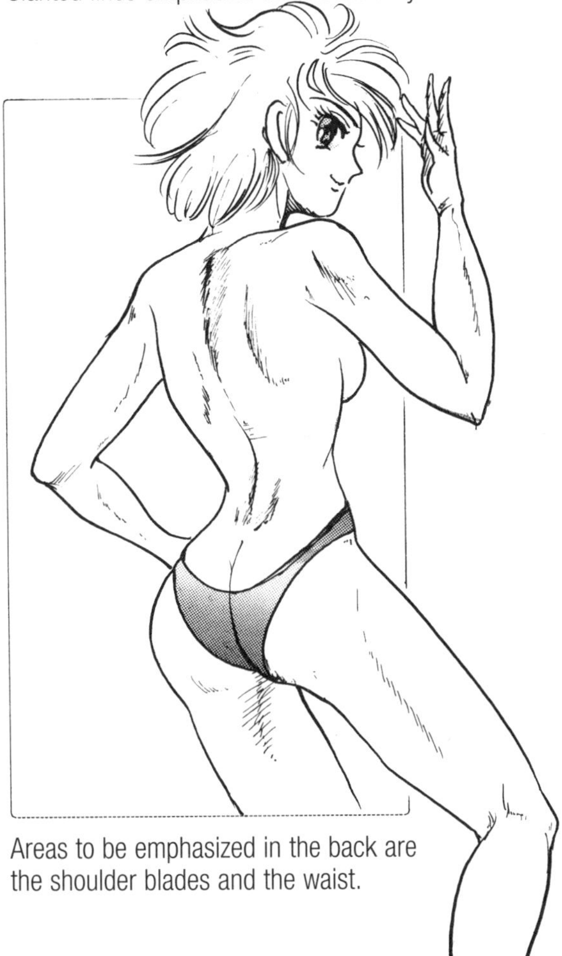

Areas to be emphasized in the back are the shoulder blades and the waist.

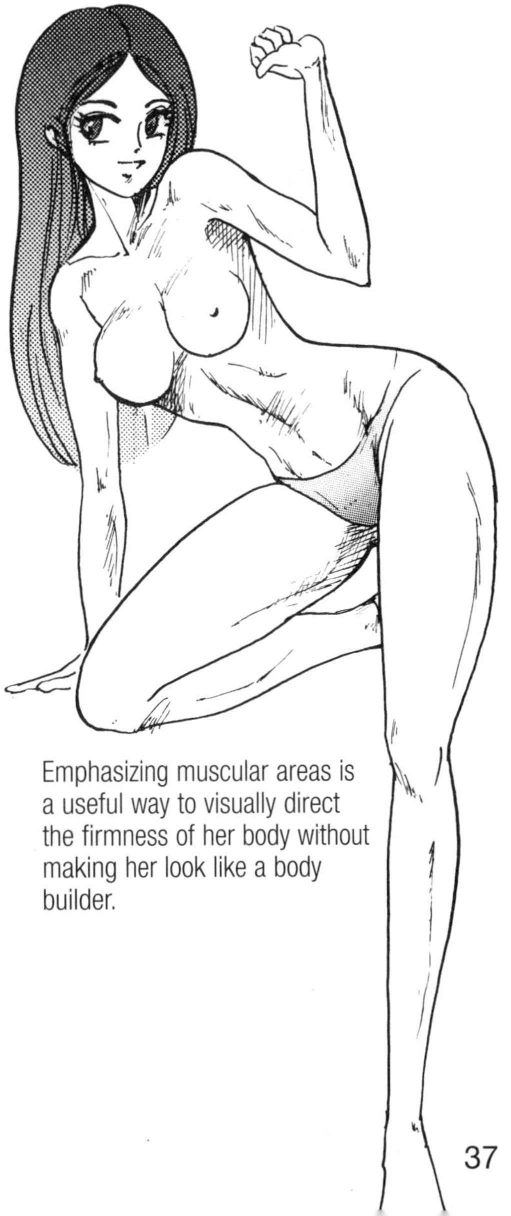

Emphasizing muscular areas is a useful way to visually direct the firmness of her body without making her look like a body builder.

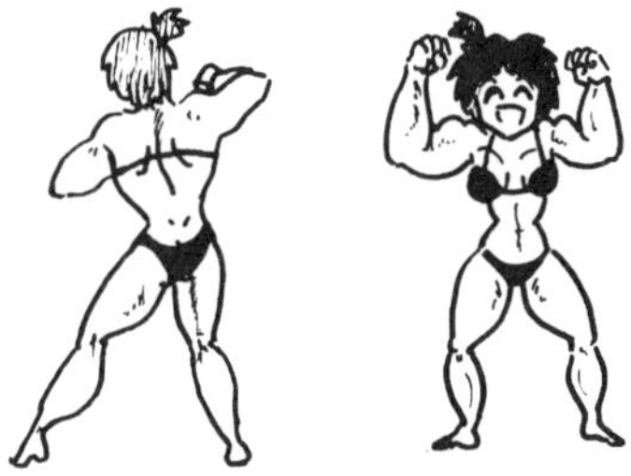

Reference: Macho figures

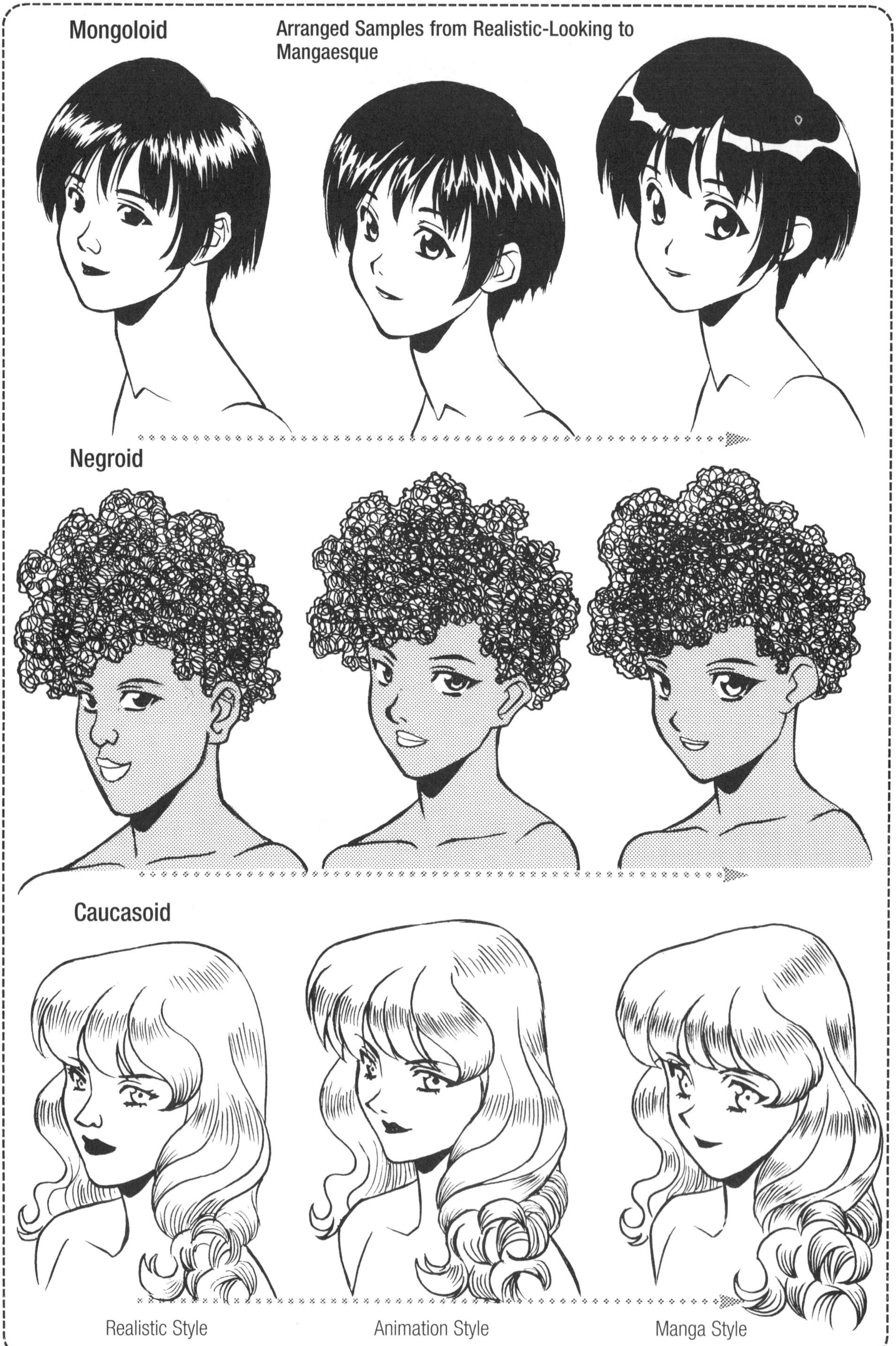
Mongoloid
Arranged Samples from Realistic-Looking to Mangaesque
Negroid
Caucasoid
Realistic Style
Animation Style
Manga Style

Chapter 2

How to Draw Bishoujo From Different Countries and Regions

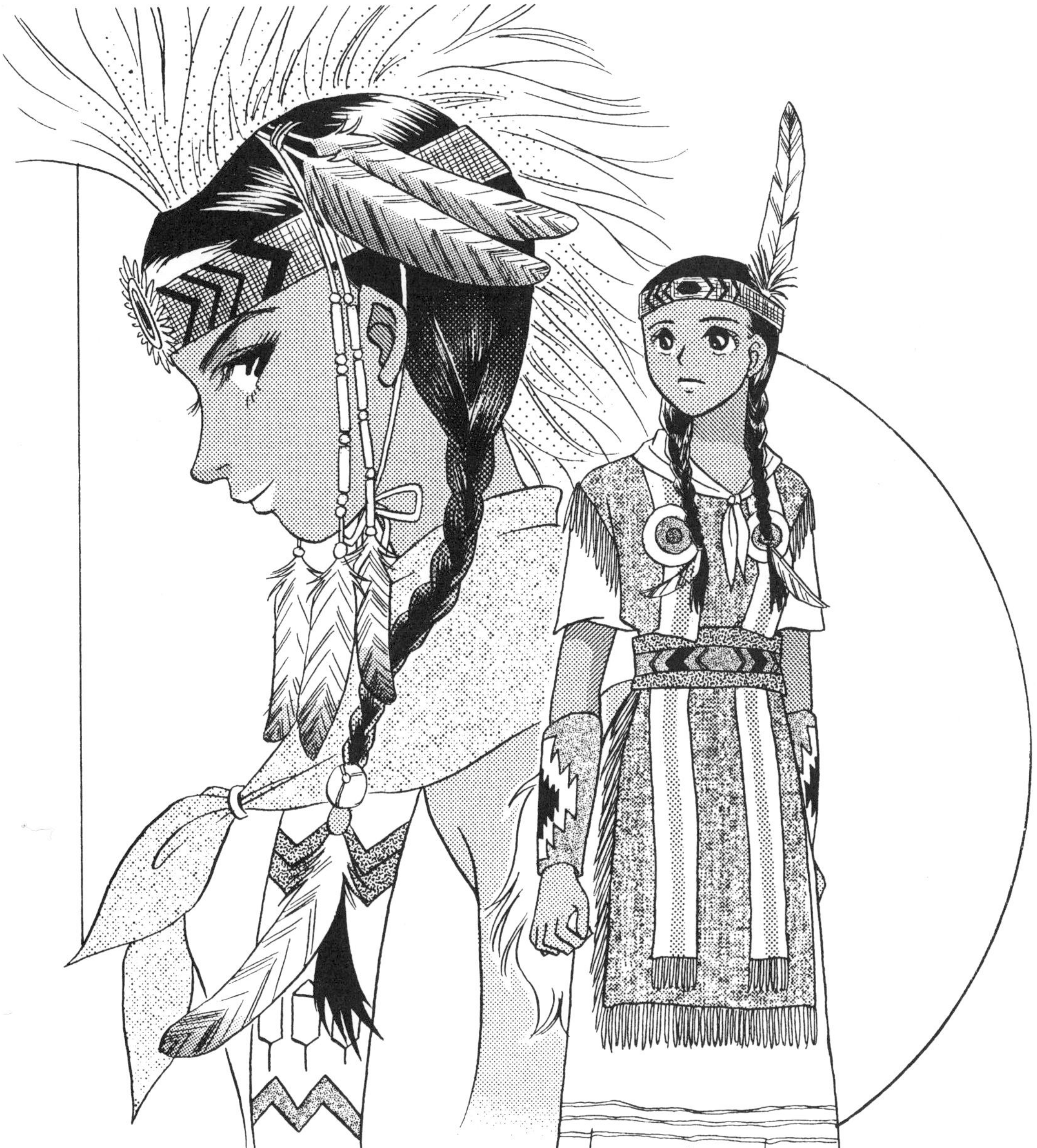

Learning About the Countries of the Girls You Want to Draw

All bishoujo around the world fall into three categories; the question is which one, Mongoloid, Caucasoid or Negroid.

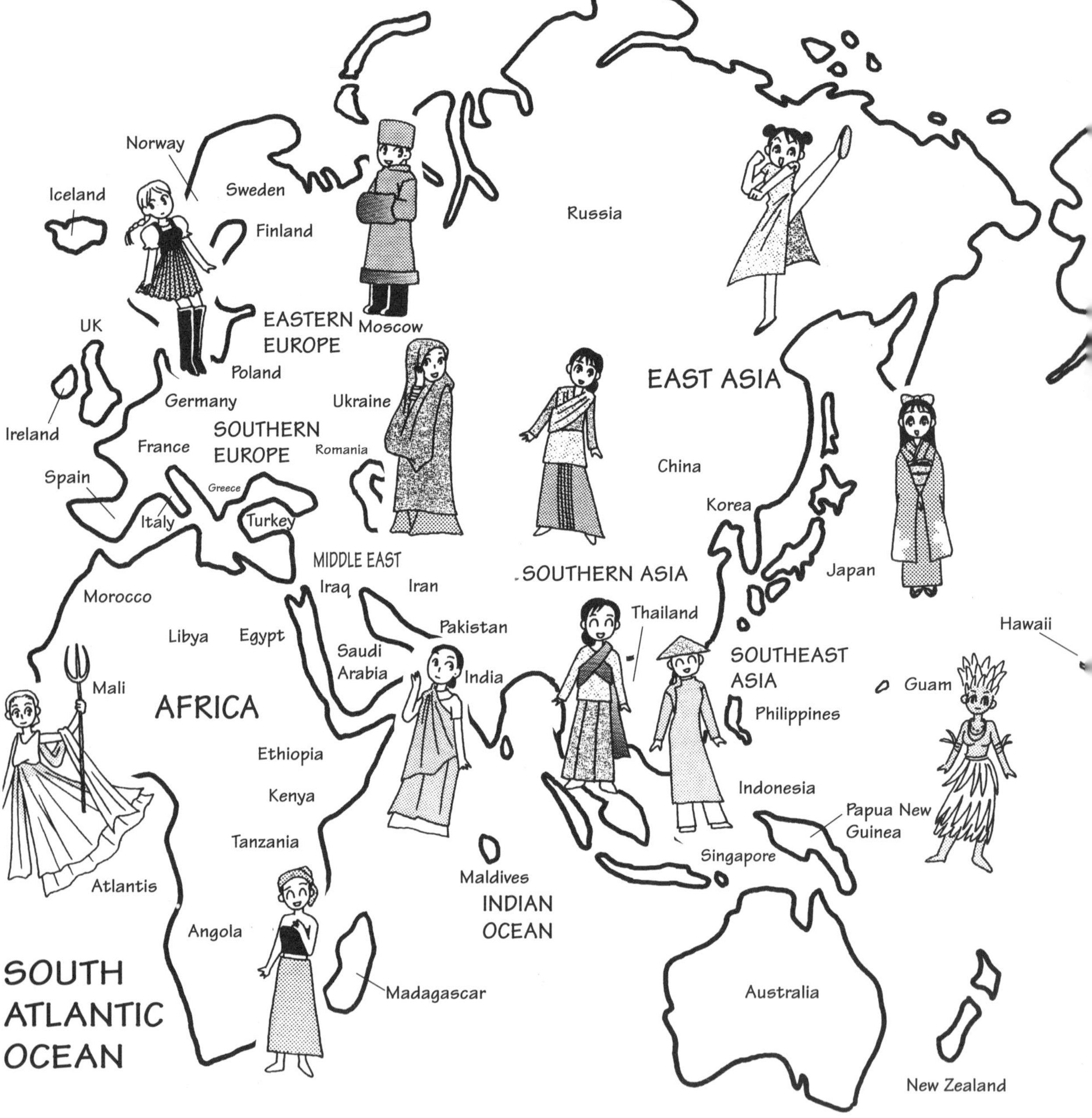

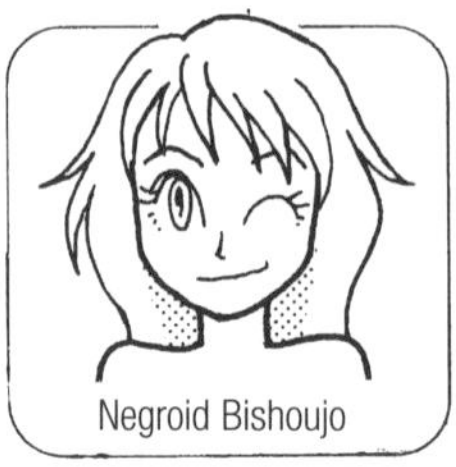

Negroid Bishoujo

- Wavy hair
- Light blue to black eyes
- Adult face with a defined noseline

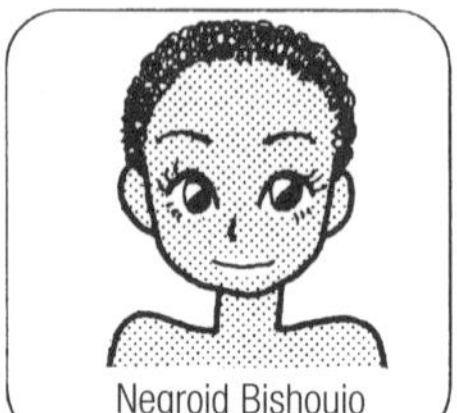

Negroid Bishoujo

- Curly hair
- Brown to black eyes
- Cute round nose

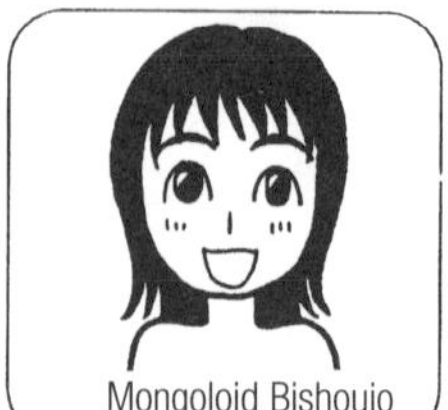

Mongoloid Bishoujo

- Straight hair
- Brown to black eyes
- Baby face with a smooth noseline

To draw foreign bishoujo:

- Bring out distinctive features in the body types.
- Visually direct things such as fashion.

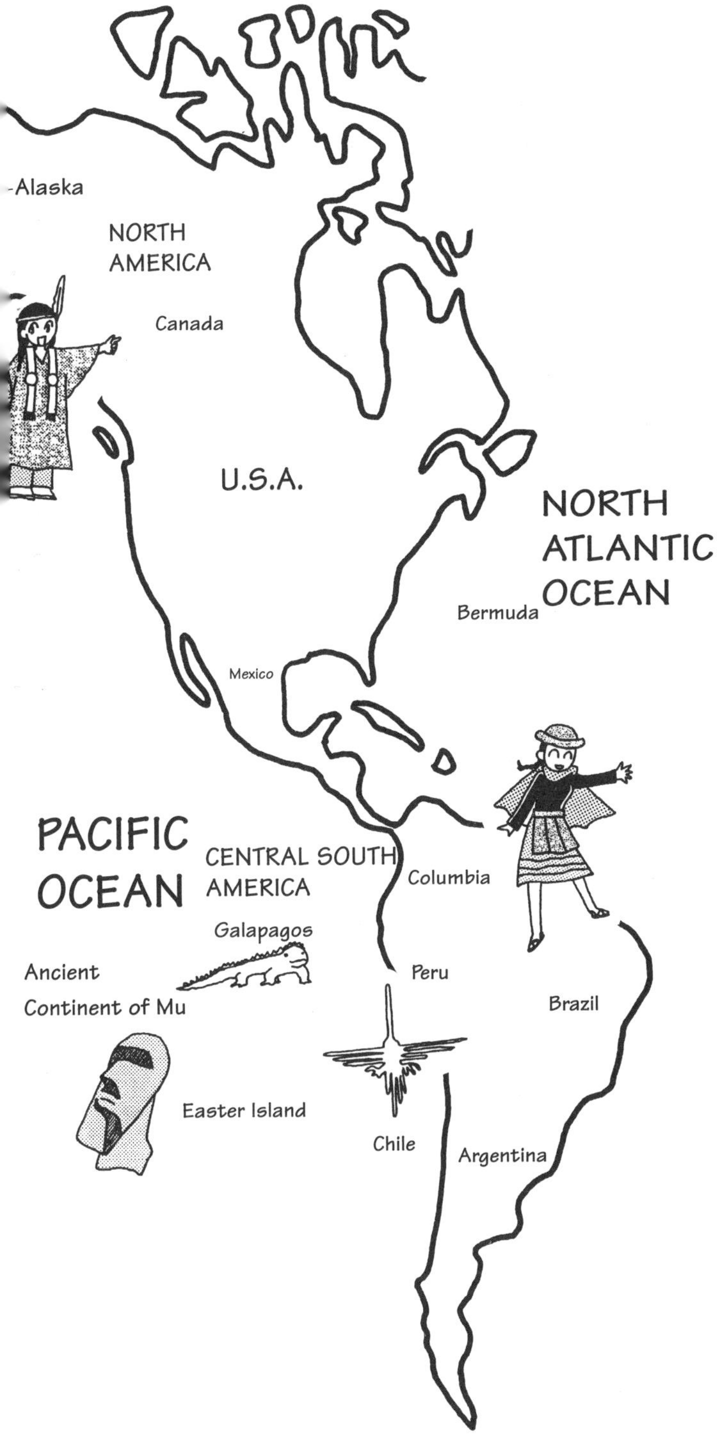

People Are All the Same

Appearances may be deceiving!!

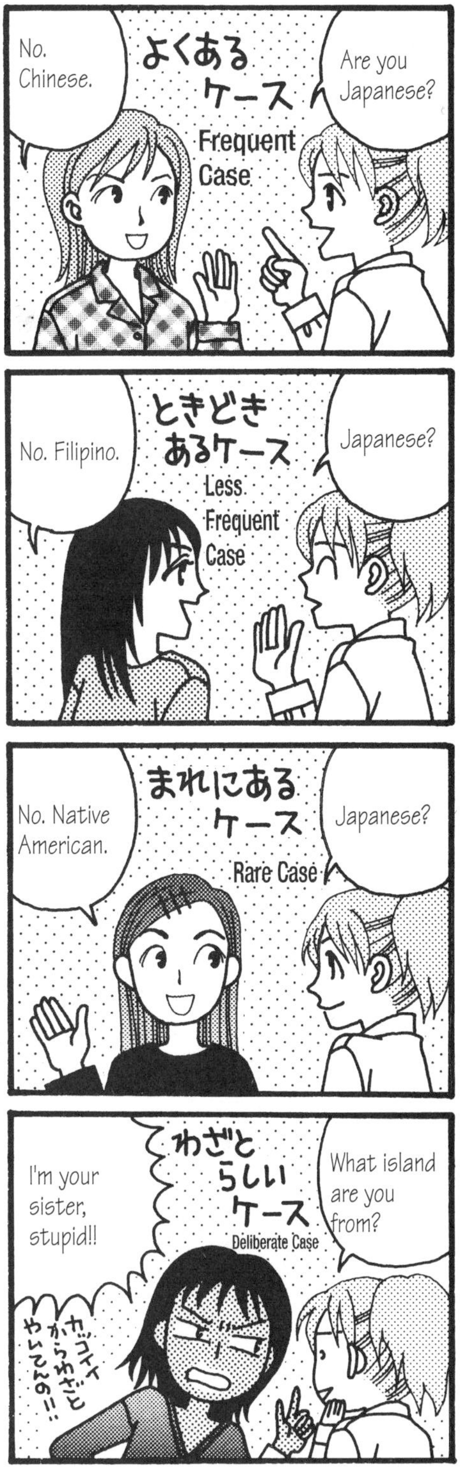

This is a tan!

Often times, we won't know where people are from until we ask them. Character introduction is indispensable to manga. In addition to using visual direction and easily identifiable fashion, make sure you give distinction to the looks of each character.

Drawing Girls of Unknown Nationalities

Fashion and Makeup

Modern day makeup and fashion are ever-changing. Do your best to incorporate these elements into your visual direction and design.

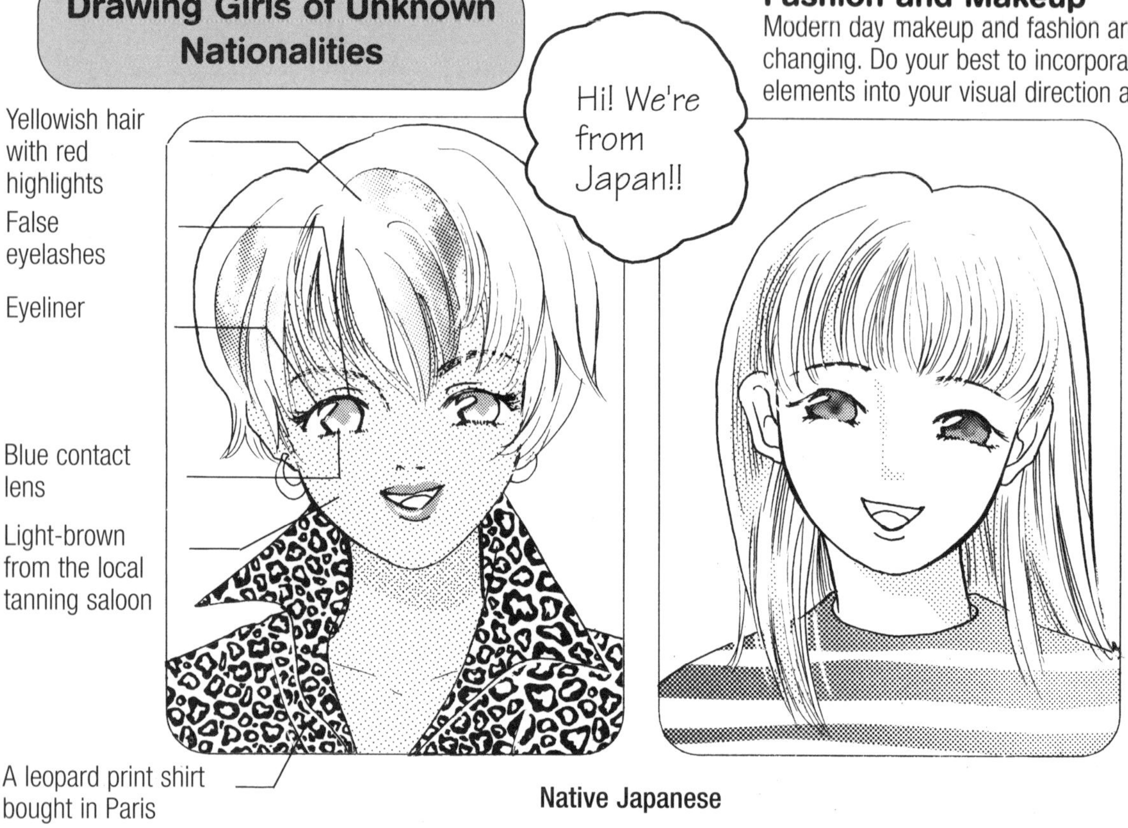

Native Japanese

Differences in Time Periods and Appearances of Girls

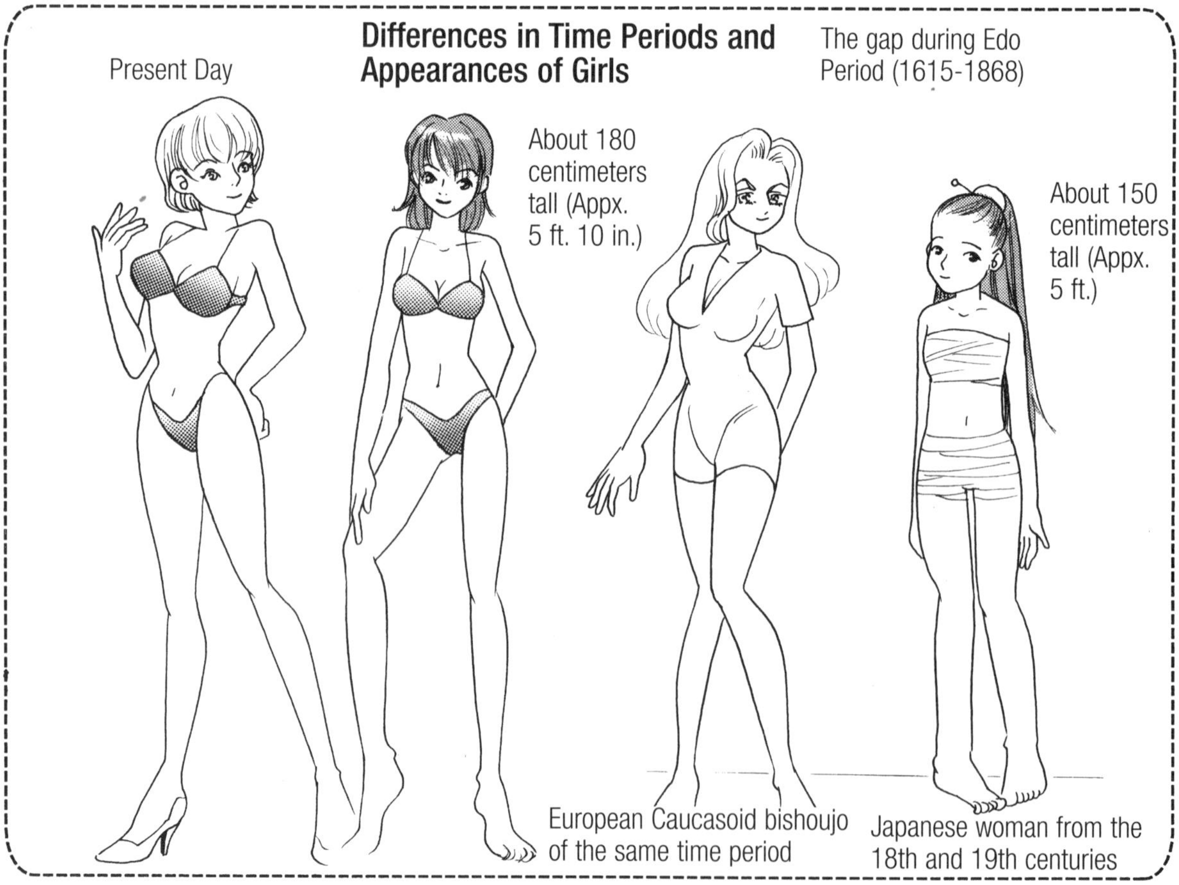

Racially Mixed Girls

People of mixed race possess a combination of their parents' special features. Unfathomable character heredity and genetic constitution from dominant and recessive genes seen in DNA are all permitted in the world of manga.

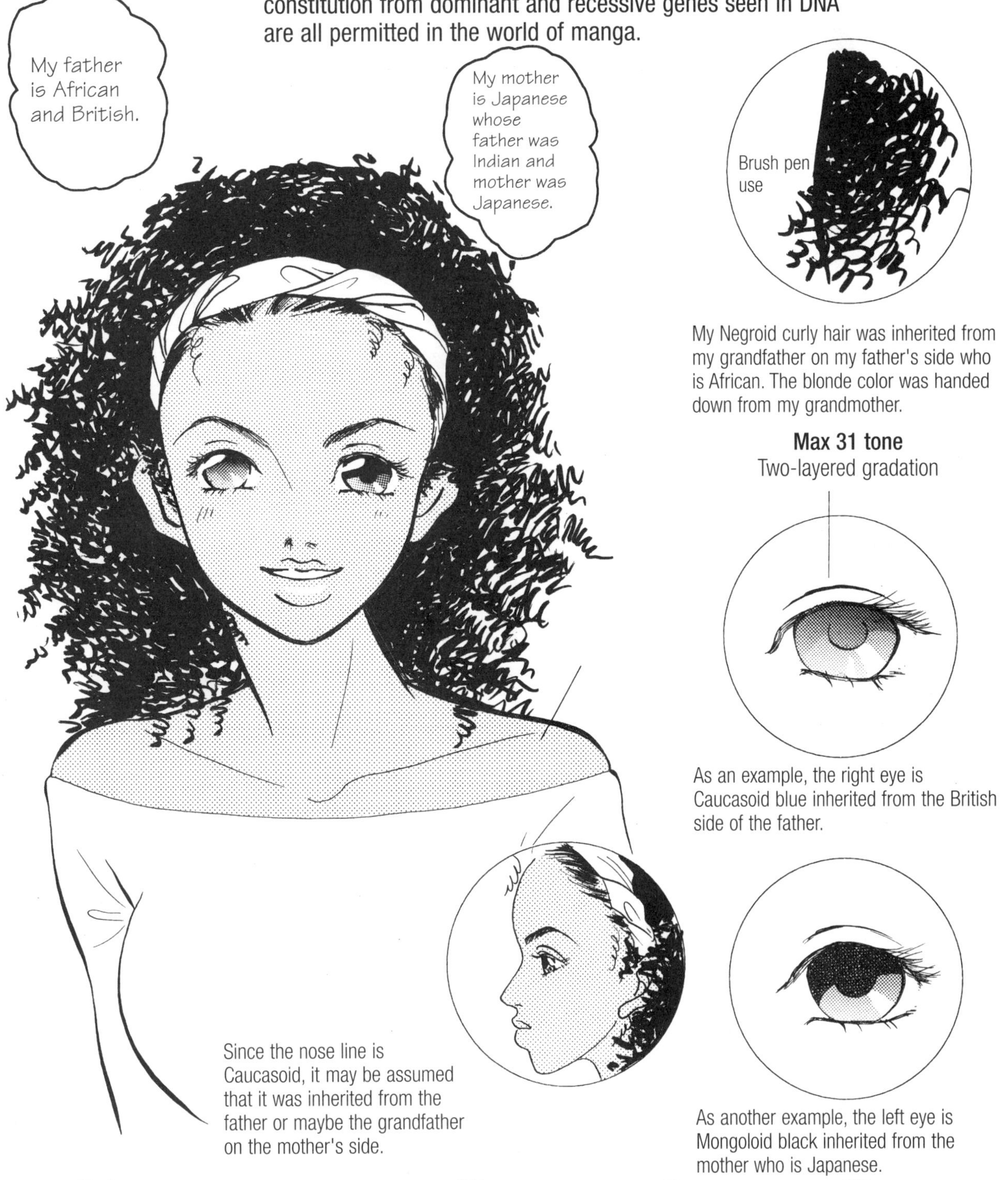

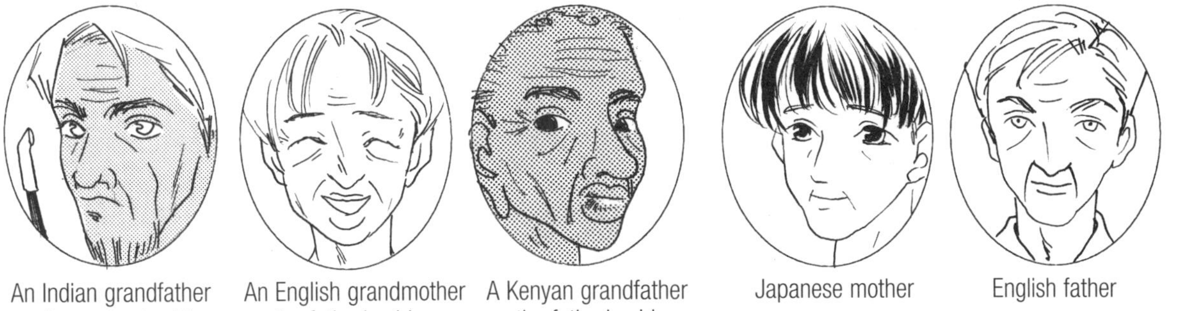

An Indian grandfather on the mother's side | An English grandmother on the father's side | A Kenyan grandfather on the father's side | Japanese mother | English father

East Asian Bishoujo
from Japan, China and Korea

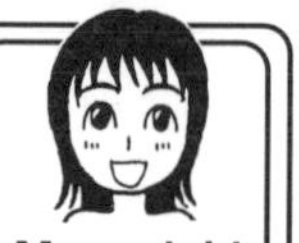
Mongoloid

East Asian bishoujo when lined up look almost like sisters. As a rule, visually direct these characters with well-known fashion and costumes.

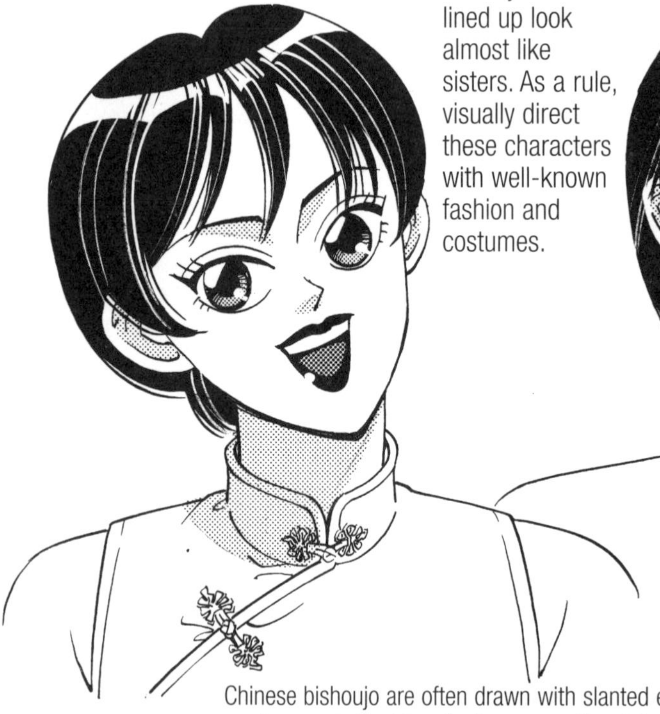

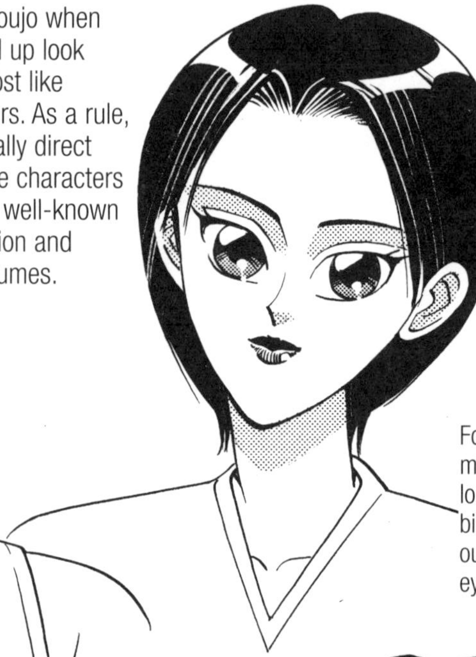

For Korean bishoujo, try making the neck a bit long and plenty slim. The bishoujo nature comes out by making the slanted eyes large.

Chinese bishoujo are often drawn with slanted eyes that are long and slim. Visually direct a continental sense of open-heartedness by making the mouth and eyes on the large side while widening the breadth of the shoulders.

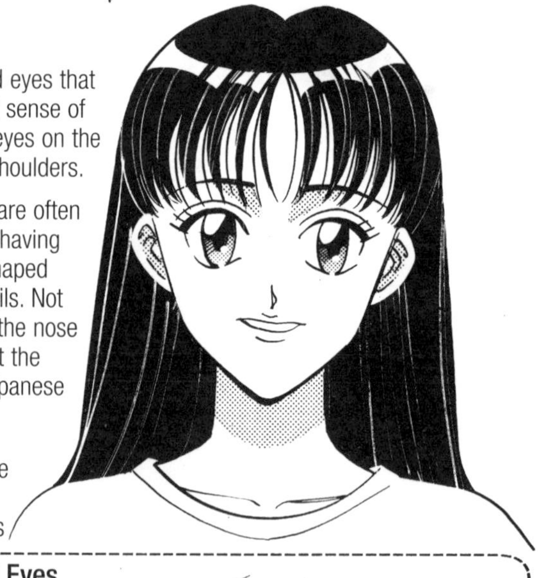

Japanese bishoujo are often designated as girls having relatively almond shaped eyes with large pupils. Not defining the line of the nose too much brings out the Mongoloidesque Japanese nature.

Chinese, Japanese and Korean simplified versions

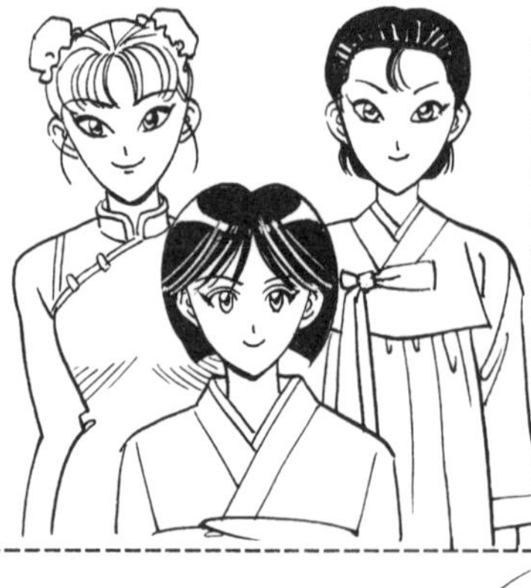

Various Slanted Eyes

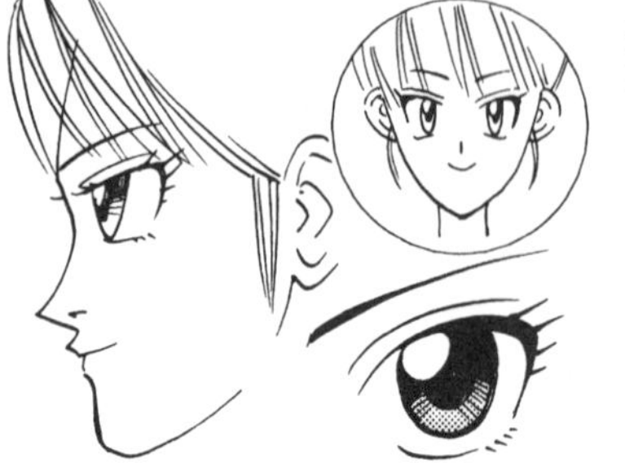

The lower eyelids are level or hanging down.

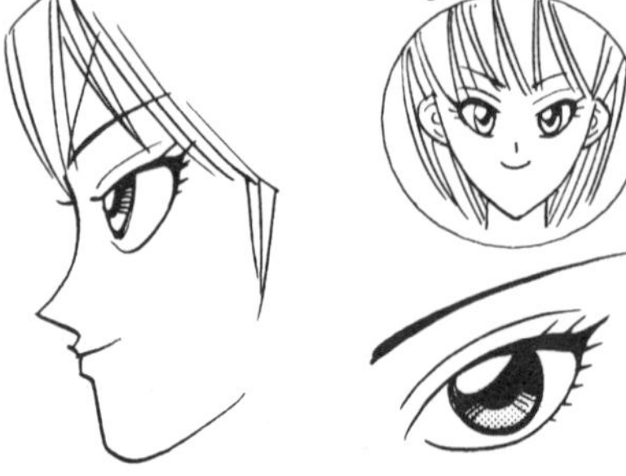

The lower eyelids are also upturned.

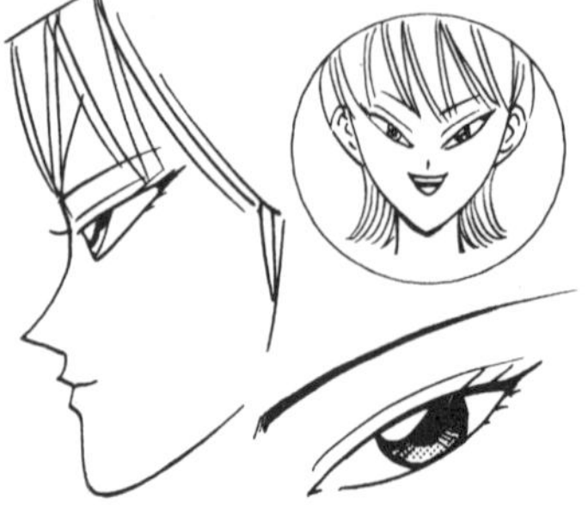

Thin-eyed

Korean Girl

Chima and Chogori
Garments

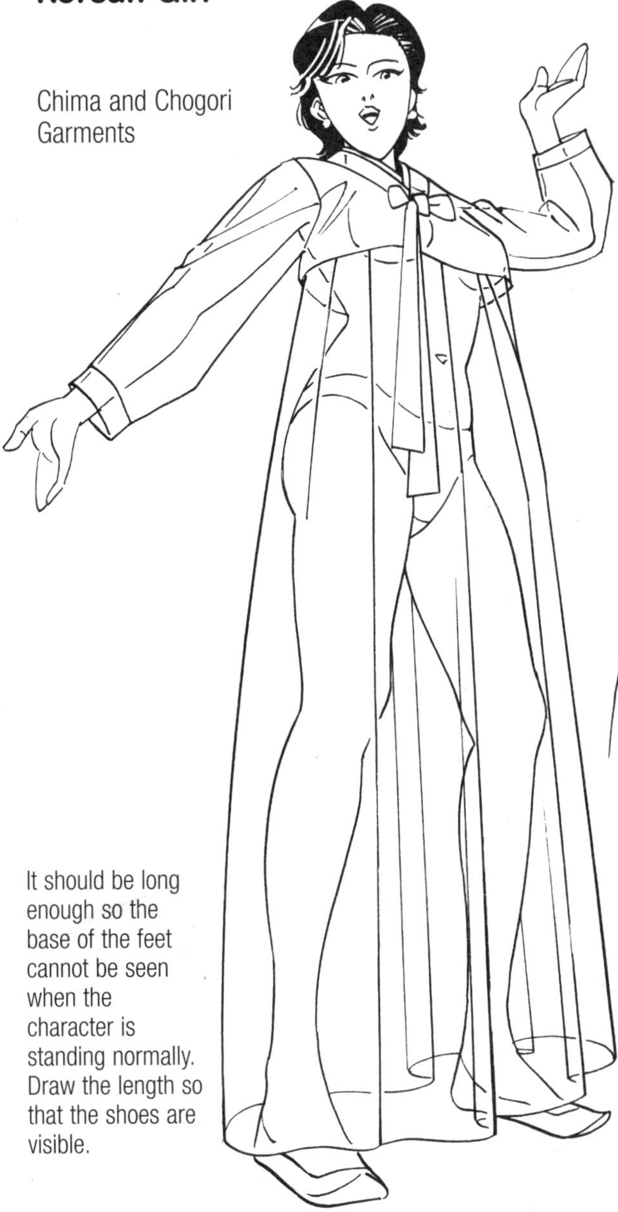

It should be long enough so the base of the feet cannot be seen when the character is standing normally. Draw the length so that the shoes are visible.

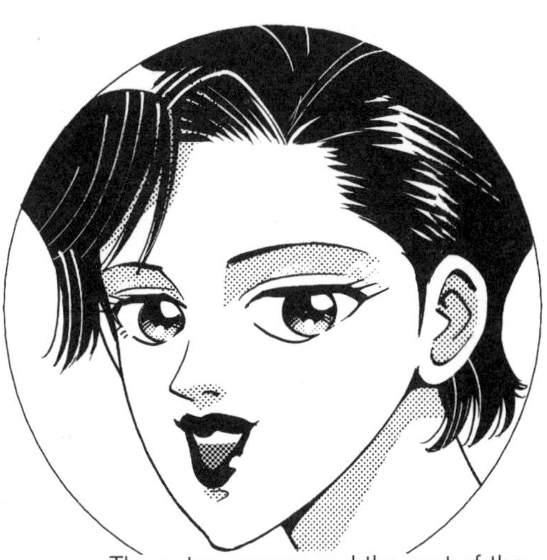

The outer corners and the cast of the eyes are strong in this makeup version.

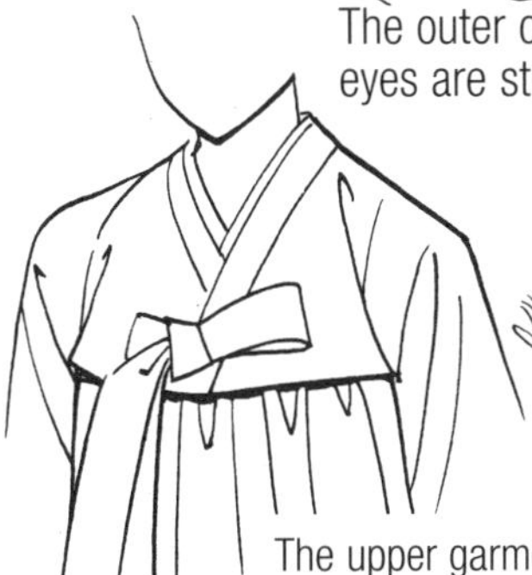

The upper garment known as a 'chima' is about 30 centimeters tall.

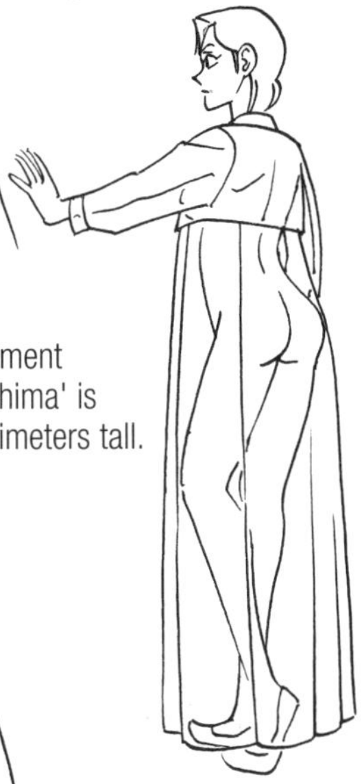

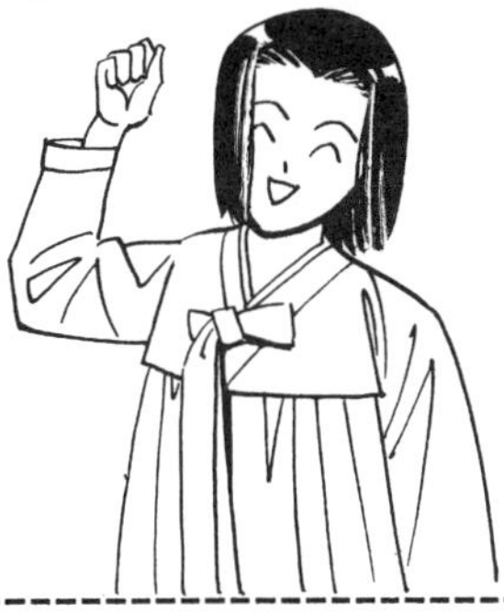

Steps to Putting On Chimas and Chogoris

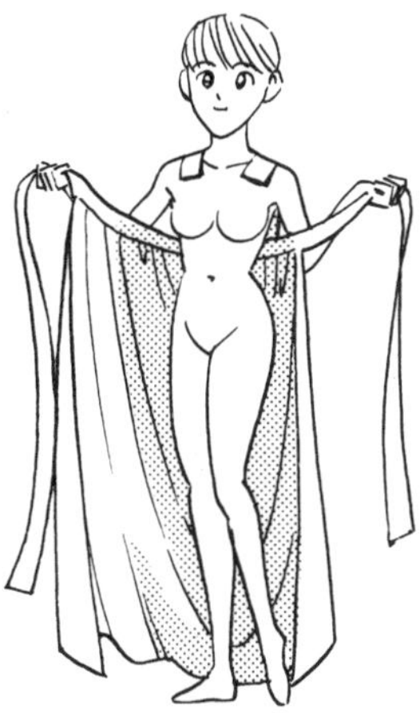

This is a single sheet of cloth like a one-piece dress.

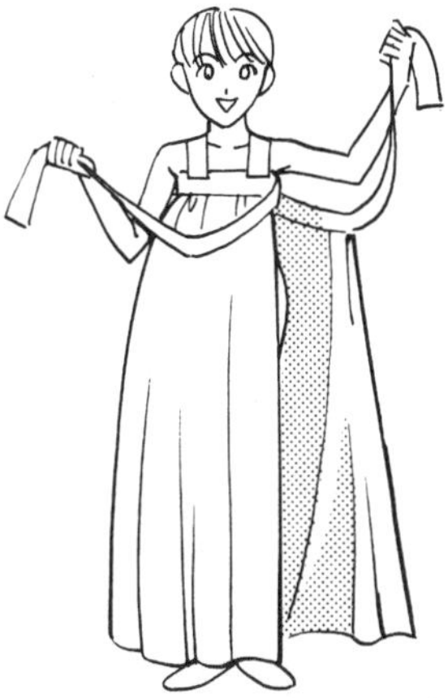

Tie it in the middle.

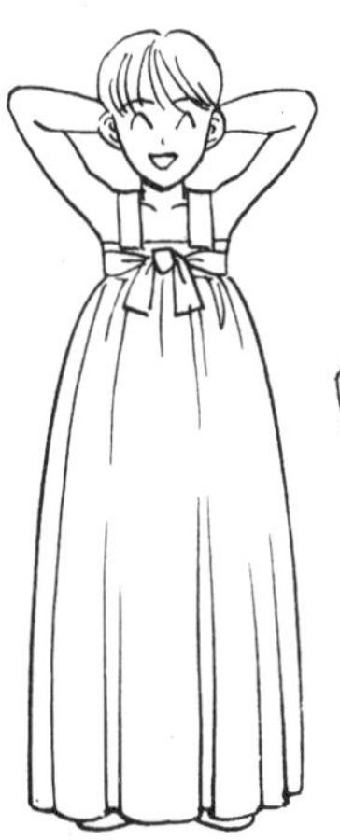

This garment is called a 'chogori'.

Put on the chima.

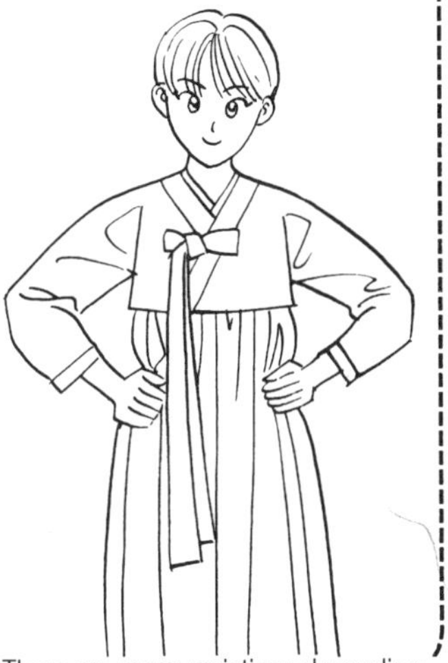

There are many variations depending on the colors and type of bow.

China Dress Girl

China Dress

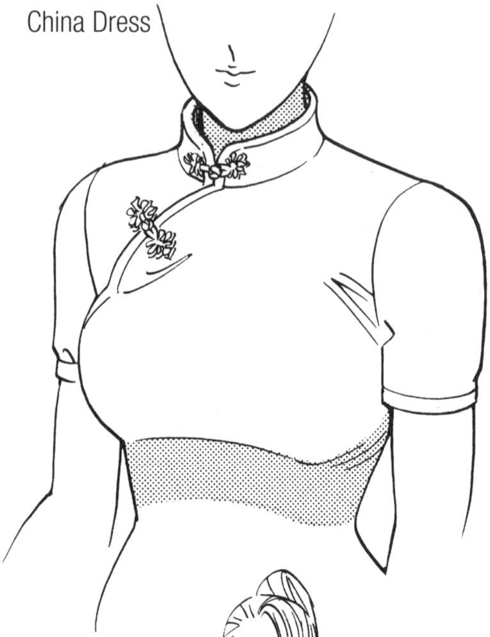

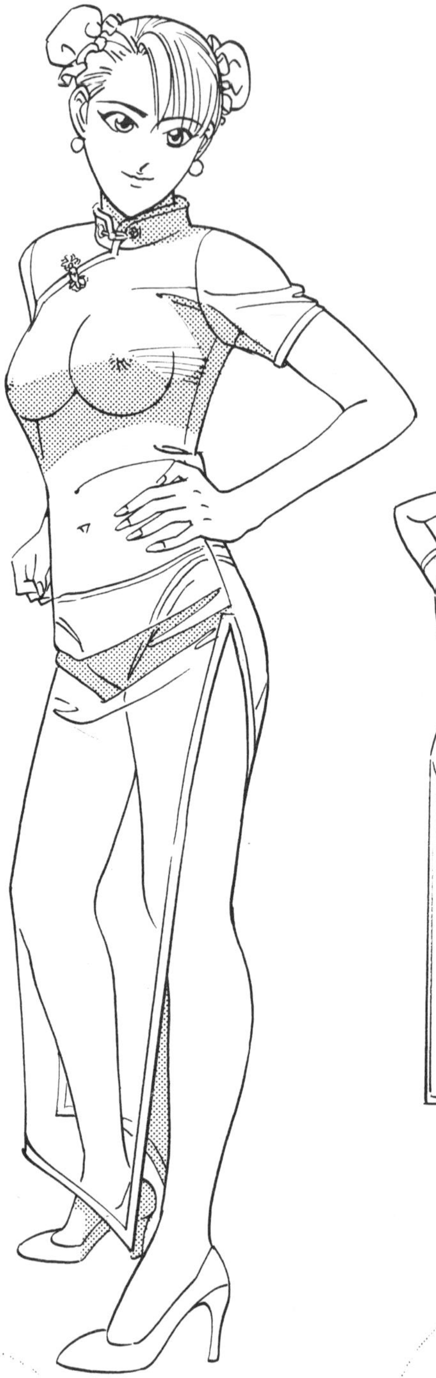

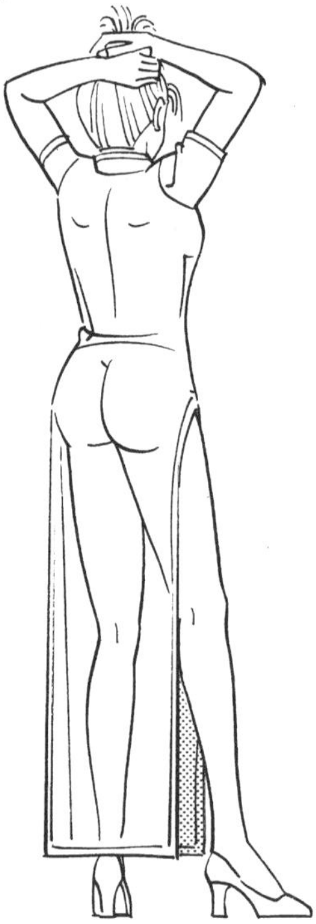

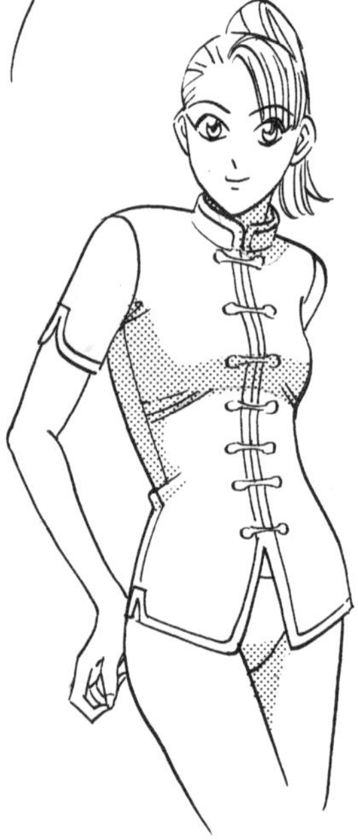

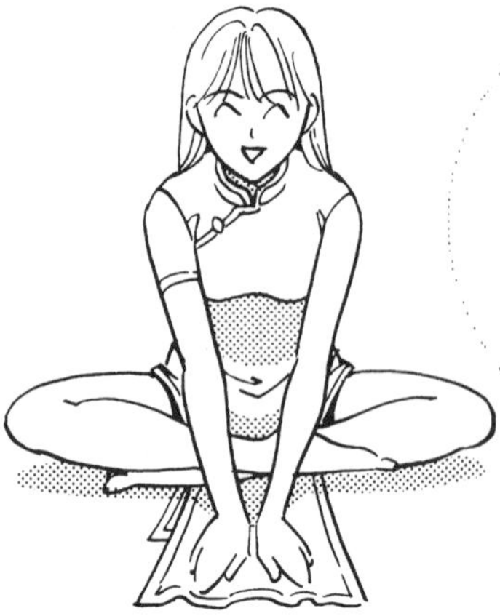

The slit in the dress depends on your design. They can be on the left, right, or on both sides.

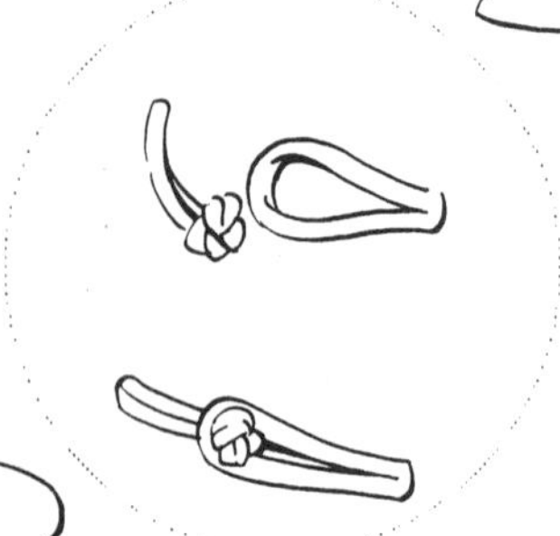

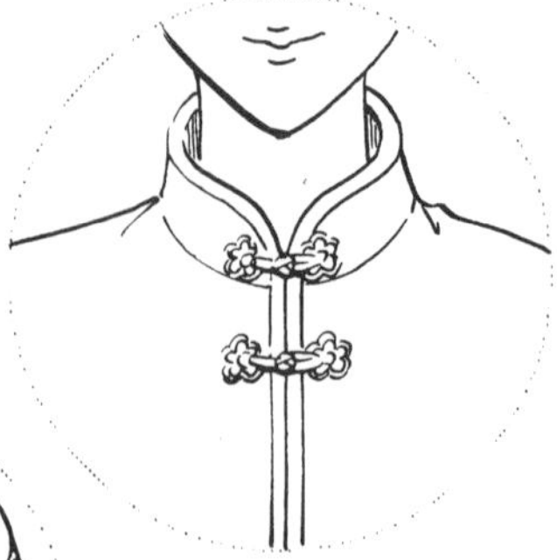

Doing the collar with a "Y-shaped" curve makes her look fashionable.

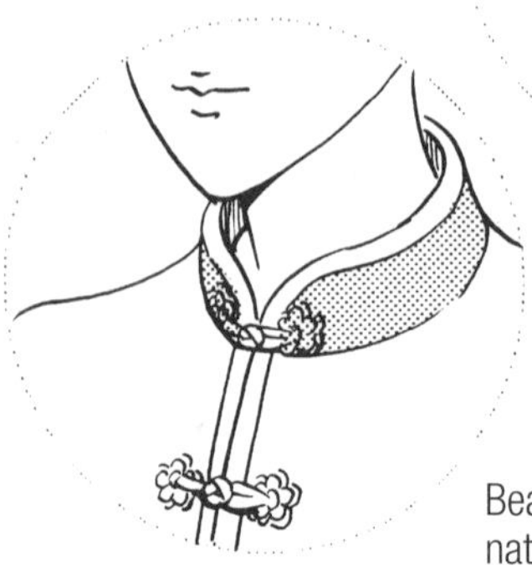

Bearing in mind the cylindrical nature of the neck makes the curved lines easy to draw.

Kimono Girl

Just because a girl is wearing a kimono does not mean she is a "geisha". Nowadays, very few Japanese people have ever seen an actual geisha. At any rate, kimonos are an example of traditional Japanese clothing.

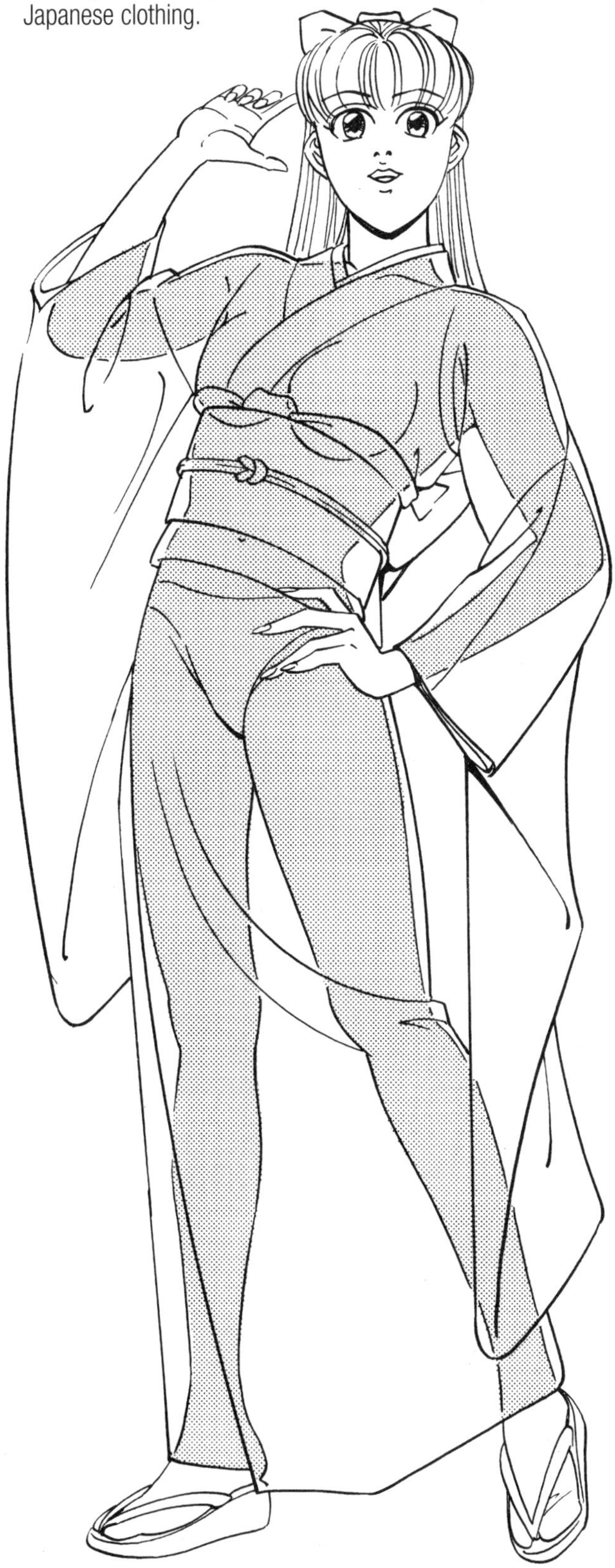

Doing Hair Up China Style

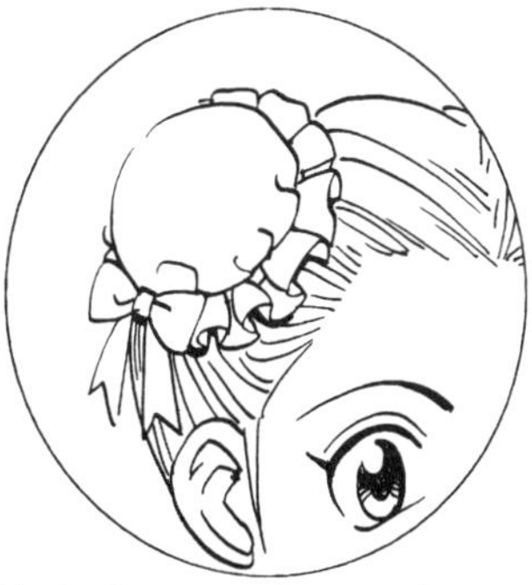

Undo the cover to reveal...

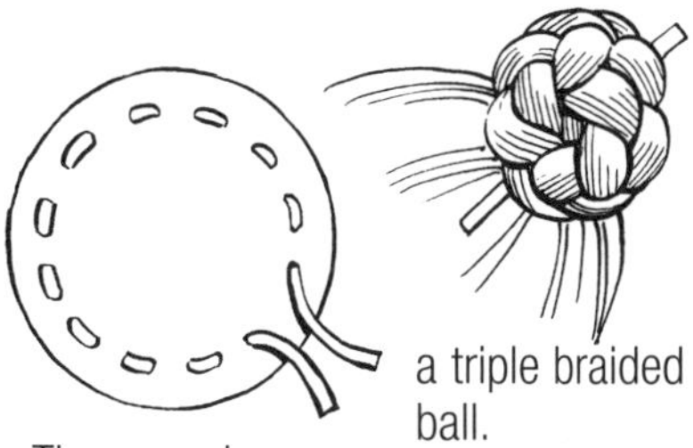

a triple braided ball.

The cover is round with a string threaded through it.

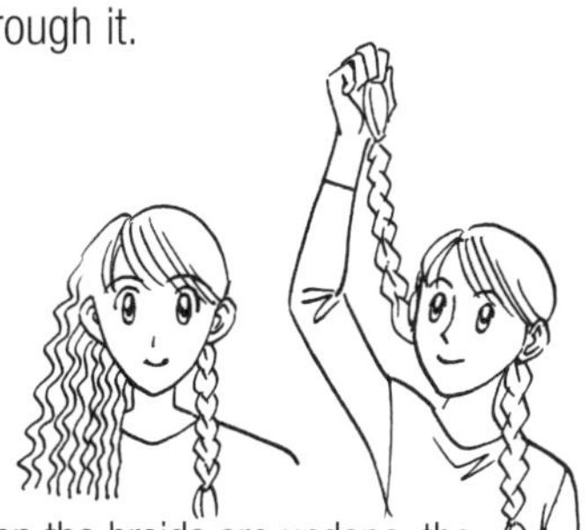

When the braids are undone, the hair looks like a sauvage style.

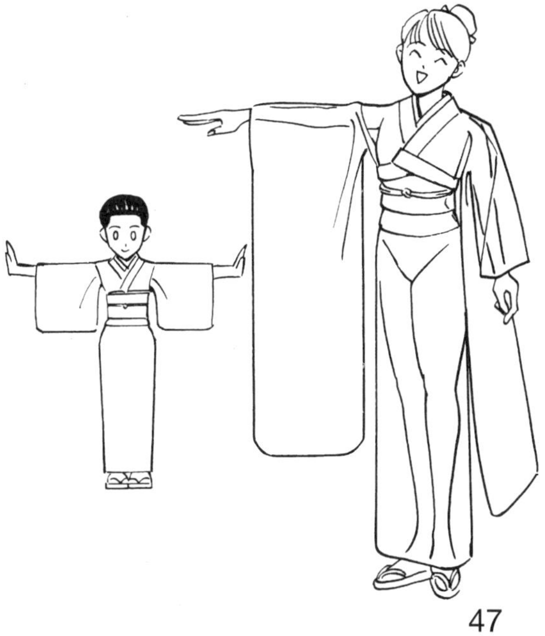

East Asian Bishoujo

from Thailand, Vietnam, Philippines and Indonesia

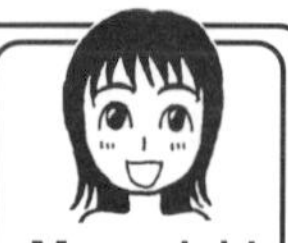

Mongoloid

This Filipino girl has a cute, strongly built jawline keeping with the line of the nose.Draw the facial distinctions a bit on the circular side and the mouth a bit larger bringing out a mood of Southern open-heartedness. The eyes are brown.

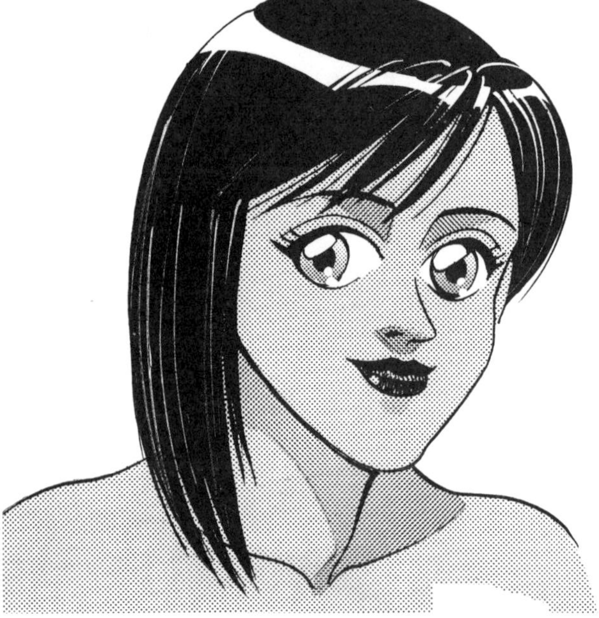

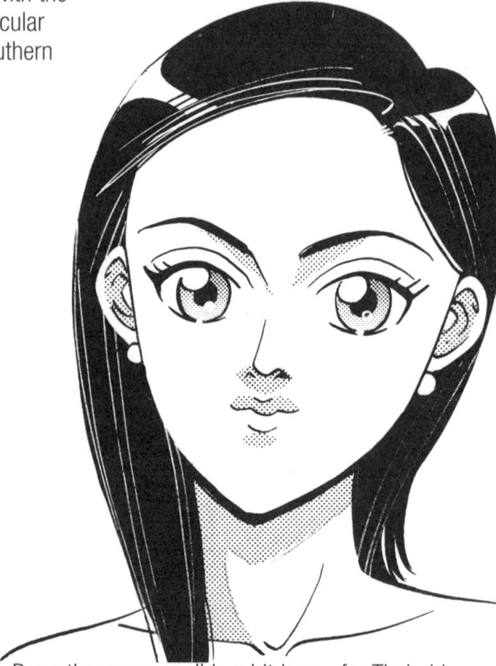

The skin color is a healthy, light brown. Use 10% type tones. Since these characters are Mongoloid, their facial features do not differ much from Japanese. Make the eyes something other than black, mainly brown, and devise a means to distinguish these characters from Japanese.

Draw the upper eyelids a bit heavy for Thai girls. Also, since girls with clear-cut facial features are not uncommon, draw the line of the nose accordingly. The mouth is small, and the hair is black.

The hair and eyes are both black for Vietnamese girls. The facial features are almost the same as Japanese girls. Placing a characteristic Vietnamese palm leaf hat brings out the individuality.

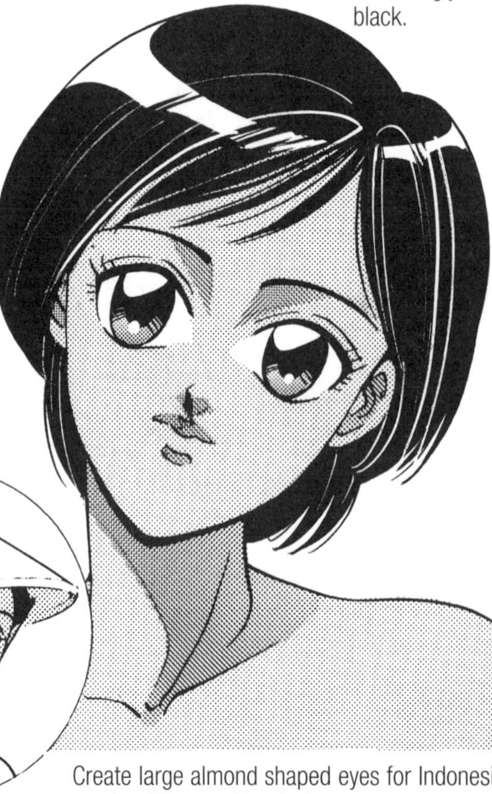

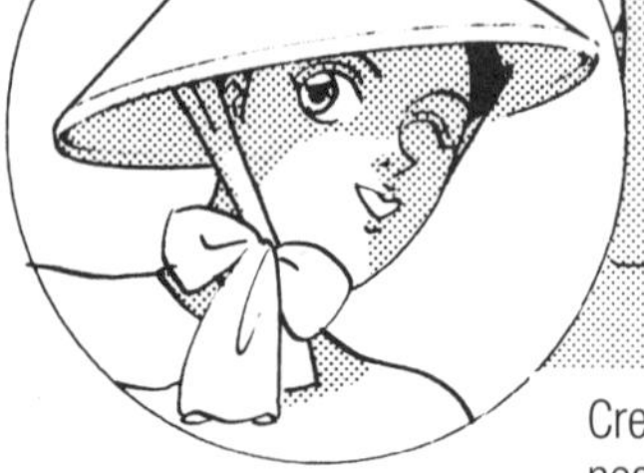

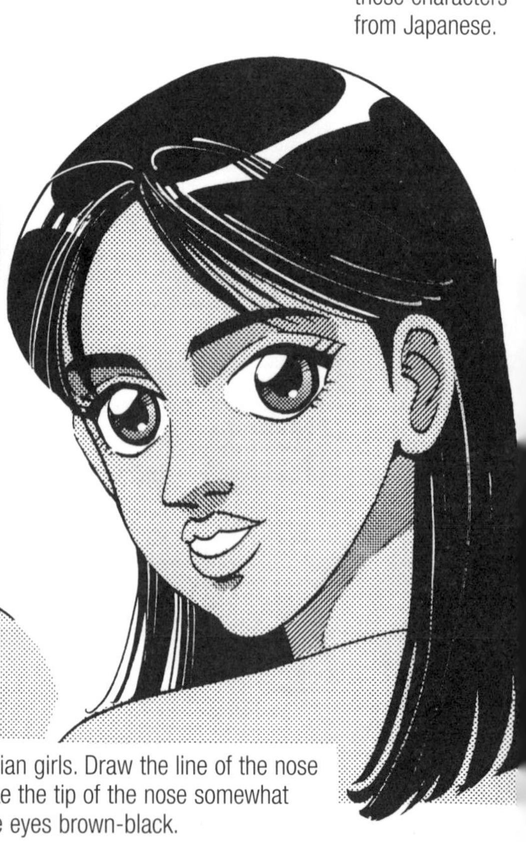

Create large almond shaped eyes for Indonesian girls. Draw the line of the nose neatly without making it show too much. Make the tip of the nose somewhat round and the lips on the thick side. Color the eyes brown-black.

Vietnamese Ao Dai Style

The traditional 'ao dai' originally consisted of a jacket. The pants are called 'kuwan'. The combination of these two are called 'kuwan ao'.

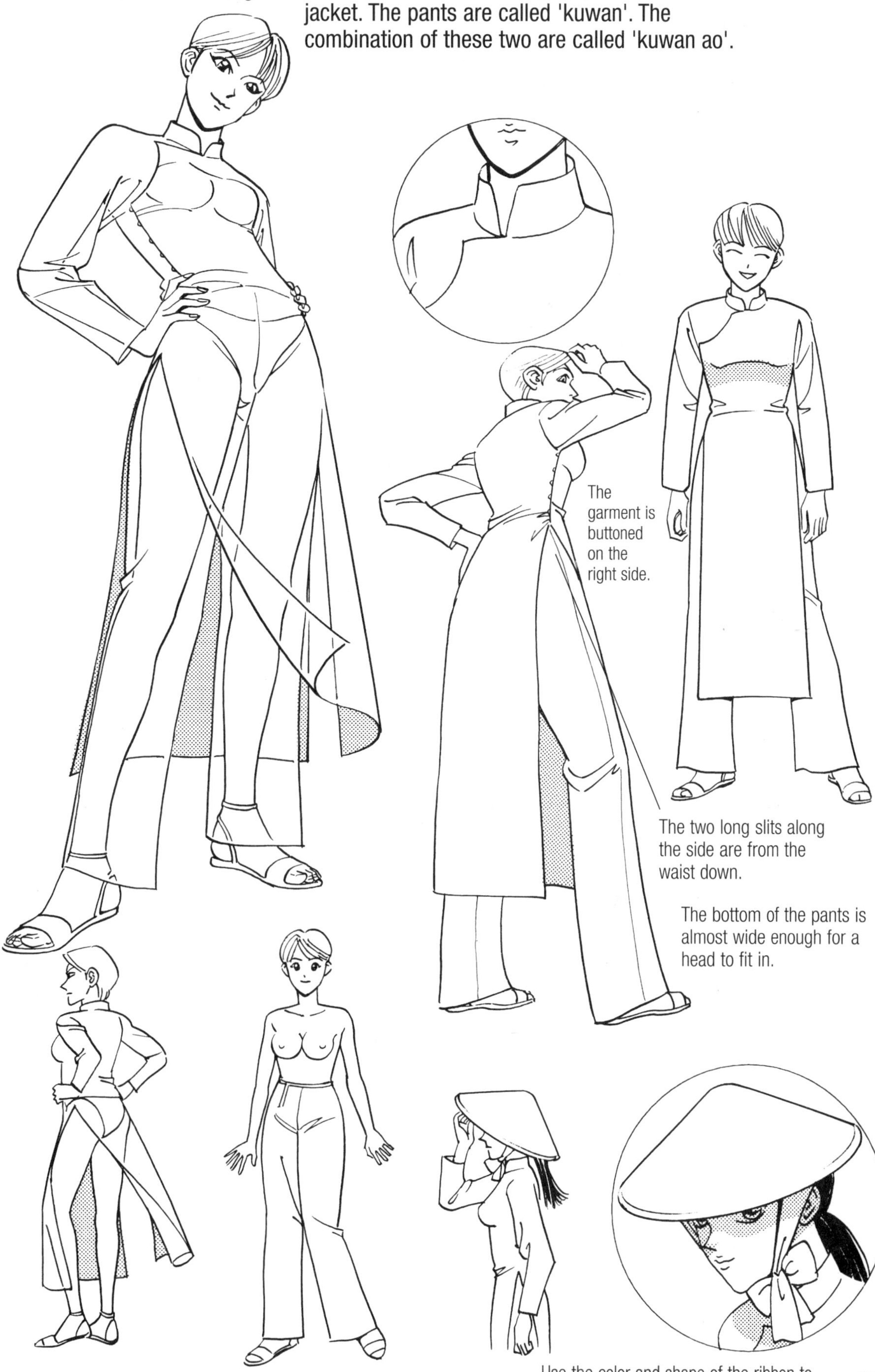

Use the color and shape of the ribbon to make elegant looking conical palm leaf hats.

Thai Bishoujo Techniques abound in traditional Thai fashion. Understanding their logic makes for powerful design reference.

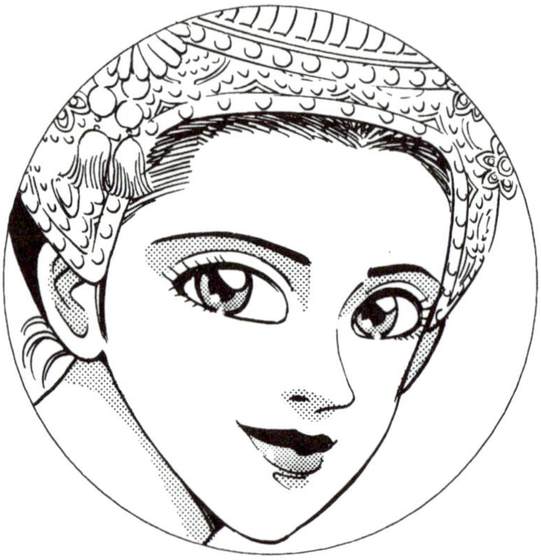

Darken the lower eyelids and edges for makeup worn during traditional dance.

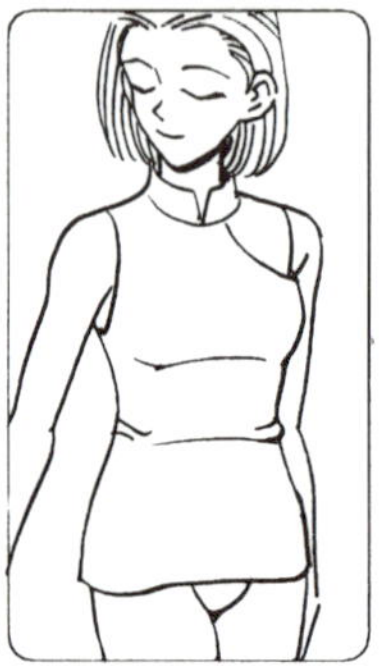

Originally, a long-sleeved or sleeveless jacket was worn before putting on the shoulder wrap.

Waist and shoulder wrap combination

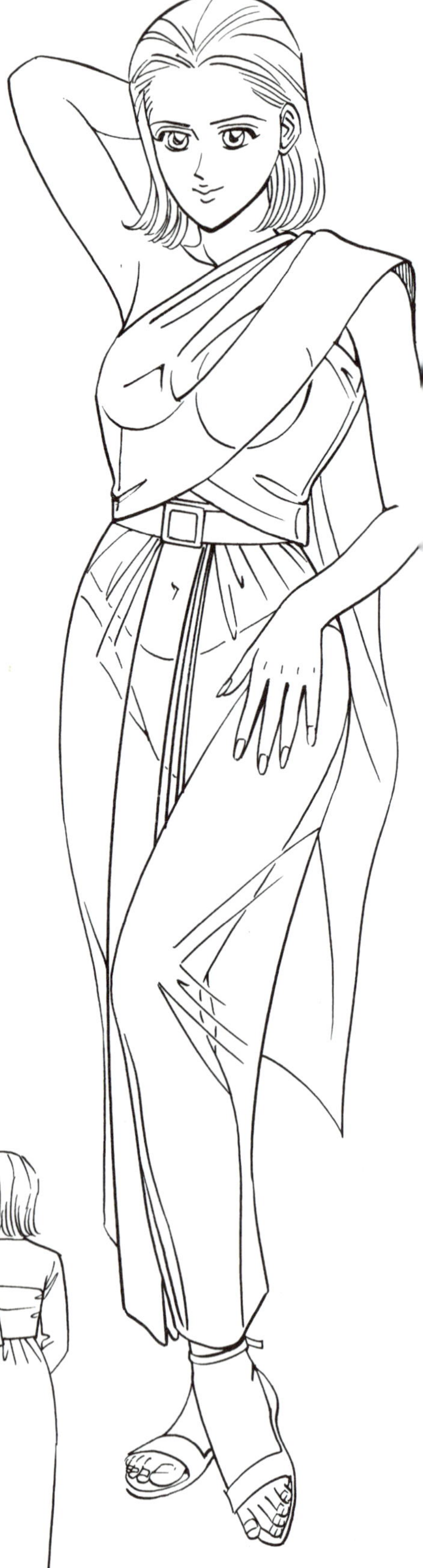

Putting On Waist Wraps

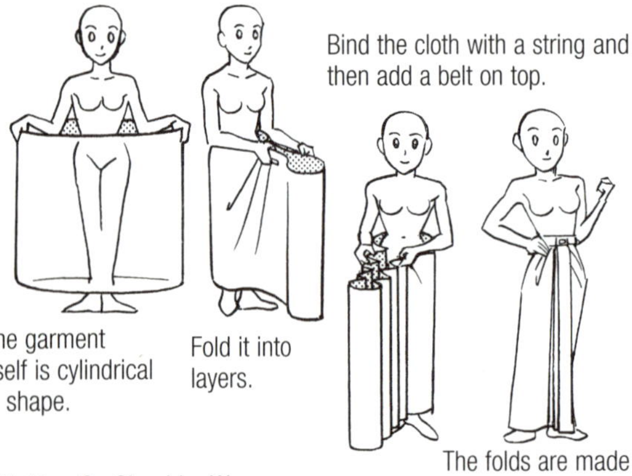

The garment itself is cylindrical in shape.

Fold it into layers.

Bind the cloth with a string and then add a belt on top.

The folds are made up into a bundle.

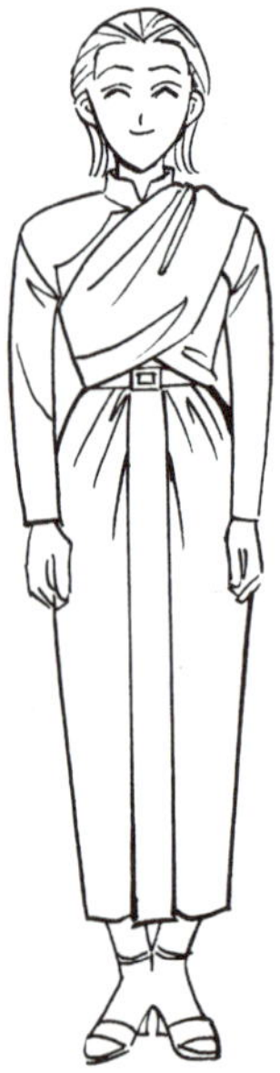

Putting On Shoulder Wraps

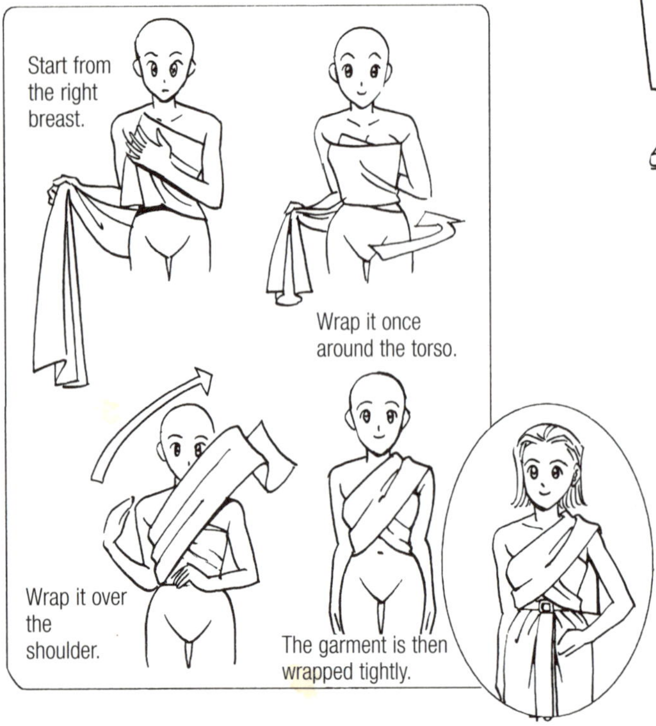

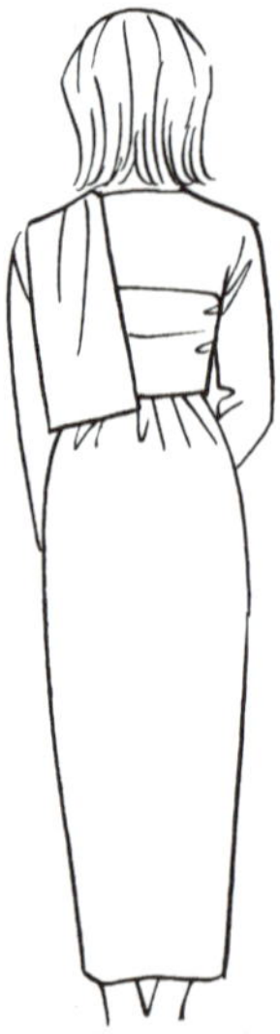

Thai Style Pants

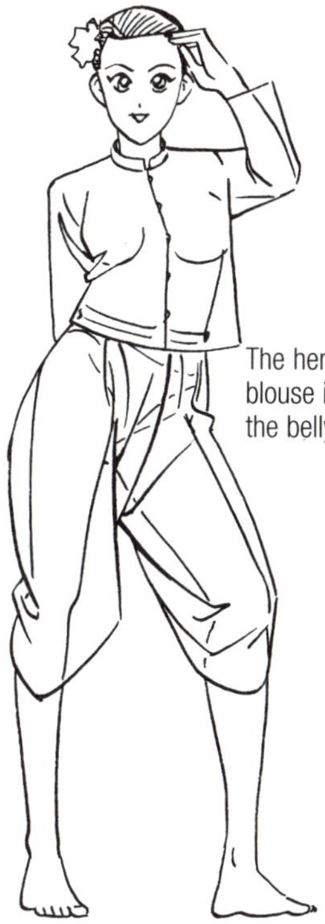

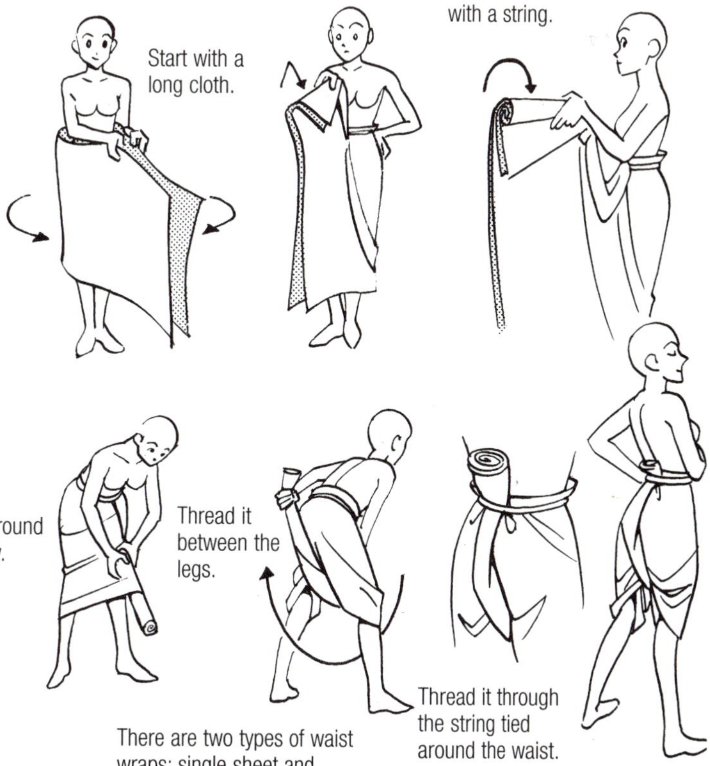

Indonesian Bishoujo

Make the jacket vermilion or add in a pattern.Use showy patterns for waist wraps.

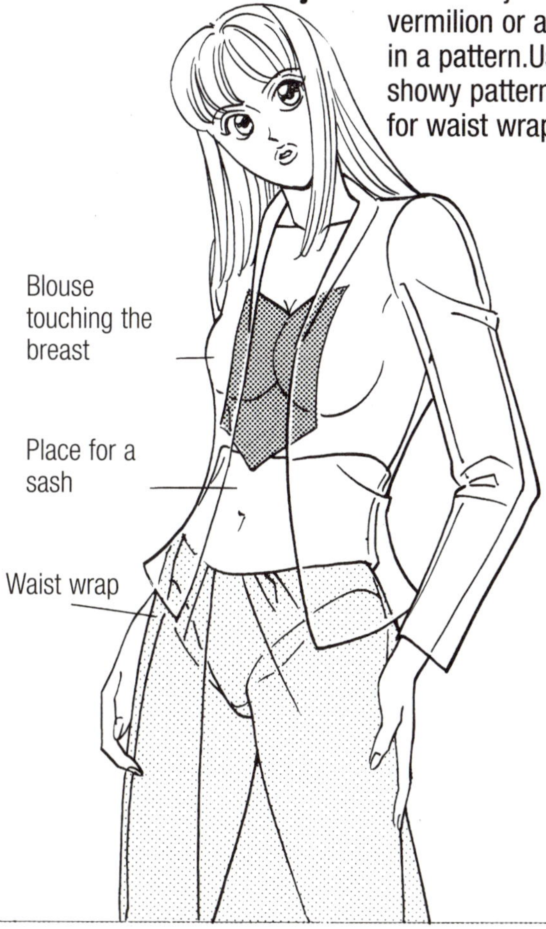

There are two types of waist wraps: single sheet and circular. The types differ slightly from island to island.

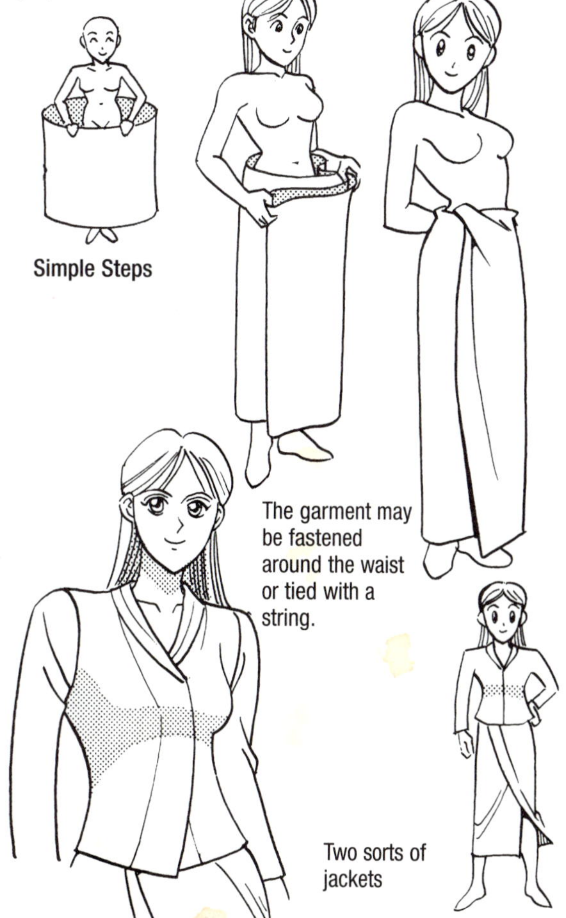

Southern Asian Bishoujo

from India, Pakistan, Nepal and Bangladesh

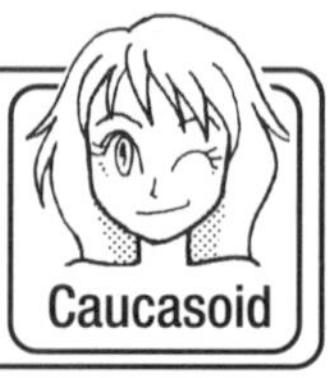

The girls from India, Nepal and Pakistan have essentially Caucasoid clear-cut facial features. However, the hair is jet black.

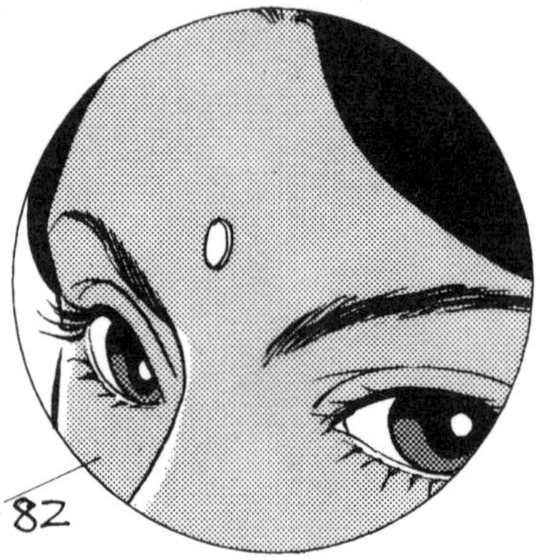

SE-82

Different castes are expressed by the color of the 'bindi' in the middle of the forehead. At times, paint is used instead.

While Indians generally have light-brown skin, in drawings, the colored in peach. As some regions have people with white skin, tones should be used accordingly. The eyes are dark brown to black and the eyelashes are long.

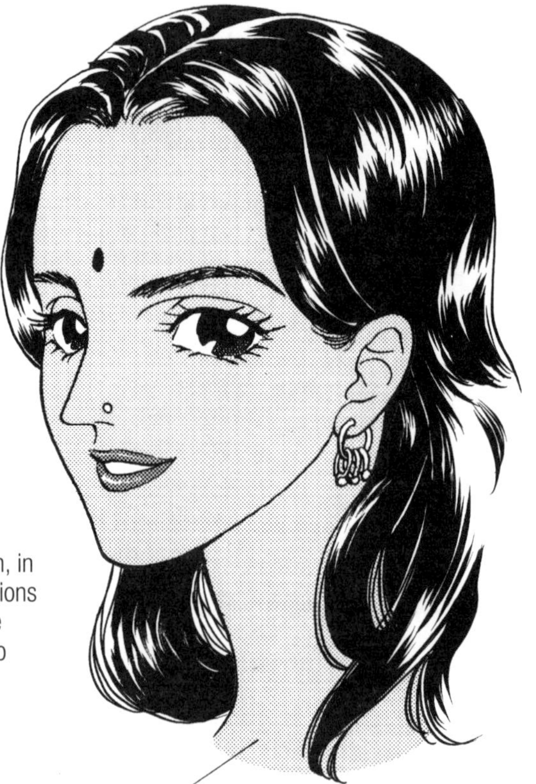

IC 71

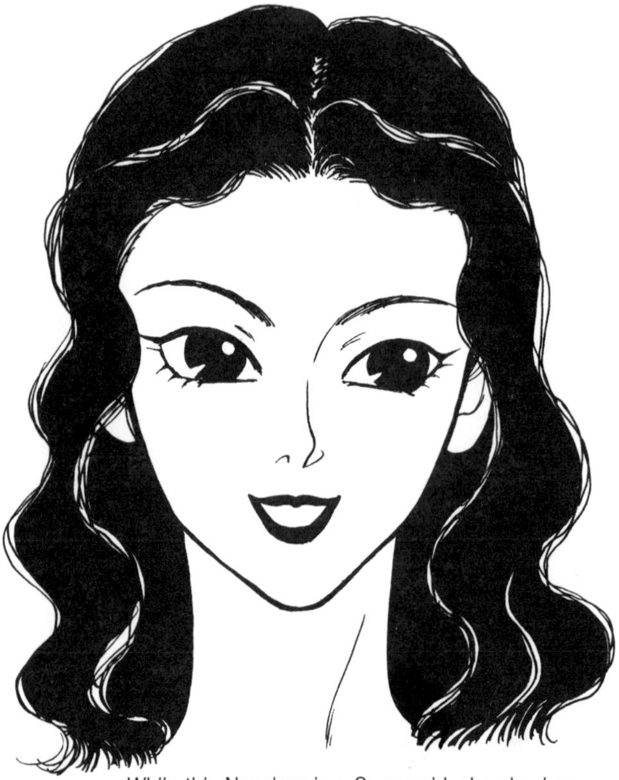

While this Nepalese is a Caucasoid, she also has Japanese features. Deepen the outline of the eyes while making her hair black and wavy.

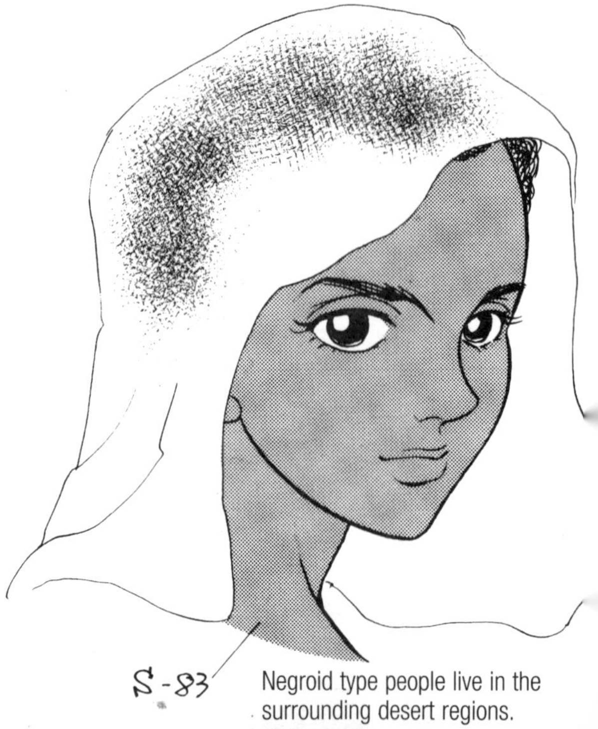

S-83

Negroid type people live in the surrounding desert regions.

Nepalese Bishoujo Characteristic jacket, waist wrap and belt combination

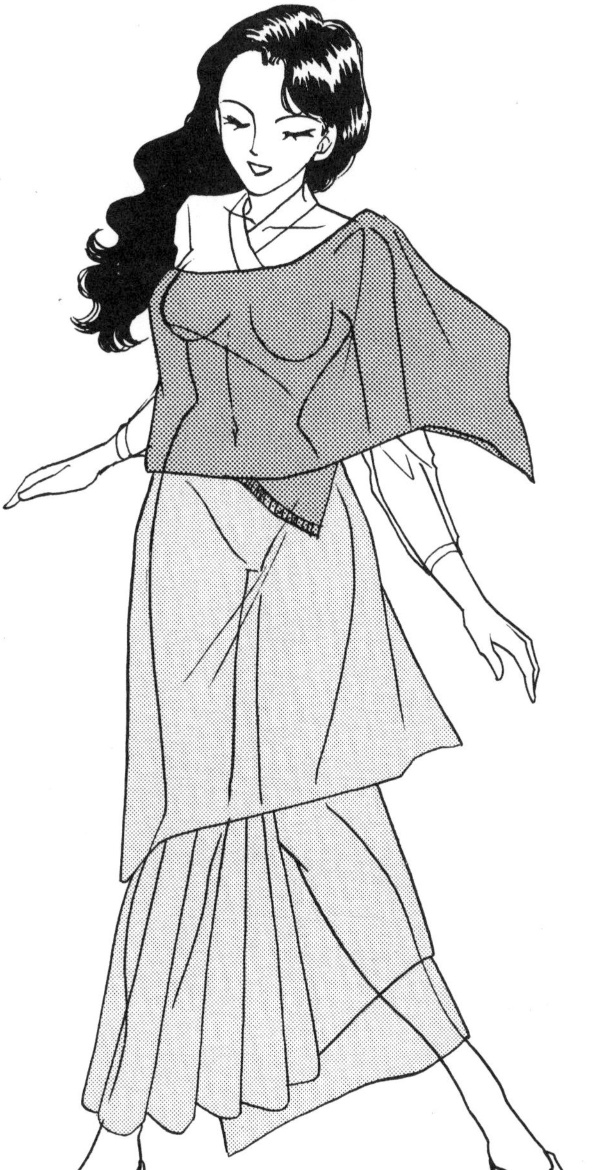

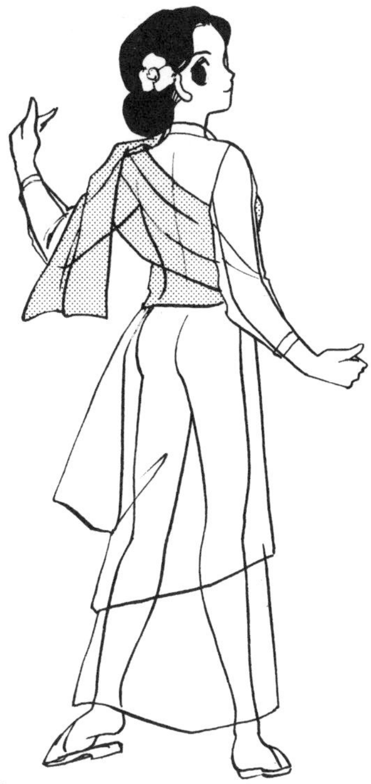

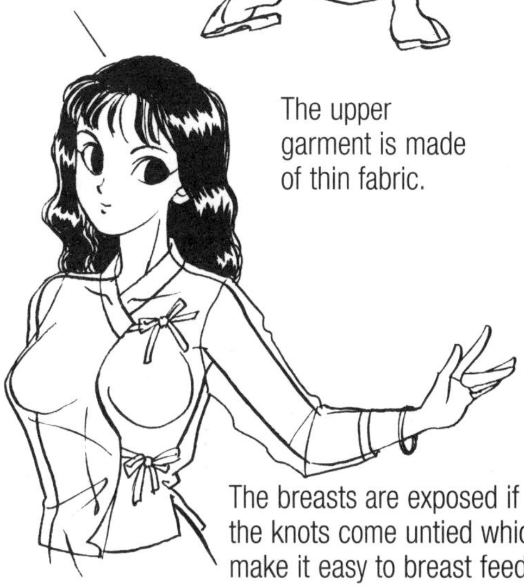

Putting on Waist Wraps

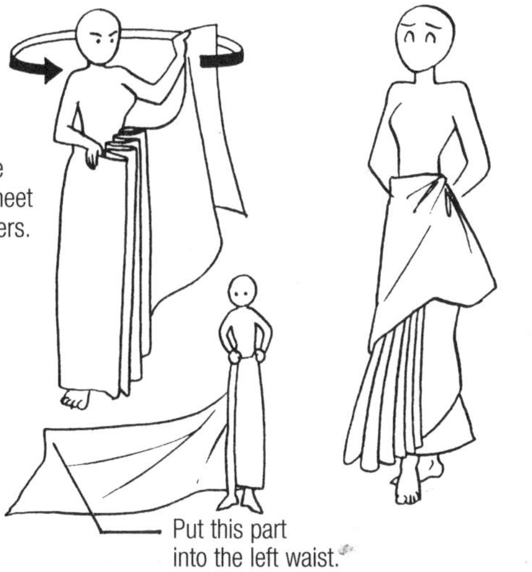

Putting on the Belt

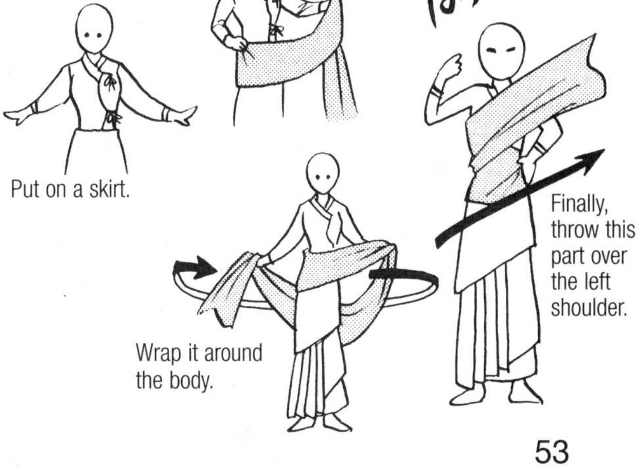

Indian Bishoujo

The clothing is varicolored, from shawls hanging from the head to ordinary clothes, depending on the region. Find the distinctive colors and patterns from regions in India and Pakistan to skillfully visually direct these characters.

Sari Undergarments

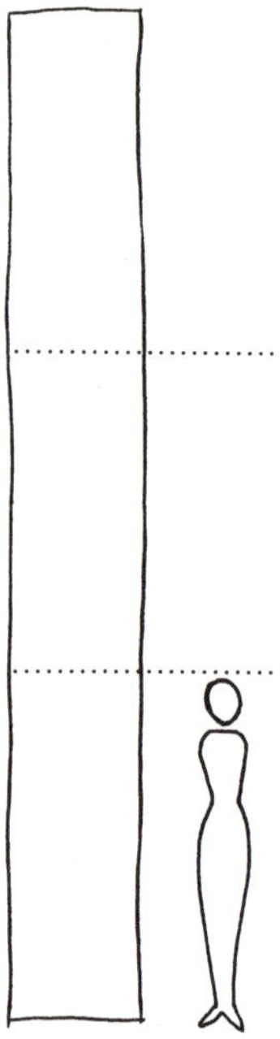

A 'sari' is length of cloth at least three times the person's height.

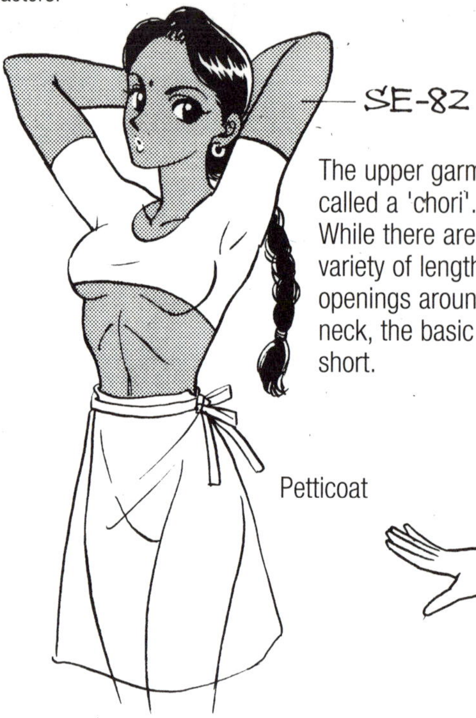

The upper garment is called a 'chori'. While there are a variety of lengths and openings around the neck, the basic style is short.

Petticoat

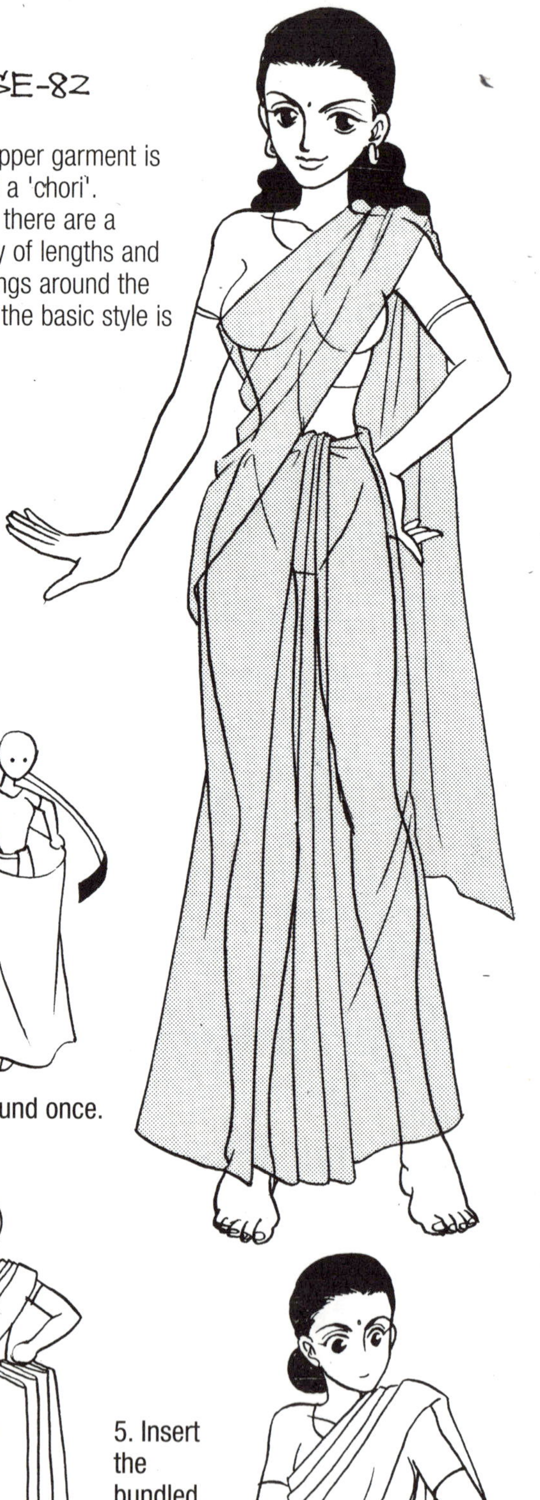

Putting On Saris

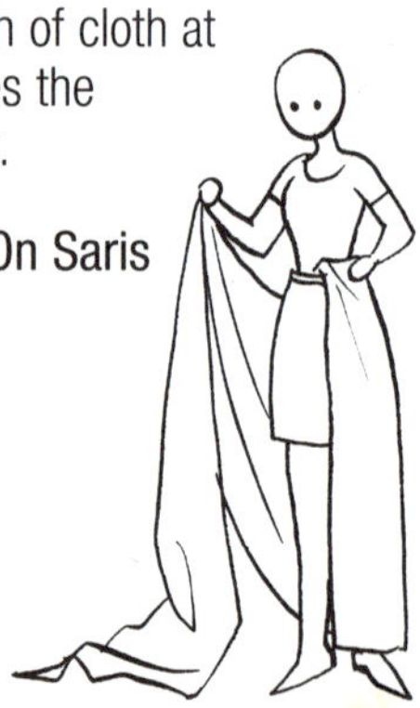

1. Insert it into the petticoat.

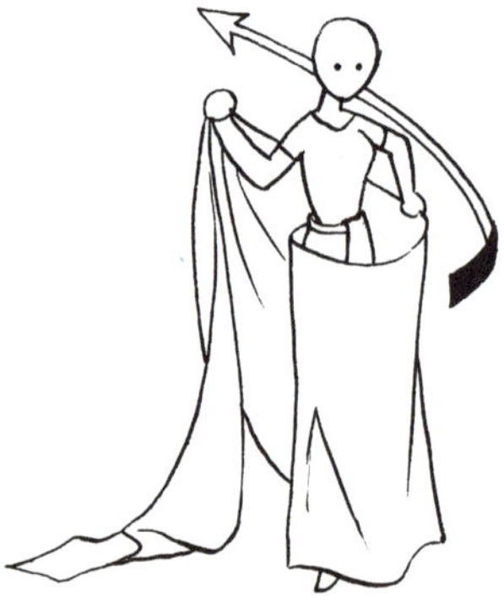

2. Wrap it around once.

Fold the edges into layers.

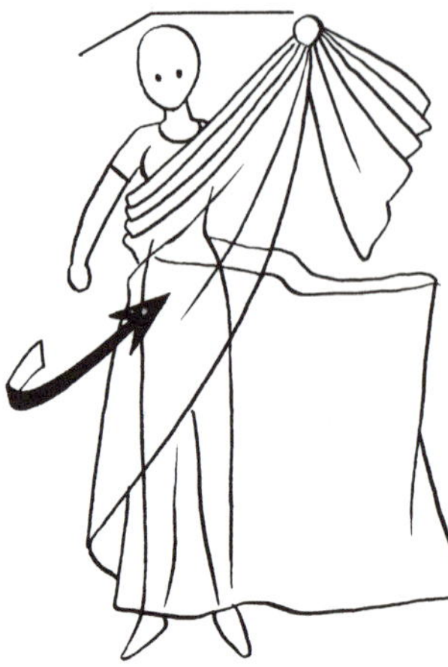

3. Wrap it over the shoulder.

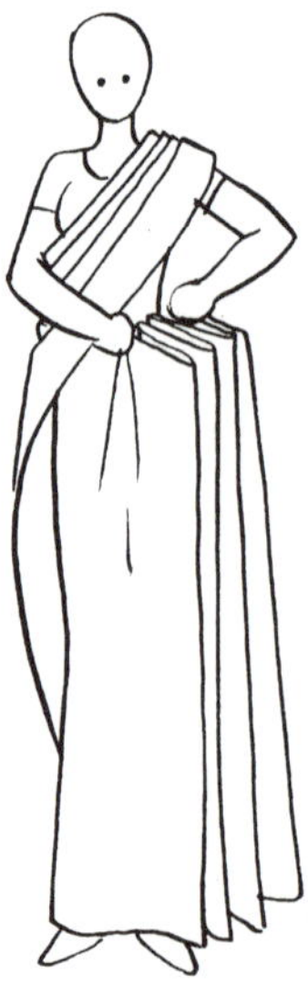

4. Fold the left over parts.

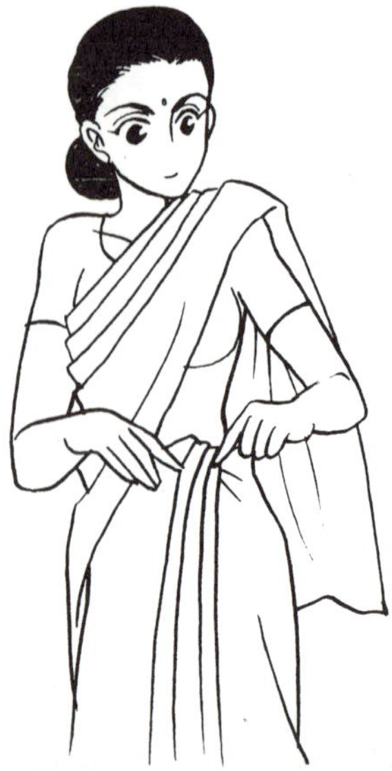

5. Insert the bundled area under the waist.

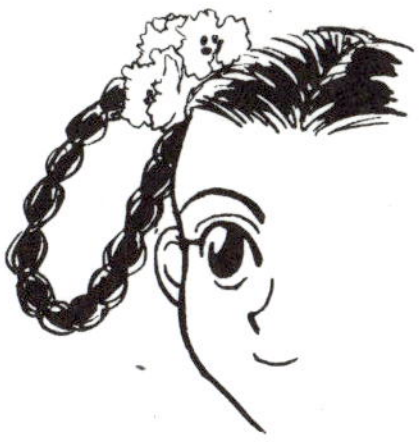

Flowers are worn in the hair for festivals and other occasions.

Girl On the Town

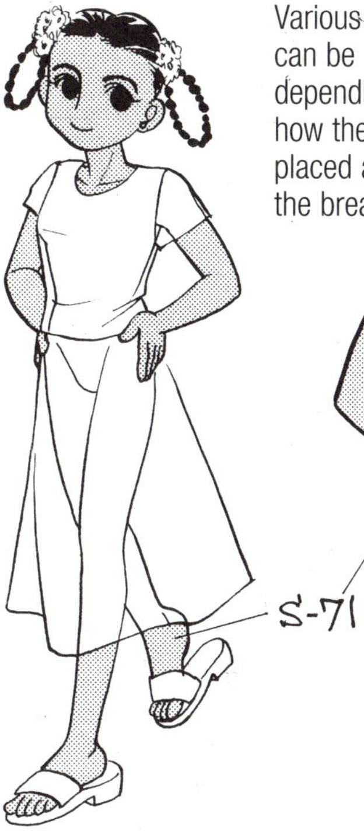

Various styles can be created depending on how the sari is placed around the breasts.

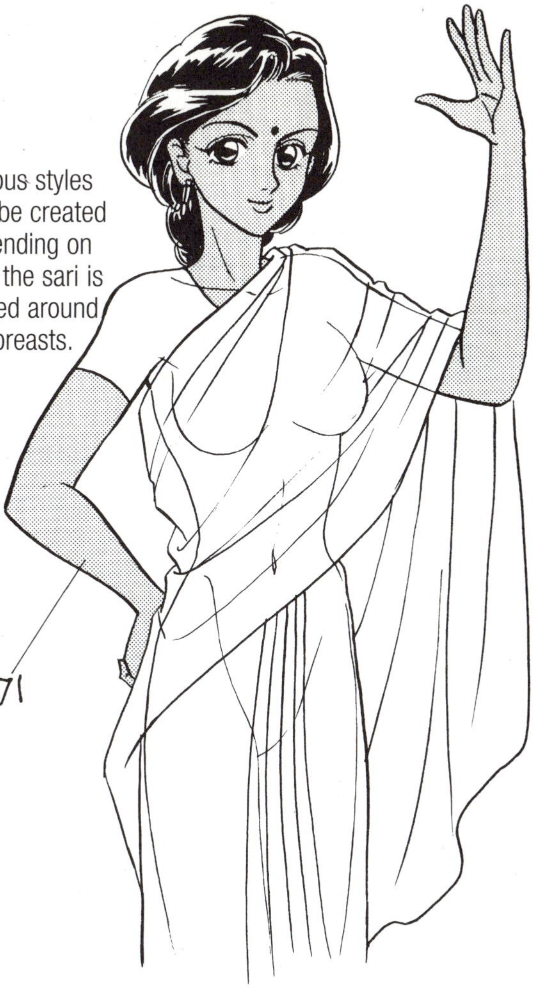

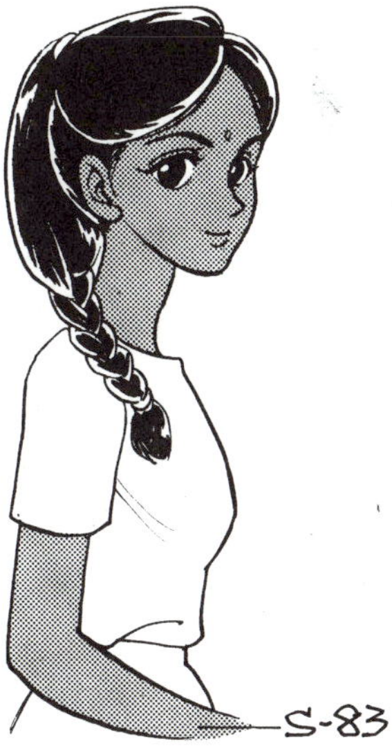

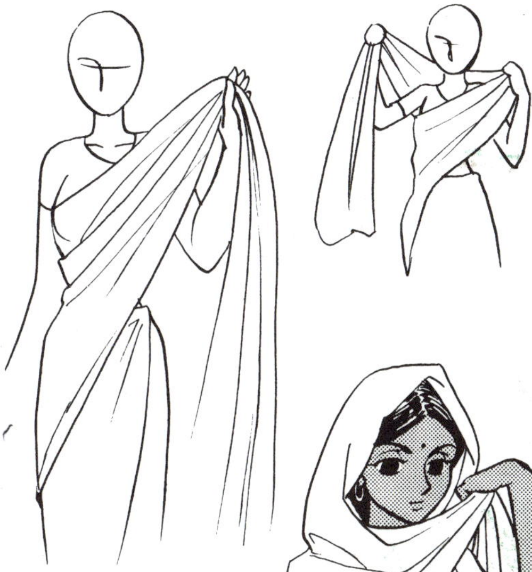

Since the cloth is quite long, it can also be used as a shawl.

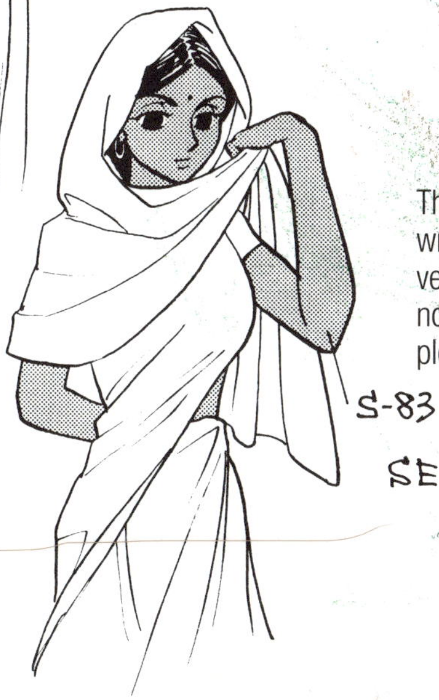

This simply wrapped version does not have pleats.

Pleated items are known as the national style.

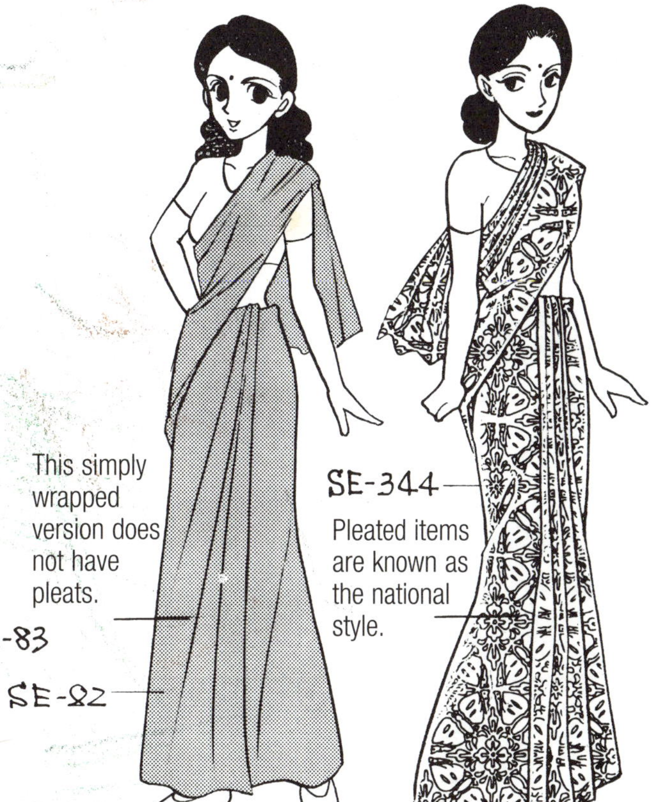

Oceanian Bishoujo

from Papua New Guinea, Micronesia and Australia

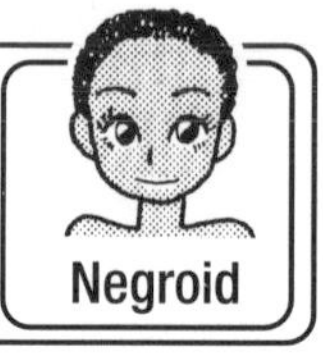

Papua New Guineans have black to brown, curly hair.
The line of the nose is firm.

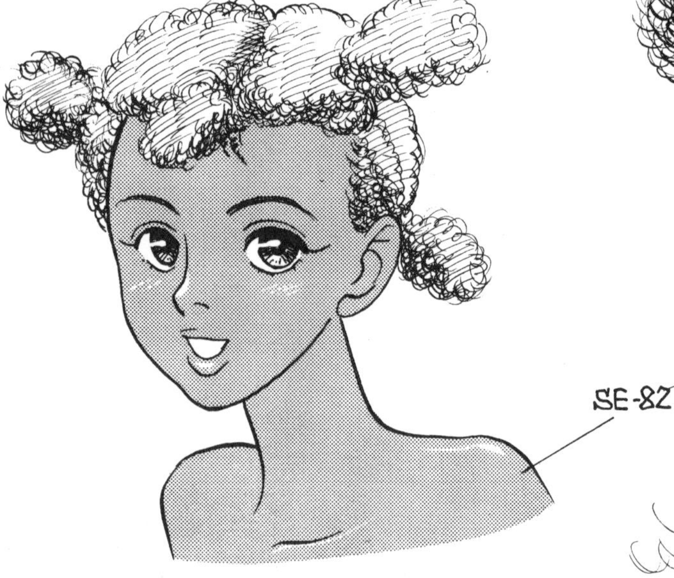

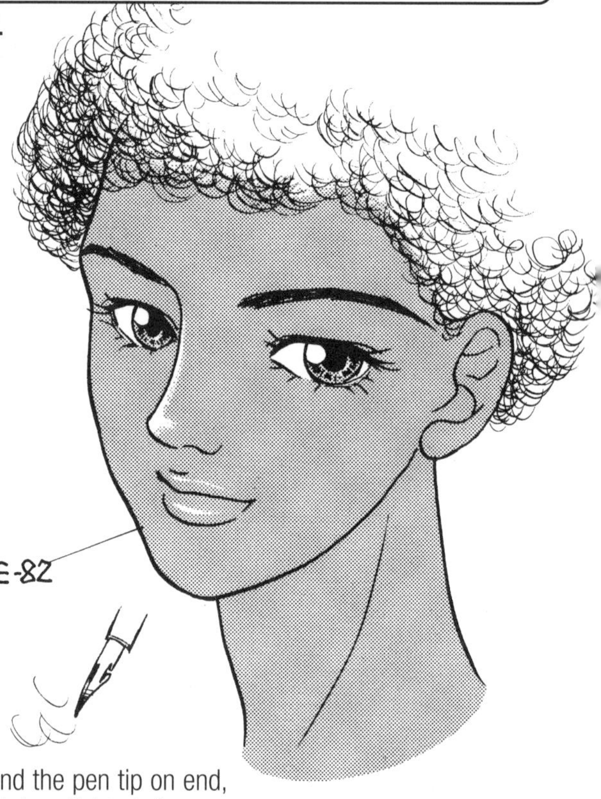

Brush pen (natural hair type)

Stand the pen tip on end, and draw light circles letting your hand almost float.

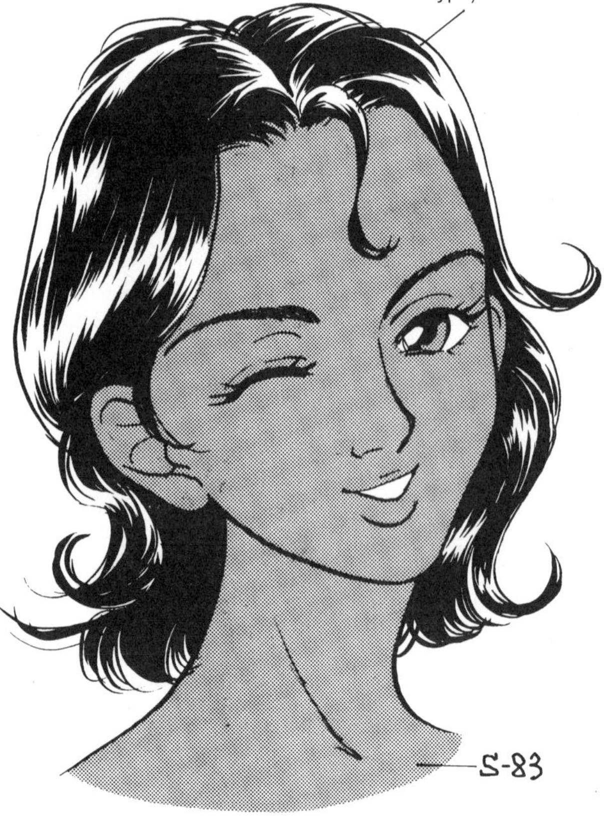

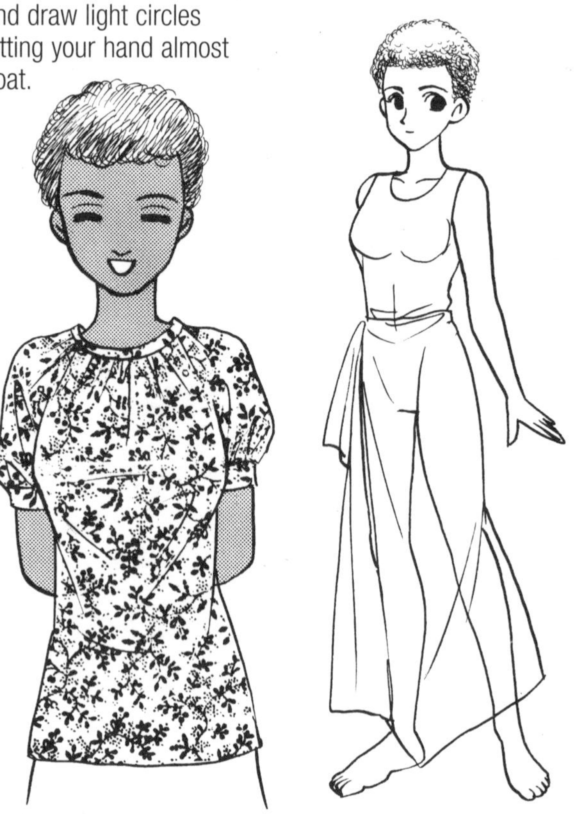

Some Micronesian girls also have straight, black hair.

The various skirts and waist wraps, which Papua New Guineans generally wear, are long. Unlike those of India which are charmingly colorful, their clothing uses more direct, showy colors.

Papua New Guinean Religious Service and Festival Clothing

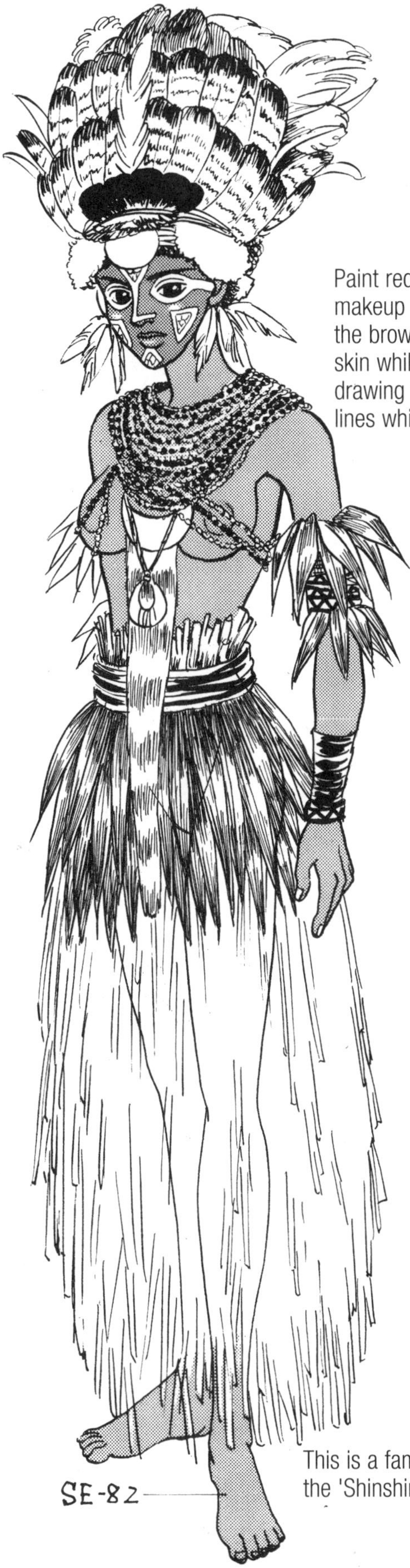

Paint red makeup over the brown skin while drawing the lines white.

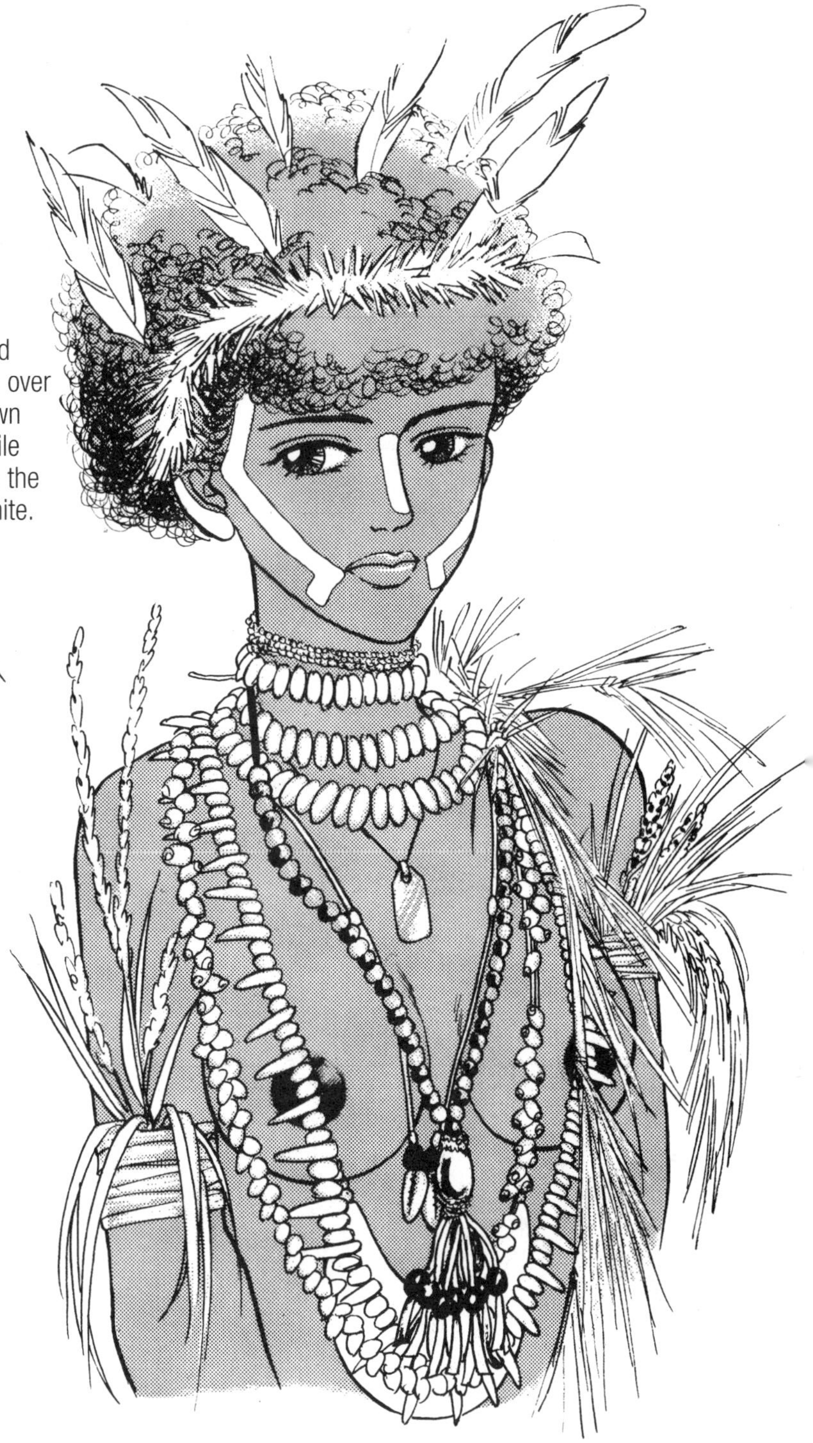

Papua New Guinea, much like prefectures in Japan, which all have their own traditional festivals and costumes, has an infinite variety of clothing styles. Each trifling ornament has deep meanings and purposes.

This is a famous costume worn for the 'Shinshin' harvest festival.

Western European Bishoujo

from England, France, Germany and Holland

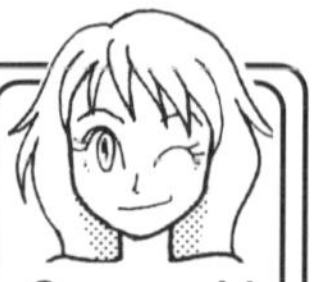

Caucasoid

These bishoujo have clear-cut facial features and hair colored from blonde to pale yellow to black. Eye colors range from blue to green with no clear tendency between nationalities.

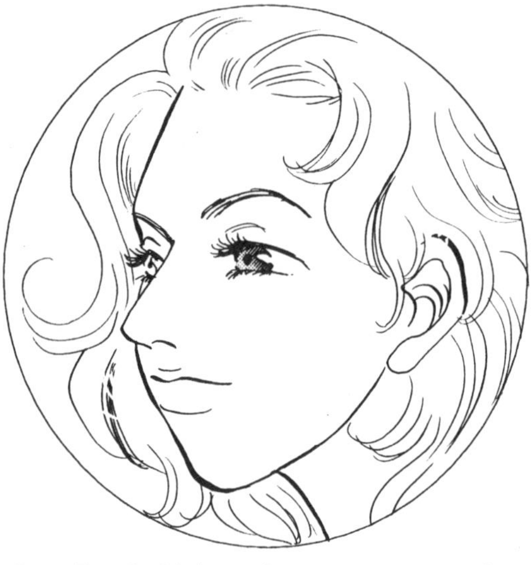

Some French girls have silvery, sauvage cuts and green eyes.

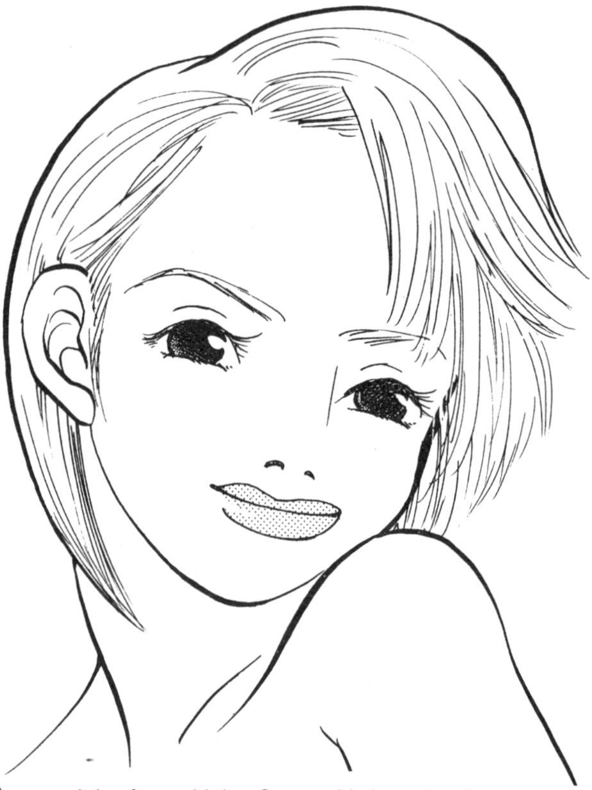

It is often said that Caucasoid characters have wavy hair. However, their hair looks straight with short hairdos. Use thin lines to express the fineness of the hair for this French bishoujo.

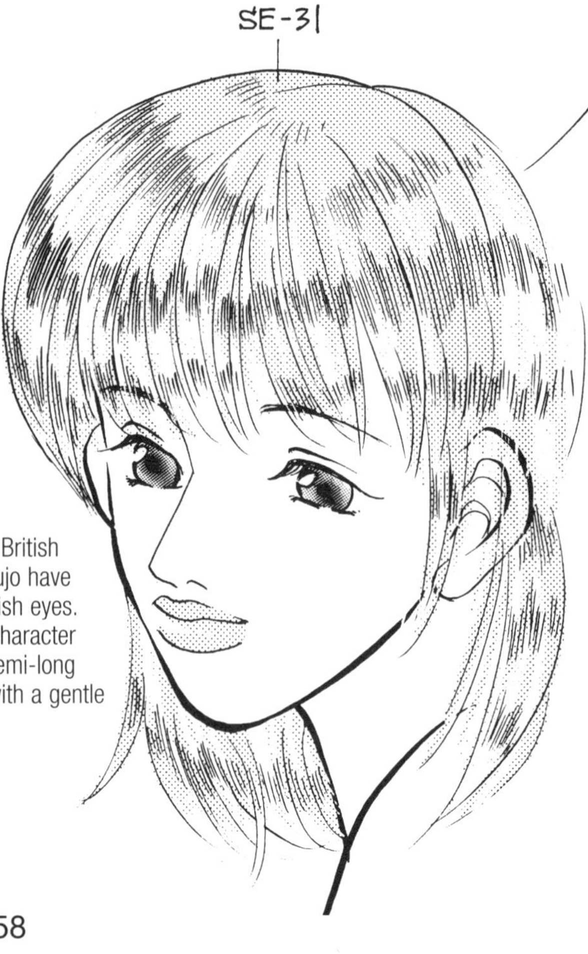

Many British bishoujo have greenish eyes. This character has semi-long hair with a gentle wave.

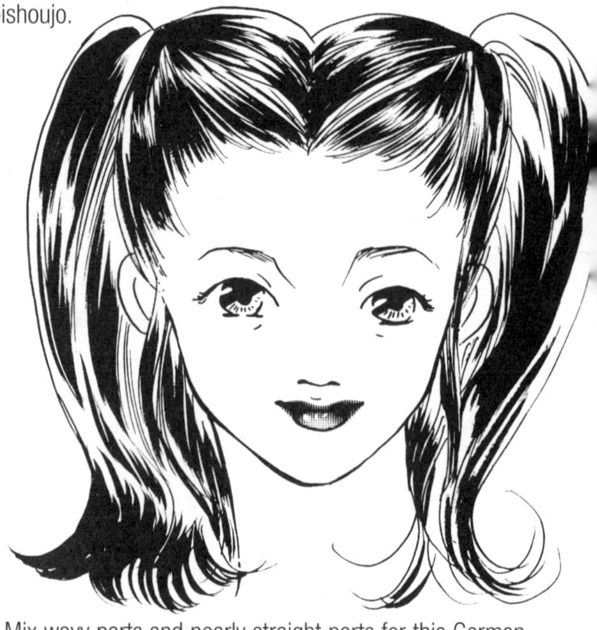

Mix wavy parts and nearly straight parts for this German bishoujo's hair. Rolling the tips is the key to drawing fine, straight hair.

German Bishoujo This traditional dress is said to be the basis of Little Red Riding Hood look.This is one style worn at the Octoberfest harvest festival.

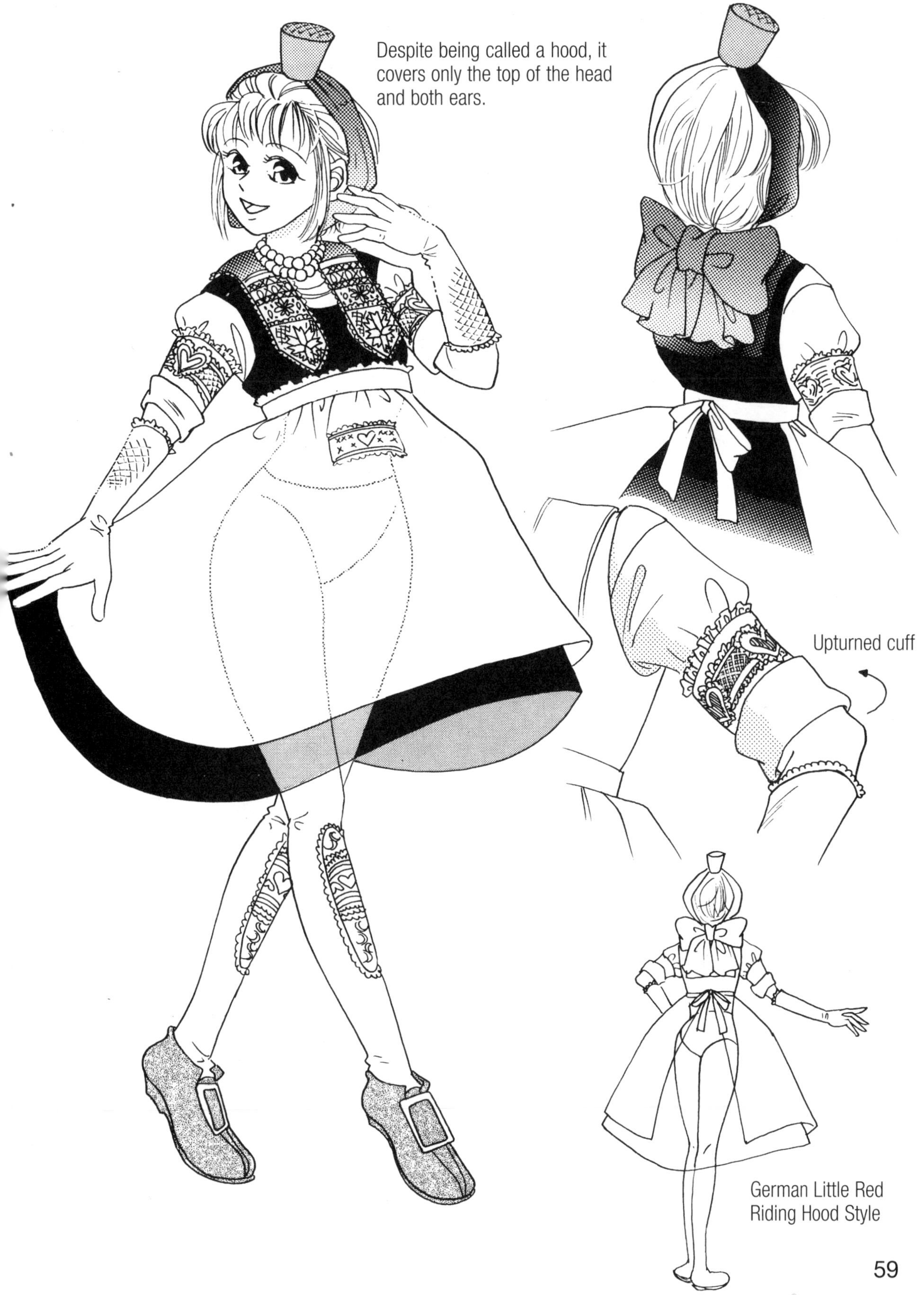

Modern Day French Fashion

French fashion is known for its distinctive coloring and coordination.

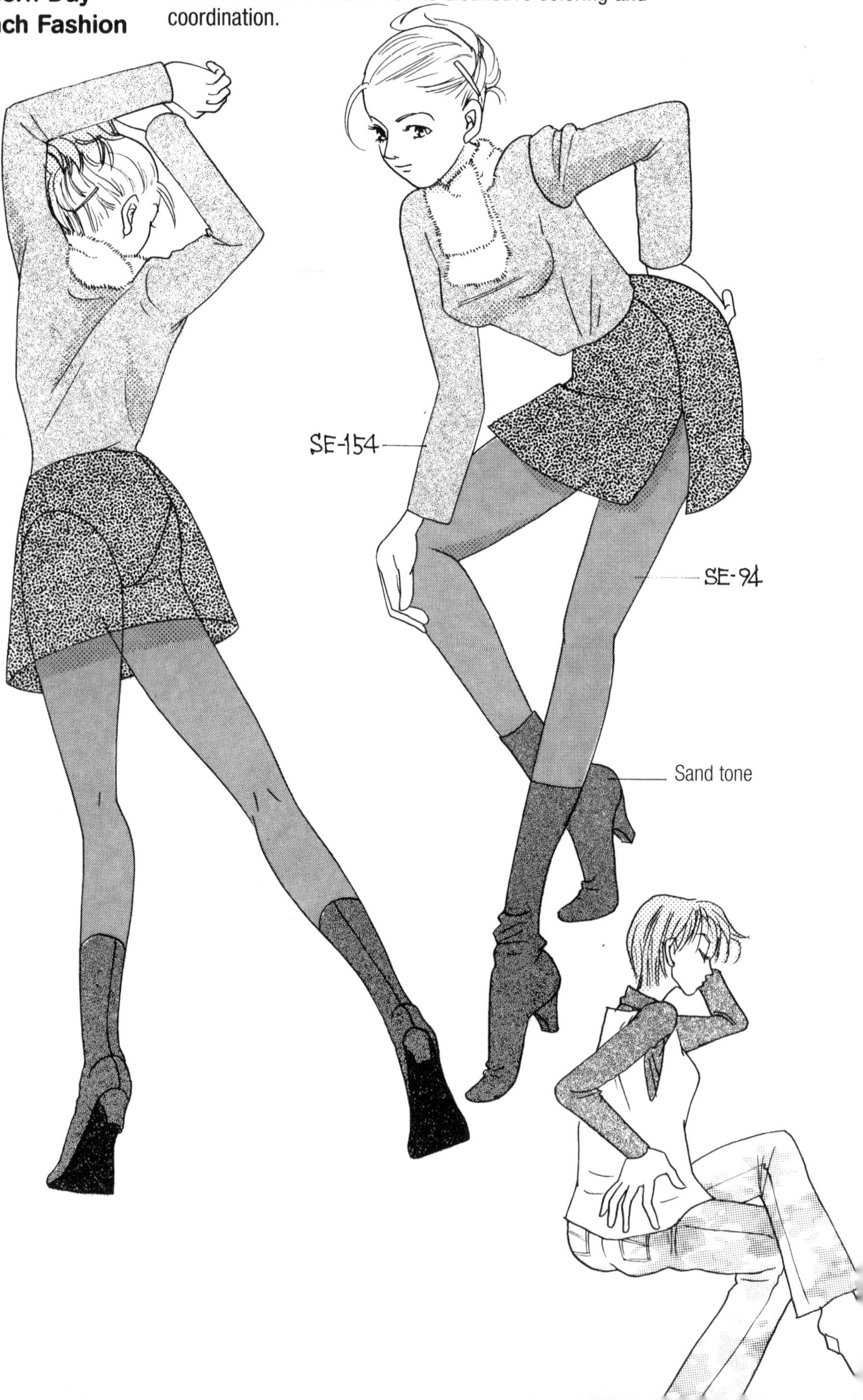

Modern Day English Fashion

Chic elegance with an orthodox mood is a distinctive characteristic of English fashion.

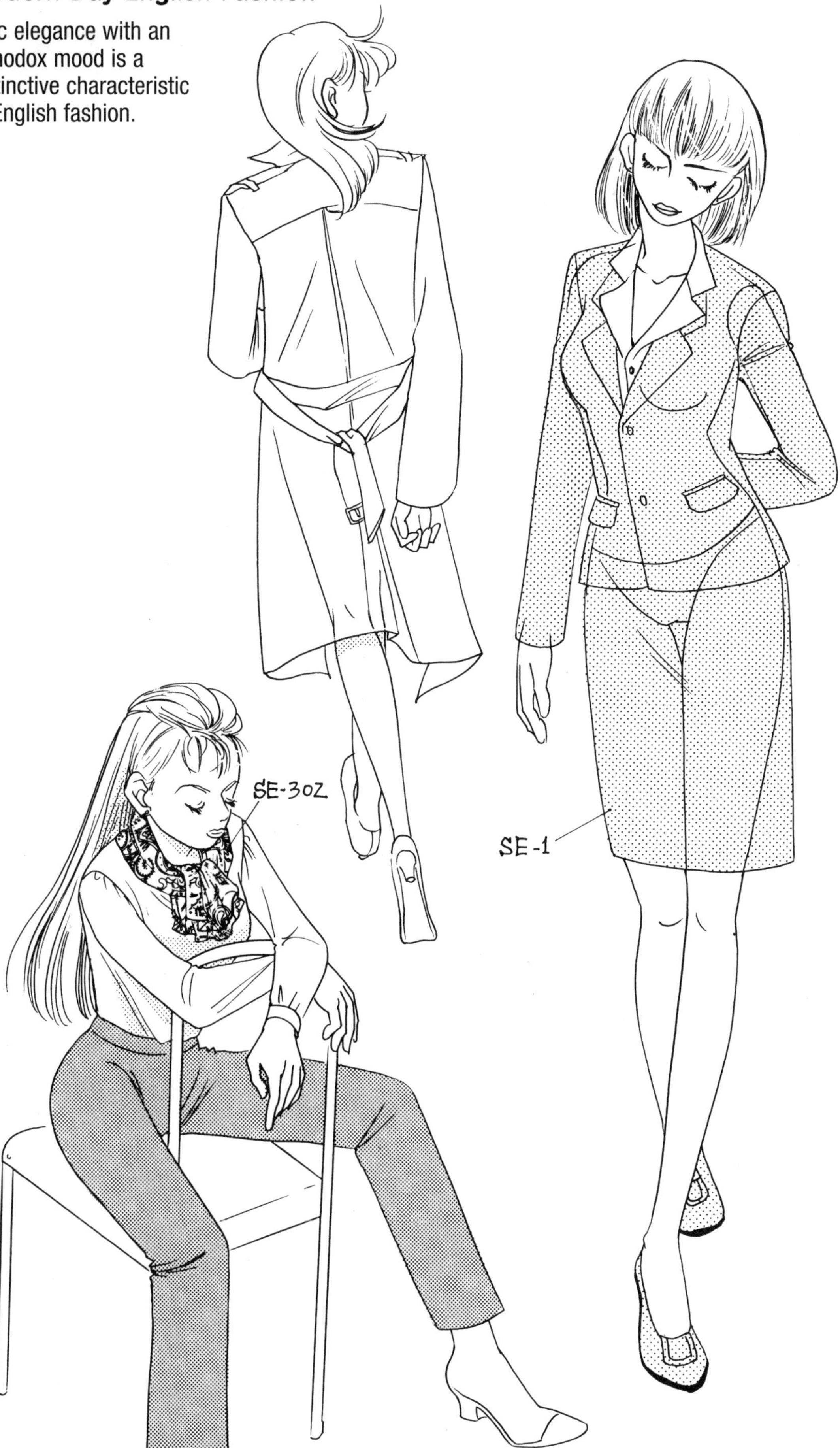

Eastern European Soviet Block Bishoujo
from Russia, Ukraine, Romania and Bulgaria

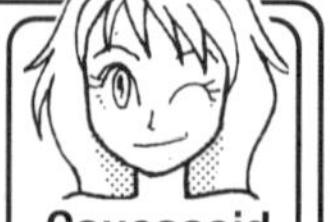

There are a wide variety of eyebrows ranging from extremely thin to thick.

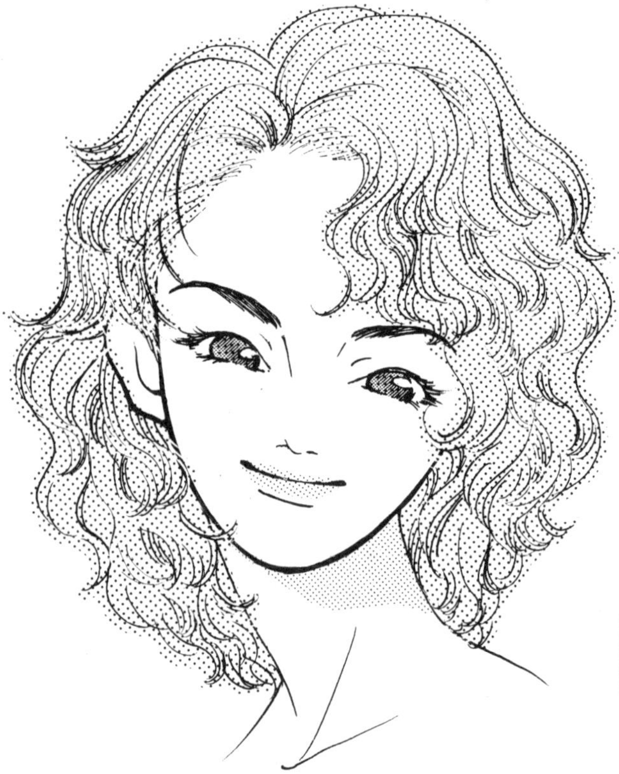

This Czech girl is blonde and blue-eyed.

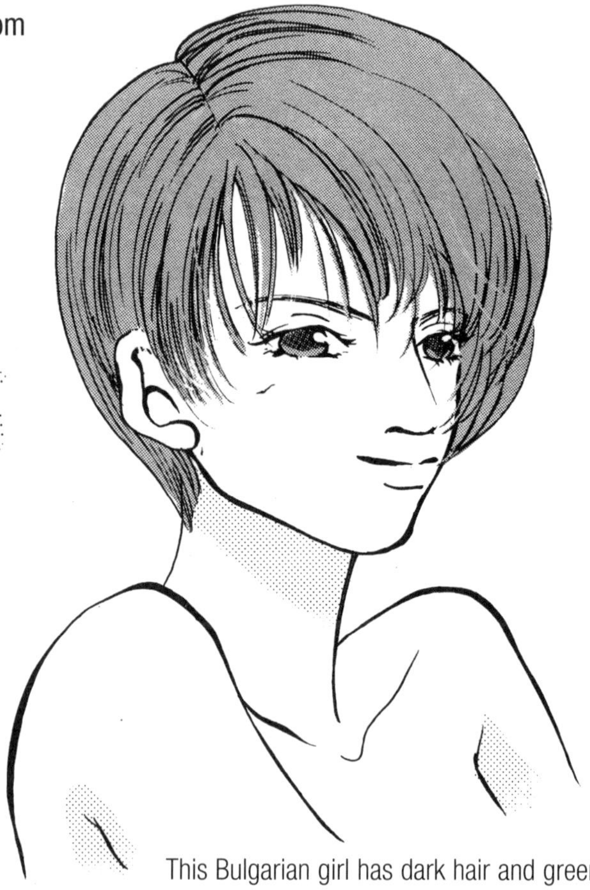

This Bulgarian girl has dark hair and green eyes.

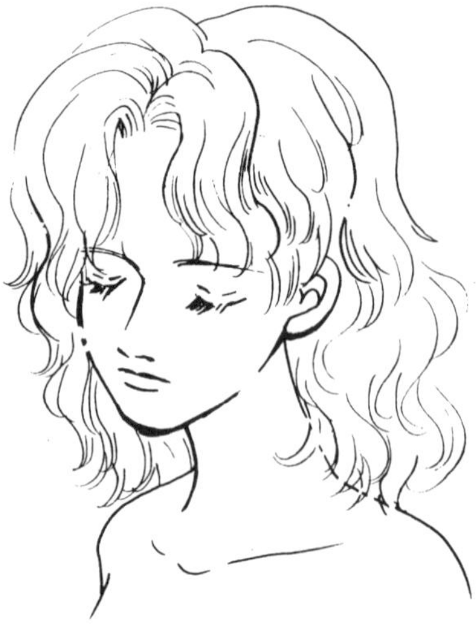

Fine, delicate silvery hair can be expressed by reducing the number of lines and weaving thick and thin lines here and there, providing contrast.

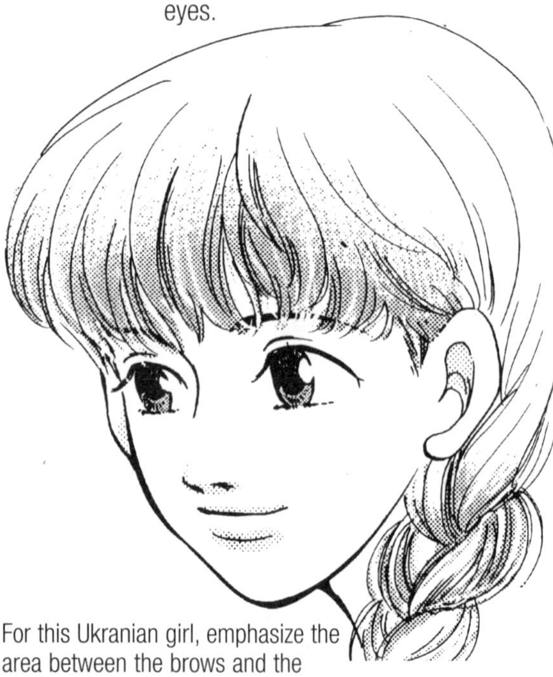

For this Ukranian girl, emphasize the area between the brows and the bottom line of the nose. The abbreviation of the nose line prevents her from appearing prim.

Traditional Czech Clothing

While the vest and the boots are masculine, the puffy sleeved blouse with ribbons and pleated skirt are girlish, keeping the drawing in check. This type of contrast is a must and should be learned in this fine example of cute visual direction.

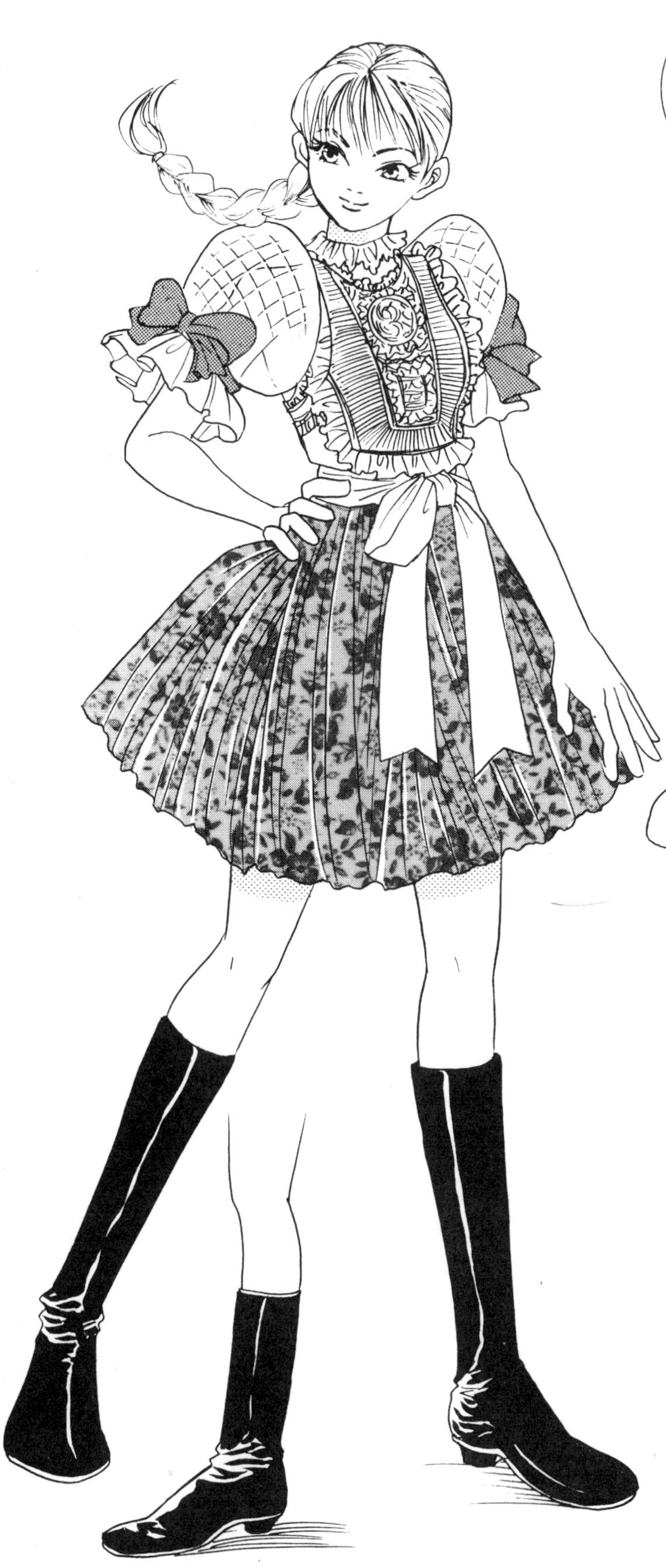

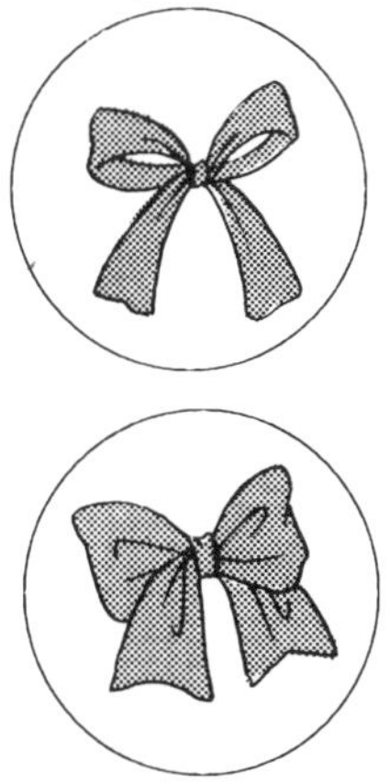

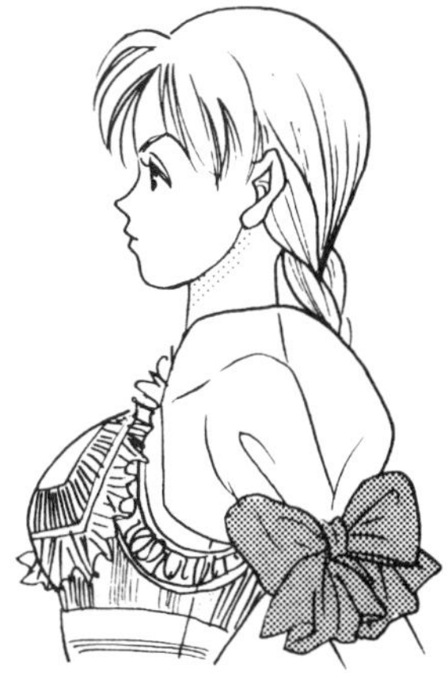

Make the puffy sleeves about the same size as the head, or make them bigger to increase the cuteness.

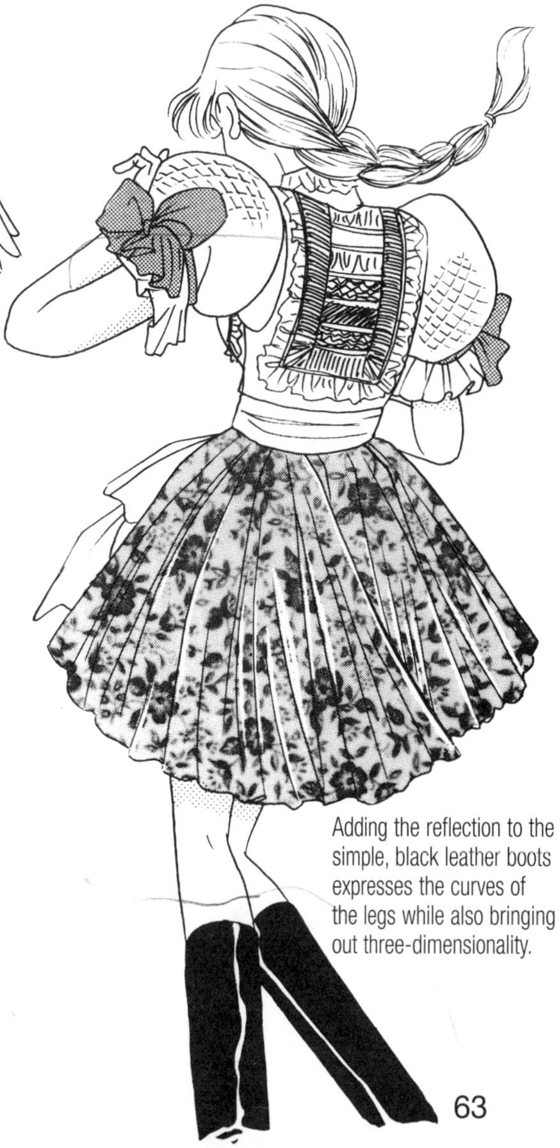

Adding the reflection to the simple, black leather boots expresses the curves of the legs while also bringing out three-dimensionality.

Northern European Bishoujo

from Iceland, Norway, Sweden and Finland

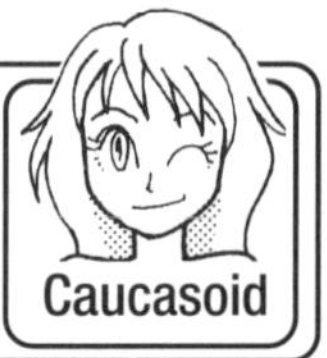

These girls live in the coldest region in Europe where the winters are long. Iceland is famous for its 'white nights'.

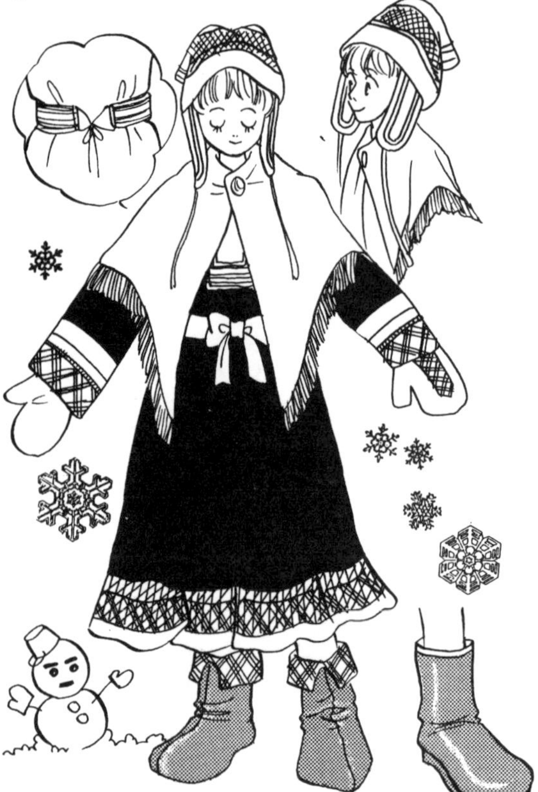

Finnish winter style

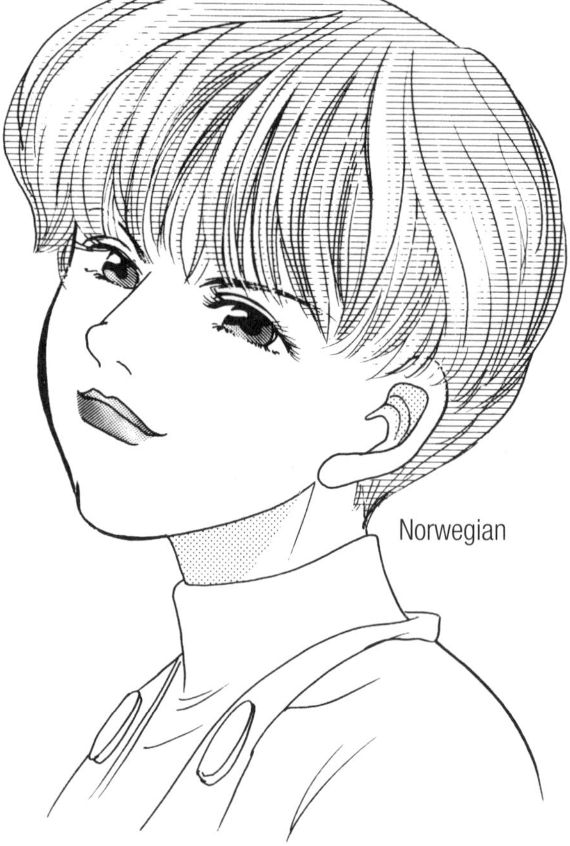

Norwegian

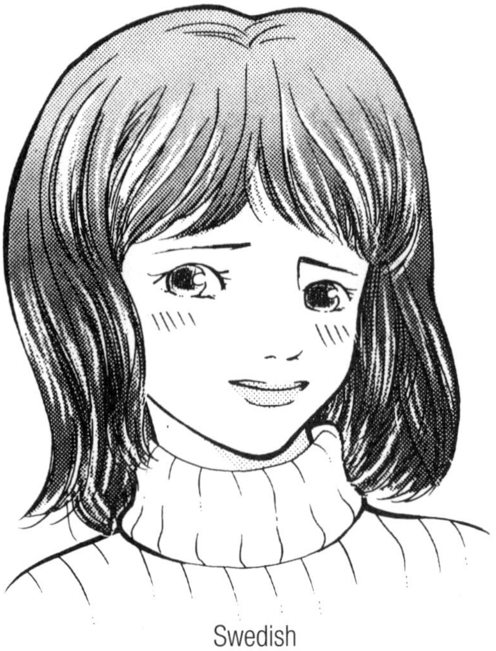

Swedish

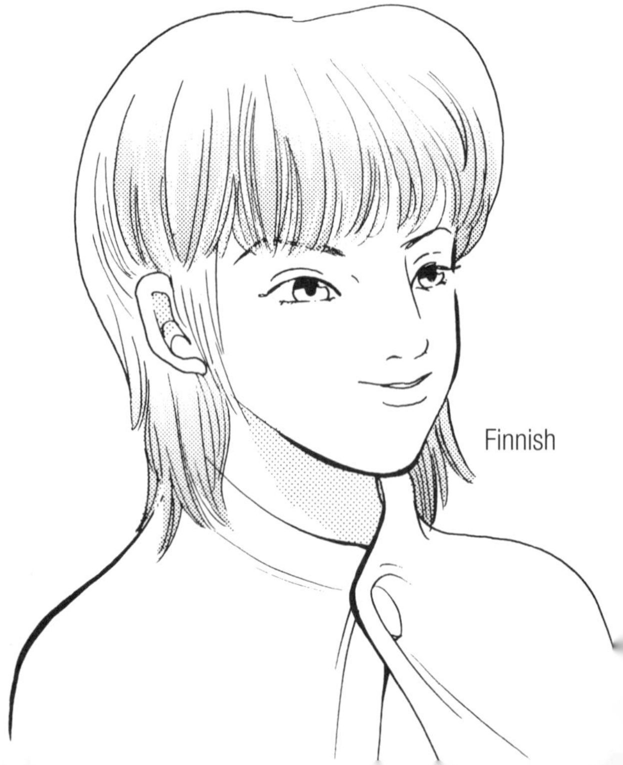

Finnish

Norwegian Apron Maiden

Minor changes in the brooch, belt and pattern of the vest worn under the jacket allows for a wide variety. These also express the ever-important European spirit of individuality.

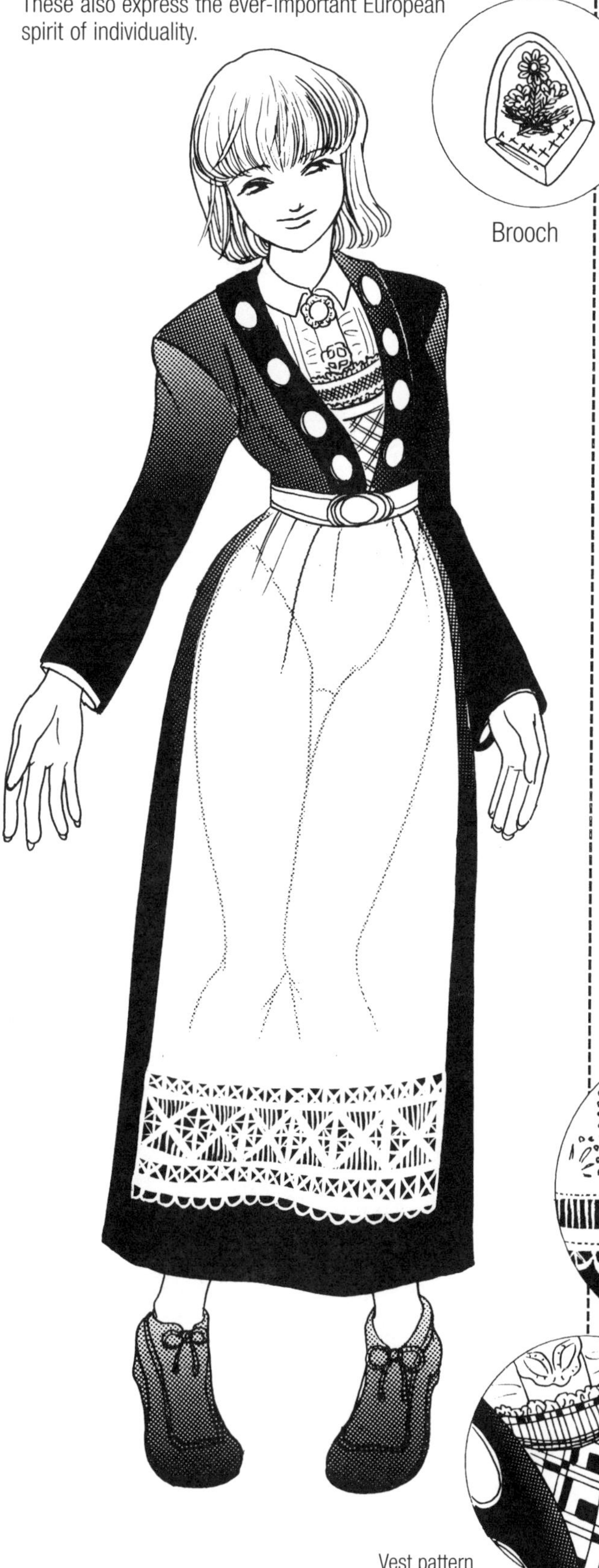

Brooch

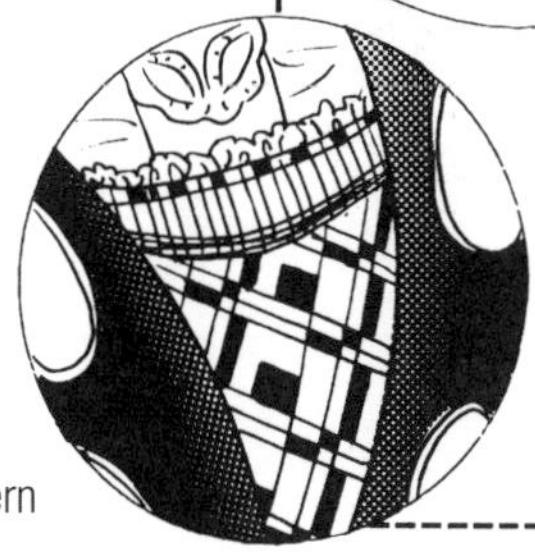

Vest pattern

White Aprons and Lace Patterns

Aprons With Notched Bottoms

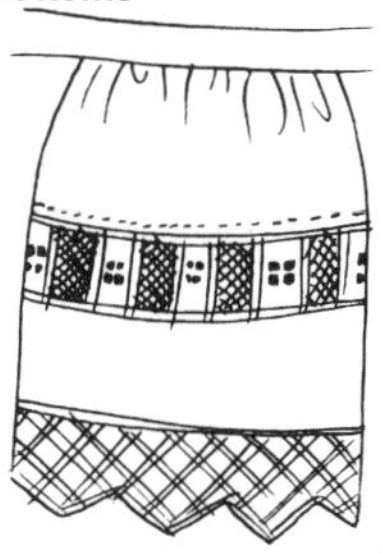

Two levels

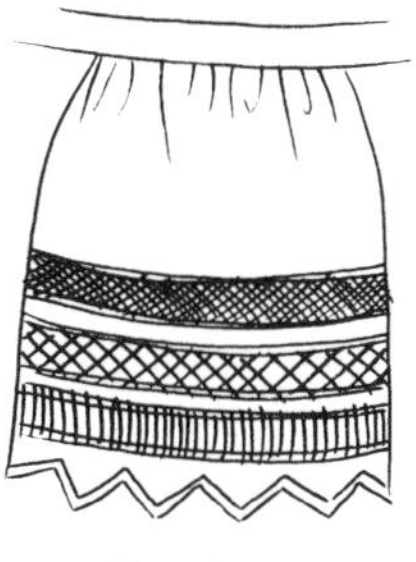

Three levels

Aprons With Hemmed Bottoms

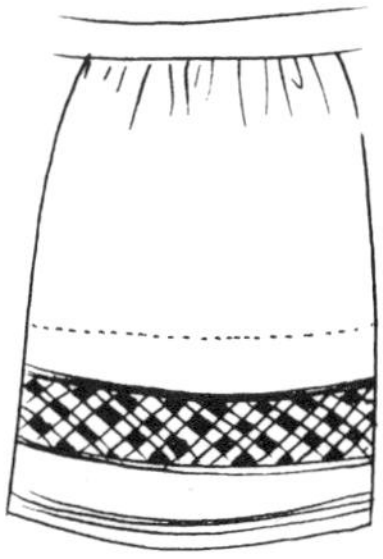

One level

Aprons With Notched Bottoms

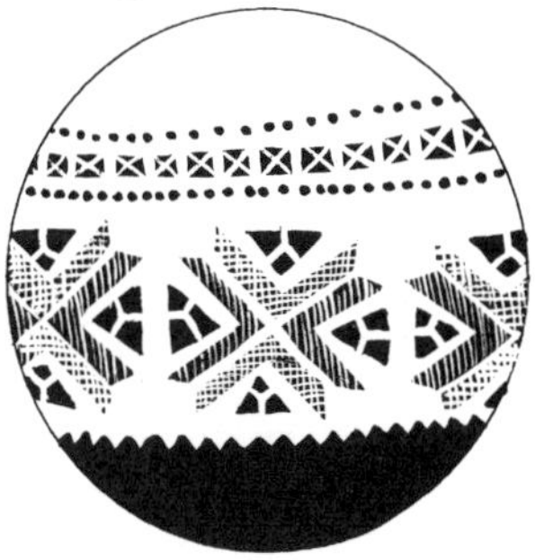

Large pattern

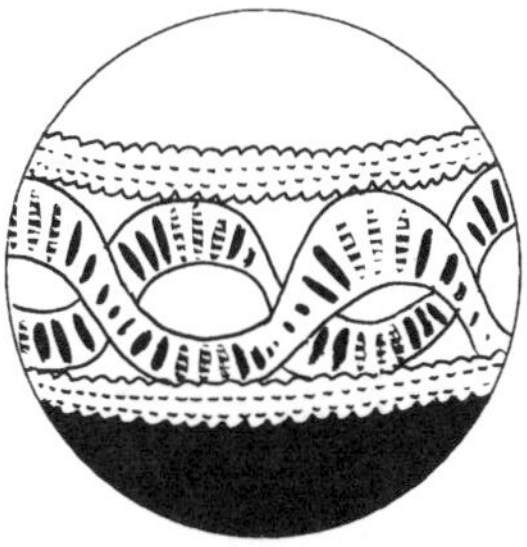

Medium-sized pattern

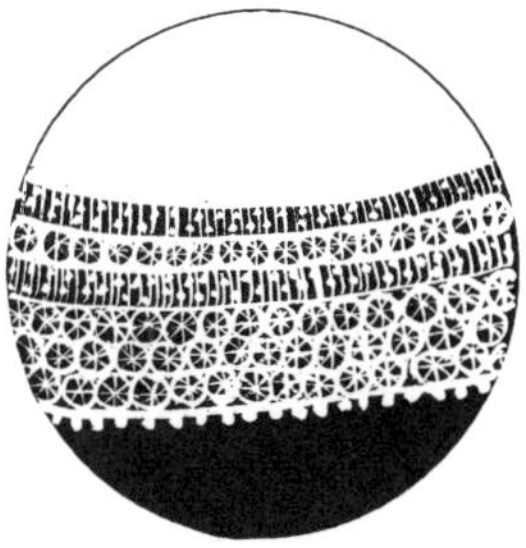

Small pattern

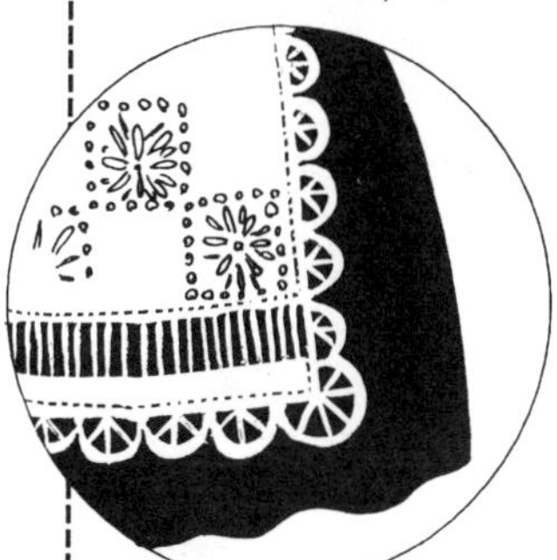

Apron Edge Patterns

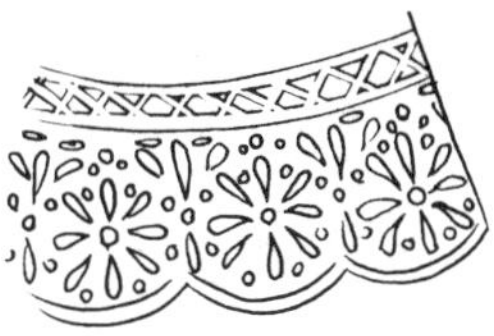

Gentle, wave-shaped edge

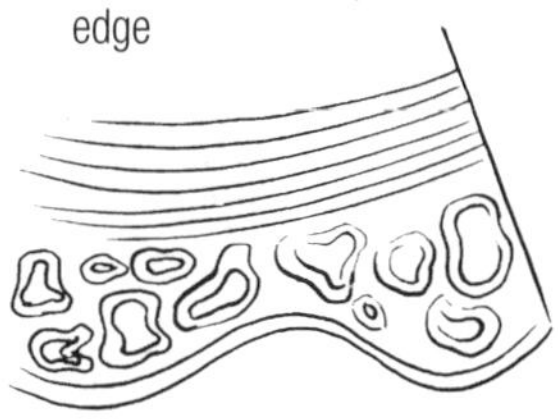

Large, wave-shaped edge

Southern European Bishoujo
from Spain, Italy and Portugal

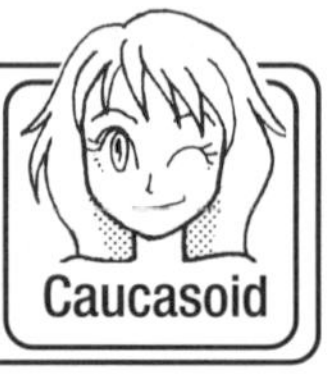

While these Caucasoid have clear-cut facial features, black hair and eyes seem to predominate. In addition, the build of the eyes, nose and mouth are relatively large. It is said that these girls are generally big-hearted, merry and passionate.
Let's study black-based hair variations.

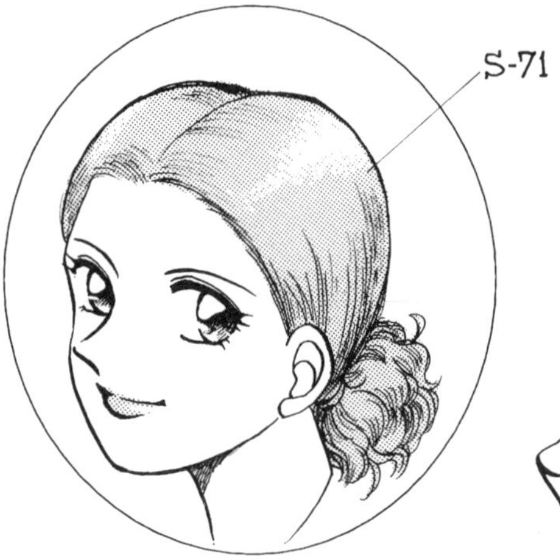

Use touches and 20% tones for hair colors other than blonde, brunette, black and brown. The lips are a bit thin.

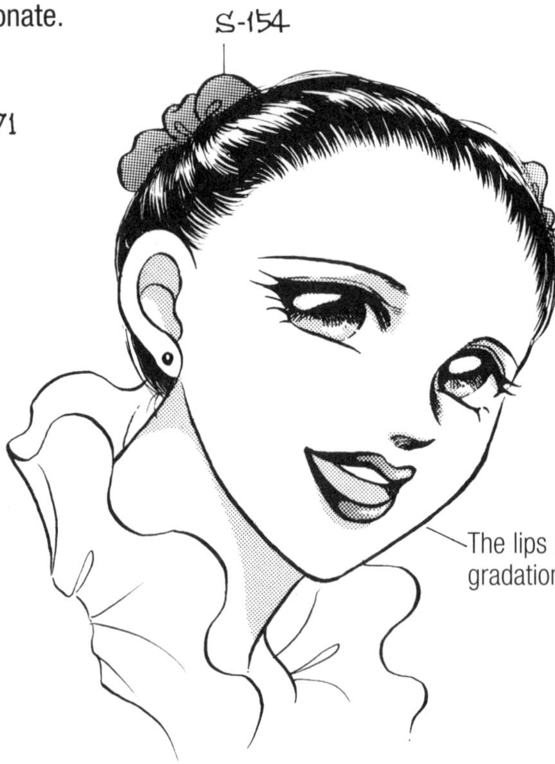

The lips use gradation tones.

This Spanish girl with black hair was drawn in the image of the musical Carmen. In reality, there are many of those with brown or dark brown hair of this type.

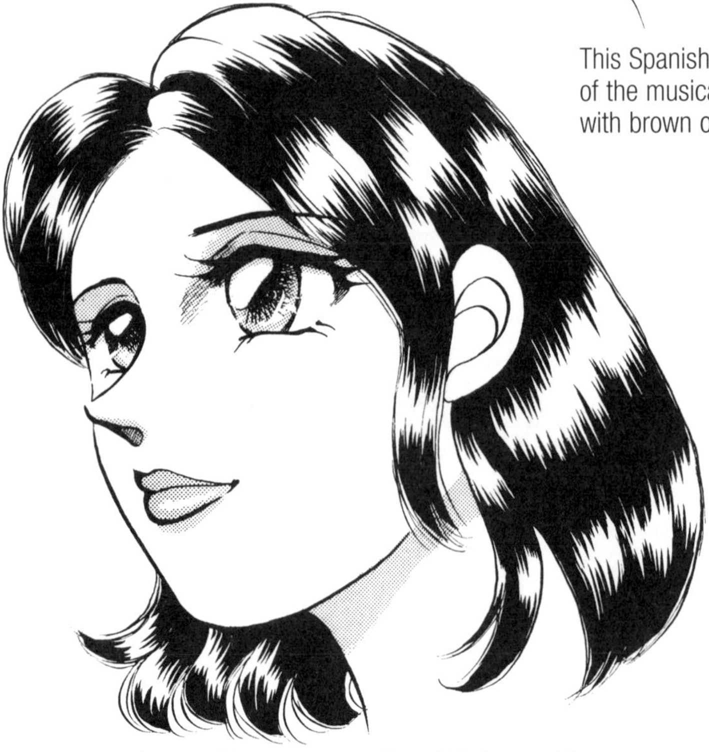

In general, larger noses are often said to be one of the distinctive characteristics of Italians. However, in order to bring out the bishoujo nature, it is best not to go for too much realism when emphasizing these features. The hair is black.

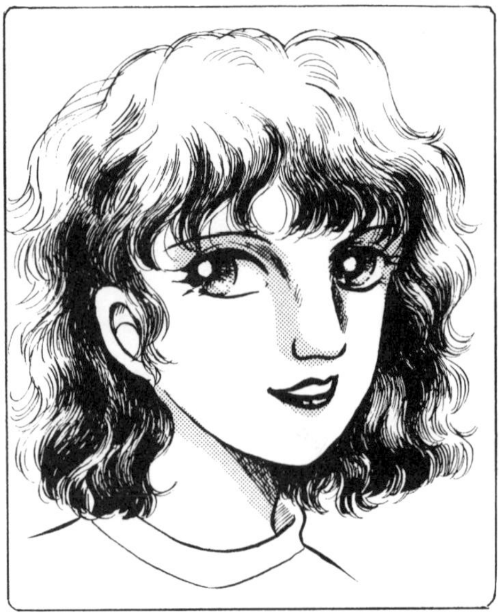

This variation of a Spanish senorita - a title used for a Spanish-speaking unmarried woman - has a high-bridged nose. When emphasizing the nose, realistic illustrations go better with it. The hair is fine and colored black and brown.

Traditional Italian Clothing

Wearing a shawl over the head not only brings out the girlish nature in the character but also can create a variety of moods and feeling of things like adultness and wildness.

Here is an example of a shawl pattern. They are usually abbreviated.

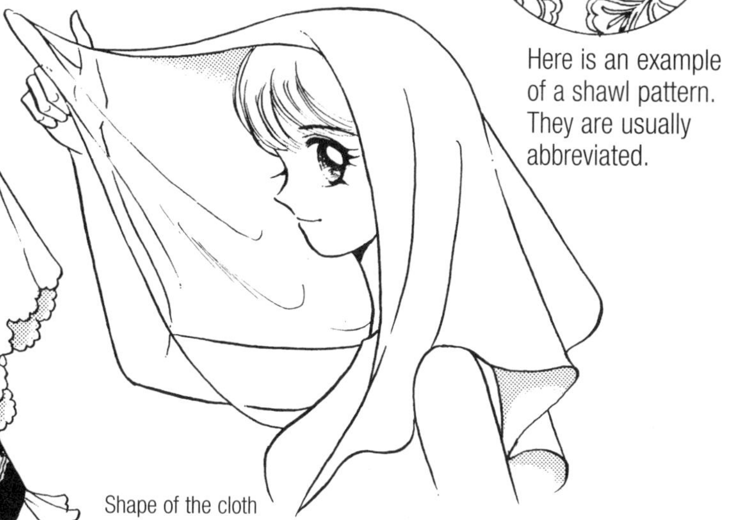

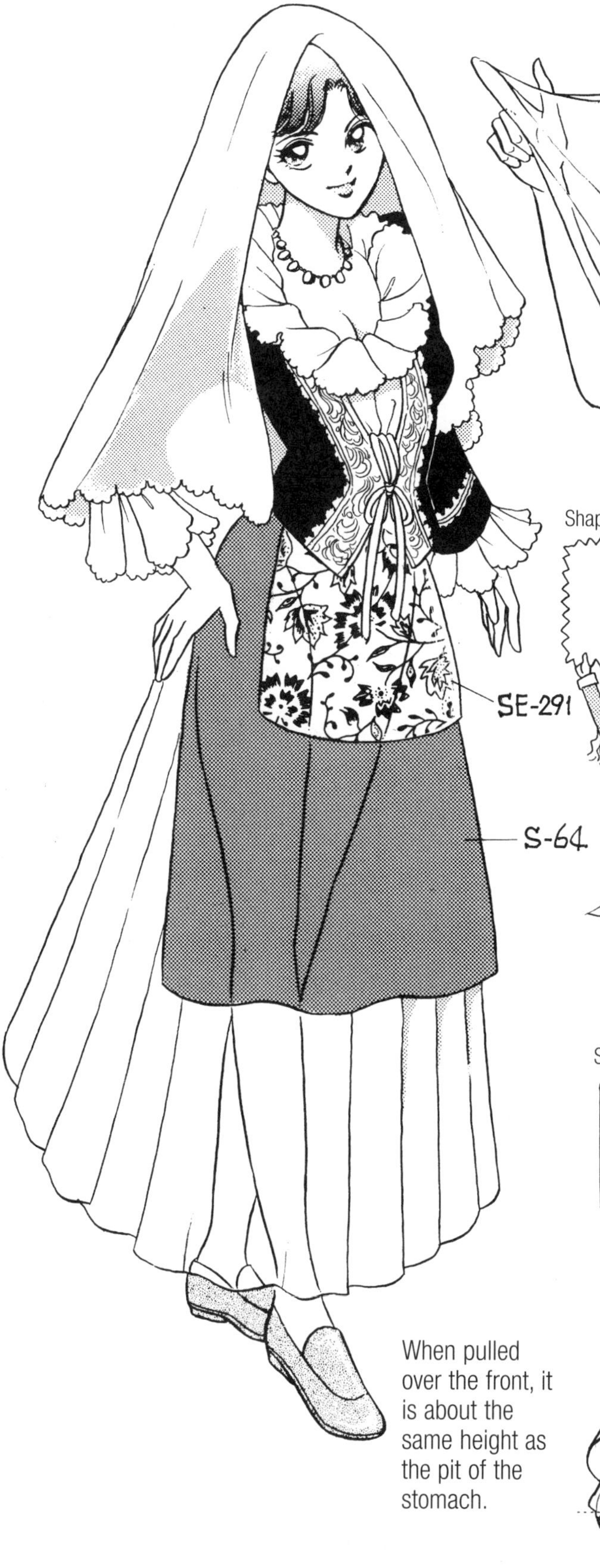

Shape of the cloth

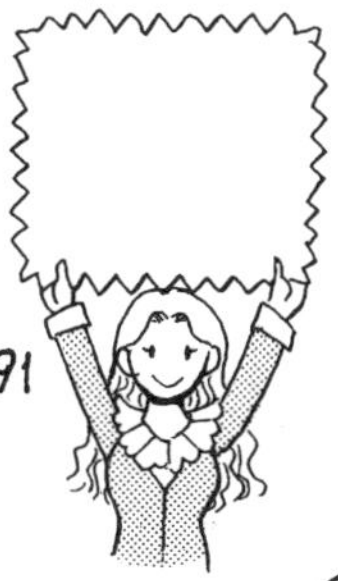

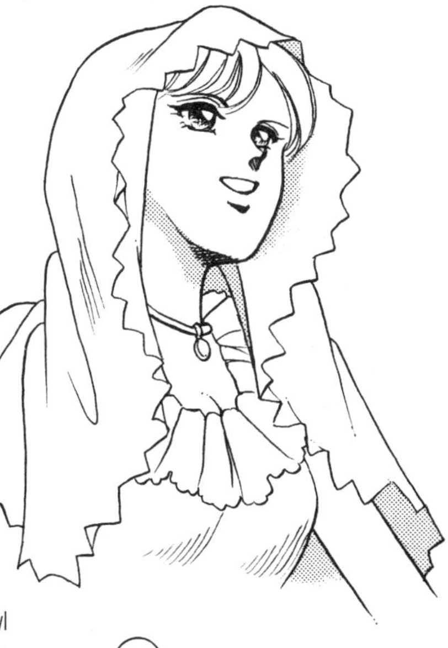

Size of the shawl

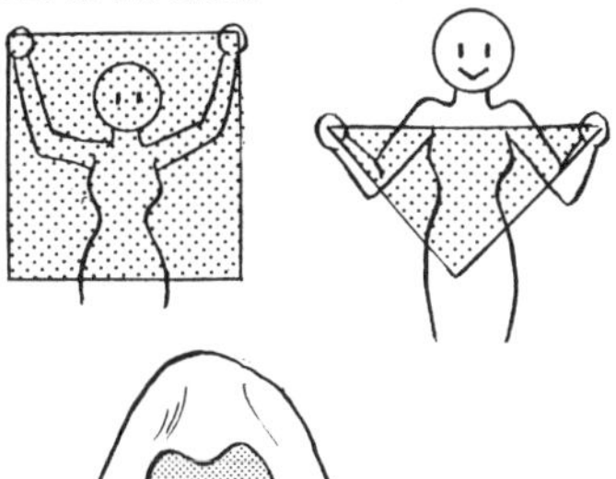

When pulled over the front, it is about the same height as the pit of the stomach.

Back side

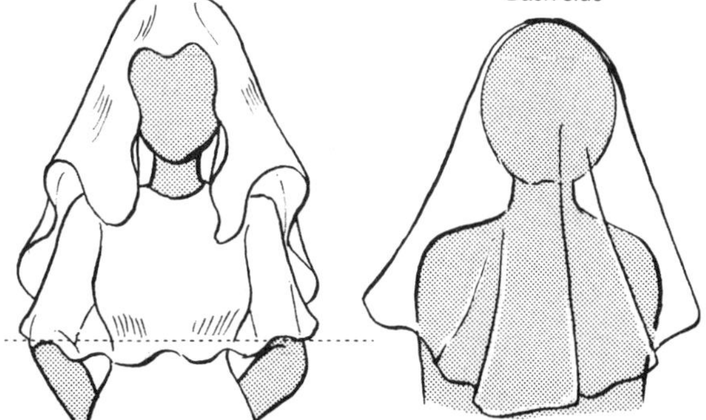

Spanish Flamenco

Flamenco fashion is reserved for festivals and dancing.

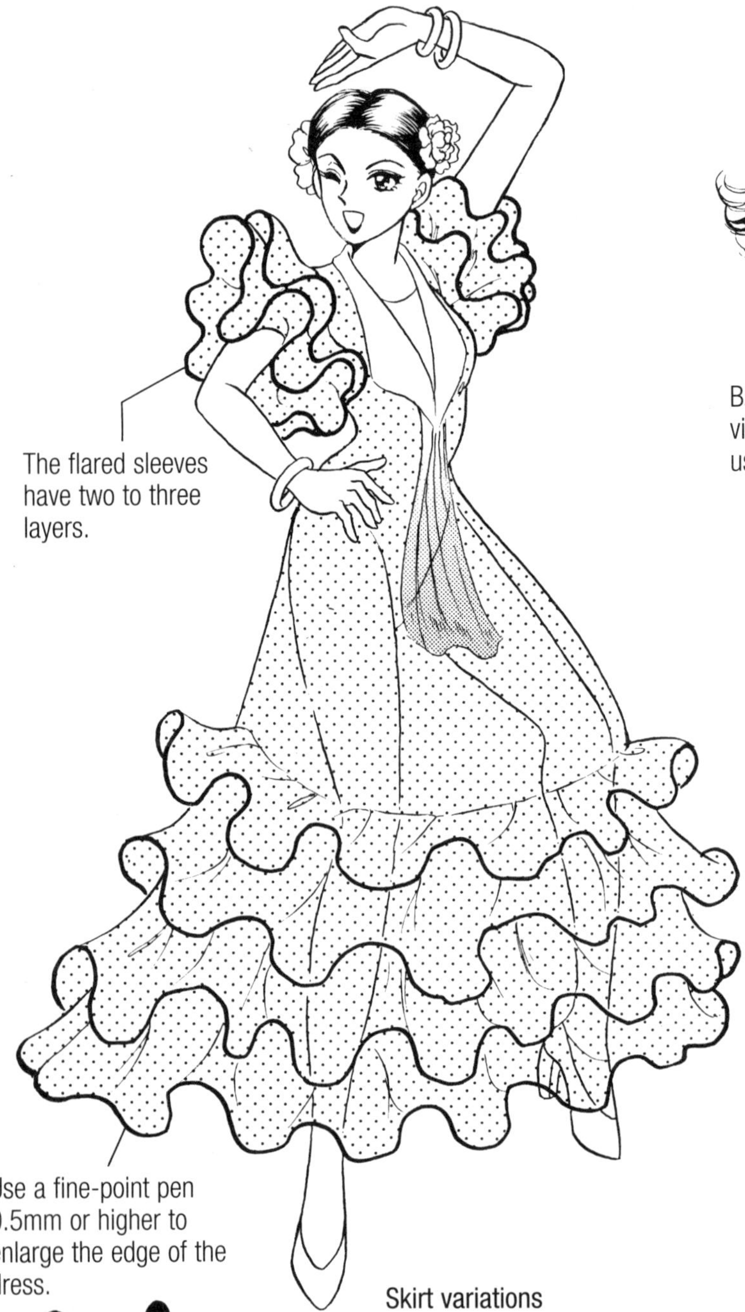

The flared sleeves have two to three layers.

Use a fine-point pen 0.5mm or higher to enlarge the edge of the dress.

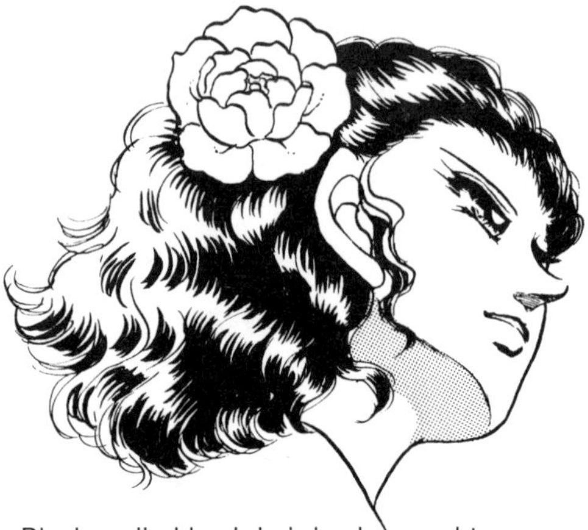

Black, pulled back hair is also used to visually direct a Gypsy nature. Flowers are useful to accentuate their beauty.

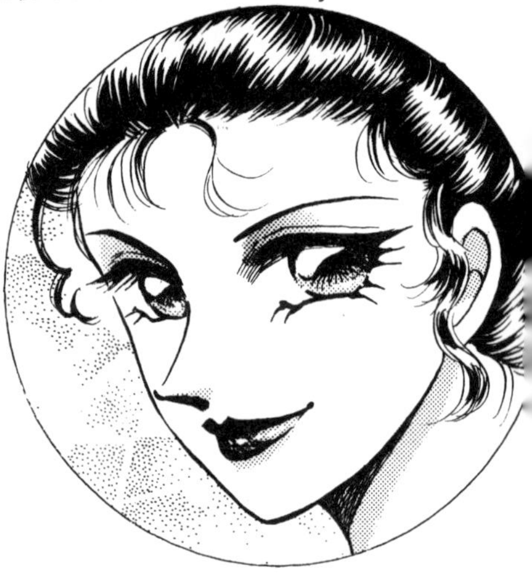

Gradation is effective for depicting the makeup on the eyes and lips.

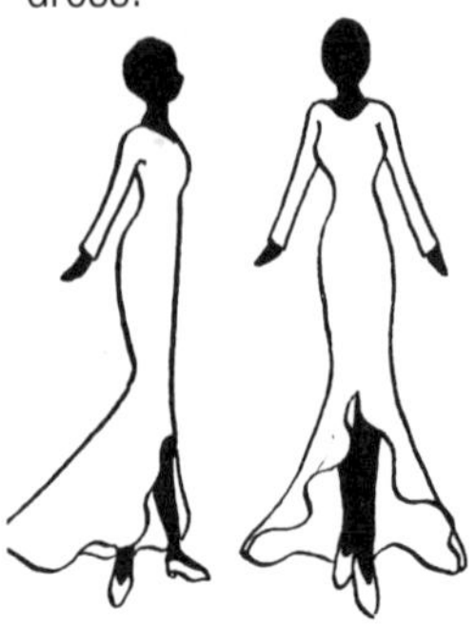

Skirt variations

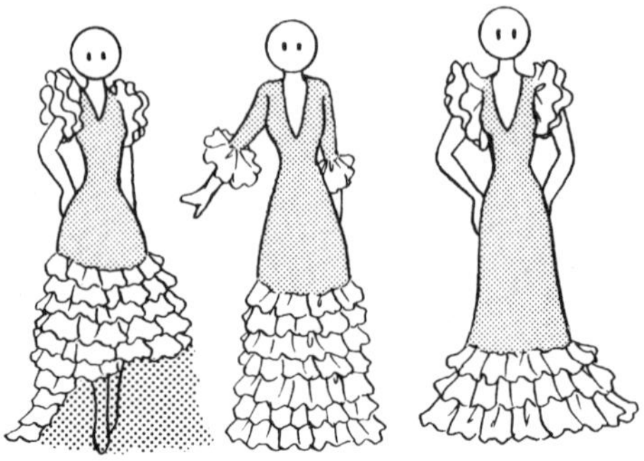

Twelve levels Seven levels Three levels

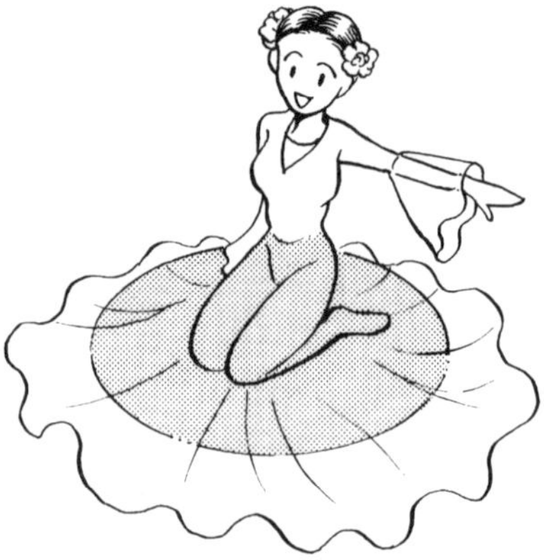

When the character is seated, the skirt spreads out like this.

Bullfighter Costume

Ranks exist amongst bullfighters whereby their clothes and roles strictly differ according to their skill and popularity. This one is the most generally known style.

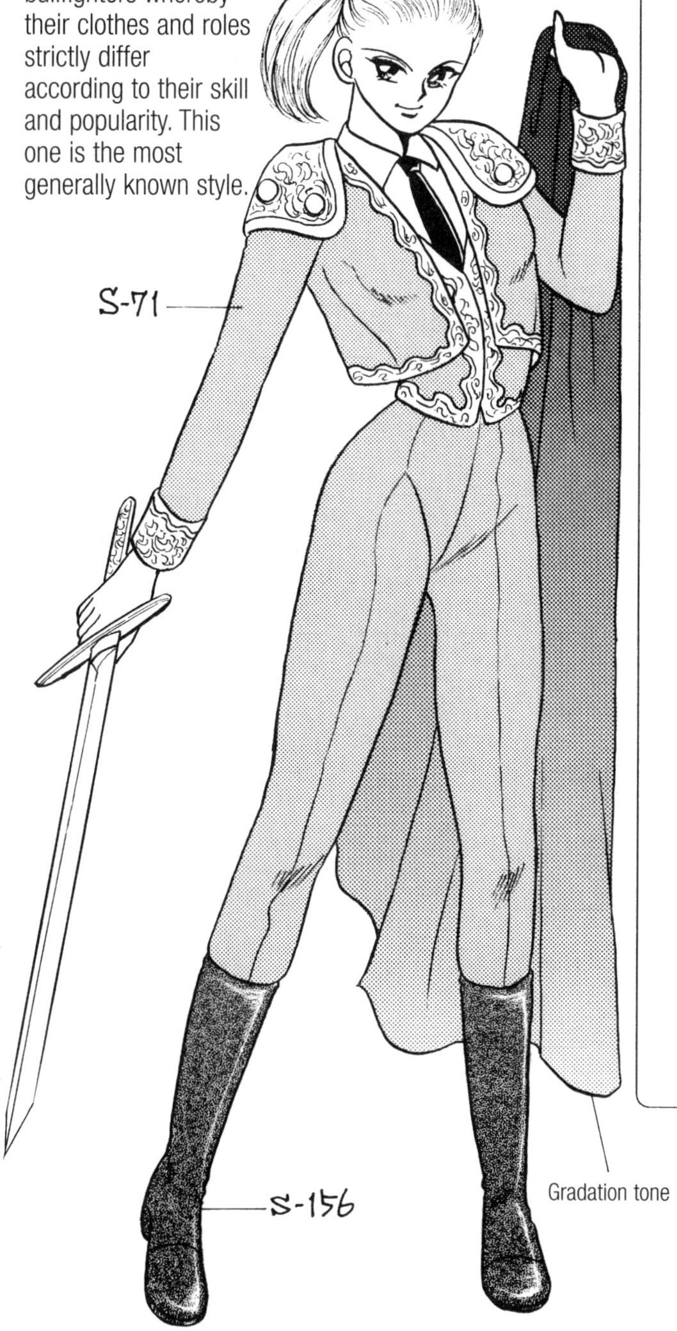

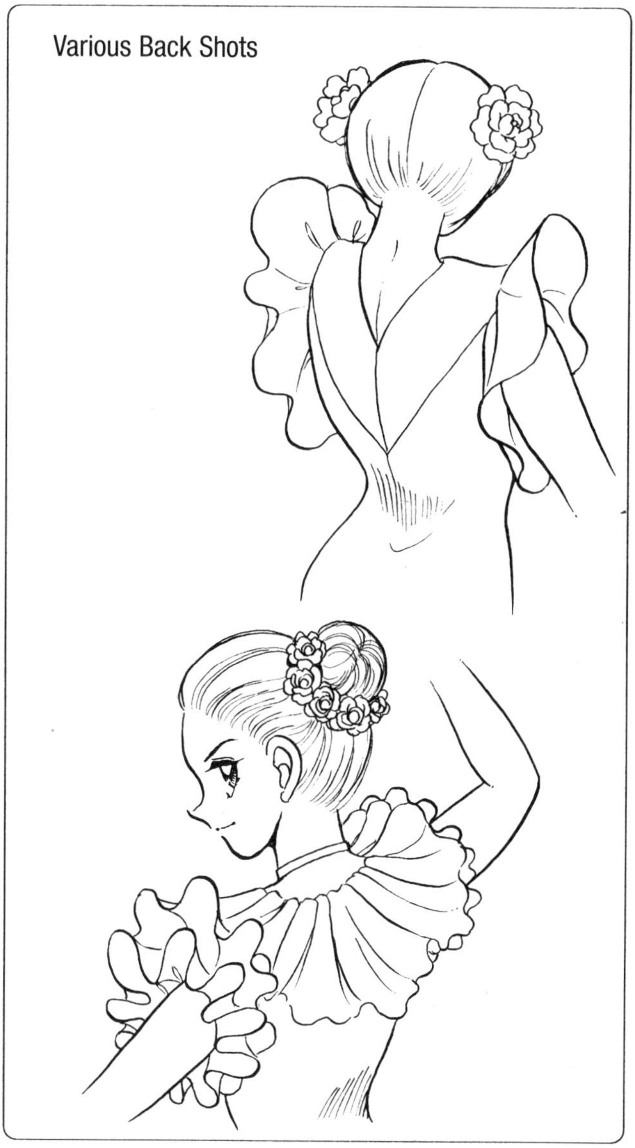

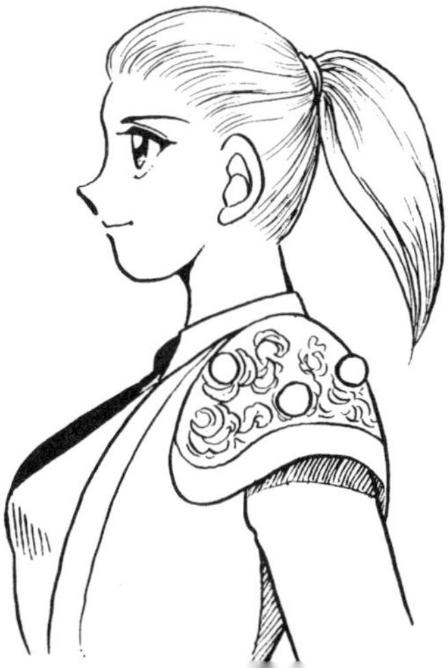

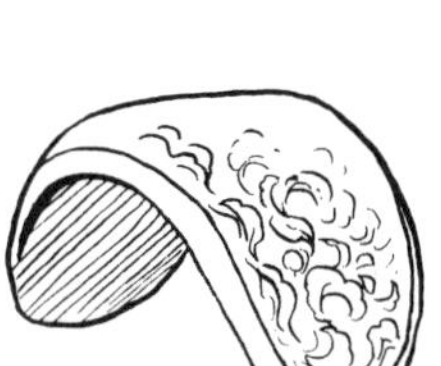

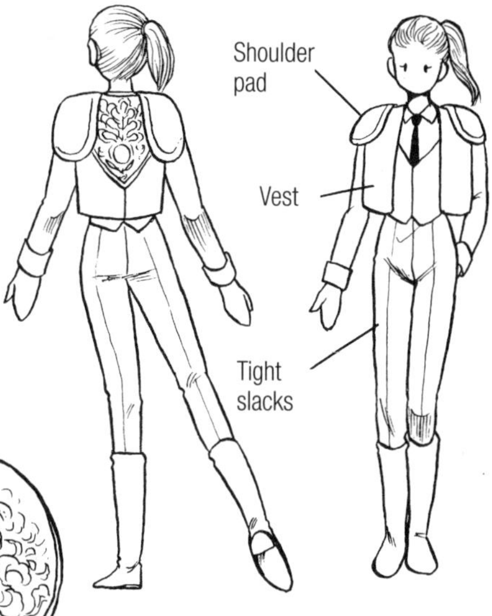

Mediterranean Bishoujo

from Egypt and Greece

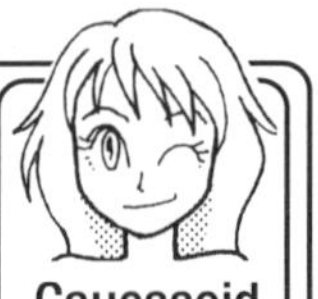

The black wavy hair comes in two types: large wavy or fine sauvage.

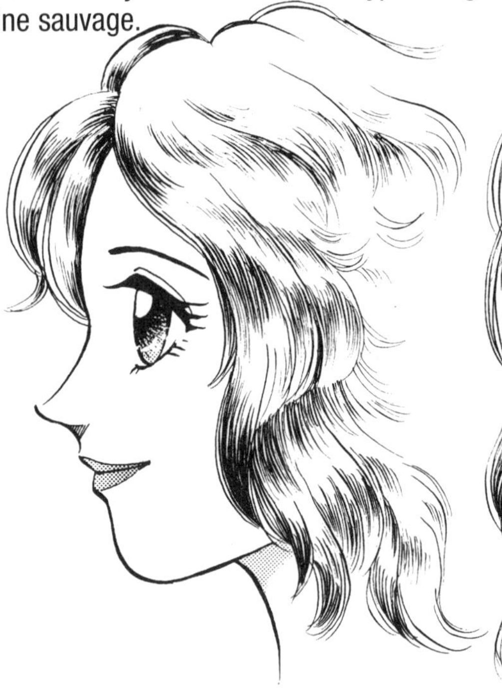

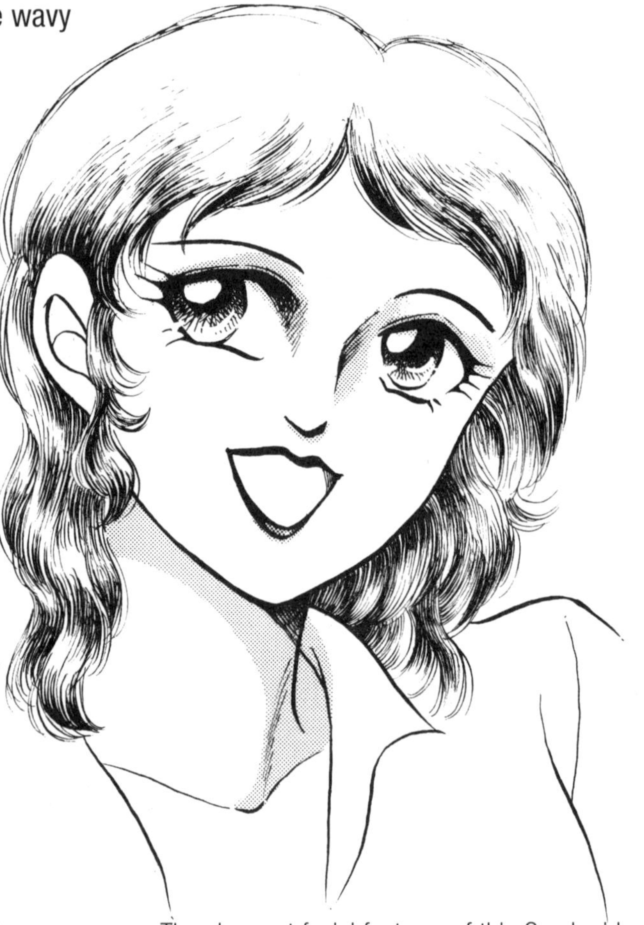

The clear-cut facial features of this Greek girl are like a sculpted figure. The hair is black while the eyes are deep-green.

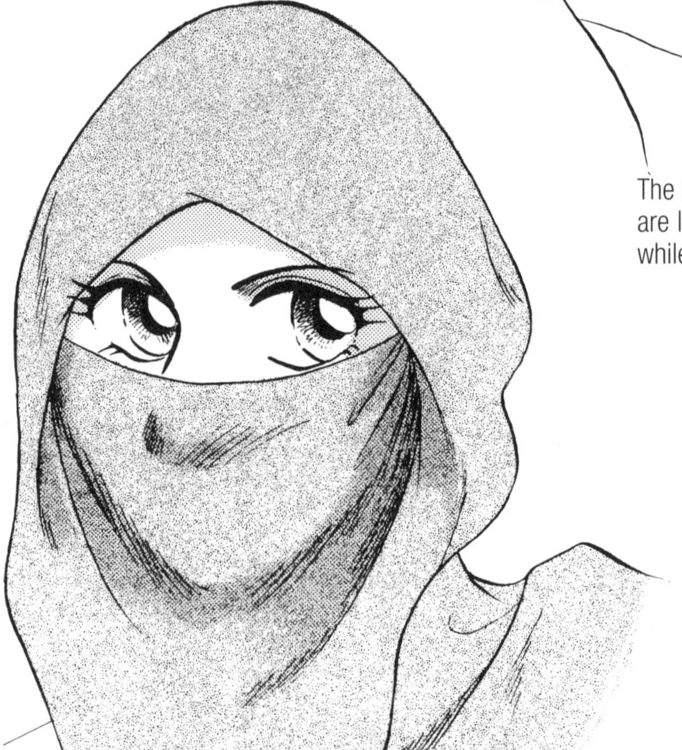

Since Egyptian girls are often drawn with the face covered, express the wide-open eyes appealingly.

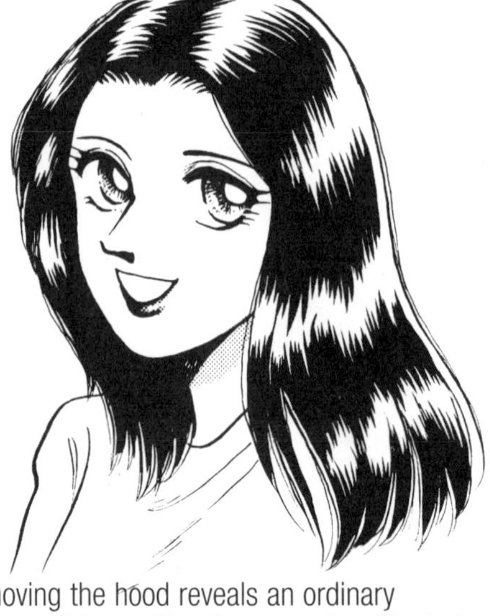

Removing the hood reveals an ordinary Caucasoid face with a fine nose line. The hair is predominantly black.

Egyptian Black Attire

The color is all black because dirt would stand out with white.

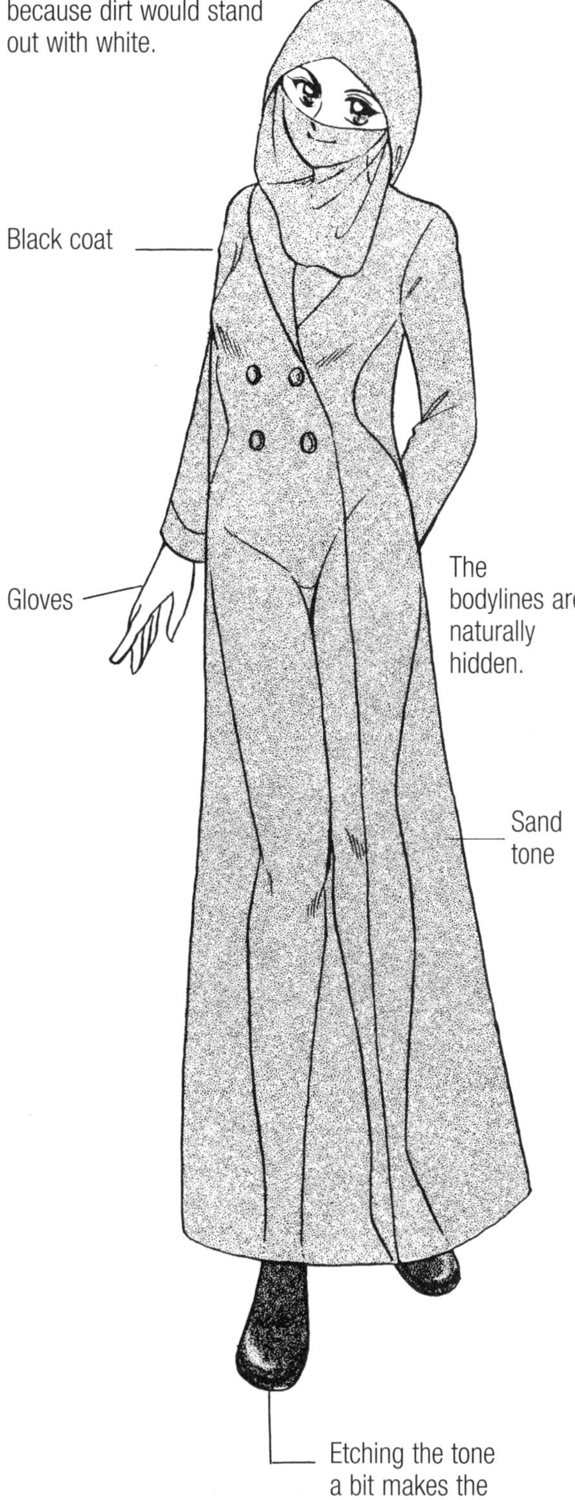

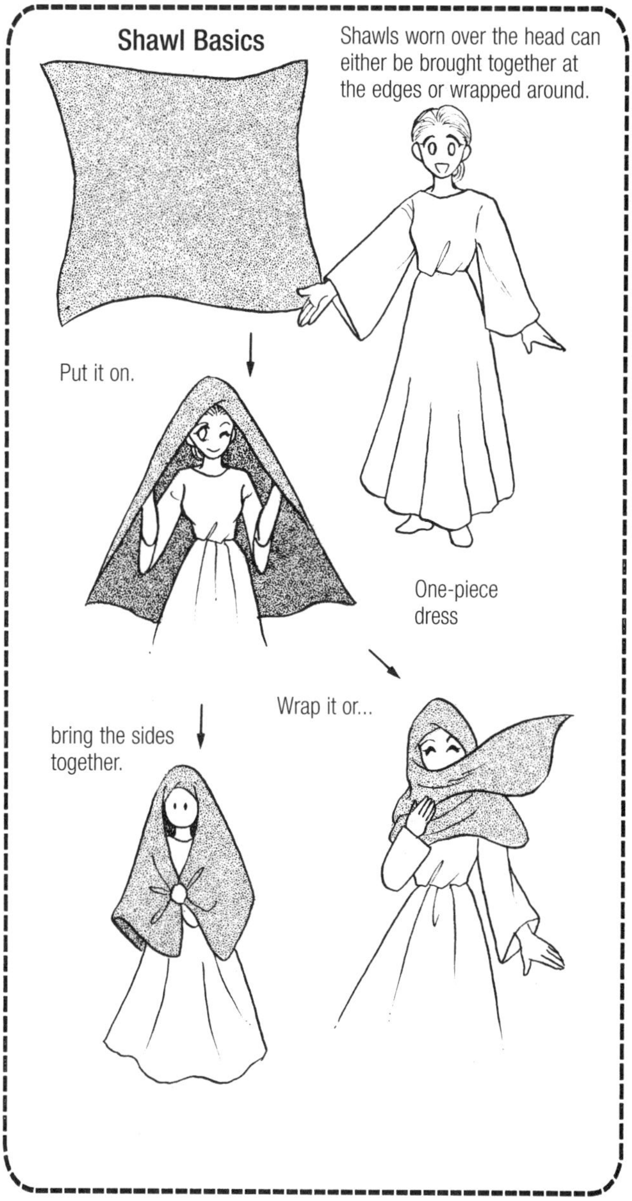

Front View

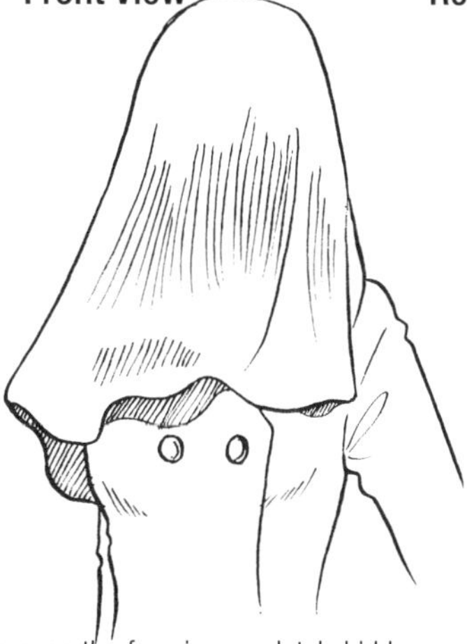

In this case the face is completely hidden from the outside. However, since the texture of the cloth is thin, the character is able to see properly.

Rear View

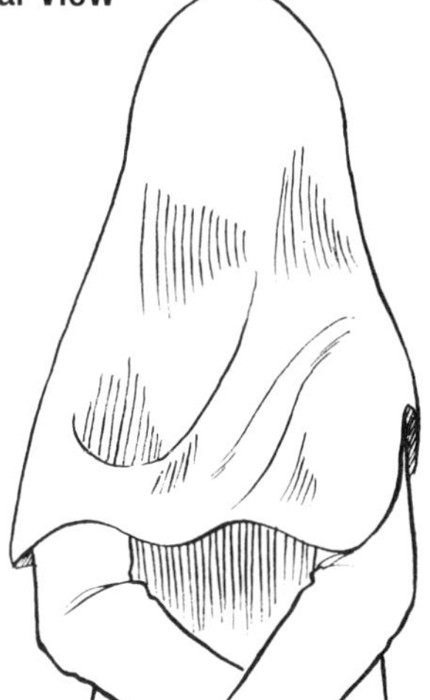

The cloth hangs downward relatively straight since the face is flat except for the nose. Shadows are used to bring out the roundness of the head.

Greek Bishoujo This traditional clothing is from the Island of Crete famous for the Knossos legendary tales of labyrinths and giants.

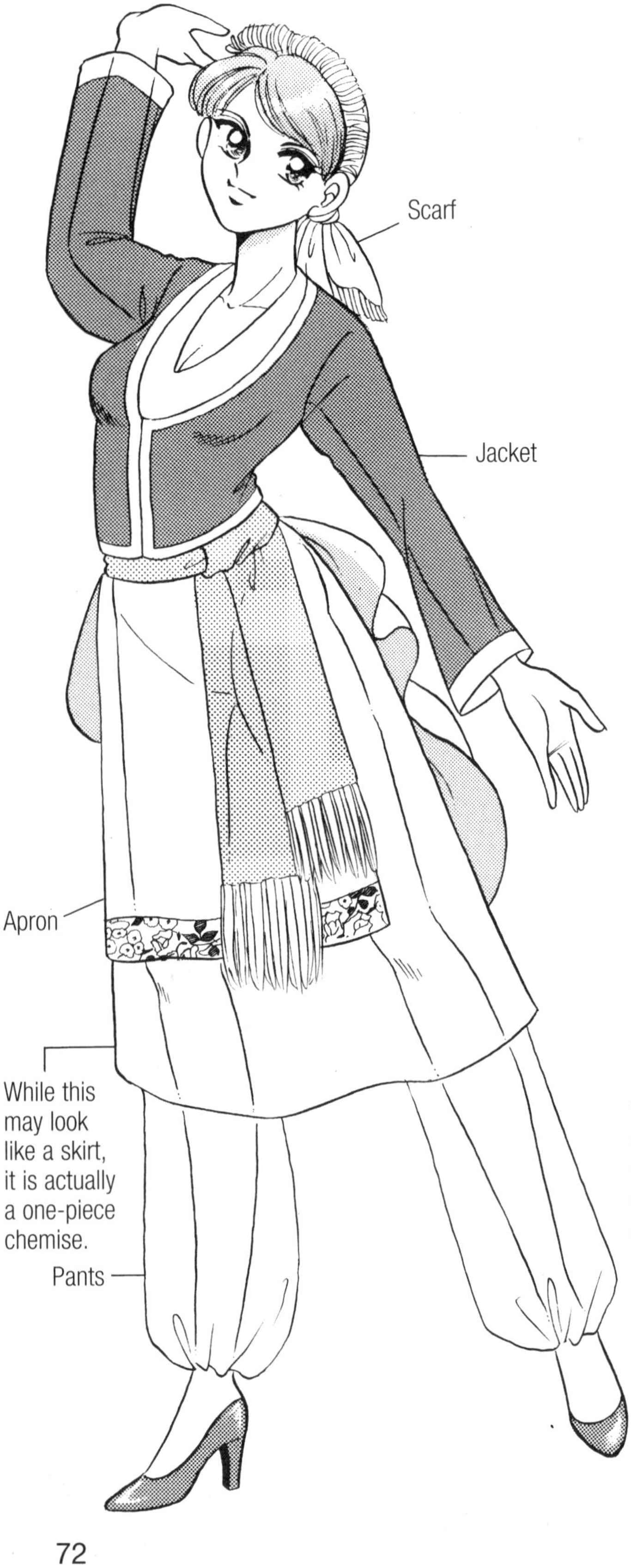

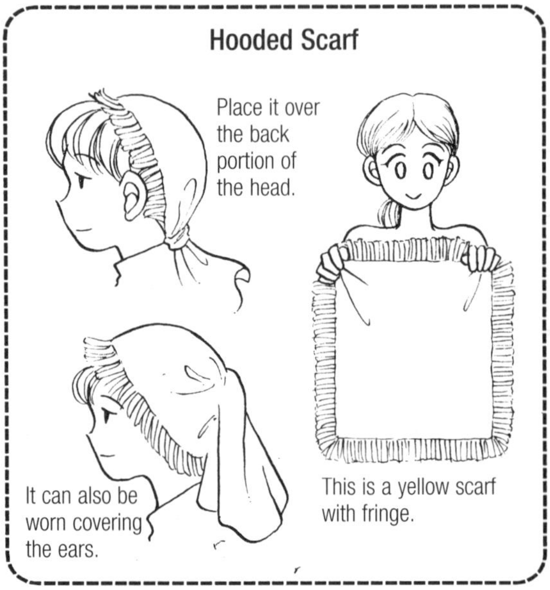

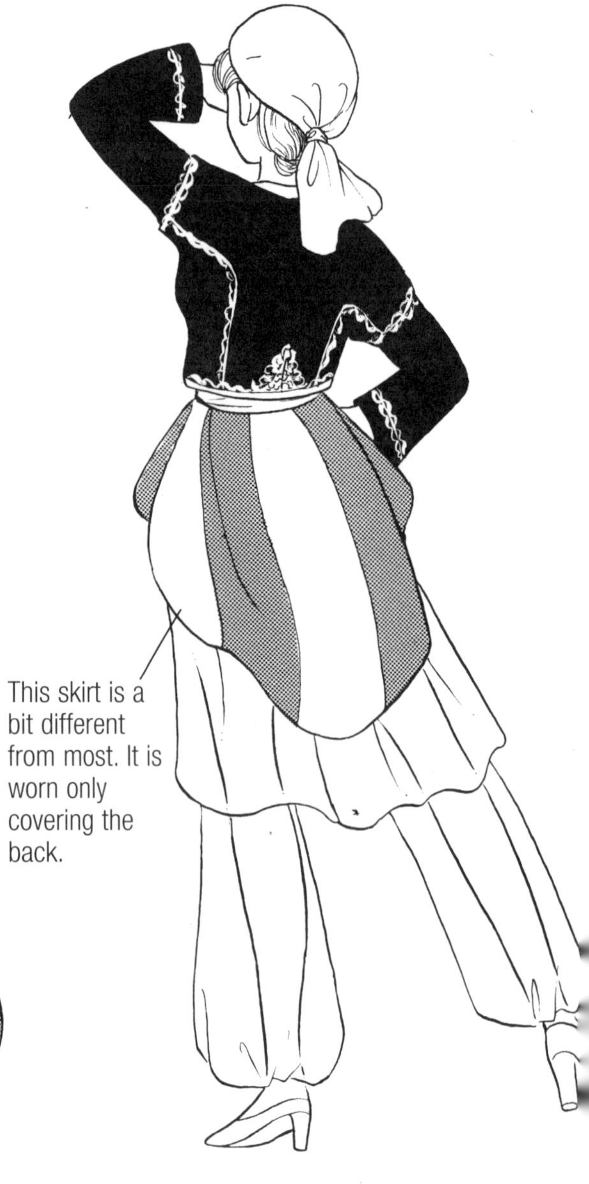

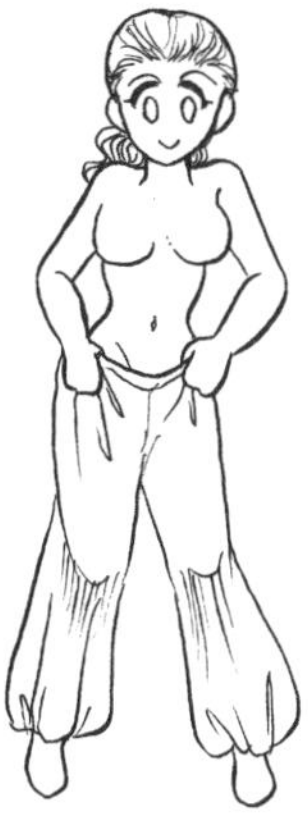

1. Put on the pants.

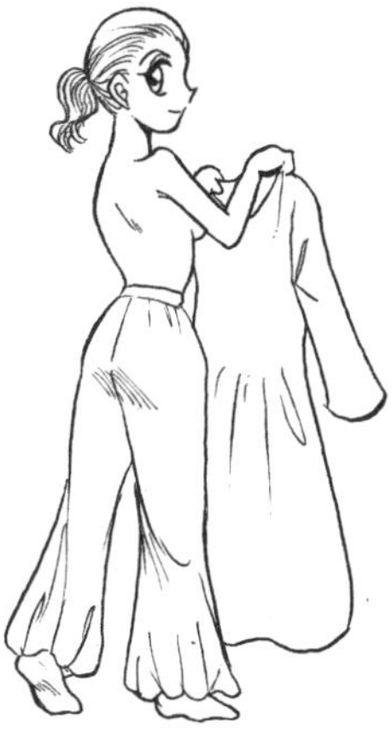

2. Put on the chemise.

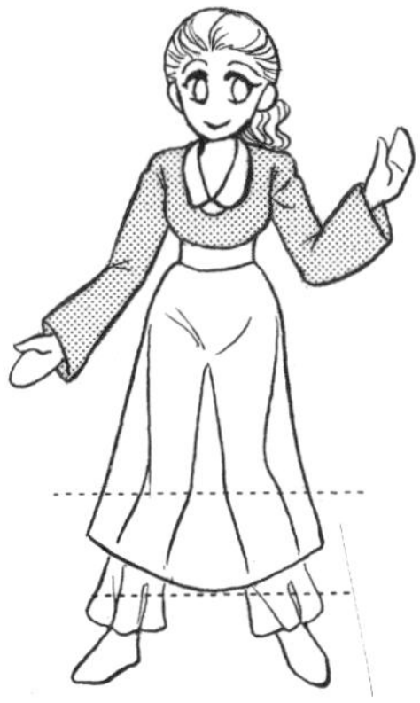

The neck area either has a collar or is a V-neck.

The hem is below the knees.

3. Put on the apron.

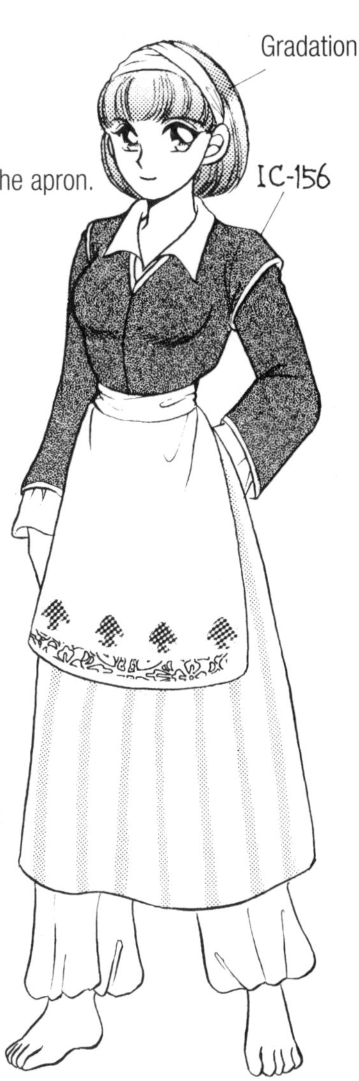

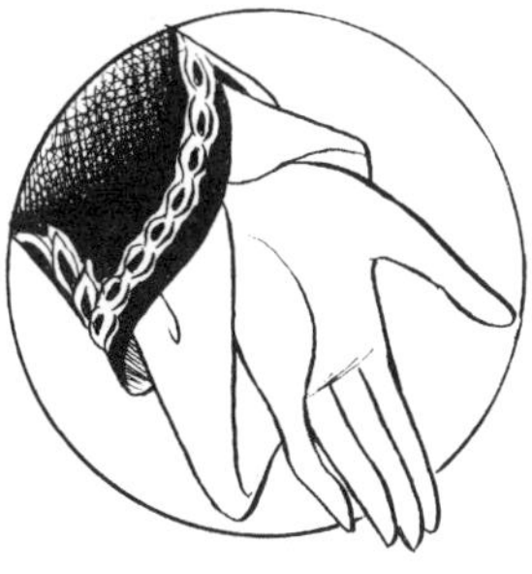

The flare type sleeves softly widen.

The apron is made of cotton. Drawing it with simple lines brings out its tough nature.

4. Put on the pleated skirt.

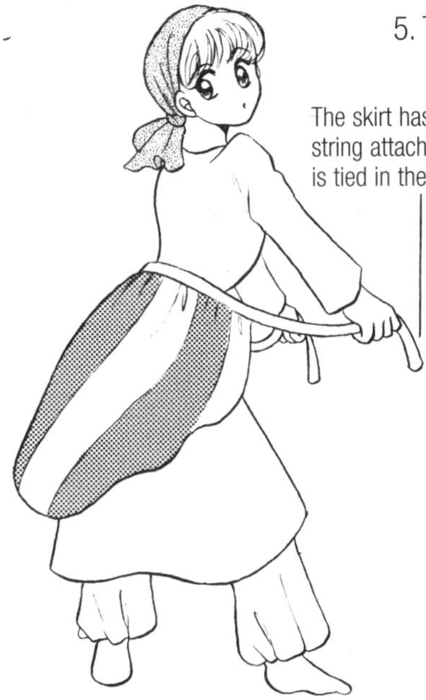

The skirt has a string attached and is tied in the front.

5. Tie the sash belt.

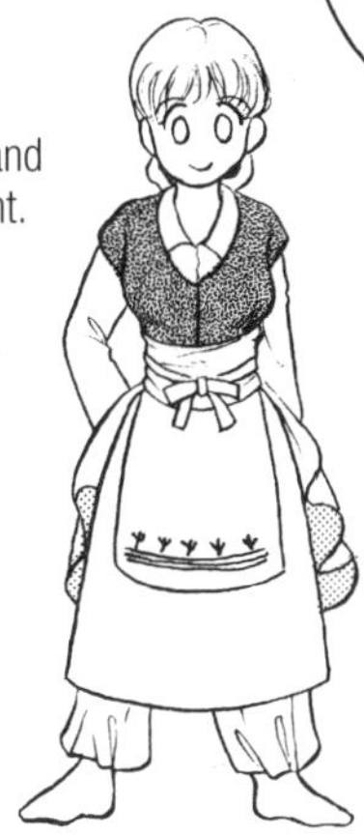

6. Finally, put on the jacket.

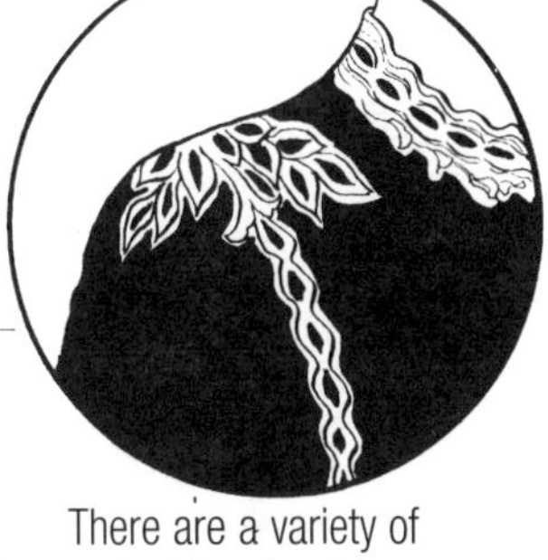

There are a variety of embroidered patterns on the shoulders and sleeves.

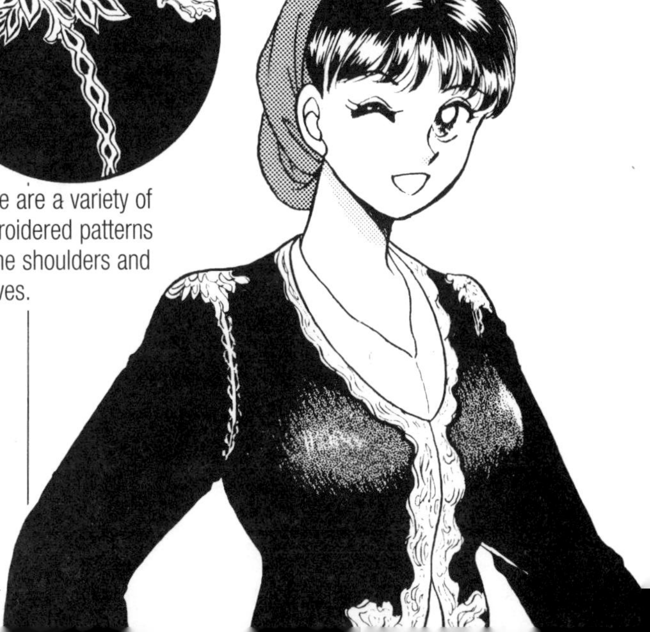

Arrangements and Accessories

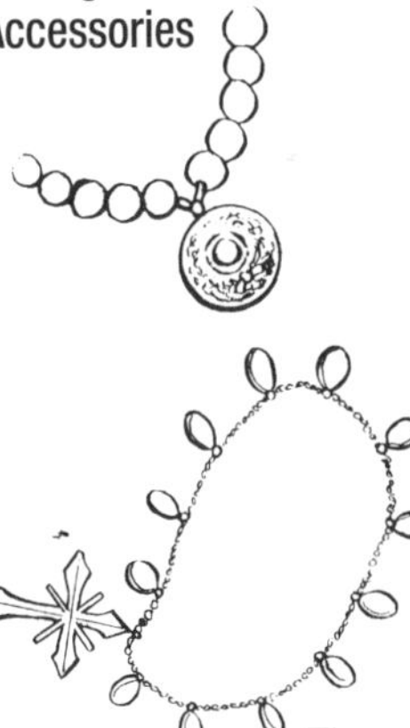

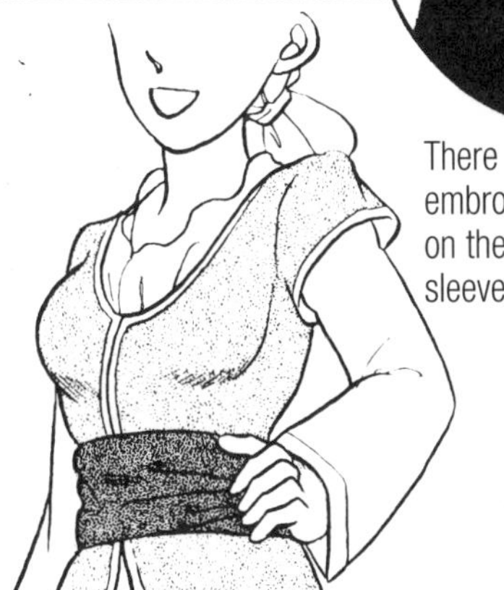

The sash can be worn facing outward.

Middle Eastern Bishoujo
from Iran, Iraq, Saudi Arabia and Turkey

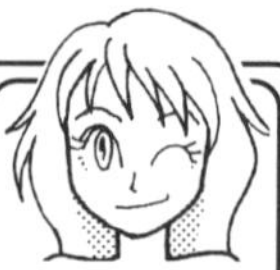
Caucasoid

Even the whitest skin turns light-brown in this sunlight intense environment. Attach skin tones accordingly. Hair colors range from pale yellow to black.

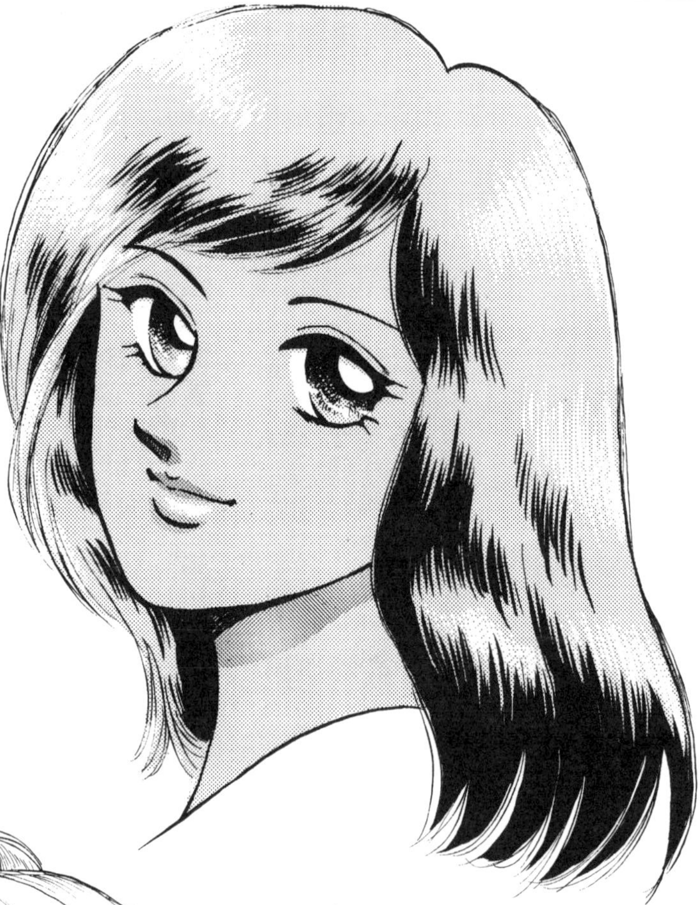

This bright-eyed Iranian girl has clear-cut facial features. Don't make the mouth too big.

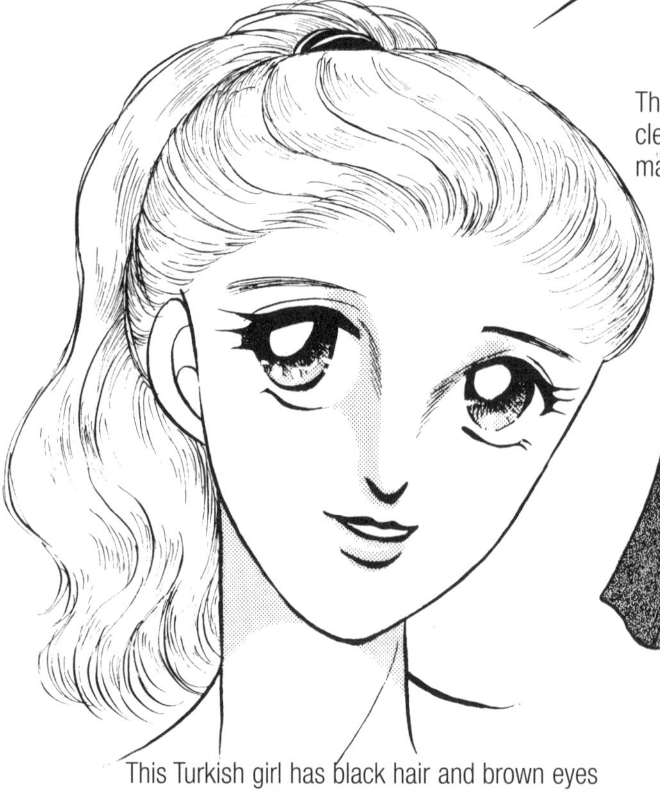

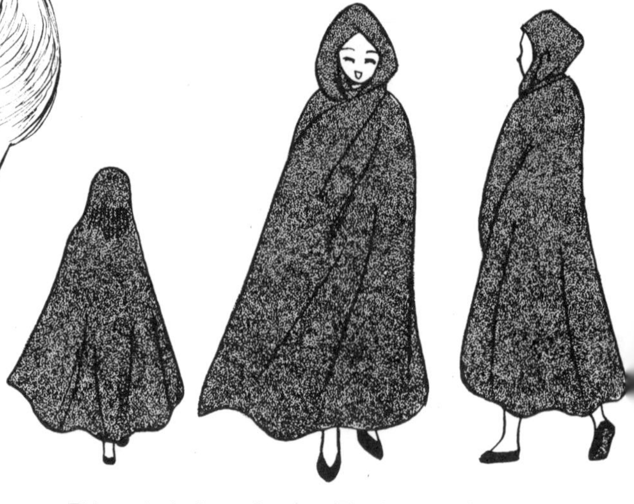

This style is for going out. The length of the garment is about mid-calf level. Since it is not too long, it is easy for the character to move about.

This Turkish girl has black hair and brown eyes with a shade of blue which are vertically long but round in a cute way.

Turkish Fashion

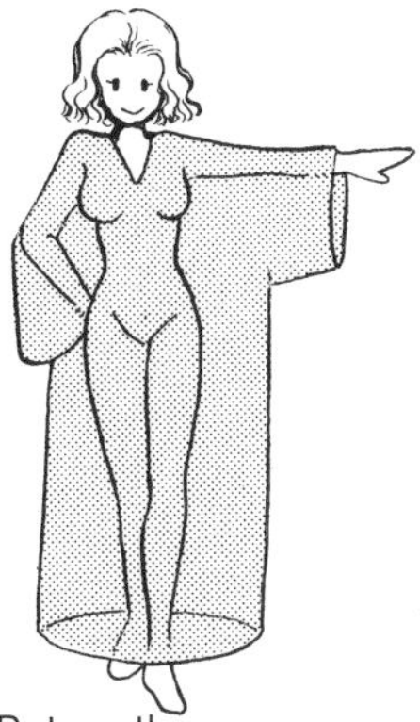

1. Put on the undergarment.

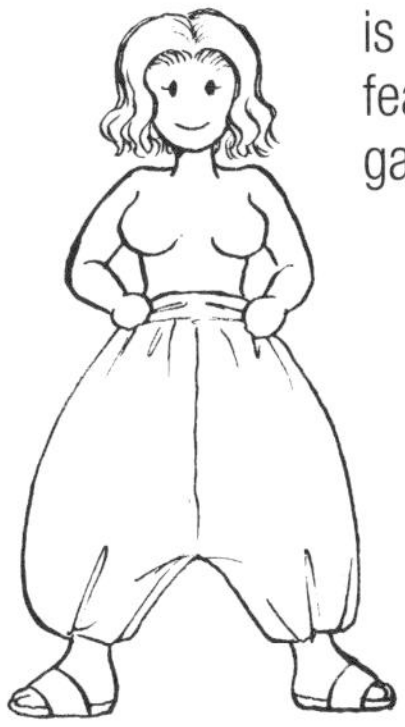

2. Put on the pants.

The deep crotch is the distinctive feature of this garment.

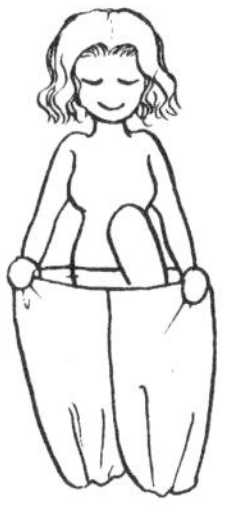

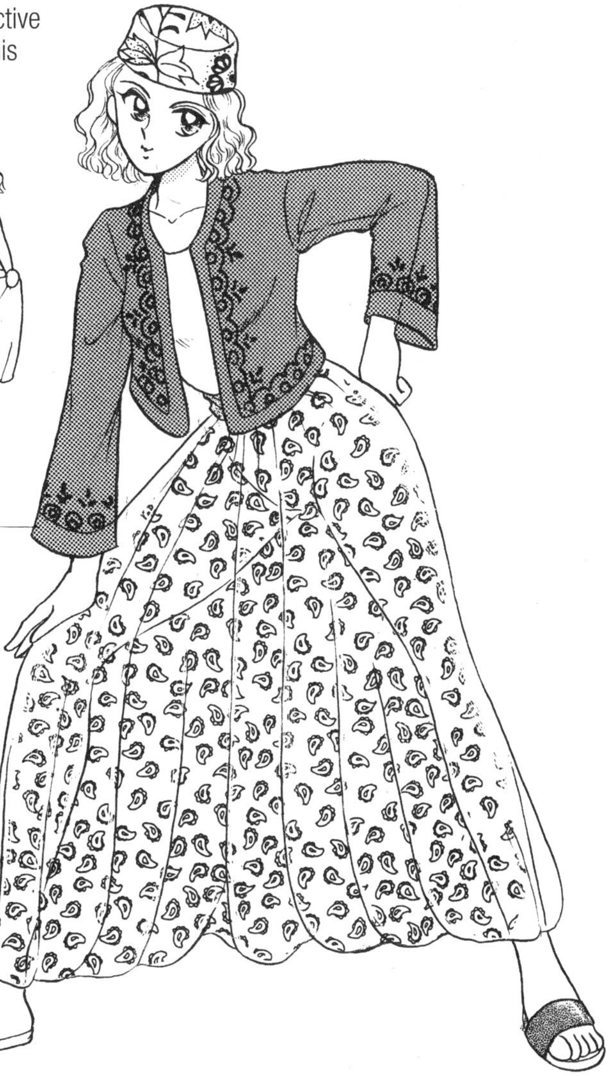

S-64

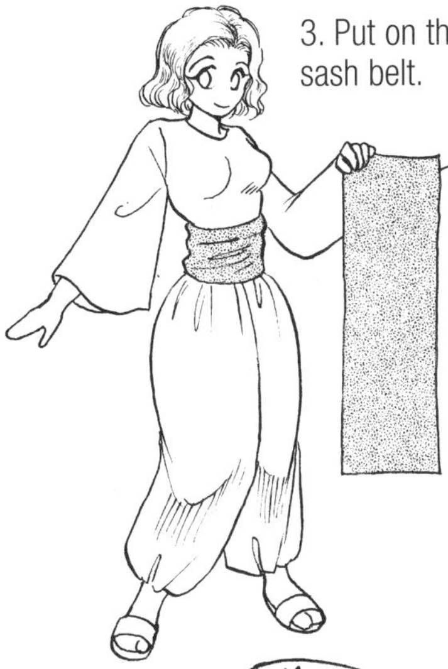

3. Put on the sash belt.

The belt is about this long.

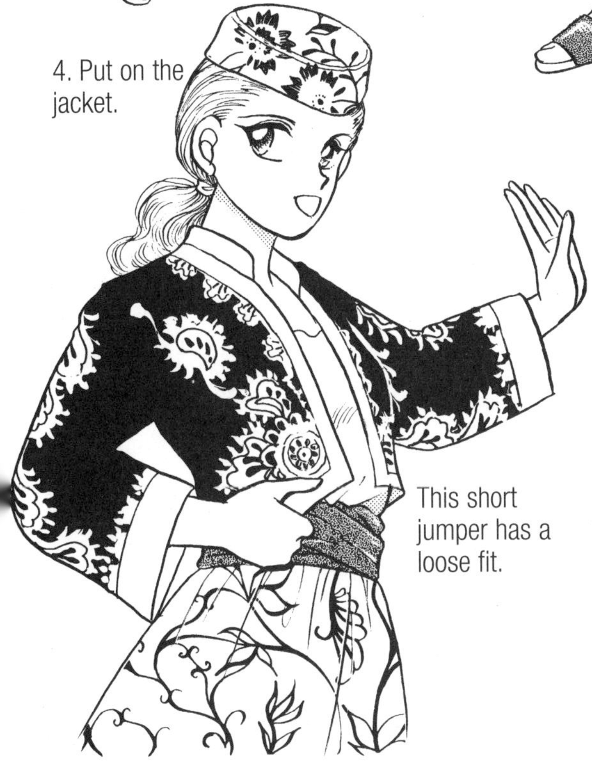

4. Put on the jacket.

This short jumper has a loose fit.

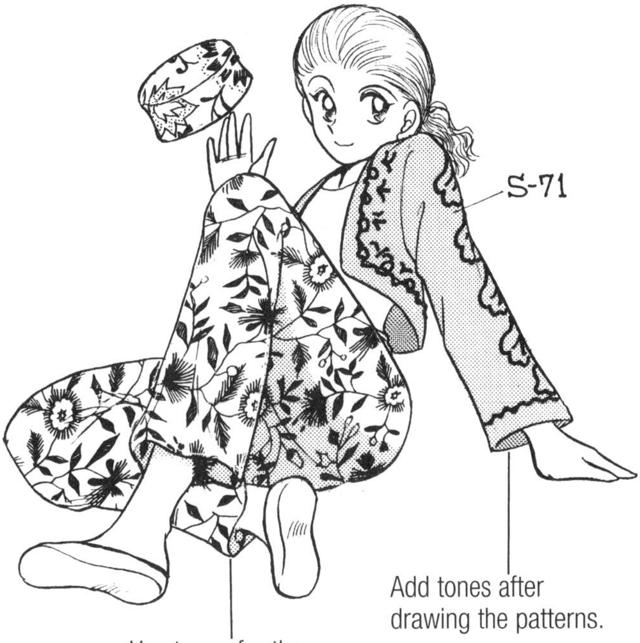

S-71

Add tones after drawing the patterns.

Use tones for the patterns in the pants.

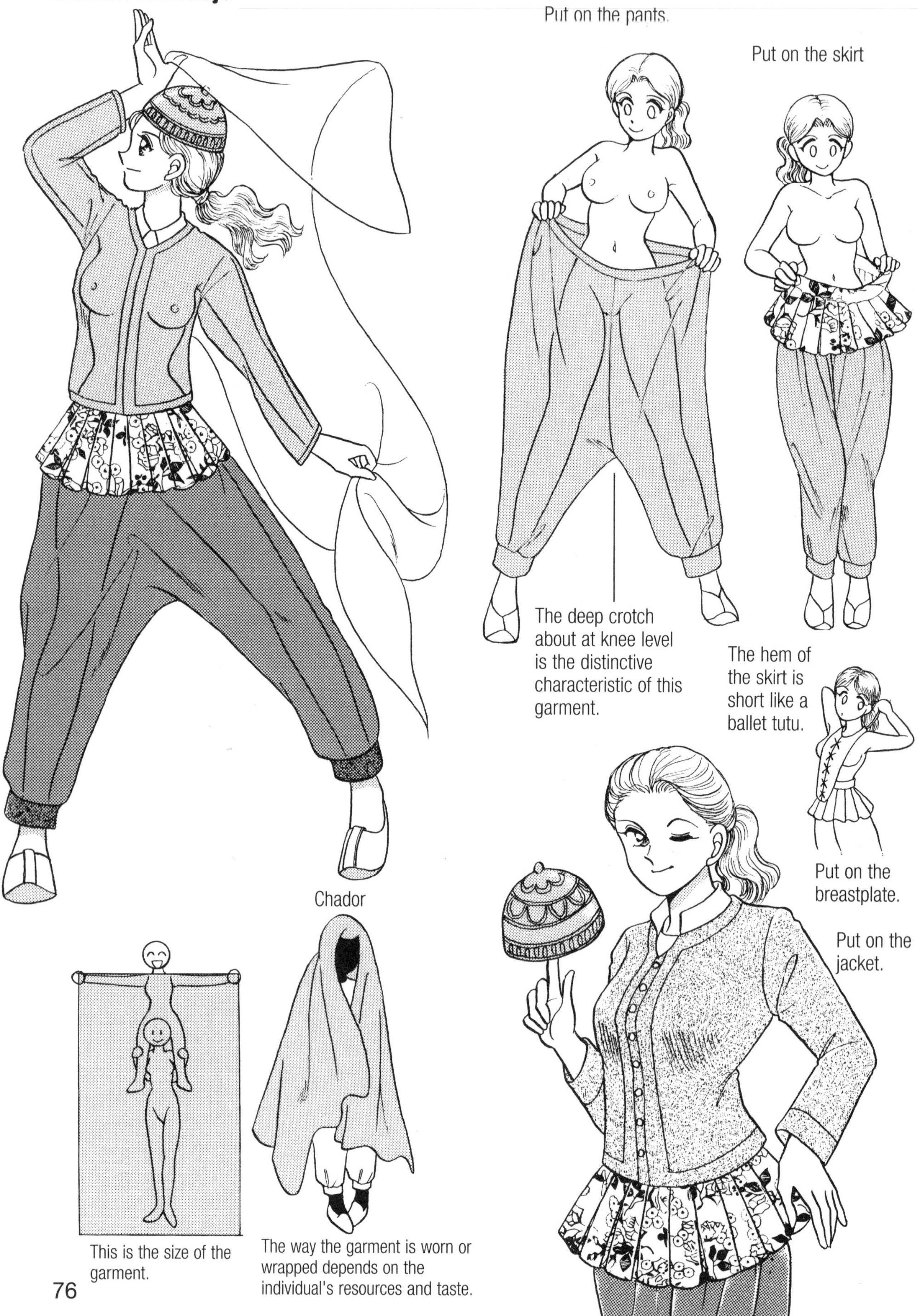

Put on the pants.
Put on the skirt
The deep crotch about at knee level is the distinctive characteristic of this garment.
The hem of the skirt is short like a ballet tutu.
Put on the breastplate.
Put on the jacket.
Chador
This is the size of the garment.
The way the garment is worn or wrapped depends on the individual's resources and taste.

Arabian Nights Belly Dancers

Arabia is famous for belly dancers. However, belly dancers also dance in the Middle East, England and America. It is said that the dance was developed from an ancient harvest prayer. Modern belly dances are differentiated into various styles like Gypsy, Pharaoh and Saber.

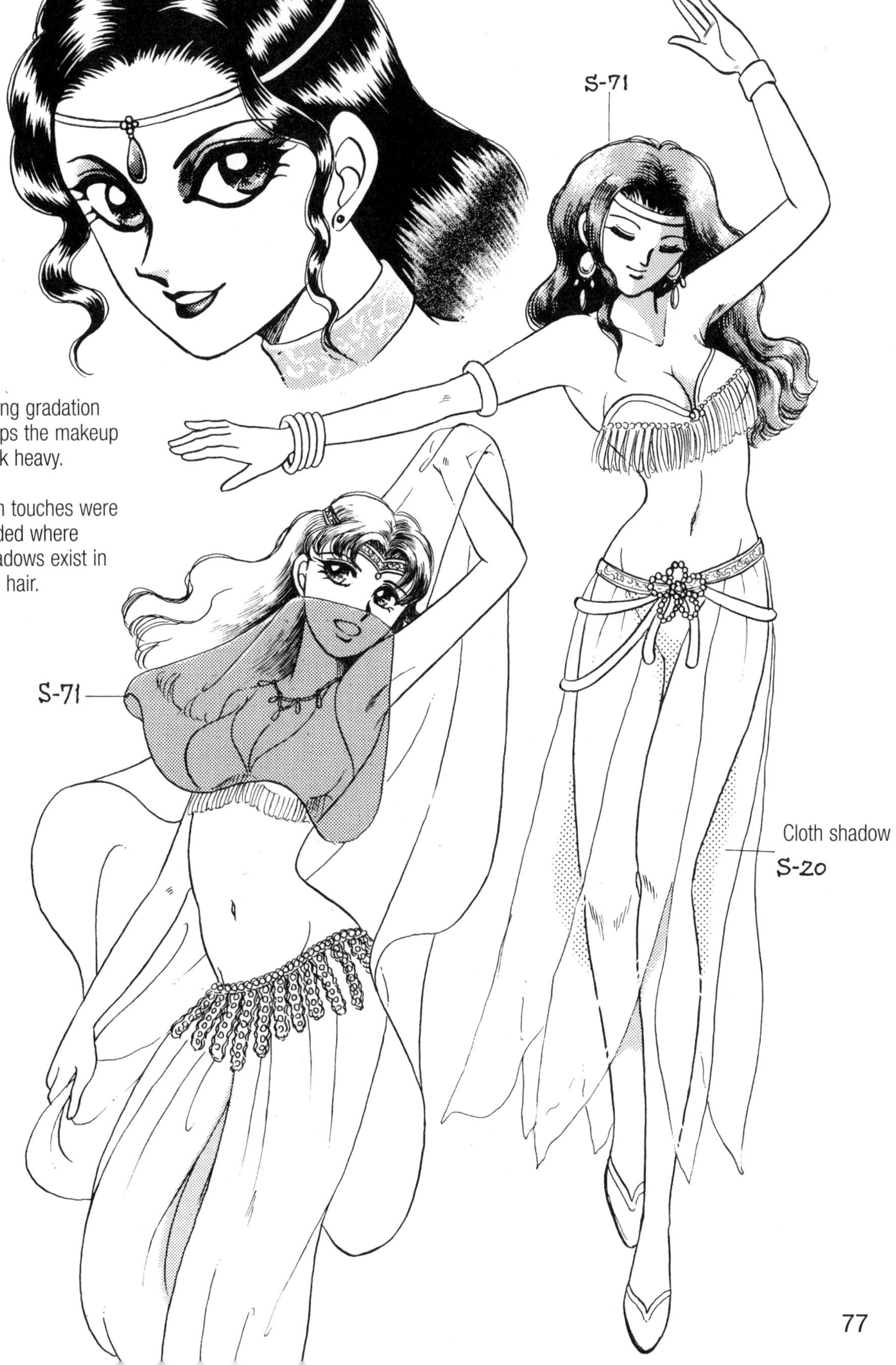

Using gradation helps the makeup look heavy.

Pen touches were added where shadows exist in the hair.

African Bishoujo
from Kenya, Tanzania, Ethiopia and Liberia

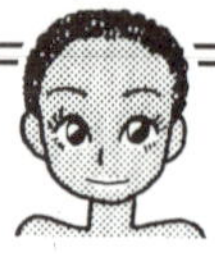
Negroid

Both long and round-faced types exist. Be sure to heavily draw the twofold eyelids which emphasize the three-dimensionality of the face. In addition, making the line of the nose shorter on round-faced girl makes her cuter.

This is a variation on the braided hair.

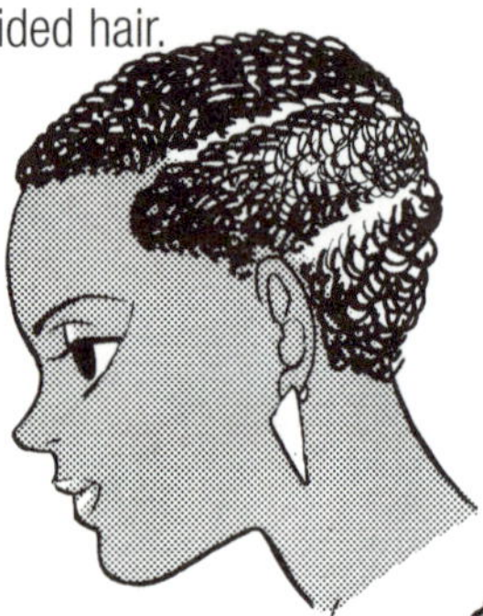

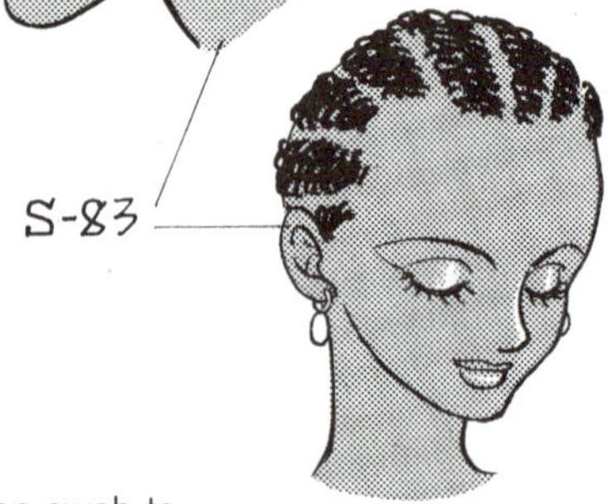

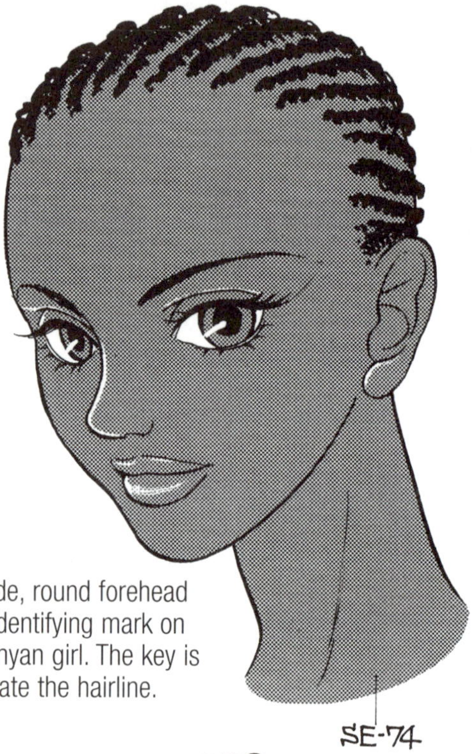

The wide, round forehead is the identifying mark on this Kenyan girl. The key is to gradate the hairline.

Use a cotton swab to draw Afro-puff.

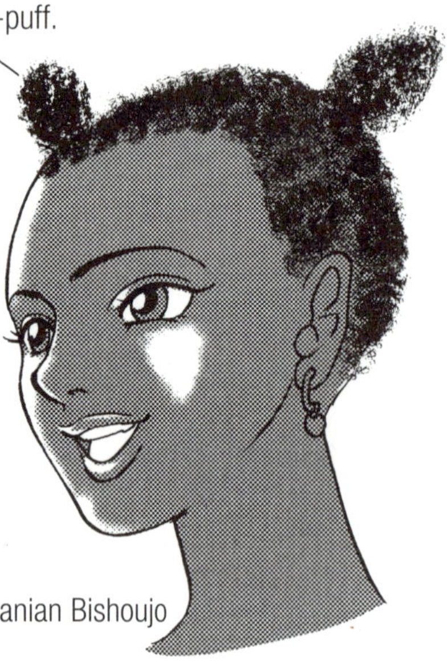

Tanzanian Bishoujo

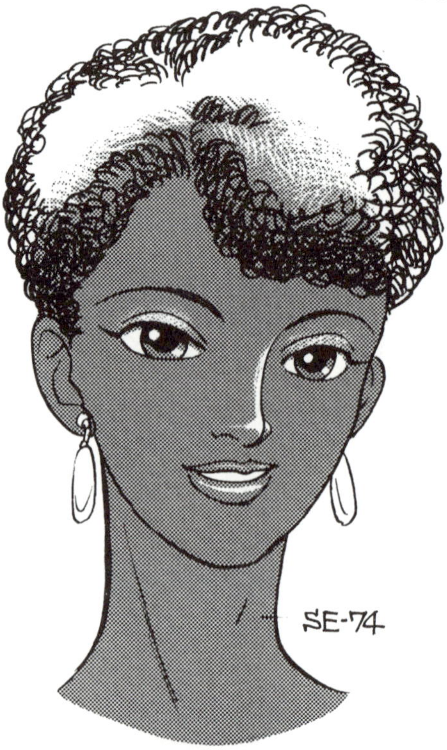

Tanzanian Bishoujo

The traditional waist wraps are still in active service. They are often wrapped around the head like a turban. Born out of need to be fit for the climate, they are used to make life easier.

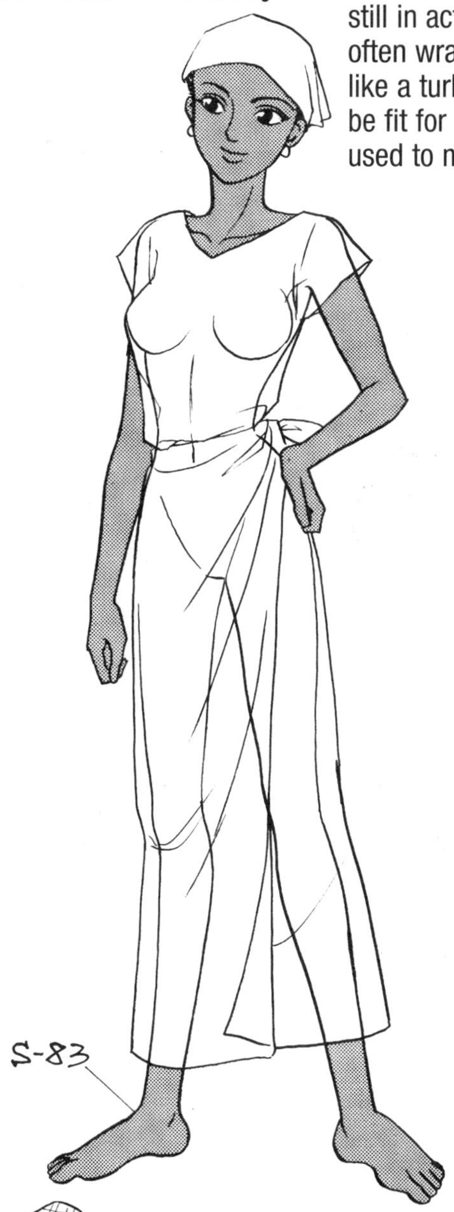

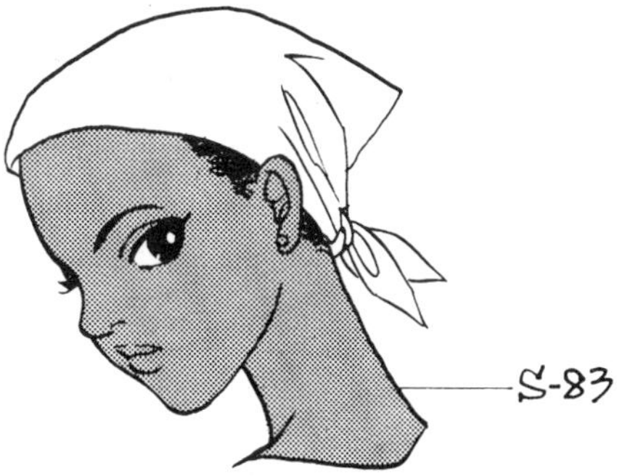

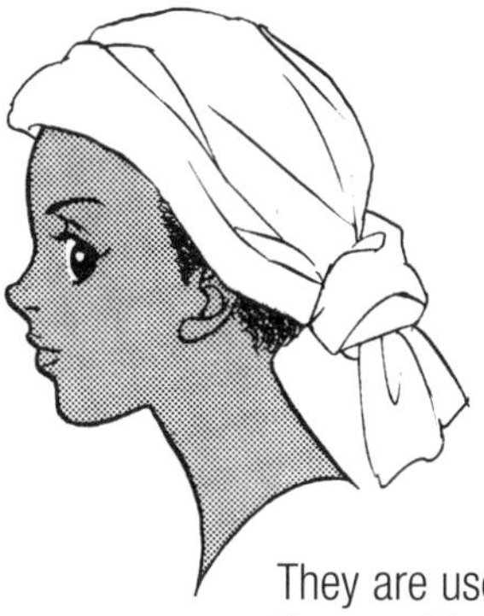

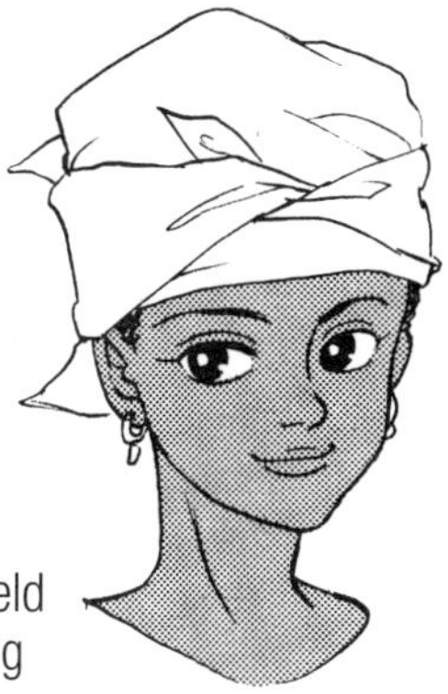

They are used to shield the sun. The wrapping method varies from person to person.

Wrapped Clothing Dress Version

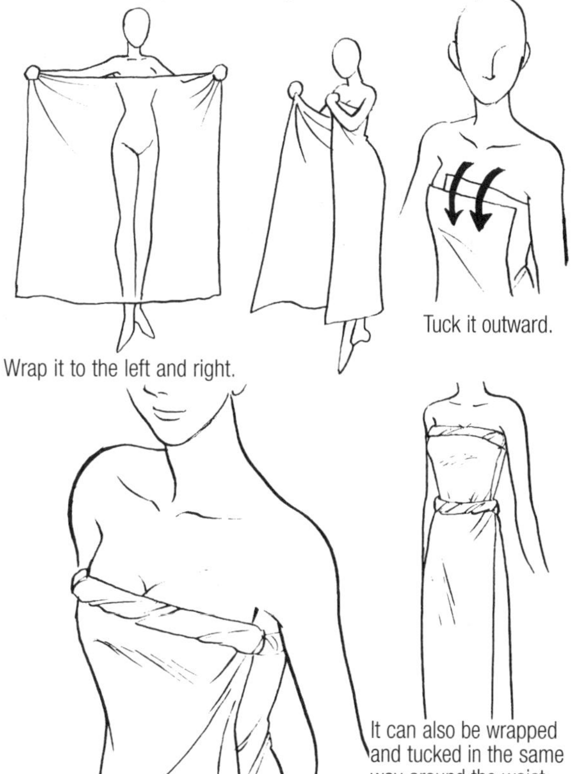

Wrap it to the left and right.

Tuck it outward.

It can also be wrapped and tucked in the same way around the waist.

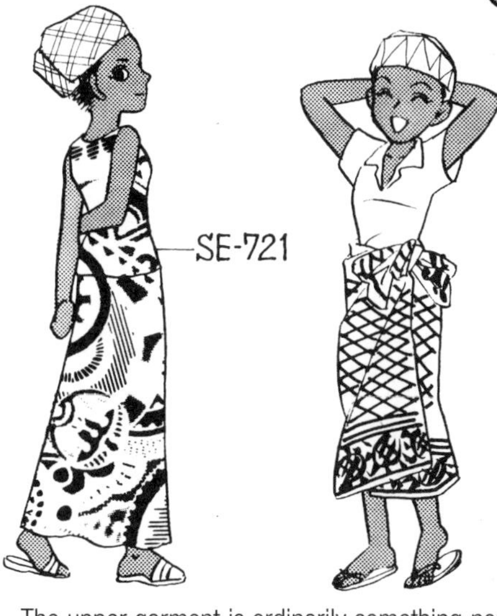

The upper garment is ordinarily something non-sleeved, a T-shirt or polo shirt. Choose colors and patterns that have sharp contrast.

North American Bishoujo
from Canada and the United States

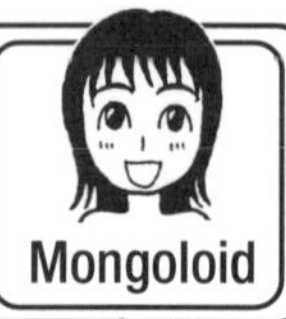

The skin is copper brown. Lightly draw the line of the nose. The black hair is lustrous and straight.

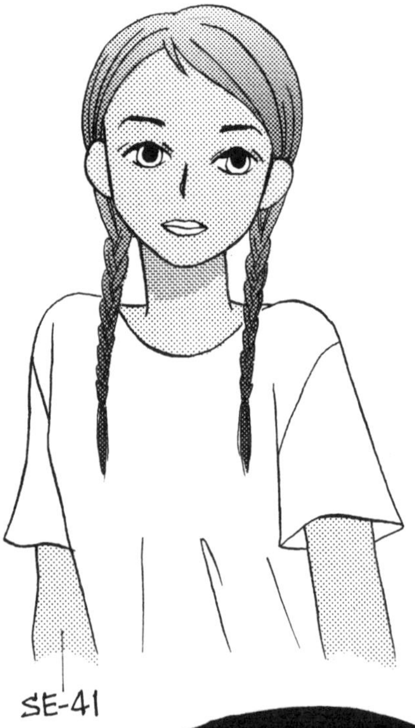

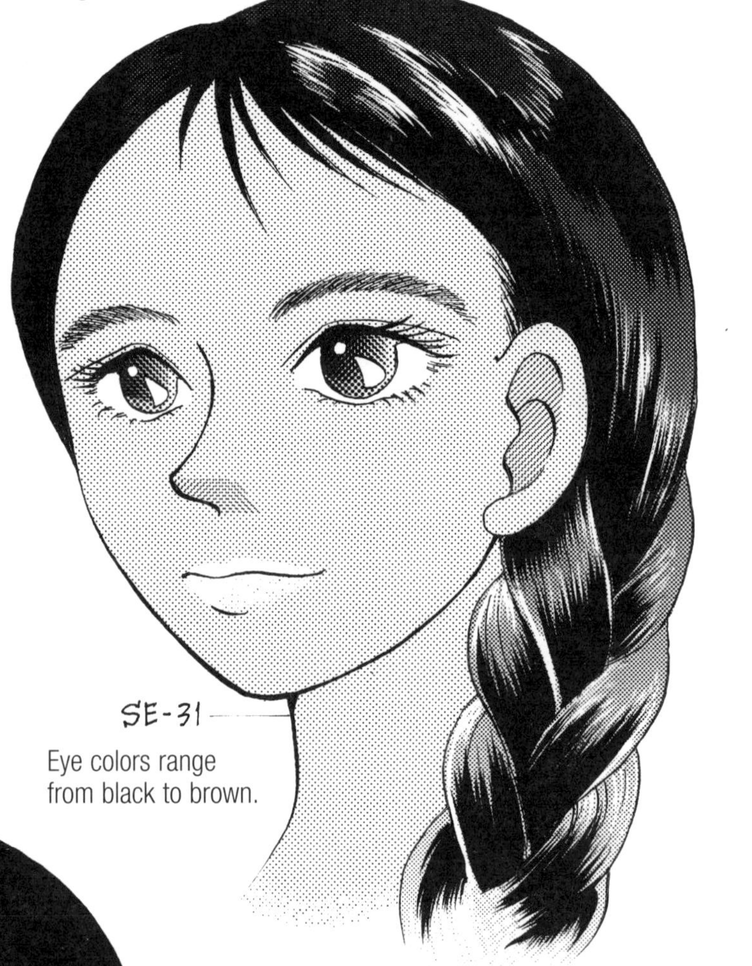

Eye colors range from black to brown.

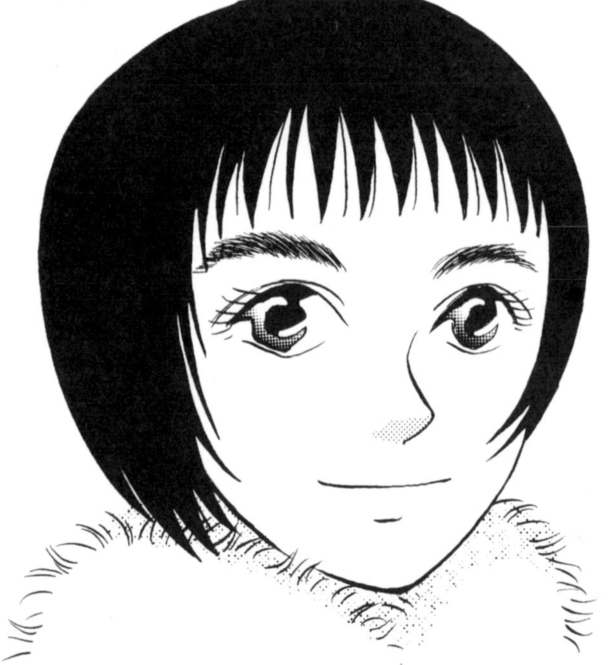

Canadian Eskimos

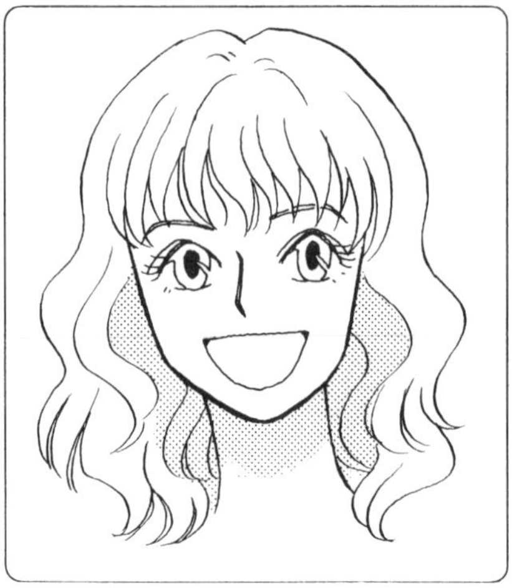

People who immigrated to Canada were usually Caucasoid.

Native American Bishoujo

A huge variety of distinctive characteristics exists in the lifestyle, culture, and physical build of these people who were the original inhabitants of the American continent. With some 600 tribes each possessing different culture, a standard Native American style cannot be defined. Use and combine a standard, virtual image created from films and television expressing a mixture of styles.

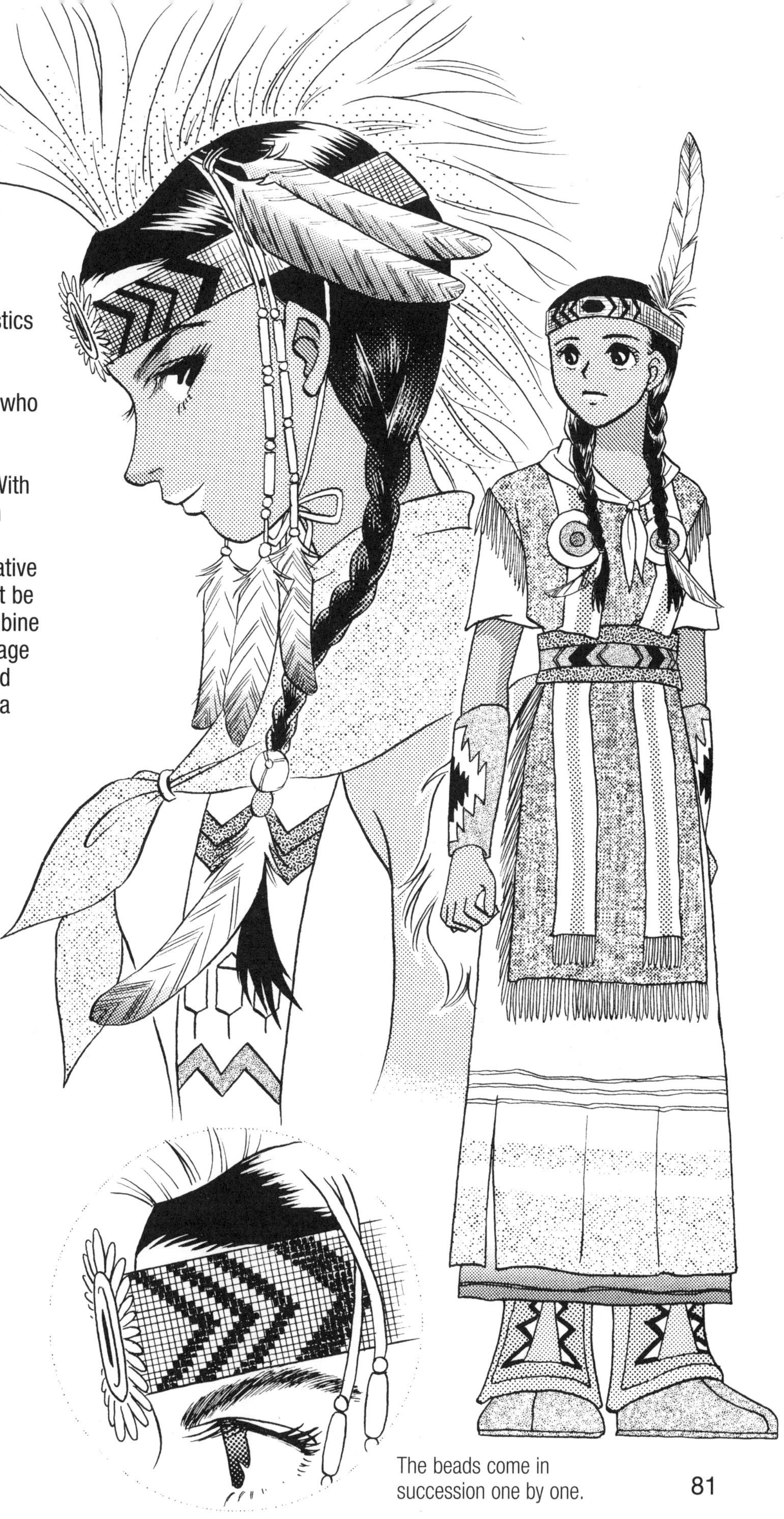

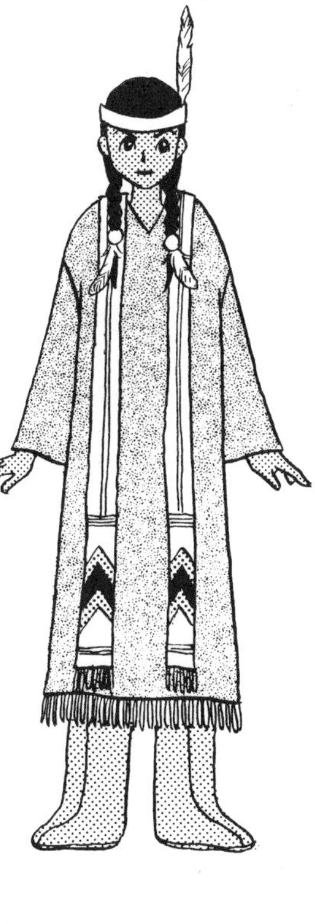

The beads come in succession one by one.

Central South American Bishoujo
from Mexico, Chile, Brazil and Peru

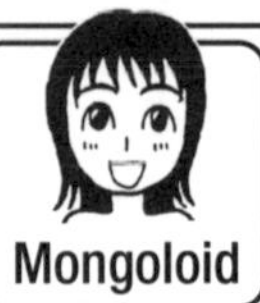

Mongoloid

Lustrous black hair seems to be common in these areas. There are also girls with dark brown hair as seen in the Rio Carnival in Brazil.

A firm noseline and distinct facial features work well with Peruvian girls.

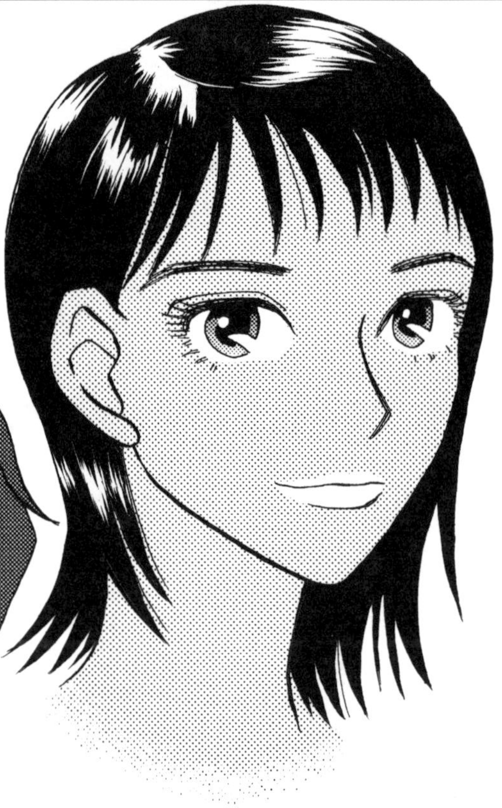

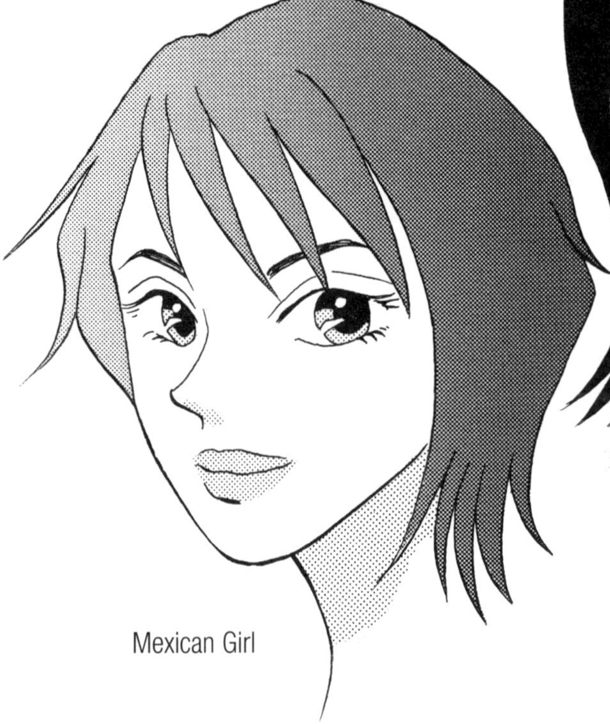

Mexican Girl

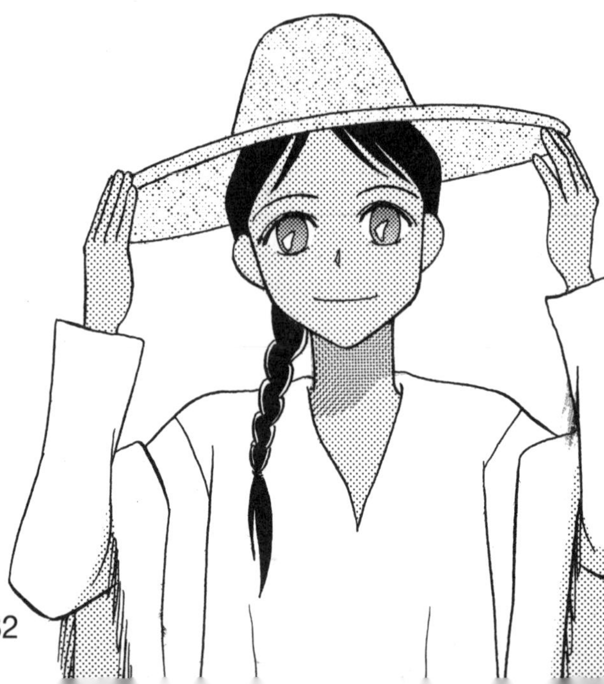

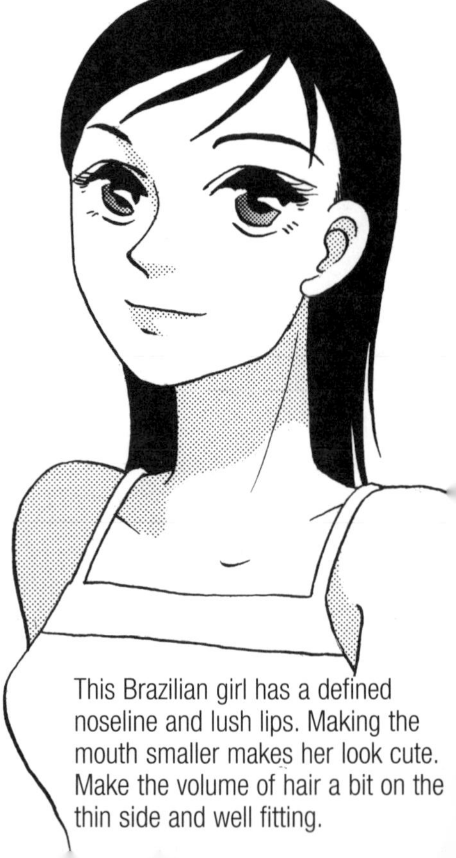

This Brazilian girl has a defined noseline and lush lips. Making the mouth smaller makes her look cute. Make the volume of hair a bit on the thin side and well fitting.

Ponchos

Since this is worn by fitting the head through the opening, the character is free to move without worrying about the clothing coming off. Bring out the soft texture when drawing ponchos for women.

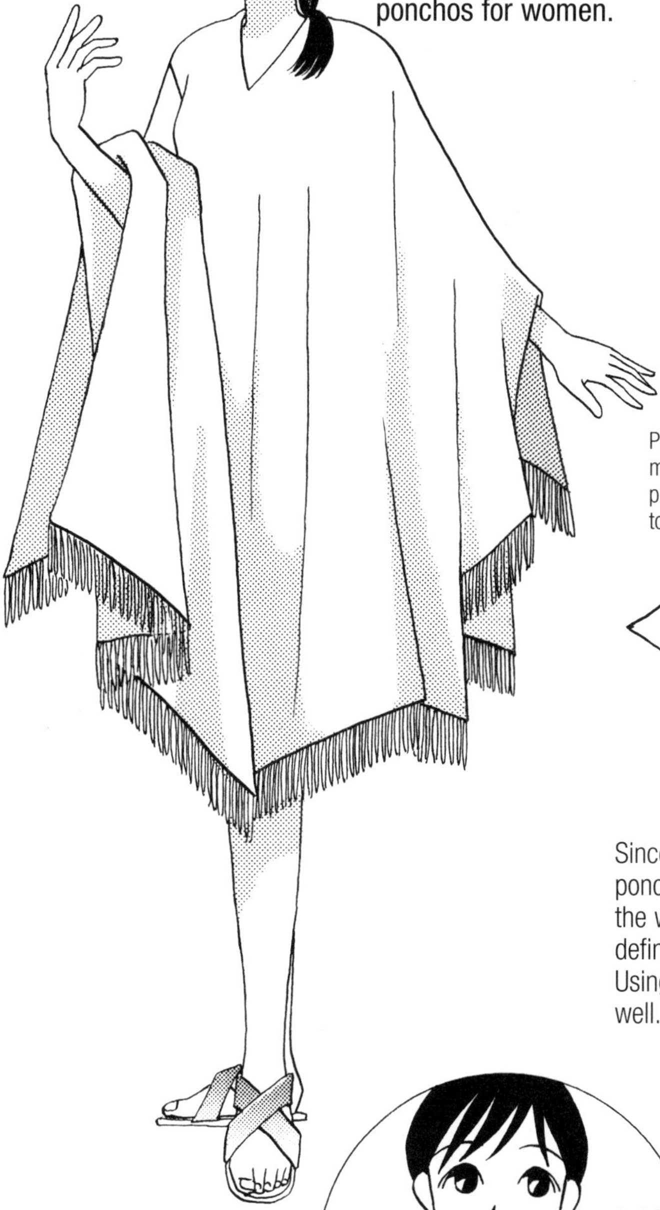

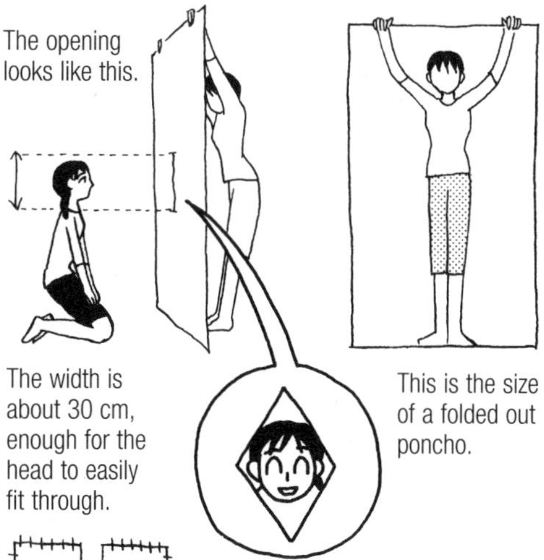

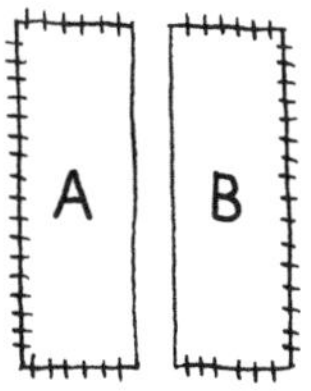

Ponchos can also be made by sewing two pieces of cloth together.

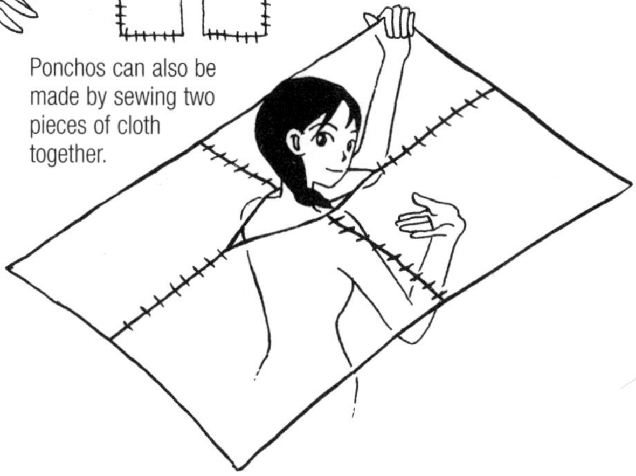

Since the texture of ponchos for boys is hard, the wrinkles are very defined.
Using rough tones works well.

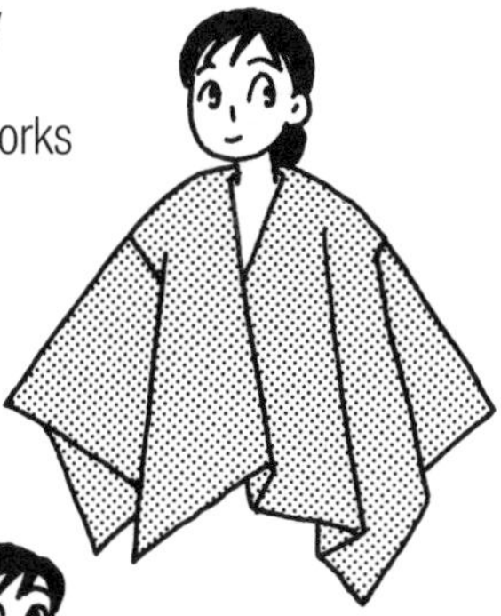

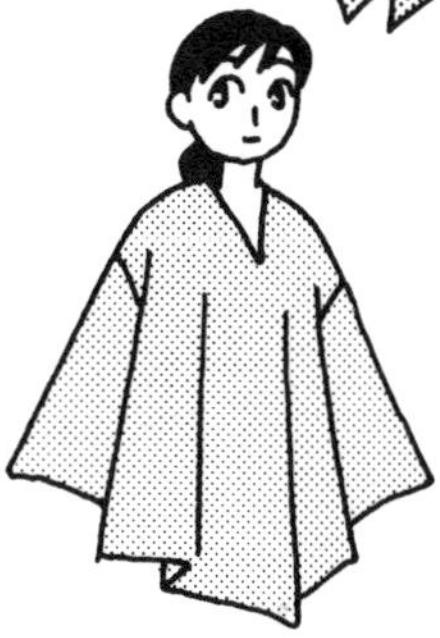

The texture of ponchos for girls is soft, and the silhouette is not very angular.
Using detailed tones works well.

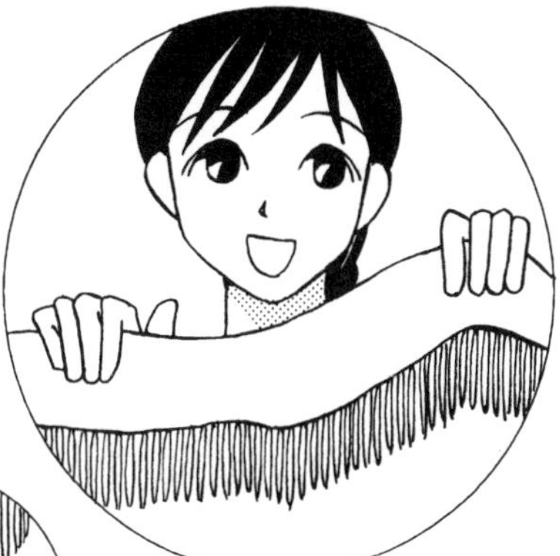

Fringe

Ways to Handle Collars

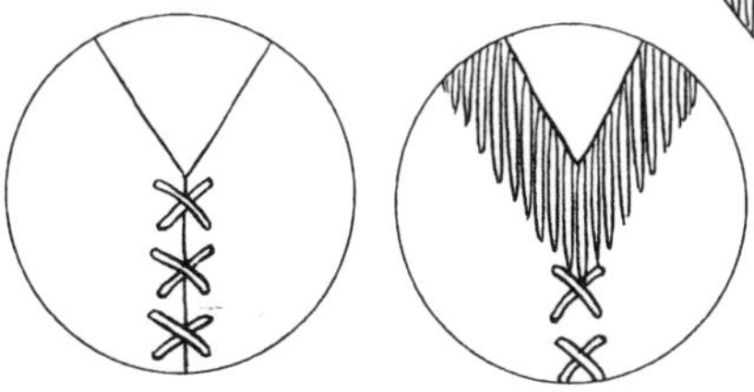

Andes Mountain Bishoujo

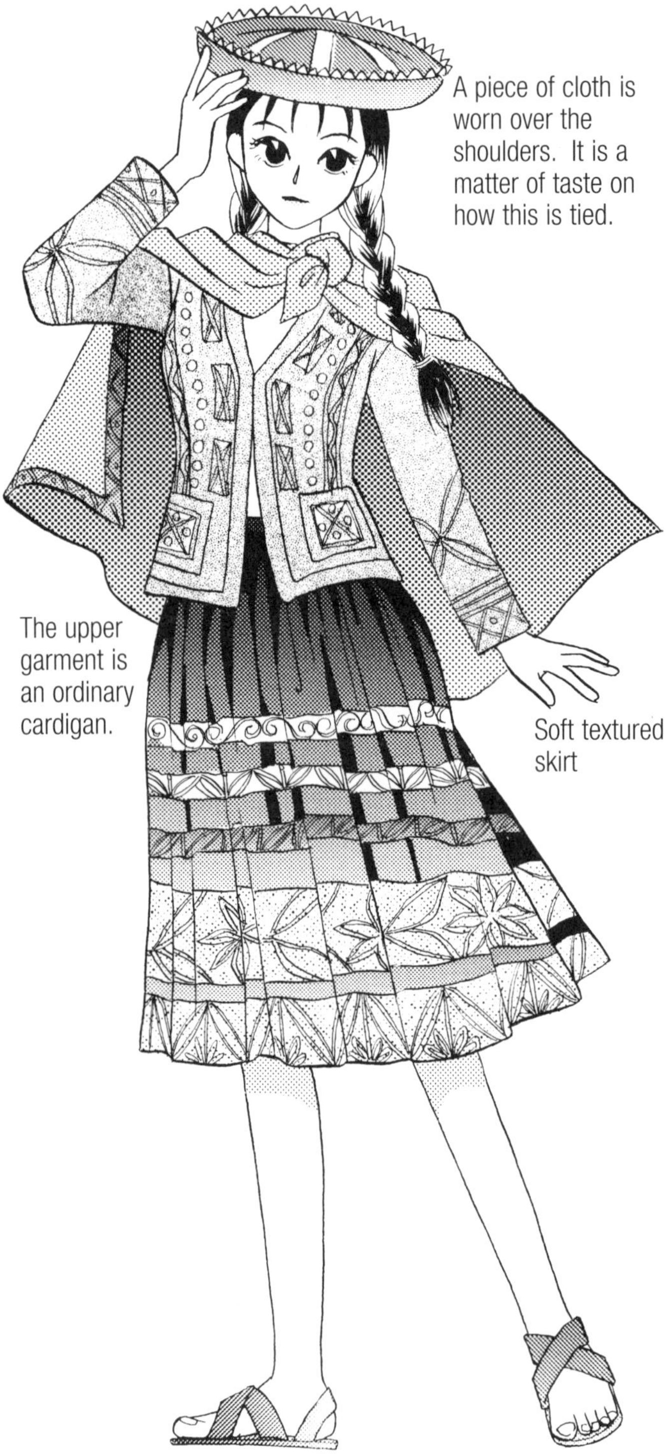

Traditional Mexican Clothing

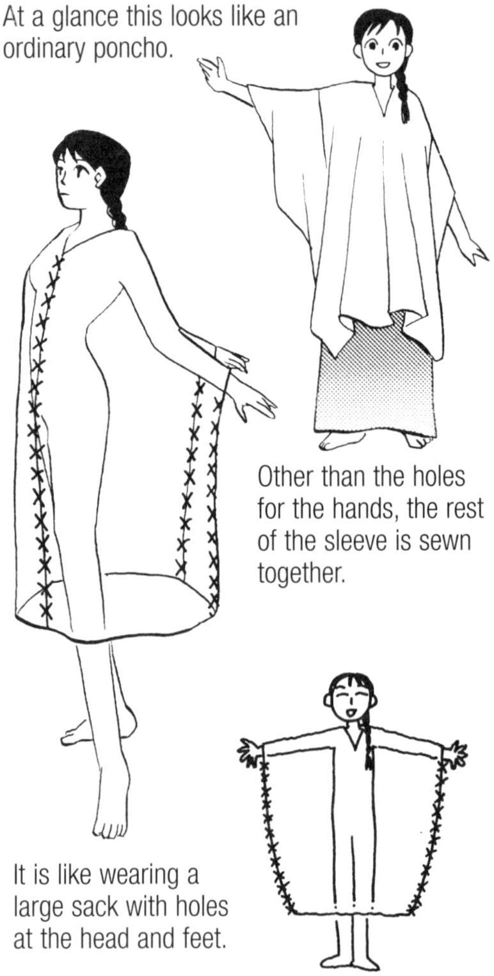

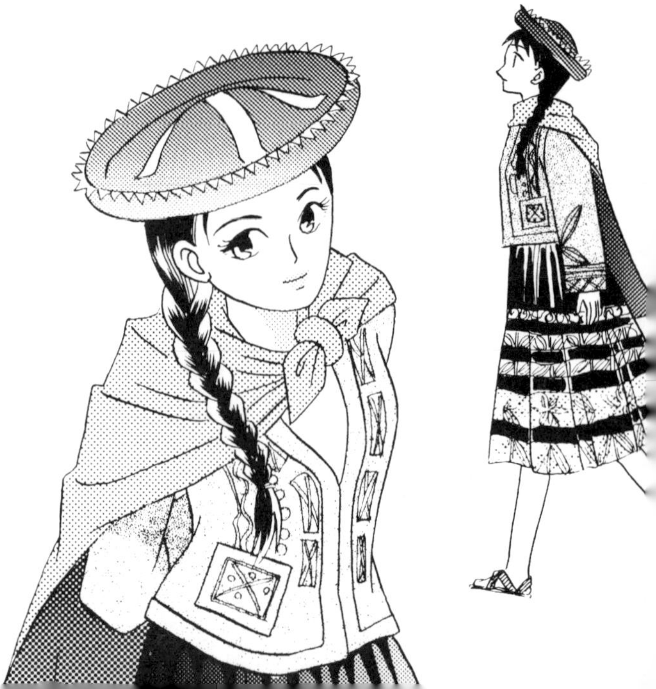

Rio Carnival Style

The carnival takes place annually in Brazil. People wear a variety of fashions as they please, ranging from well exposed to those ornately decorated. The point is to draw them as wild and showy as you can imagine.

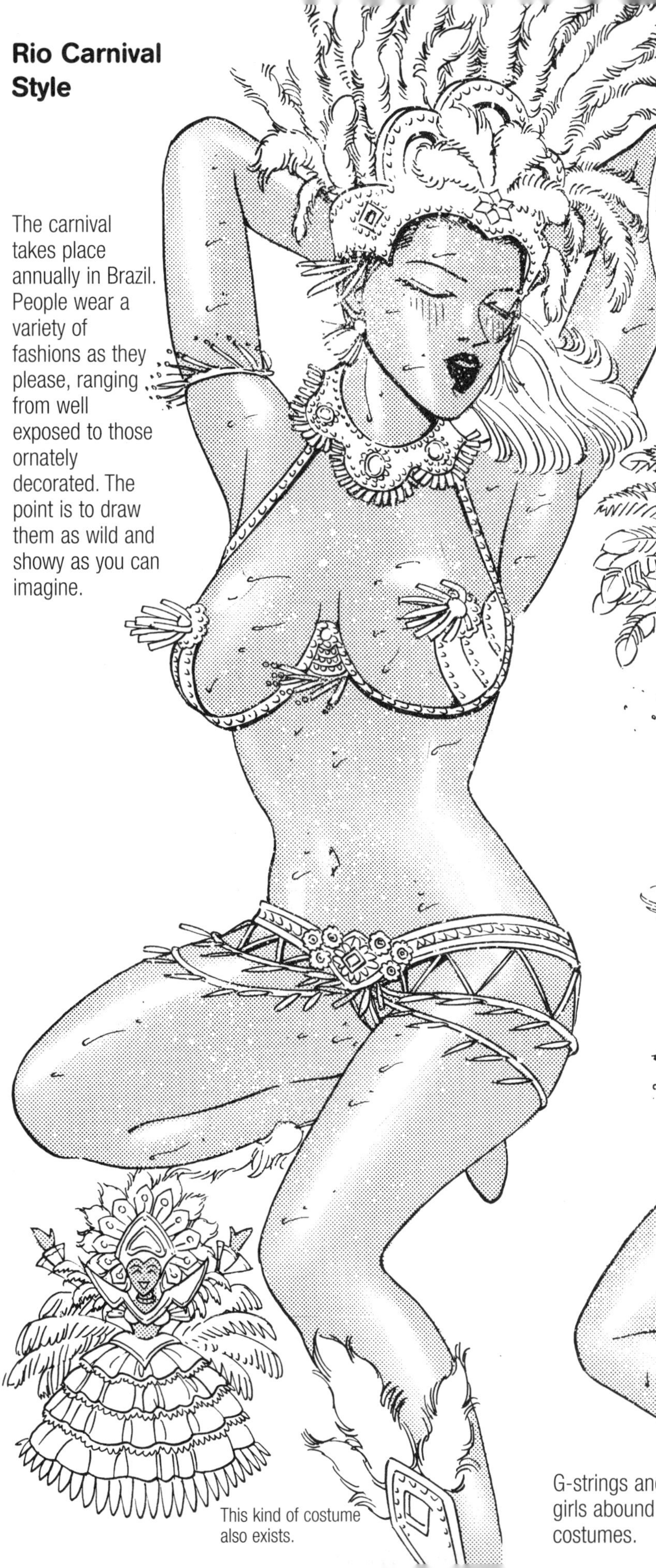

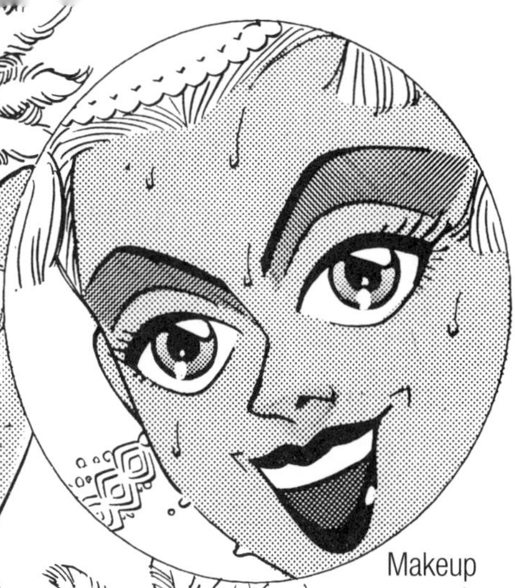

Makeup example

This kind of costume also exists.

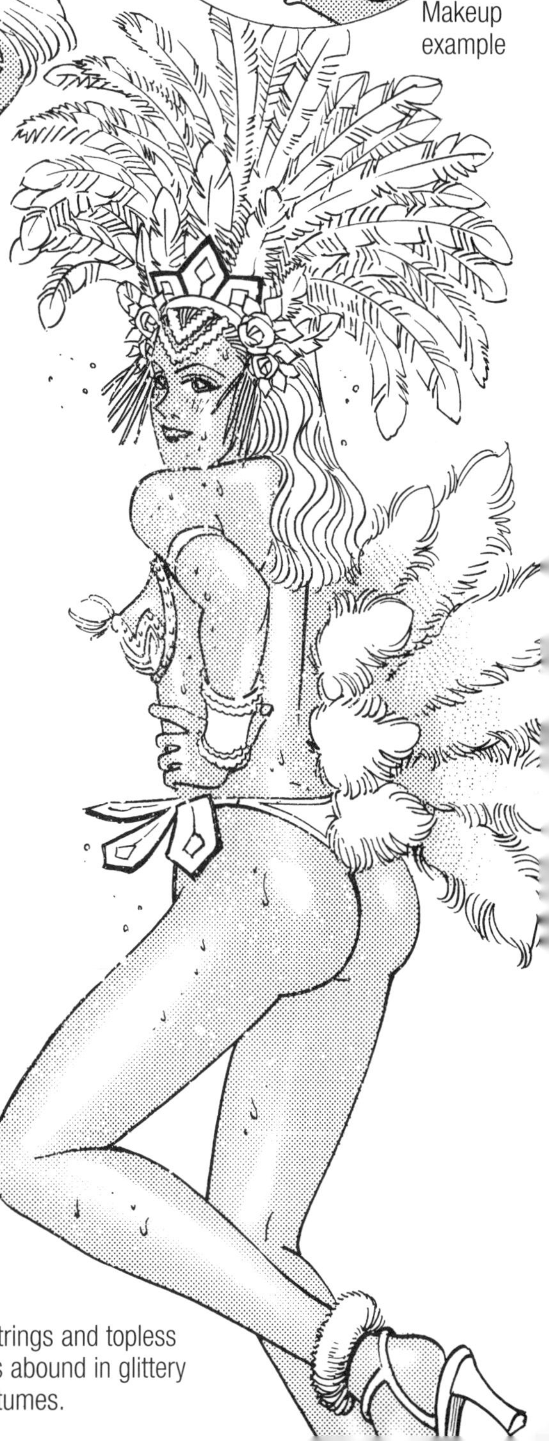

G-strings and topless girls abound in glittery costumes.

Bishoujo
from America

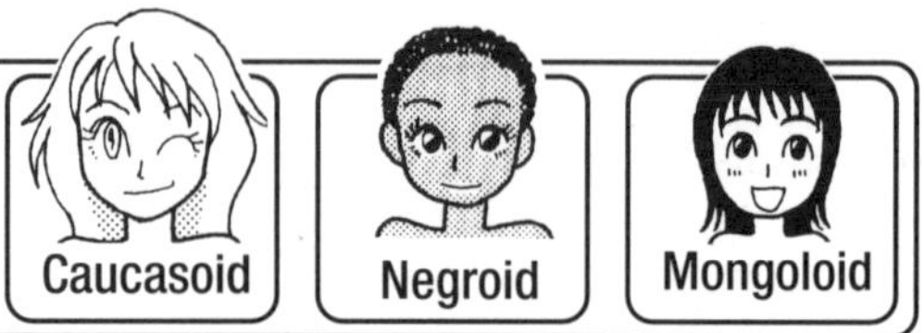

America is often said to be a melting pot where every type of girl exists. Draw with a cheerful image in mind.

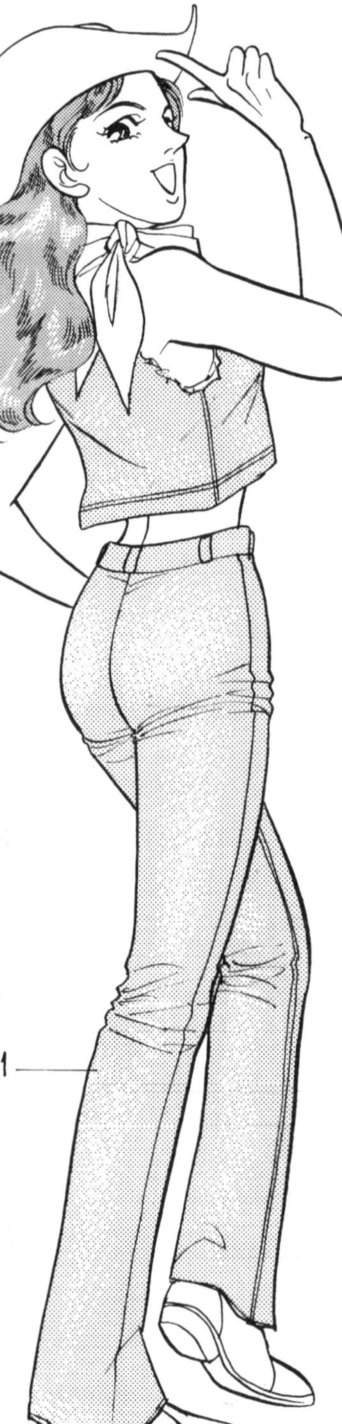

Texan maidens are lively, headstrong and apparently called termagants in the South. It is said that red hair symbolizes their headstrong nature.

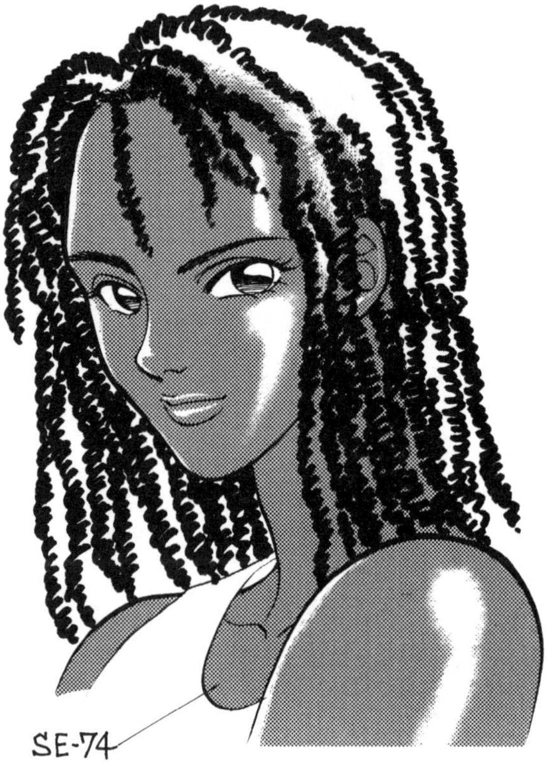

Puerto Ricans have Negroid features.

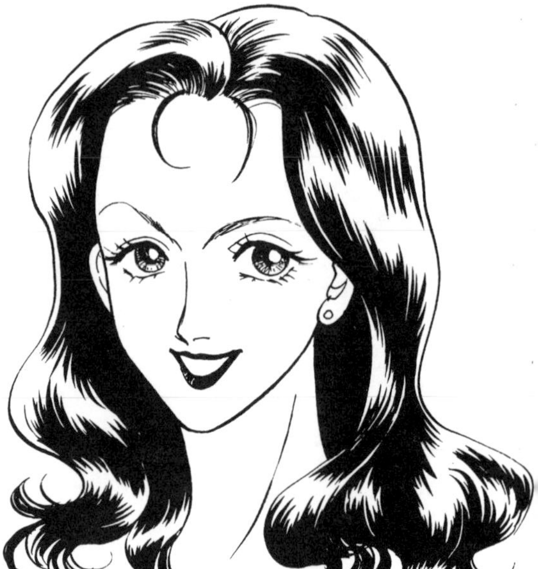

This Hispanic girl is a descendant of Spanish immigrants. Draw the hair black.

This New Yorker comes from the world capital of culture and fashion.

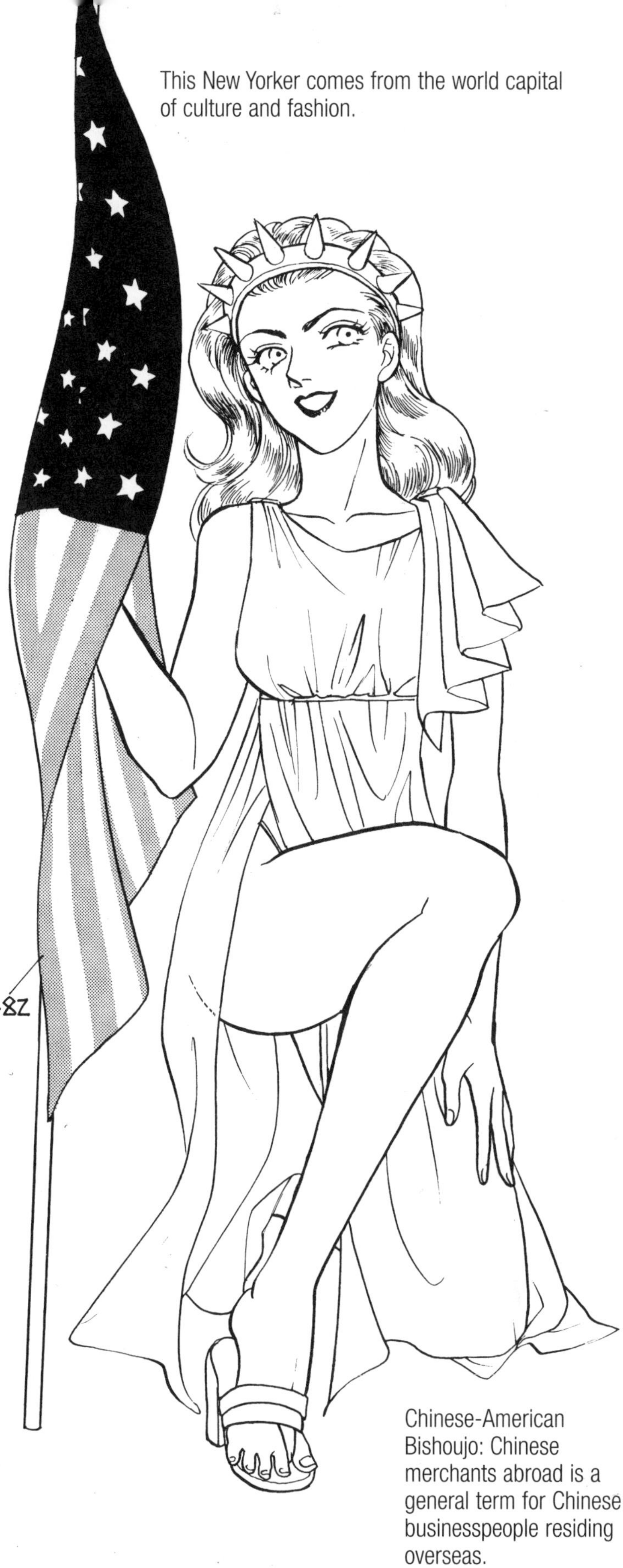

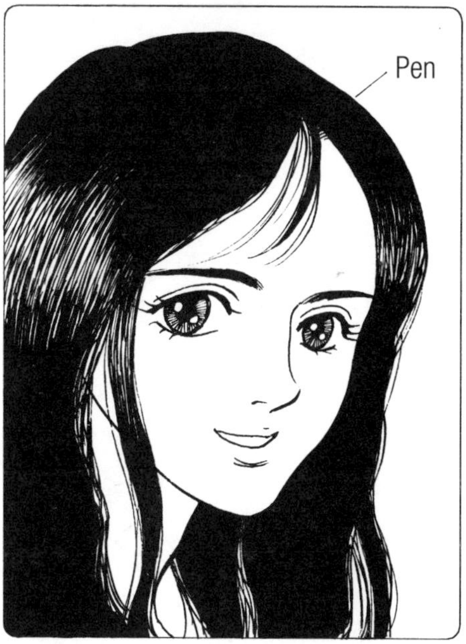

Chicanos: Americans of Mexican origin.

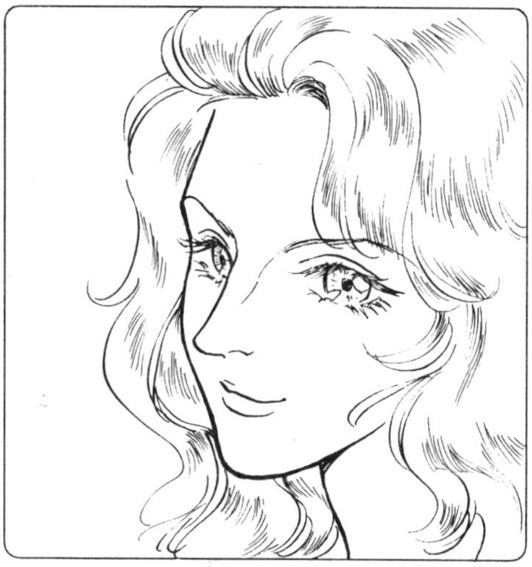

WASP: White Anglo-Saxon Protestants whose descendants where immigrants from England or Northern Europe. Recently, this appellation is looked down upon.

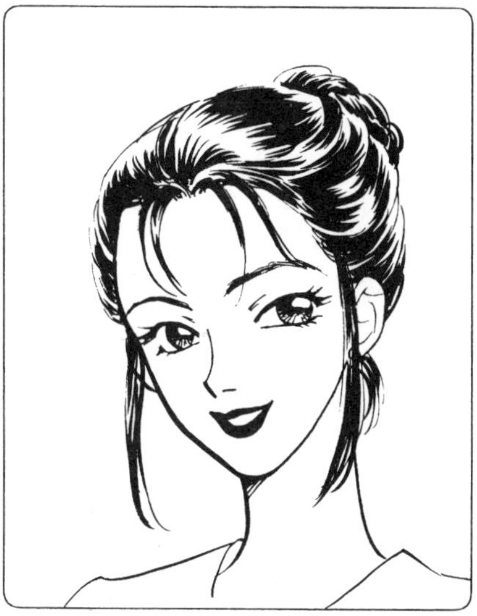

Chinese-American Bishoujo: Chinese merchants abroad is a general term for Chinese businesspeople residing overseas.

Cowgirls and Gunslingers

Cowboys and gunslingers are strictly two different things, but in films the distinction has been blurred. Jackets are either long sleeved or vest types. There is wide variation of lower garments ranging from ordinary slacks to jeans.

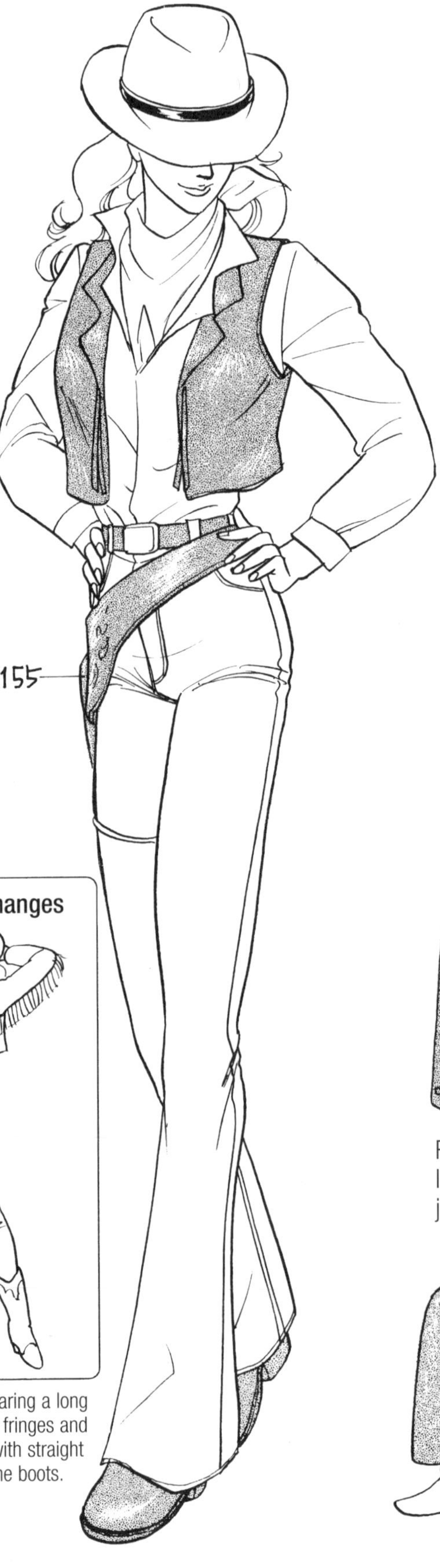

Minor Changes

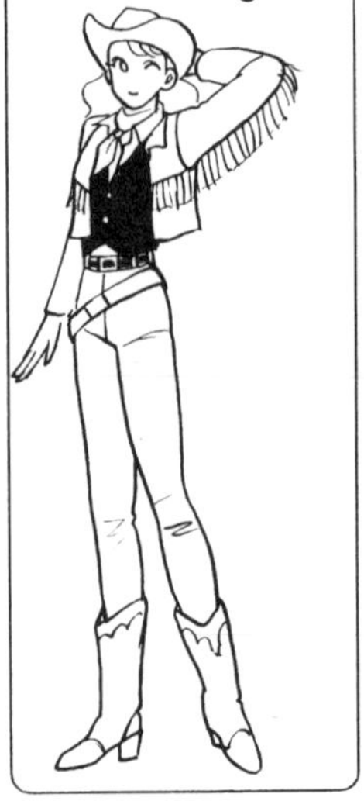

This bishoujo is wearing a long sleeved jacket with fringes and a black waistcoat with straight jeans tucked into the boots.

Put on the shirt.

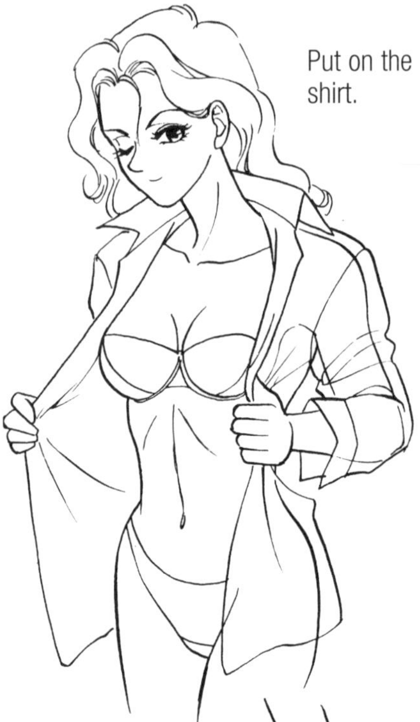

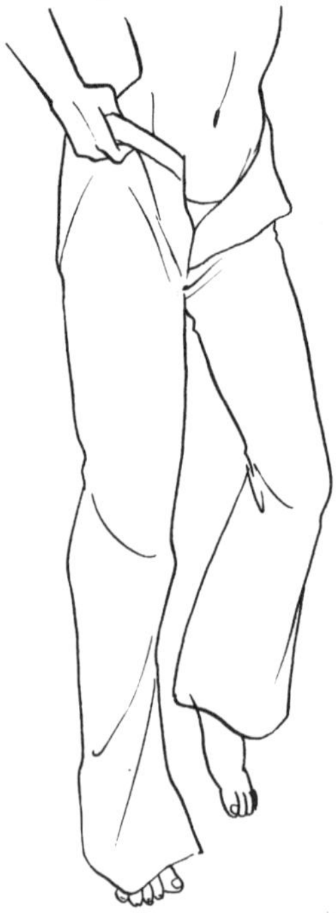

Put on the pants.

Real Cowboy Gear

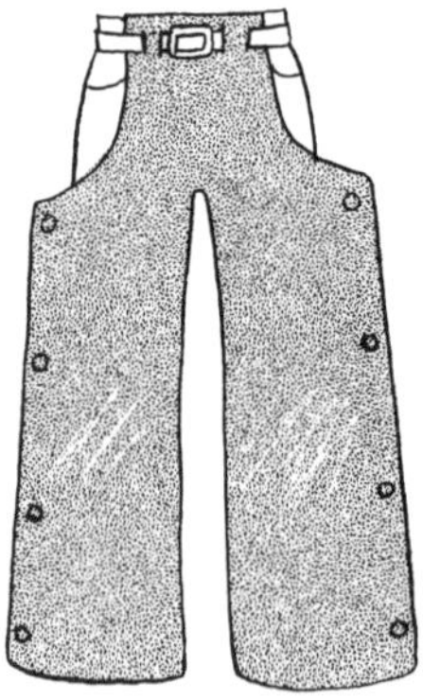

Real cowboys wear leather chaps over their jeans.

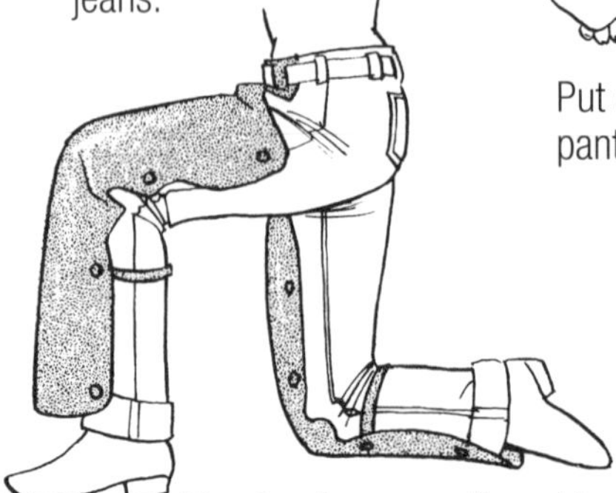

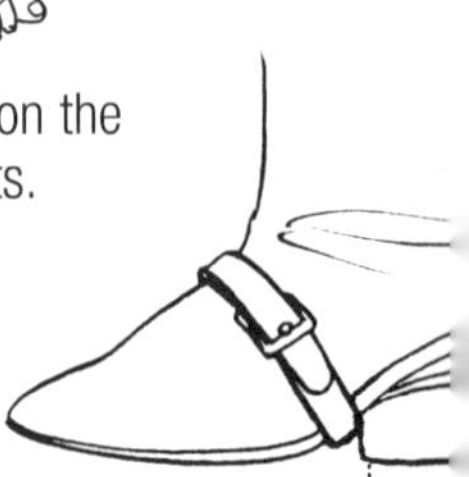

The drawings are often abbreviated as long as there is no need to portray real cowboys.

Cowboy boots

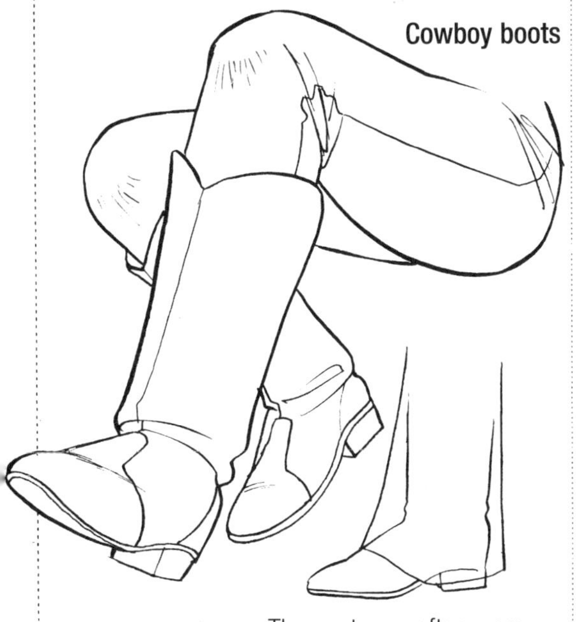

The pants are often worn outside of the boots too.

Scarves

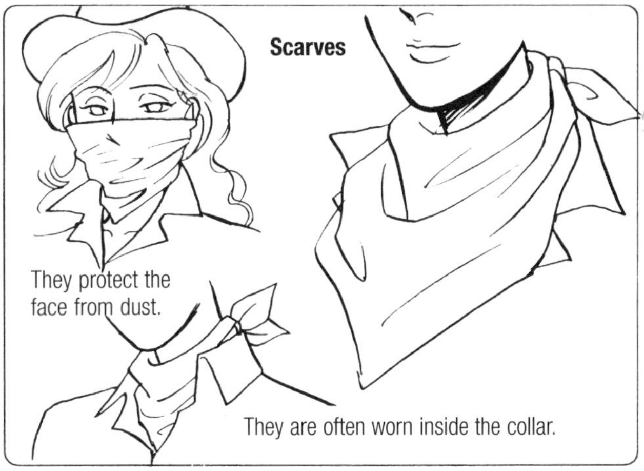

They protect the face from dust.

They are often worn inside the collar.

Gun Belts

Belt for the pants

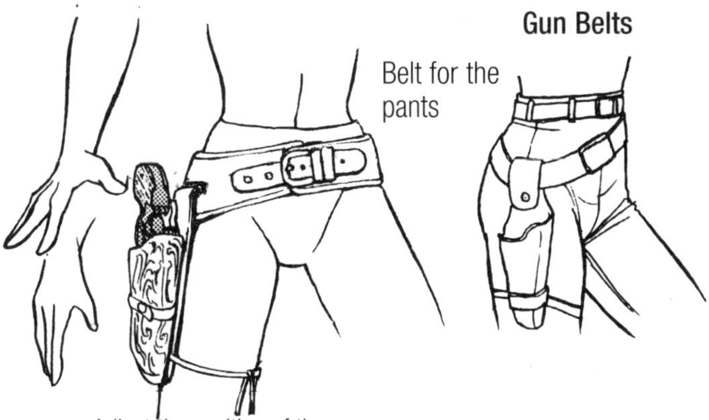

Adjust the position of the gun to the place where the hand hangs down reaching towards the gunstock.

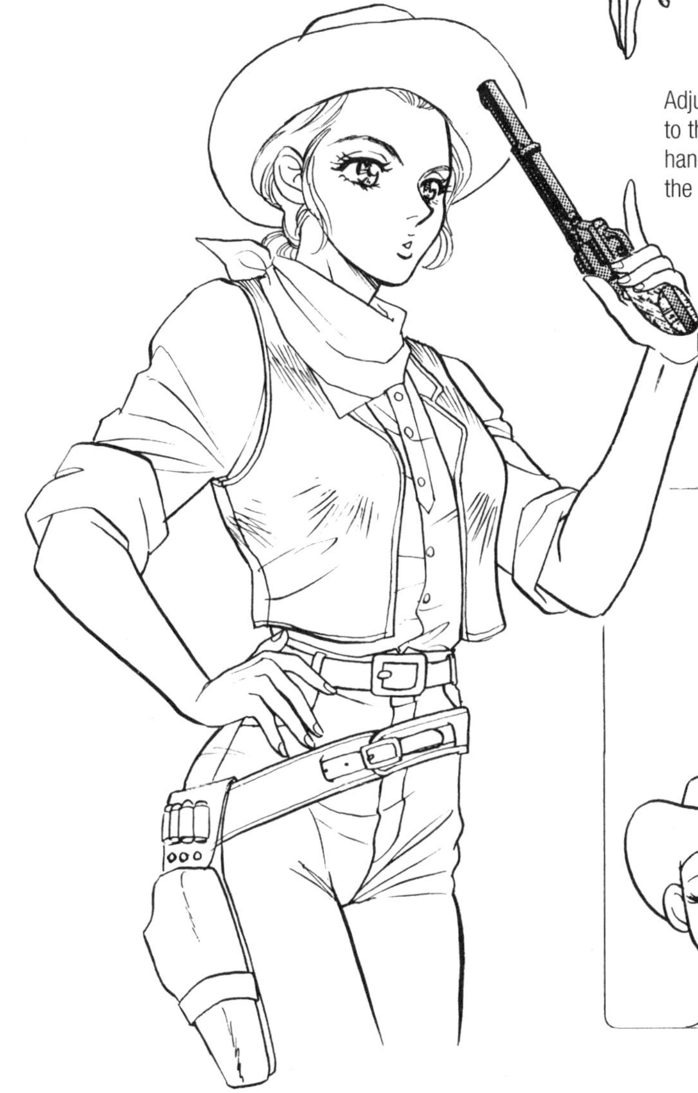

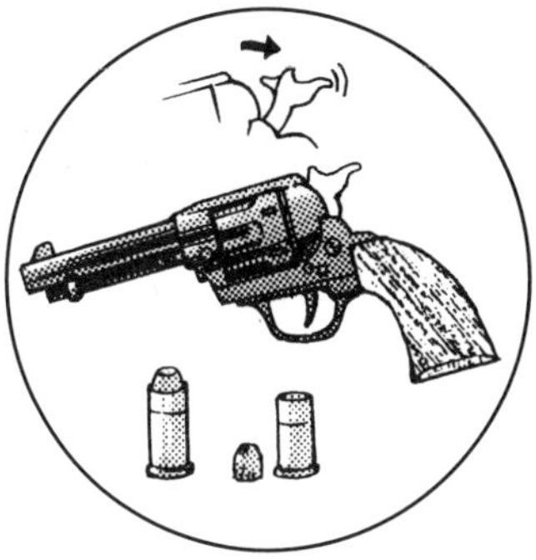

The gun that generally appears in Westerns is a Colt single action gun, nicknamed "Peace Maker". Gun barrels have various lengths. Also, be aware that guns are different on the right and left sides.

Ten gallon hat

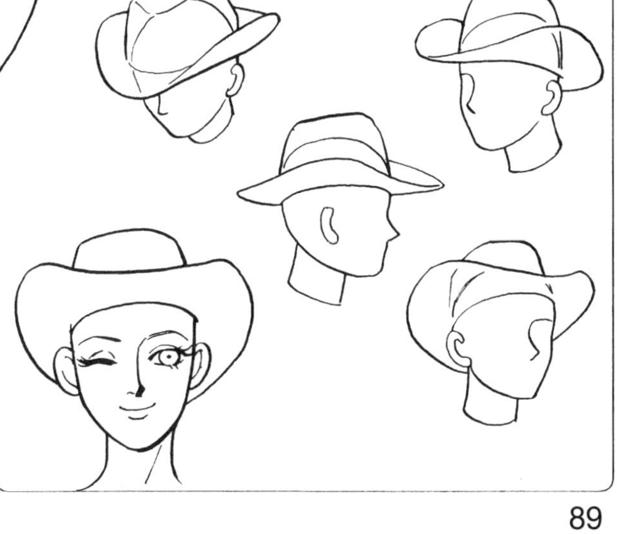

Differences Between Bishoujo and Ordinary Beauties

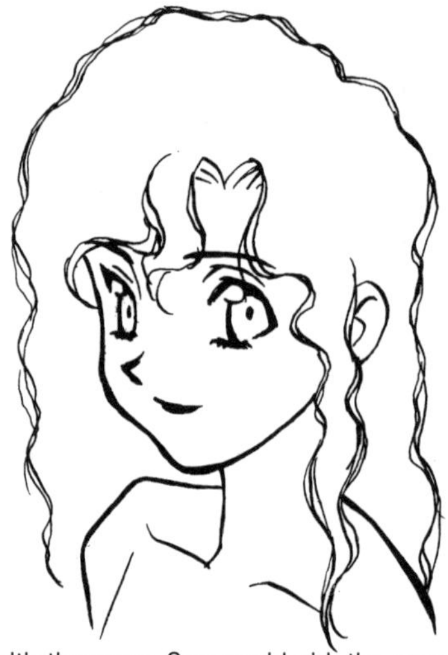

Even with the same Caucasoid girl, the overall length of the face shrinks and looks childish when making the nose shorter.

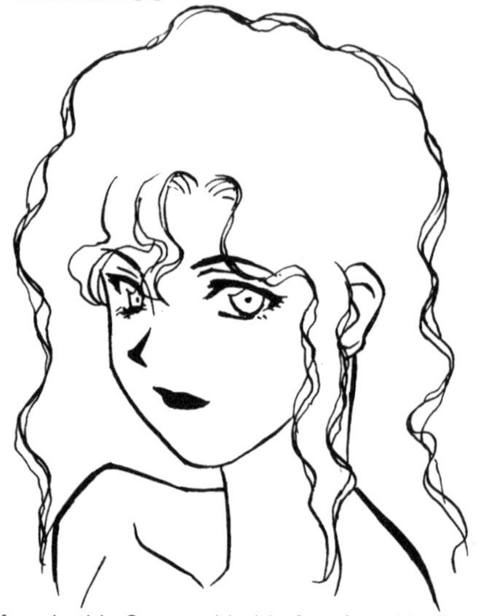

The face in this Caucasoid girl often found in Europe can easily be made to look like an adult by making the facial features clear-cut and defining the line of the nose.

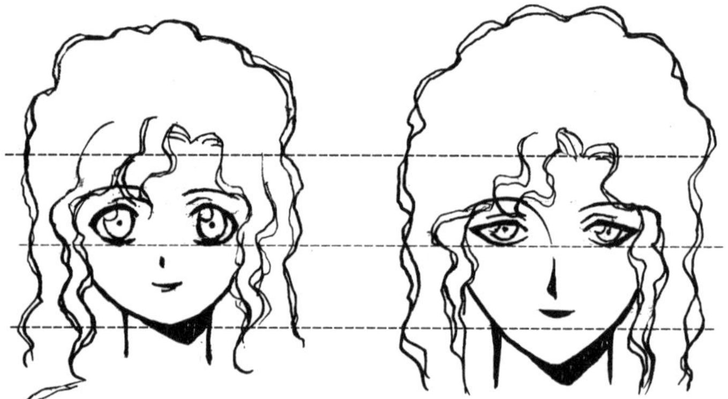

The key to drawing bishoujo is to avoid drawing girls with long faces.

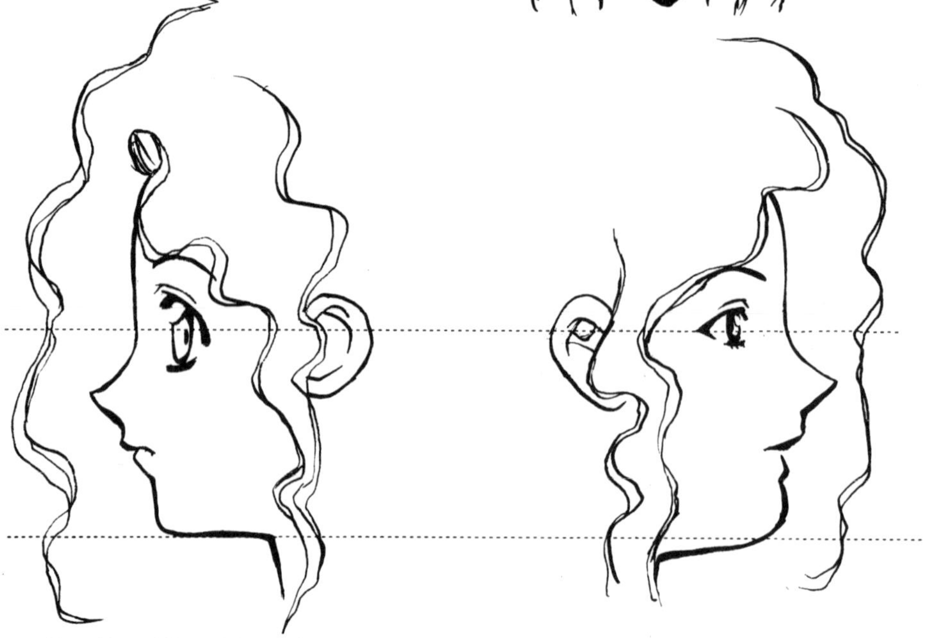

Short Faced Type: Manga design and childish face

Long Faced Type: Easy to make looking real and adult-like

Chapter 3

Ancient and Prehistoric Bishoujo

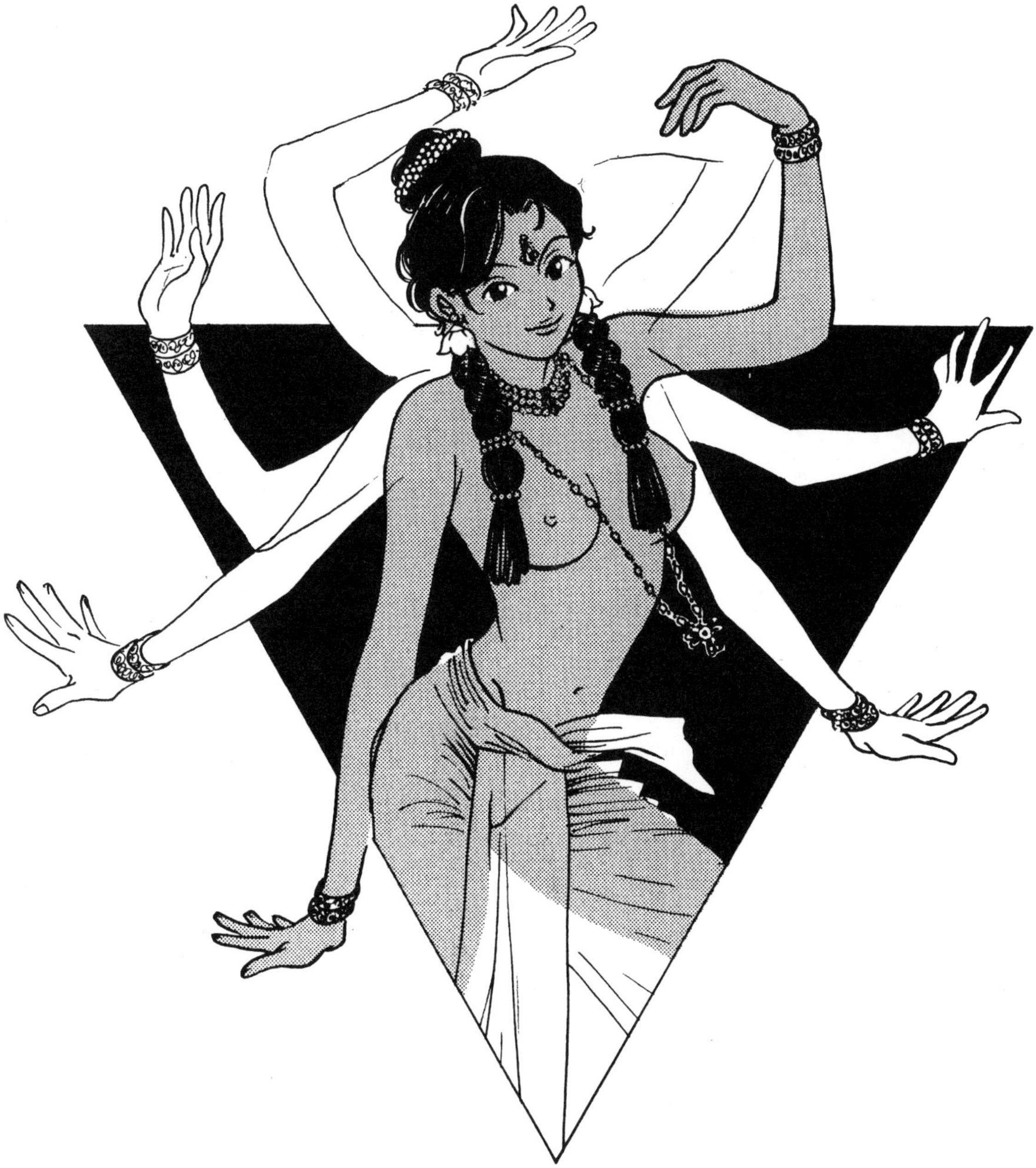

Ancient Greek Bishoujo

Caucasoid

The fashion of Ancient Greece falls into three categories. It is said that thin, see-through linen was used. Be sure to bring out the see-through nature accordingly.

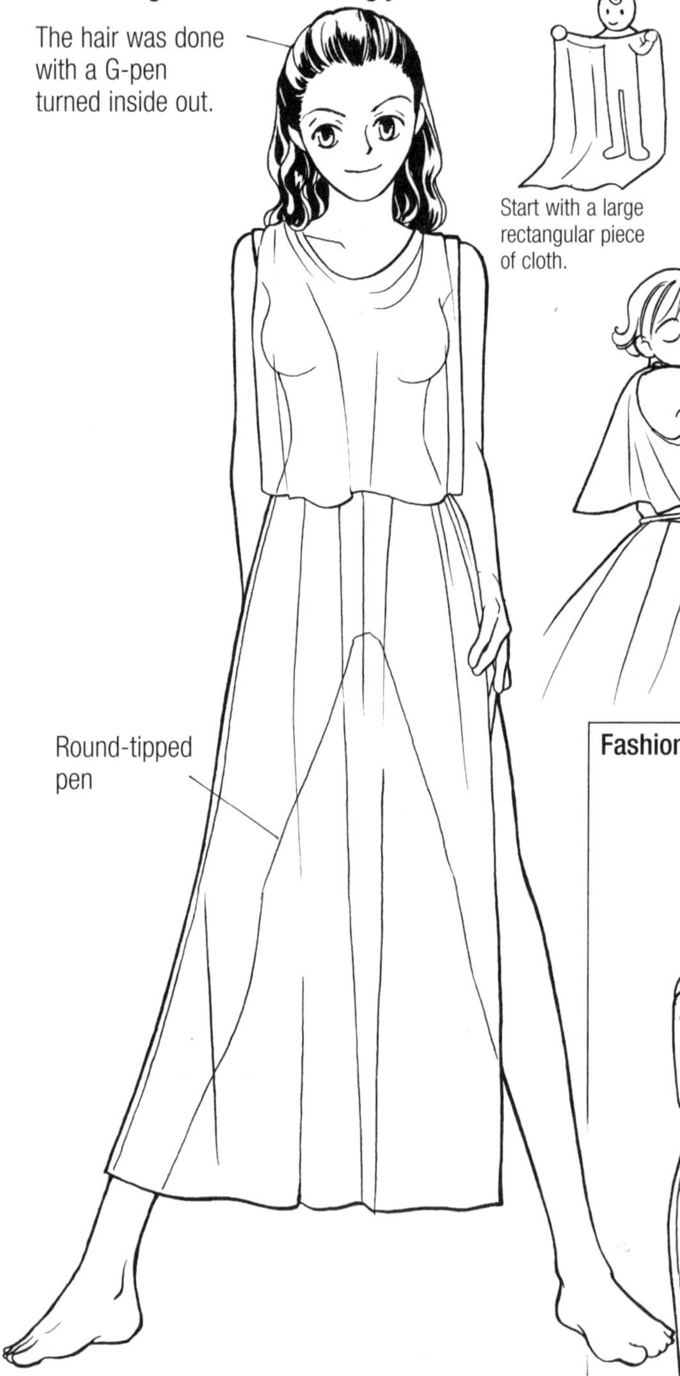

Fashion Type 1 - 'Peplos' (Doric Version Tunic)

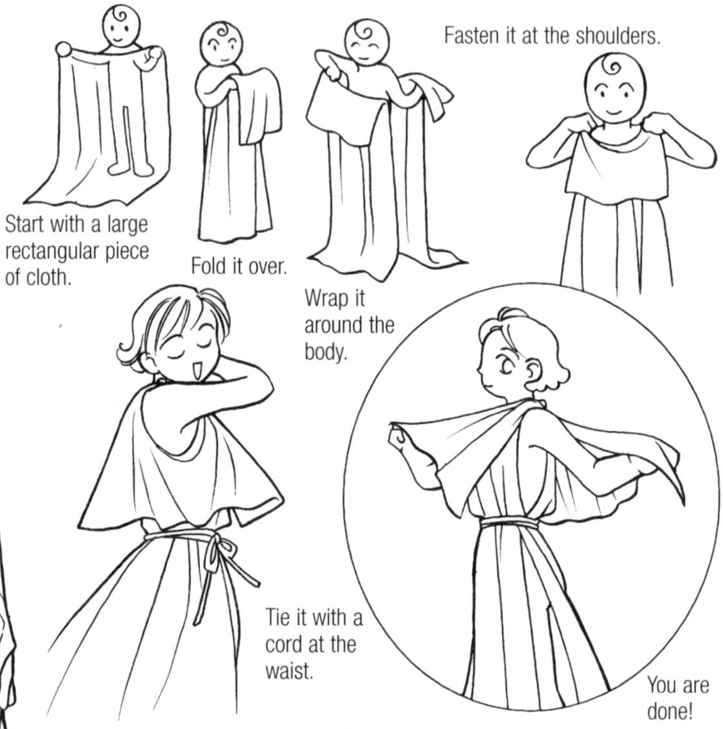

Fashion Type 2 - 'Chiton' (Tunic)

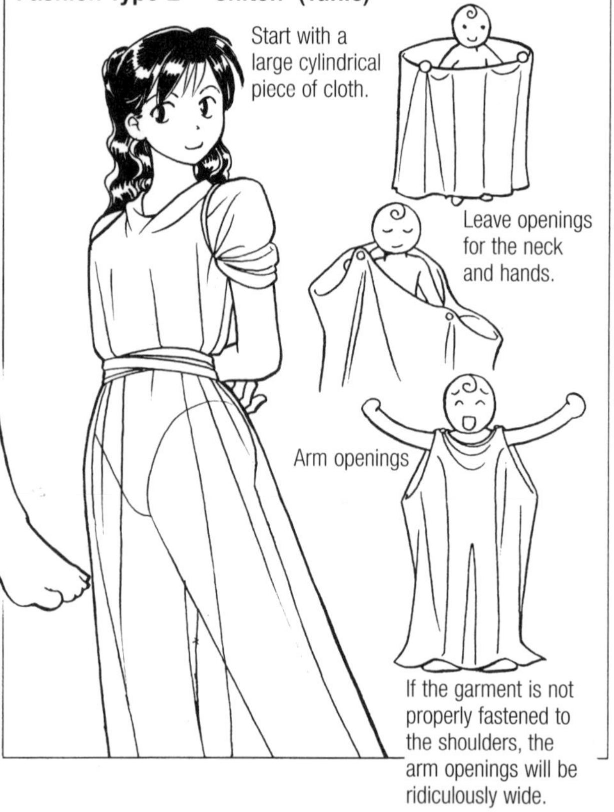

Fashion Type 3
'Chiton' (Tunic) and 'Himation' (Half-Length Coat)

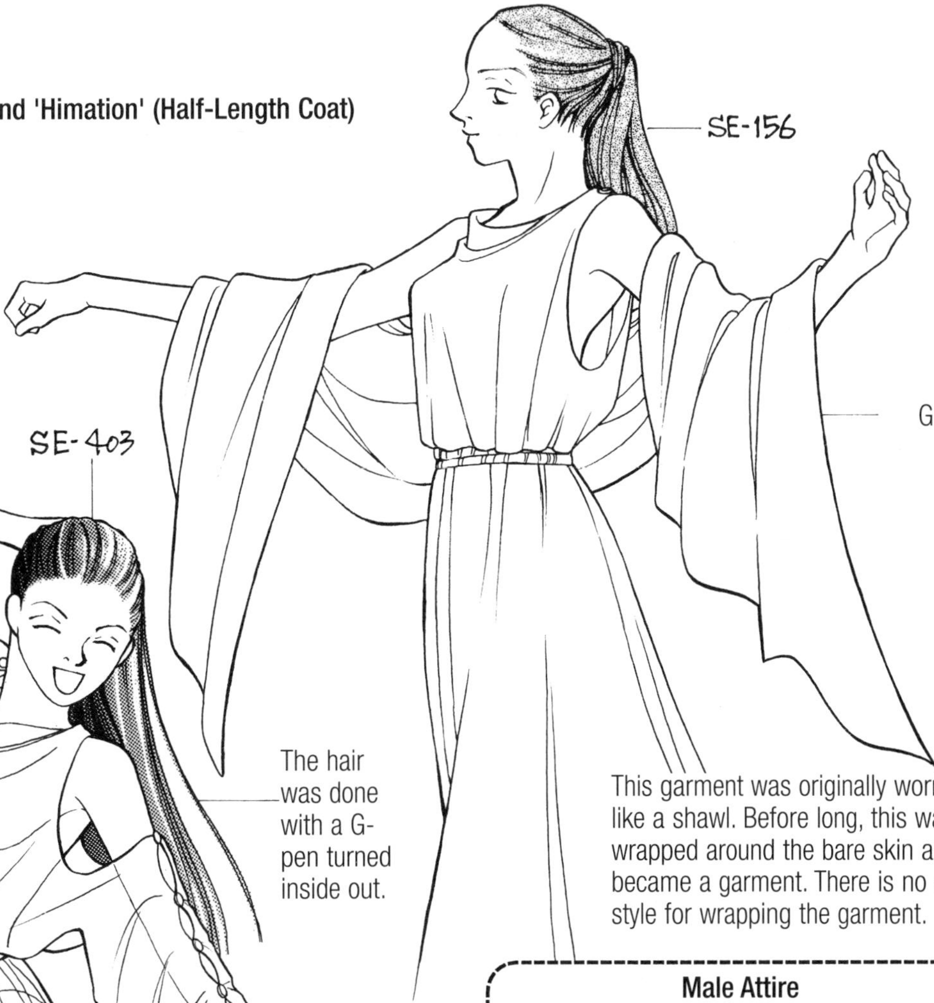

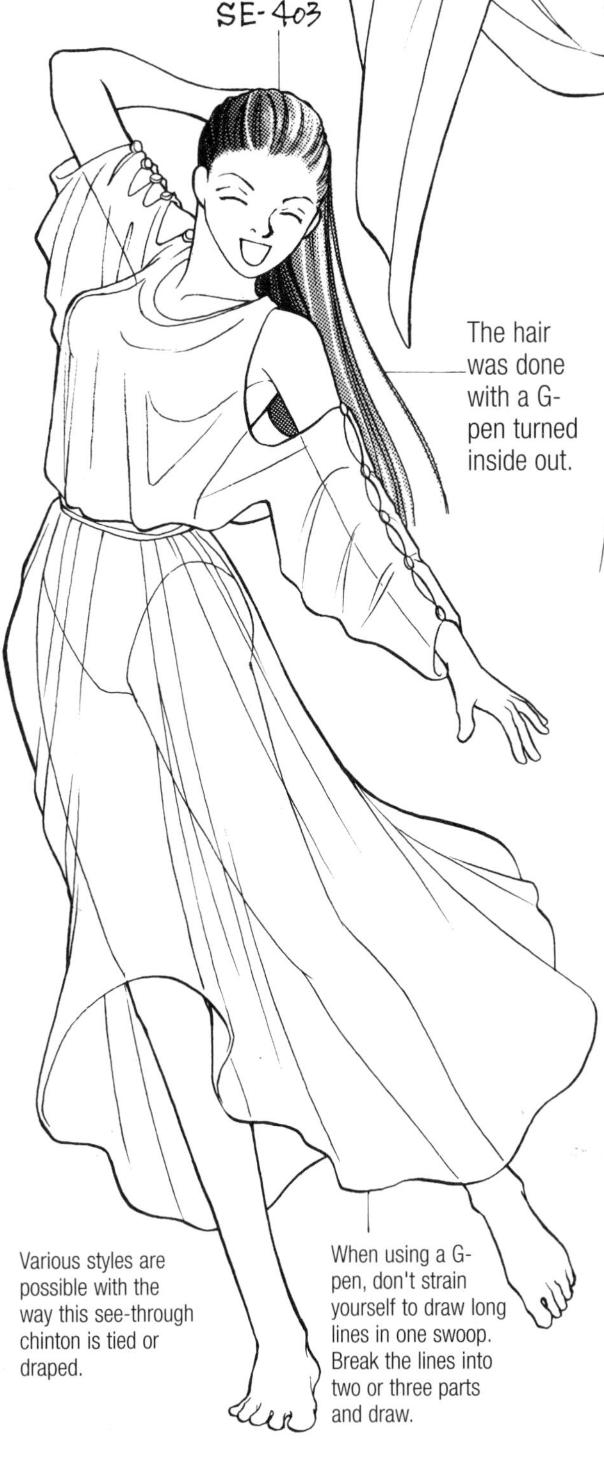

The hair was done with a G-pen turned inside out.

This garment was originally worn like a shawl. Before long, this was wrapped around the bare skin and became a garment. There is no set style for wrapping the garment.

Male Attire

The himation style of elite fashion worn by Athenian scholars, artists and statesmen, was wrapped directly over the skin.

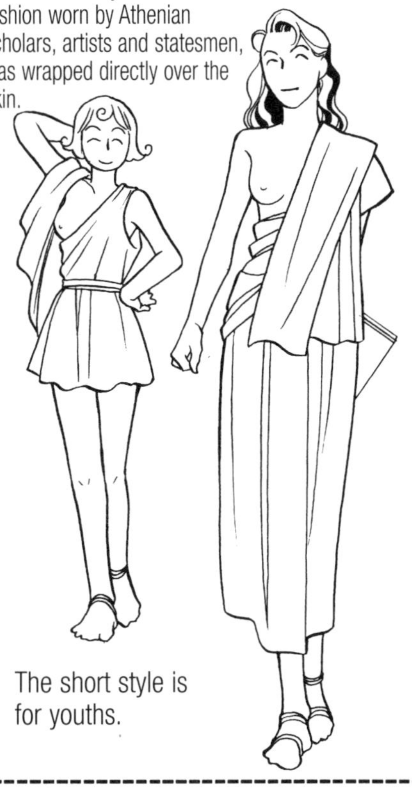

The short style is for youths.

Various styles are possible with the way this see-through chinton is tied or draped.

When using a G-pen, don't strain yourself to draw long lines in one swoop. Break the lines into two or three parts and draw.

Armor, Helmets and Amazon Girls

There was a time when all parts were bare except for the head and shins while round shields were used to guard the body.

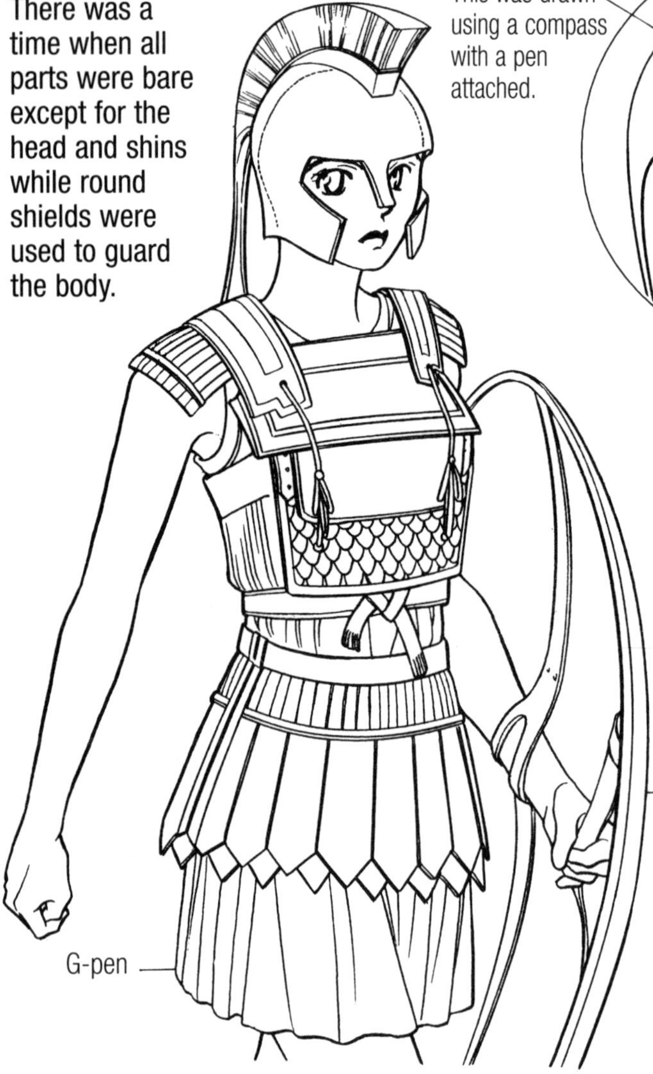

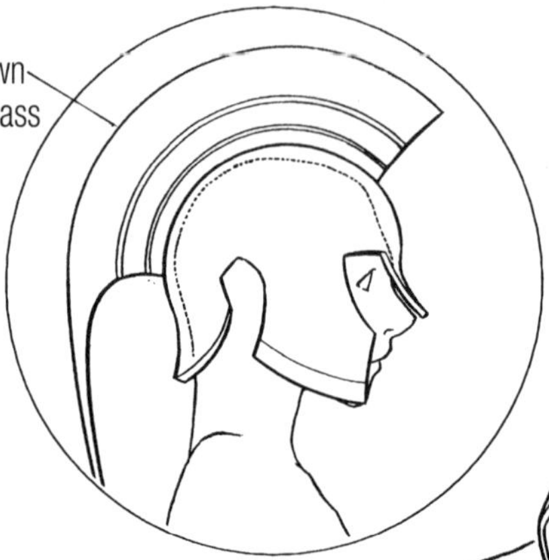

See-through drawing of the side of the head

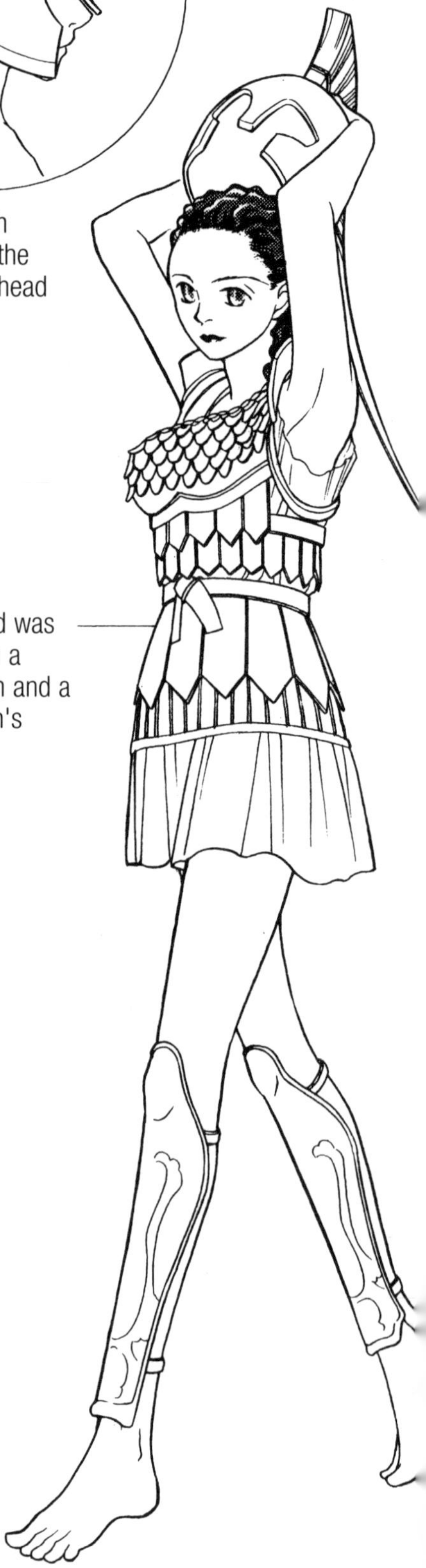

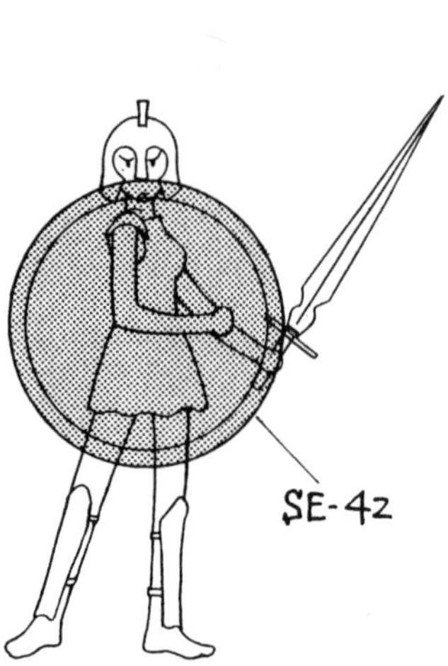

The shield guards the body from the neck to the knees.

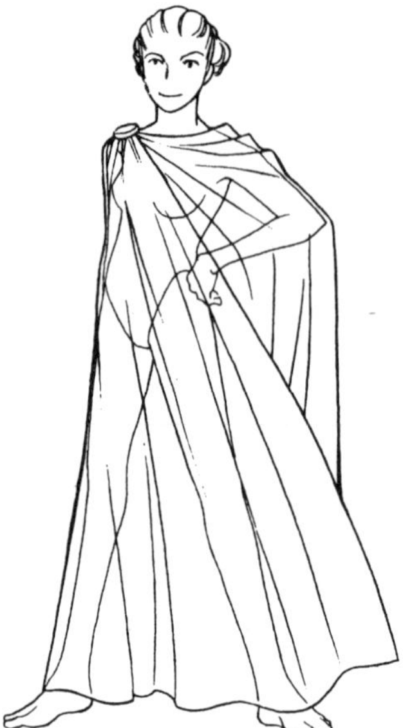

Cloak style

Drawing Seated Poses

Chitons are made of thin, plaint material. Many detailed draped areas appear on the surface. Drawing shortened versions, which did not appear in actual history, also makes for fine drawings.

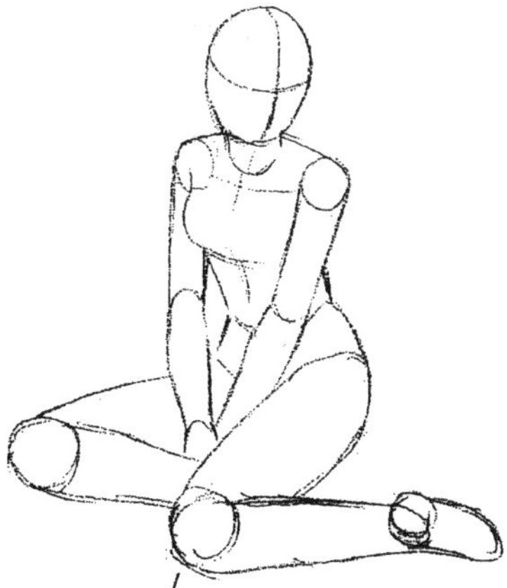

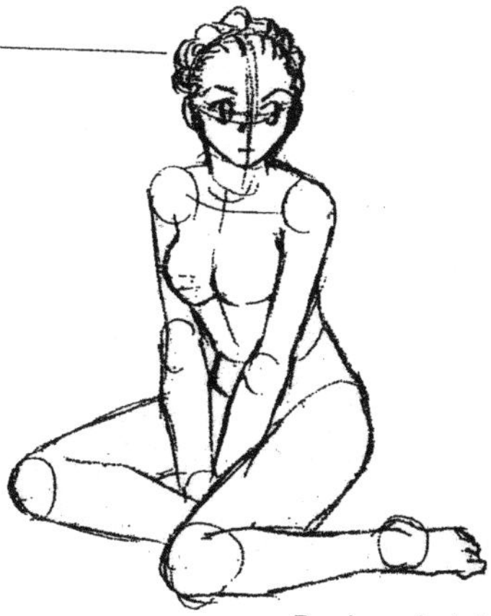

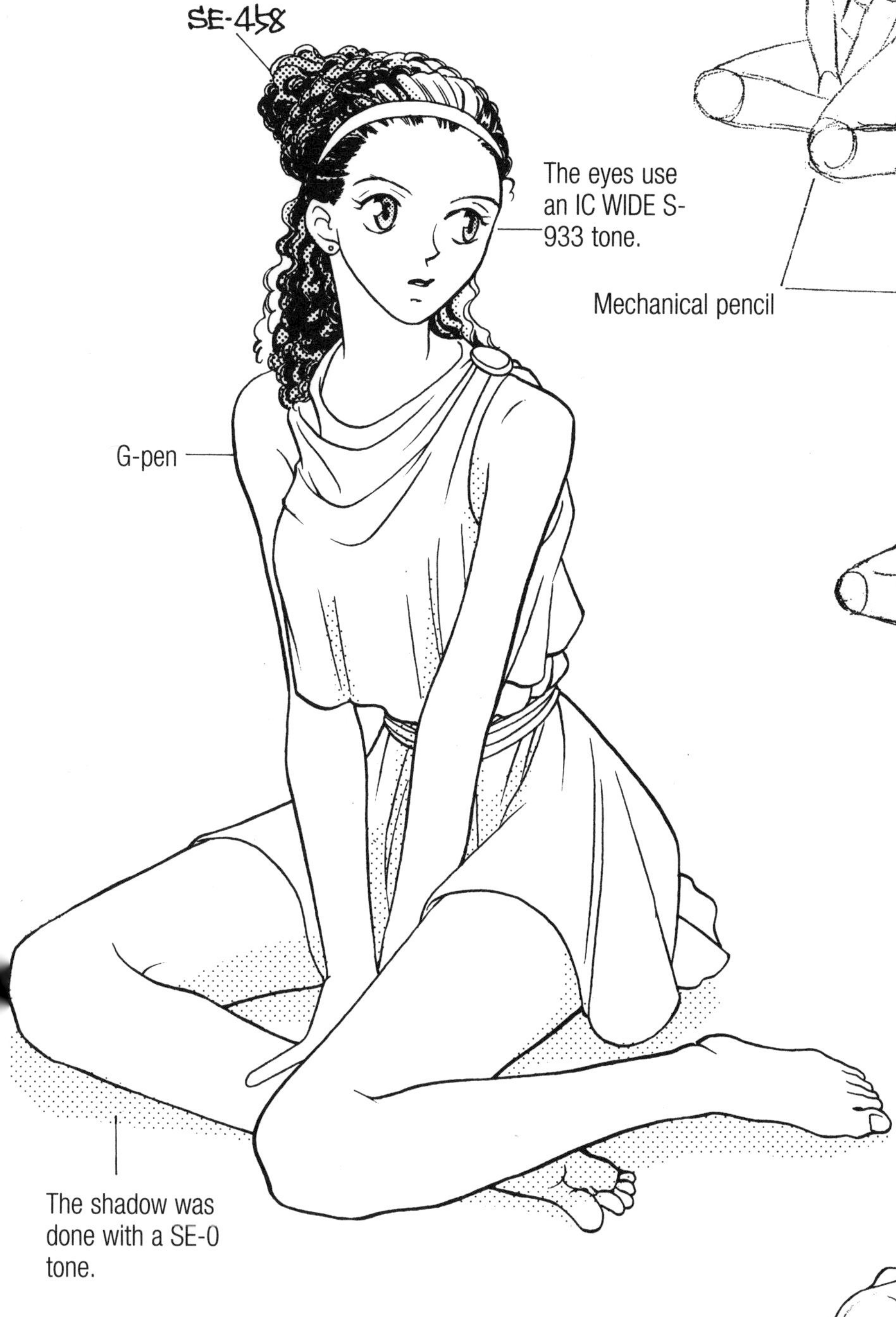

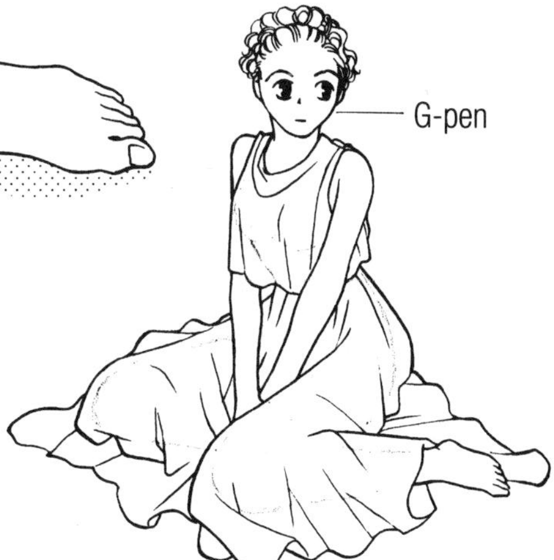

It essentially would look like this.

Ancient Germanic and Celtic Bishoujo
from Northern Europe

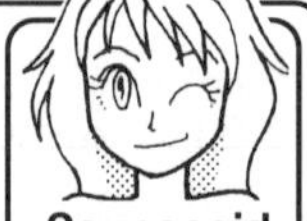

Caucasoid

While myths of Northern Europe are often introduced as Germanic and Celtic origin, in the strictest sense of meaning, the main sources for Norse mythology, Indo-European in origin, are the Icelandic folklore called Eddas which were handed down from generation to generation. Try making reference to the ancient Germanic people and their descendants, the Vikings, who were active in Scandinavian regions (Sweden, Denmark, Norway, and Iceland).

Male At

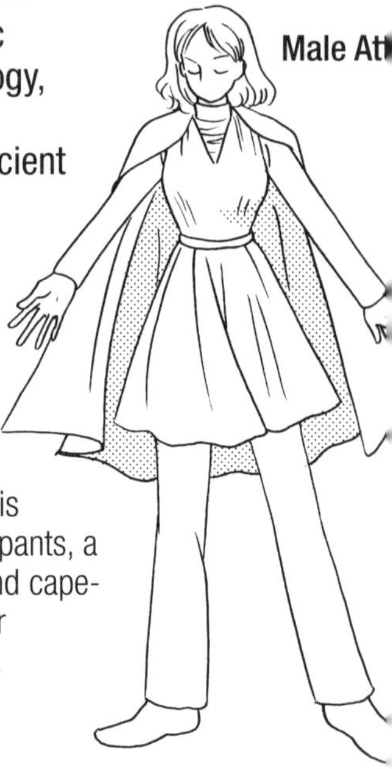

This girl is wearing pants, a jacket and cape-like outer garment.

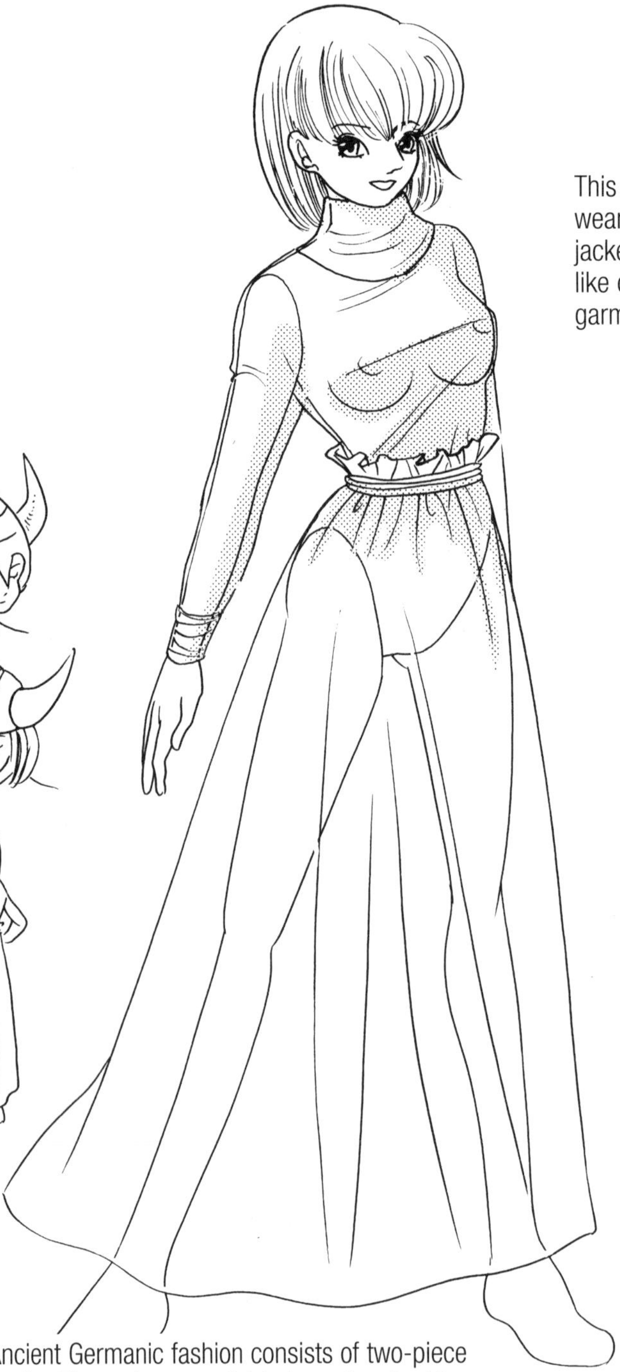

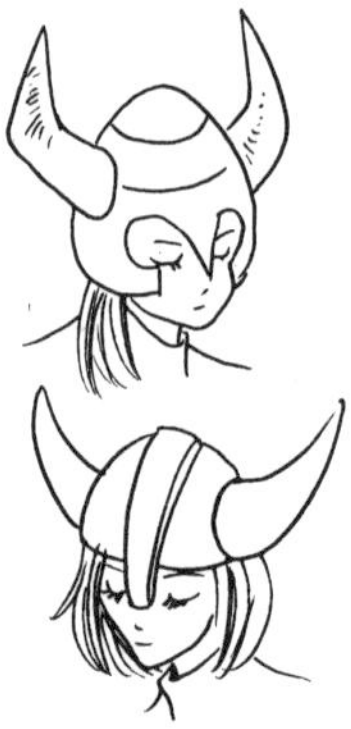

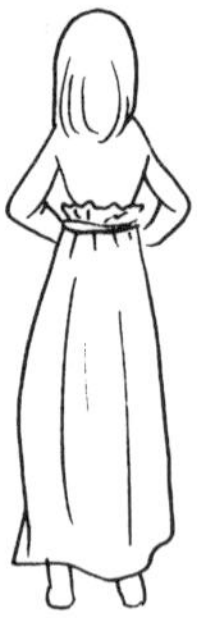

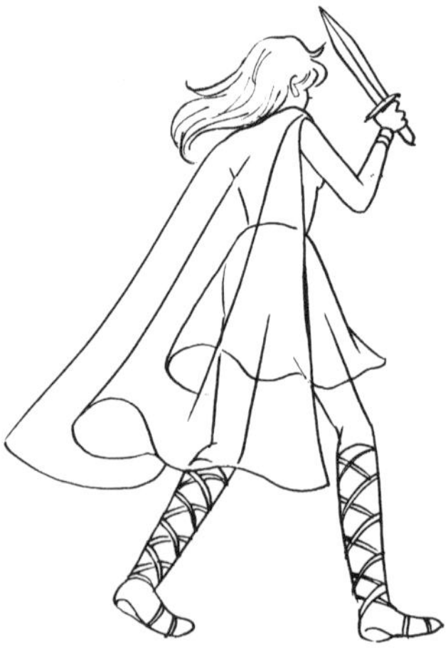

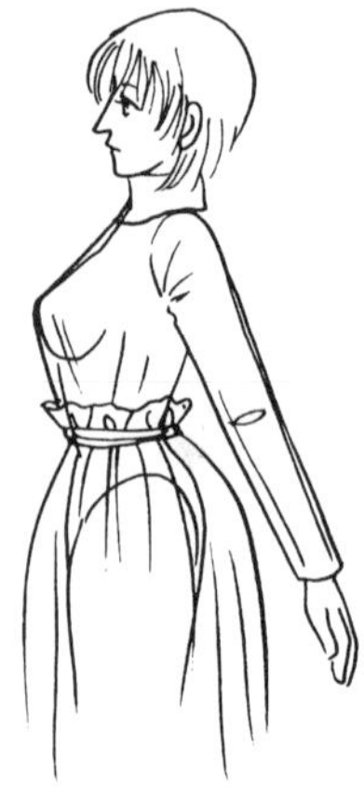

The lines of the skirt gently swell but do not widen too much. The legs cannot be seen.

Ancient Germanic fashion consists of two-piece outfits. The style was a tight sleeved under blouse with a peasant skirt.

Celtic Girls of Ireland

Celtic myths are legends from Ireland. There are very few reference materials regarding clothing. A mythical image carved into a stone monument in Gaul, a province of the ancient Roman Empire in Western Europe, remains as a reference of attire worn by a mix of ancient Romans and Germanic people.

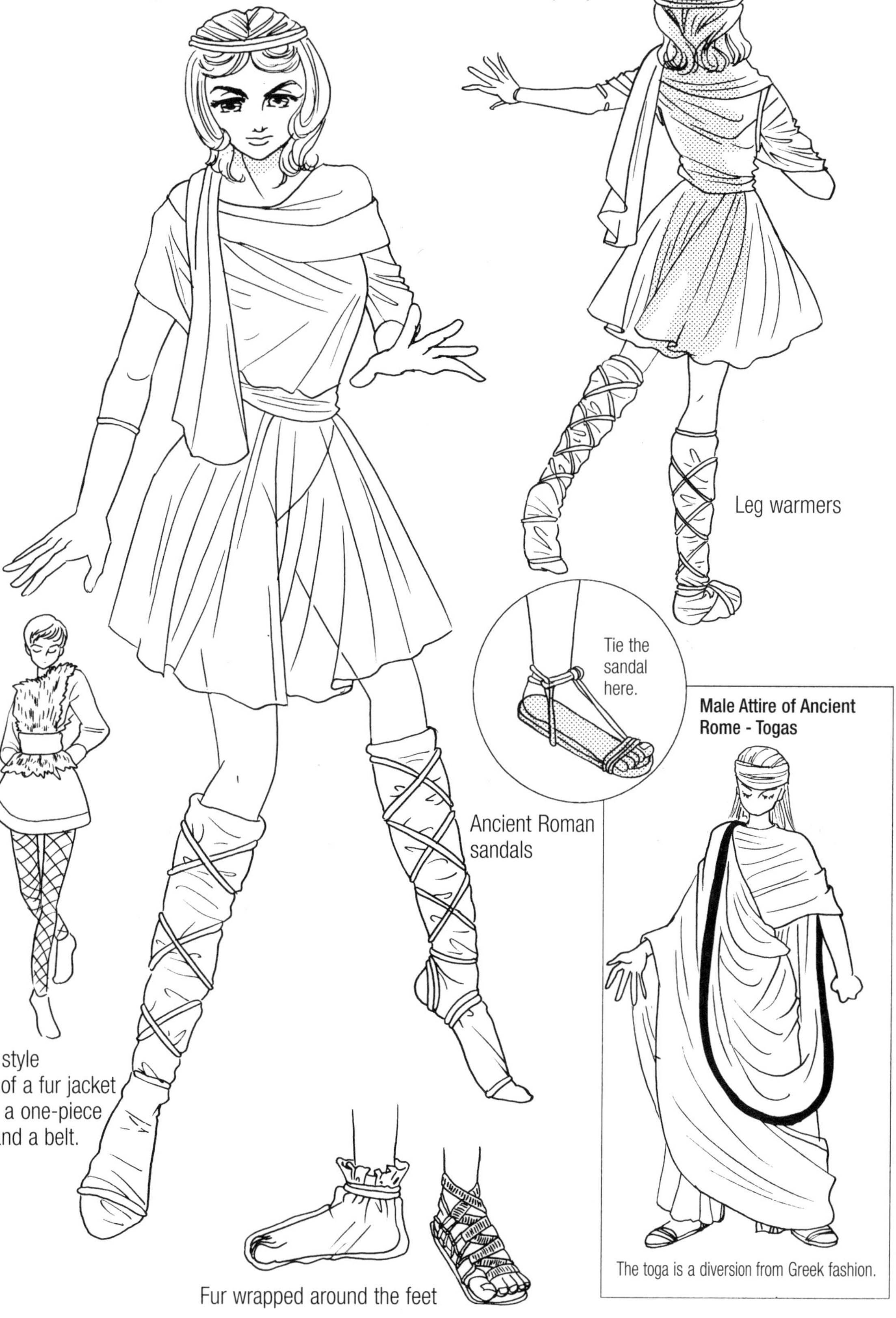

Ancient Indian Bishoujo

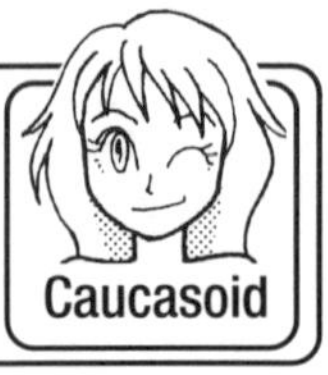

Collect various accessories based on a dhoti, a purified piece of cloth used by male ascetic practitioners of Hinduism, and ideas inferred from ancient Indian carvings and sculptures.

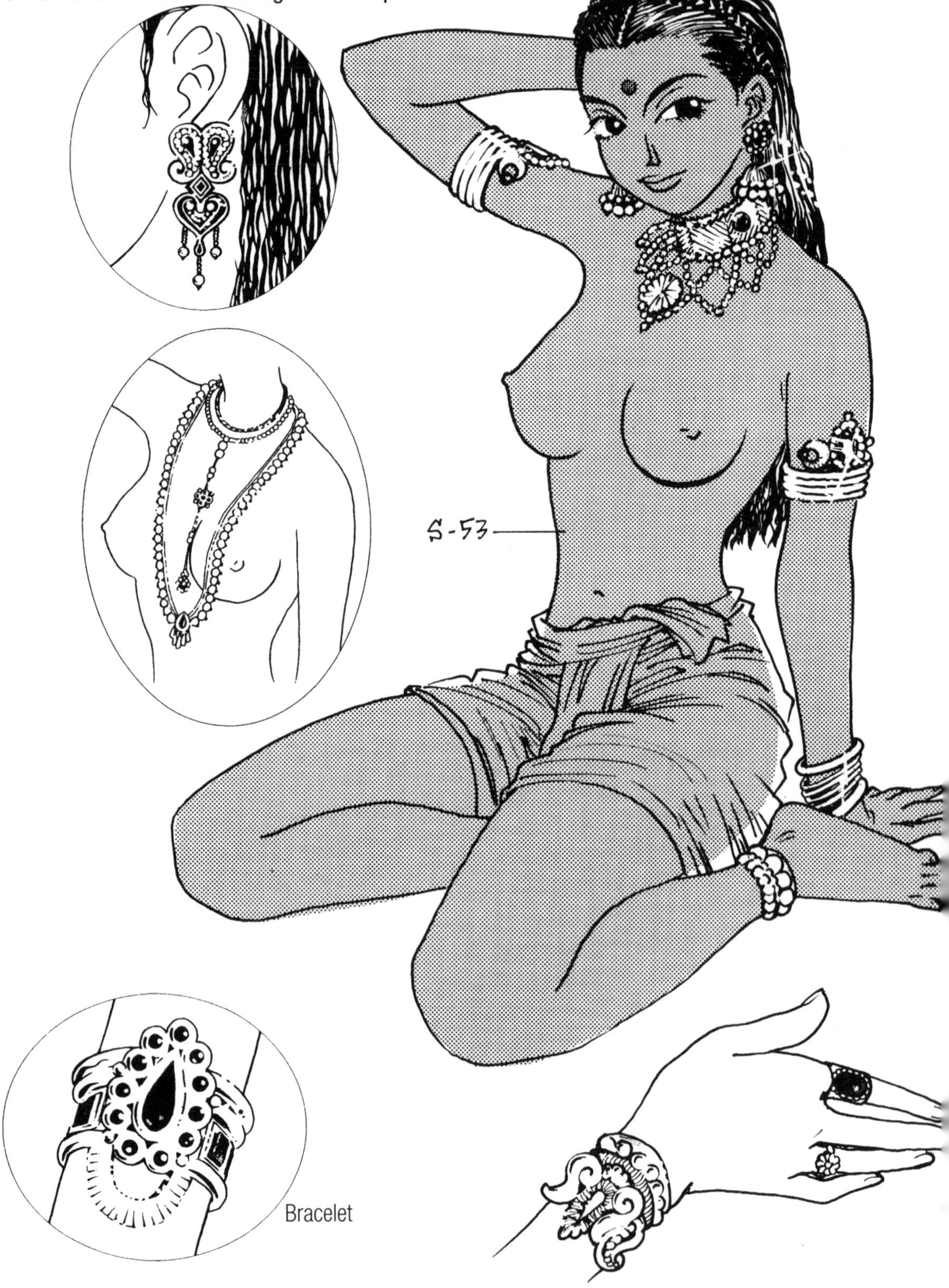

From ruins of the Indus civilization from 4,000 B.C., something similar to a dhoti was often seen in female fashion.

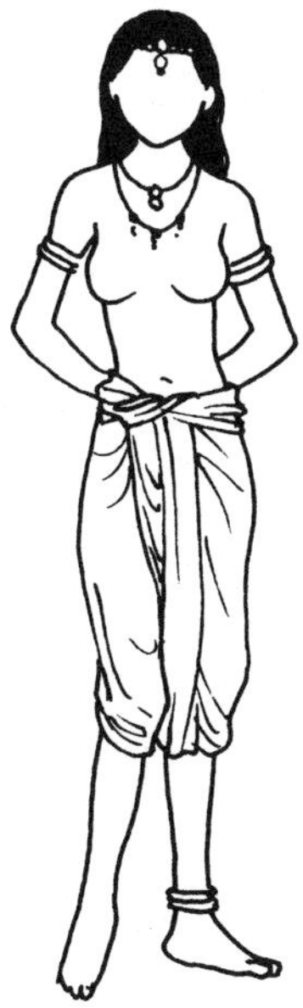

Male Attire - Dhoti Style

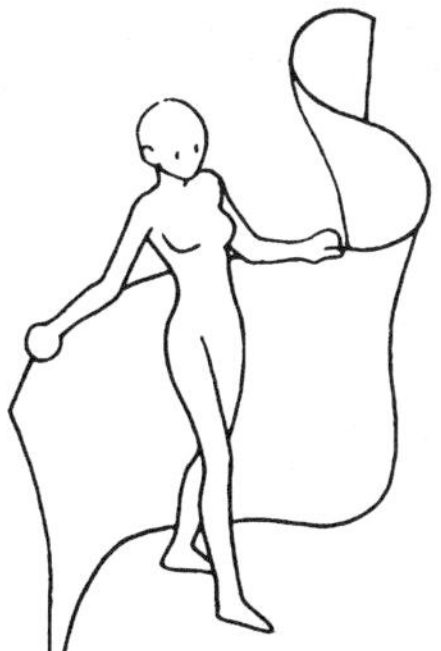

1. Start with a large piece of cloth.

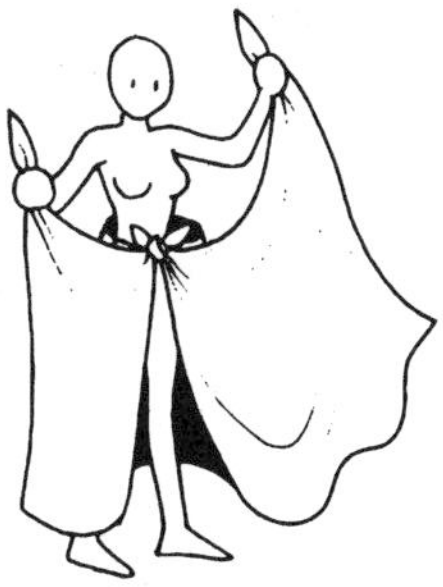

2. Tie it in the middle.

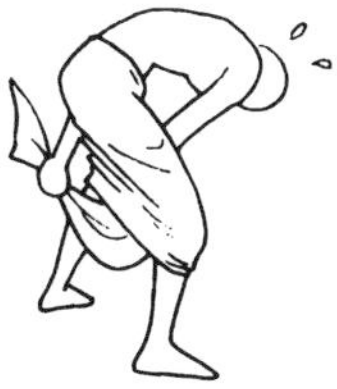

3. Holding it in one hand pass it between the legs.

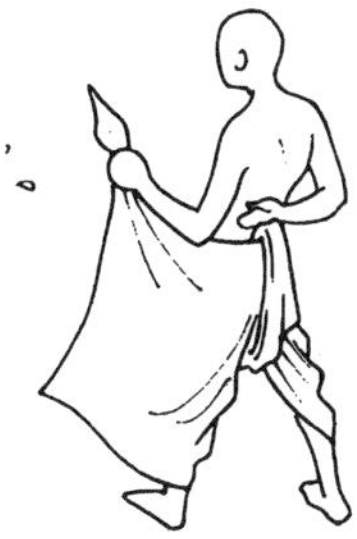

4. Insert the part you were holding in the waist area in the back.

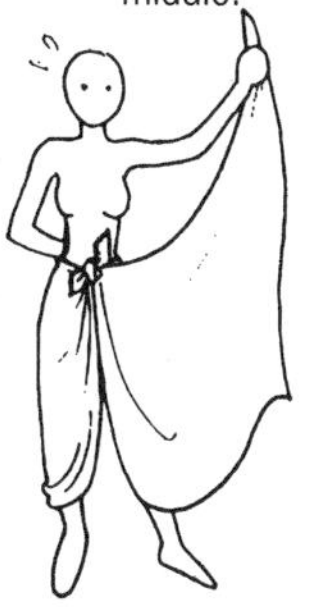

5. There is still this much left.

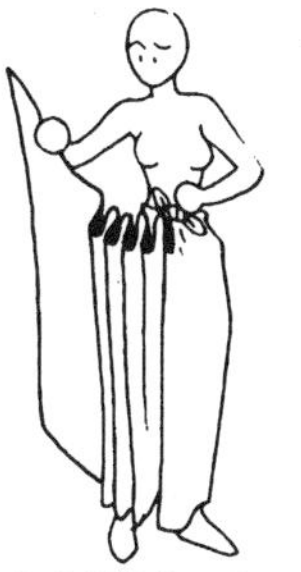

6. Fold it into layers.

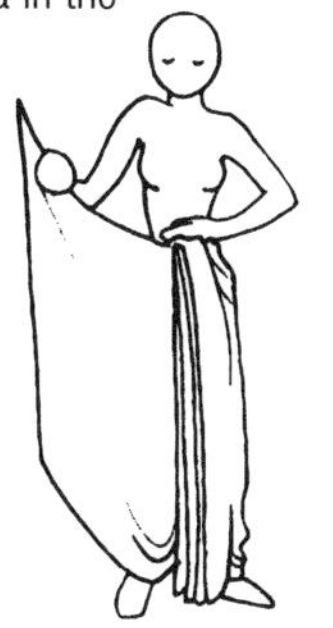

7. Insert the bundles of layers into the front.

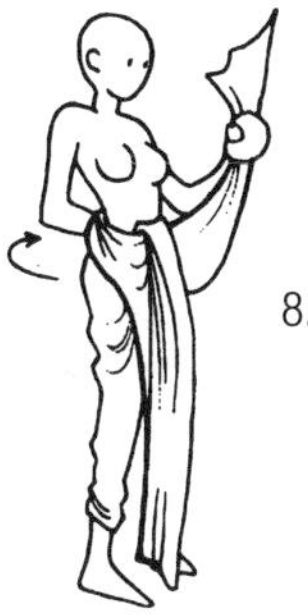

8. Wrap the leftover part around the waist.

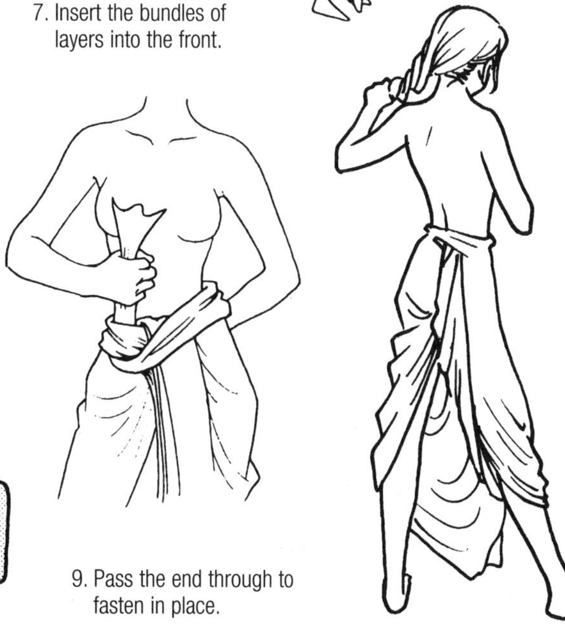

9. Pass the end through to fasten in place.

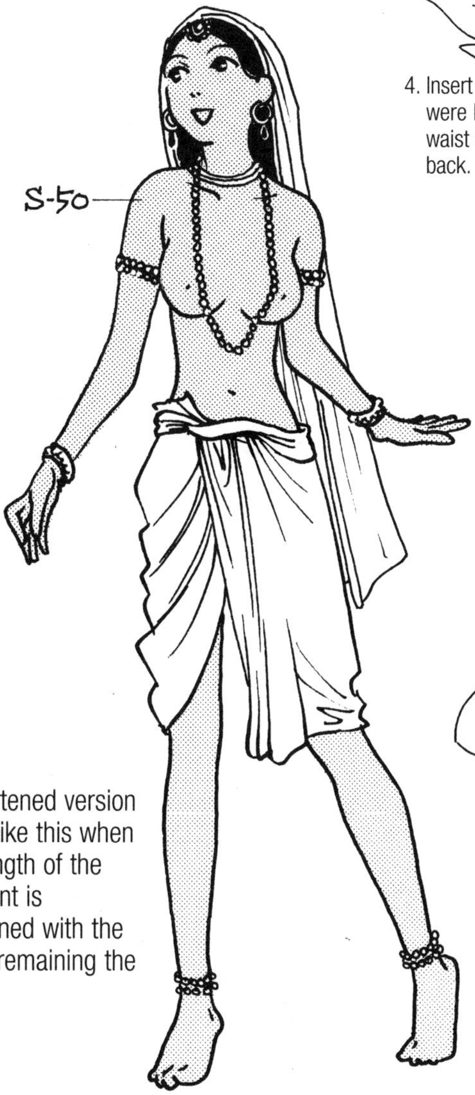

A shortened version looks like this when the length of the garment is shortened with the width remaining the same.

Dhoti Style Applications

This is a combination of a very thin dhoti with a narrow width shawl that acts as a brassiere covering the breasts with the leftover parts wrapped around the arms and shoulders.

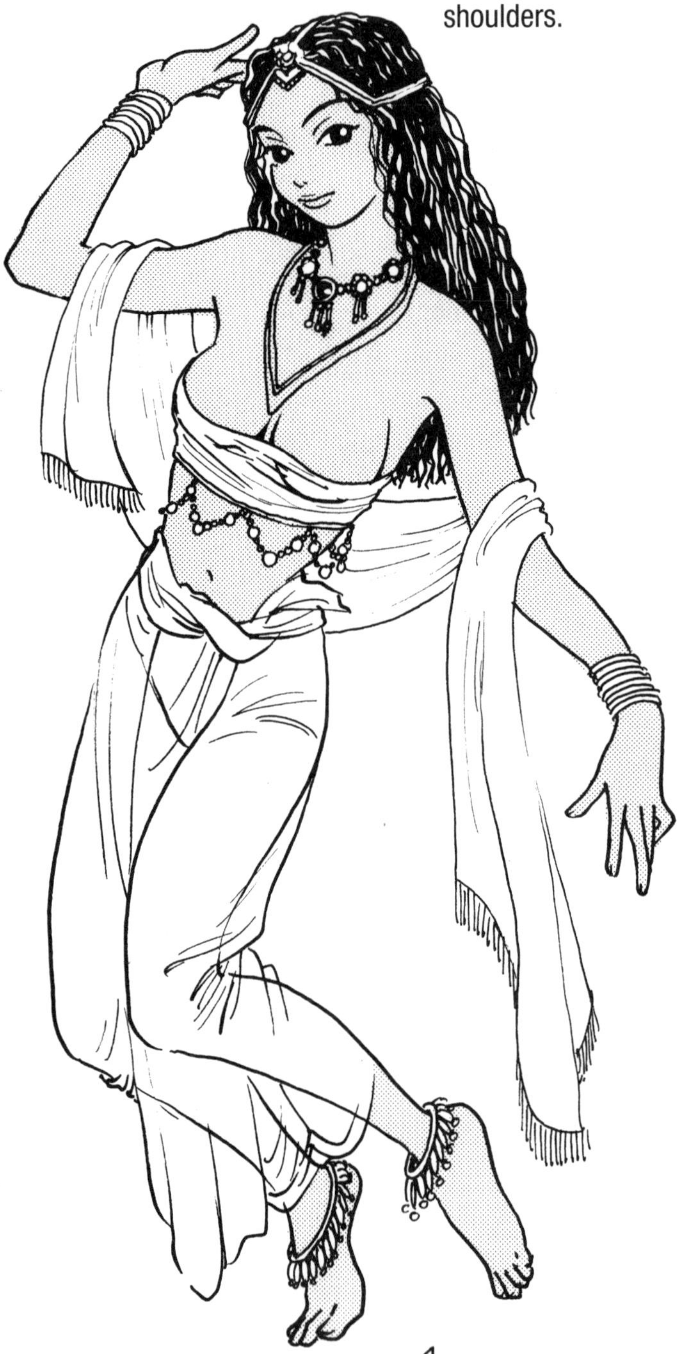

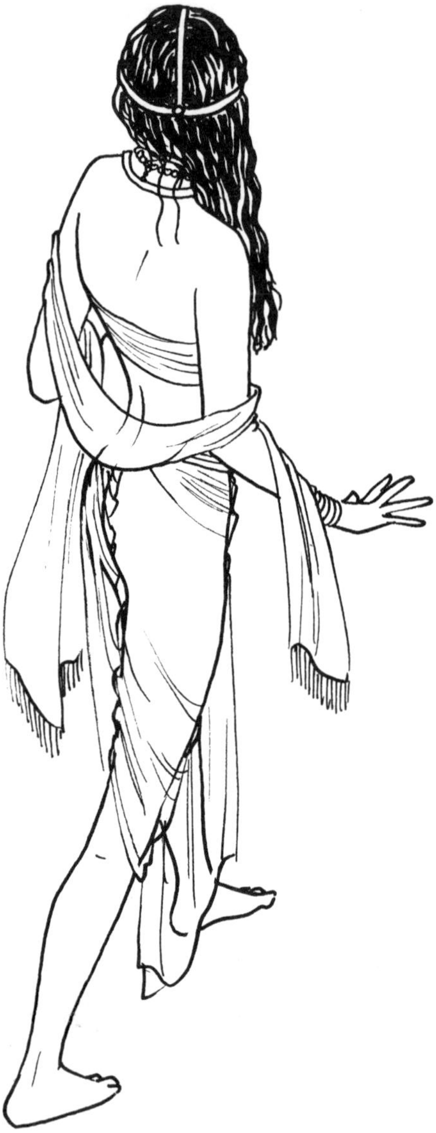

Head decorations

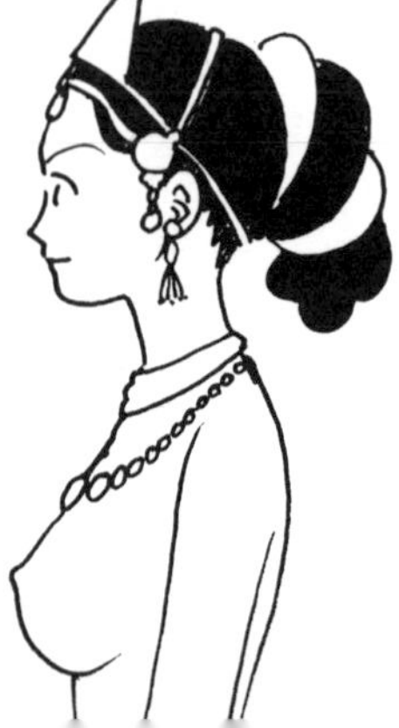

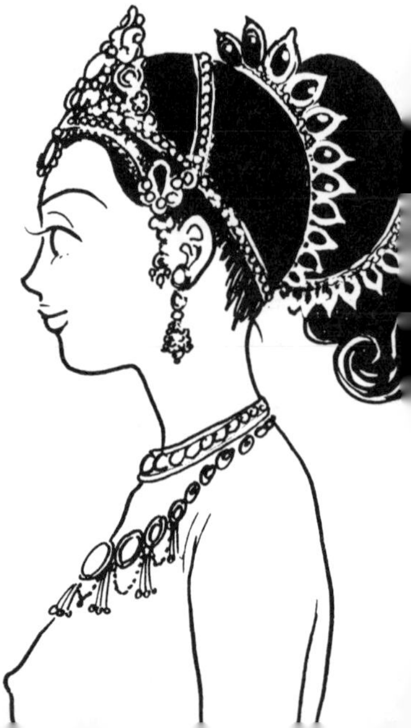

Indian Art Expression Applications

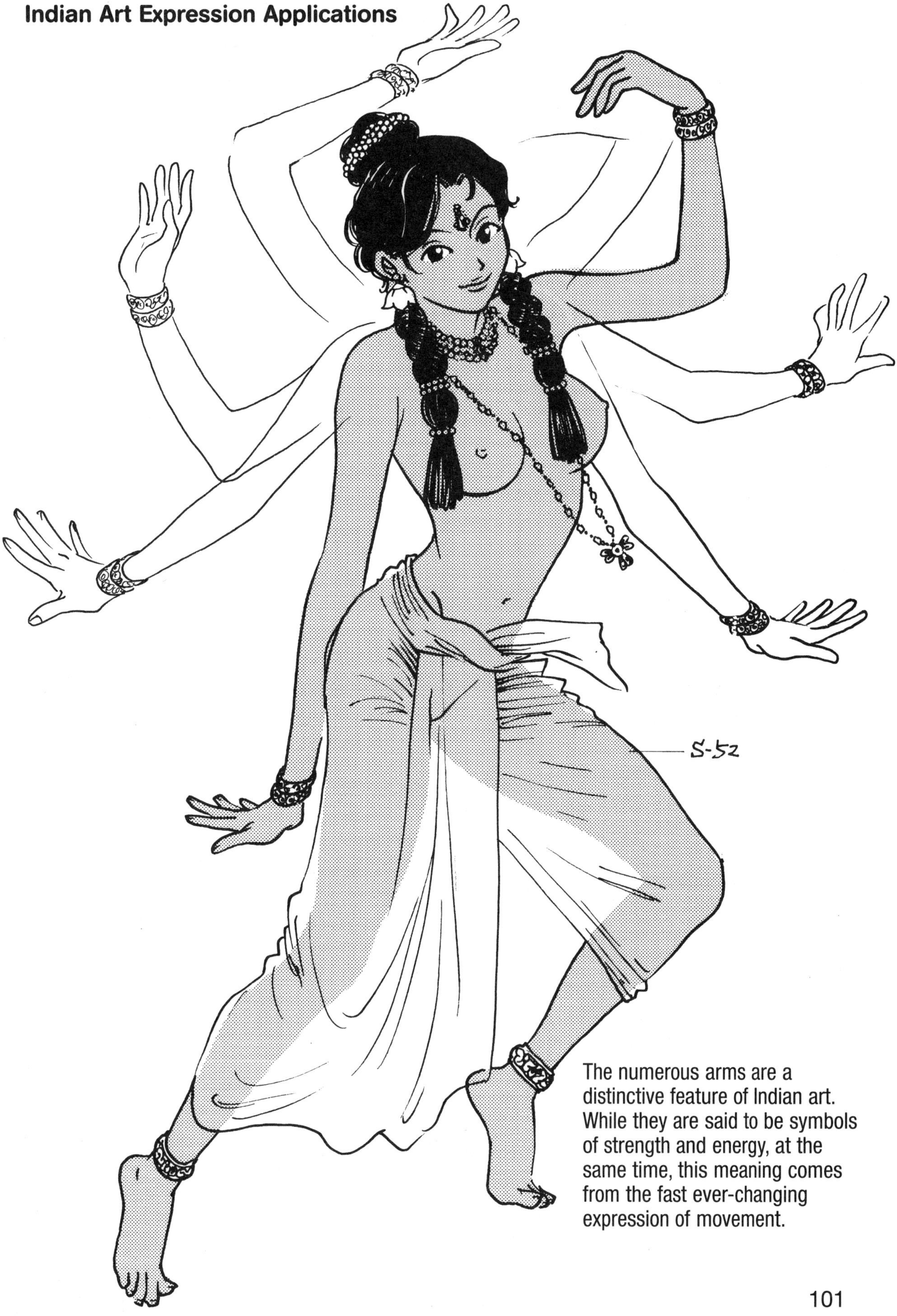

The numerous arms are a distinctive feature of Indian art. While they are said to be symbols of strength and energy, at the same time, this meaning comes from the fast ever-changing expression of movement.

Ancient Chinese Bishoujo

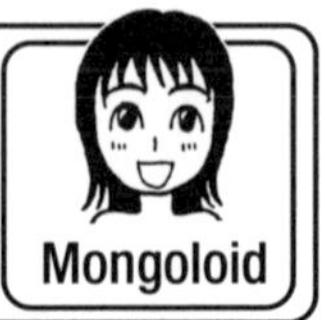

Make reference to old paintings, prints and sculptures (i.e. the 6th century Tang Dynasty) in existence, as well as, Buddhist statues.

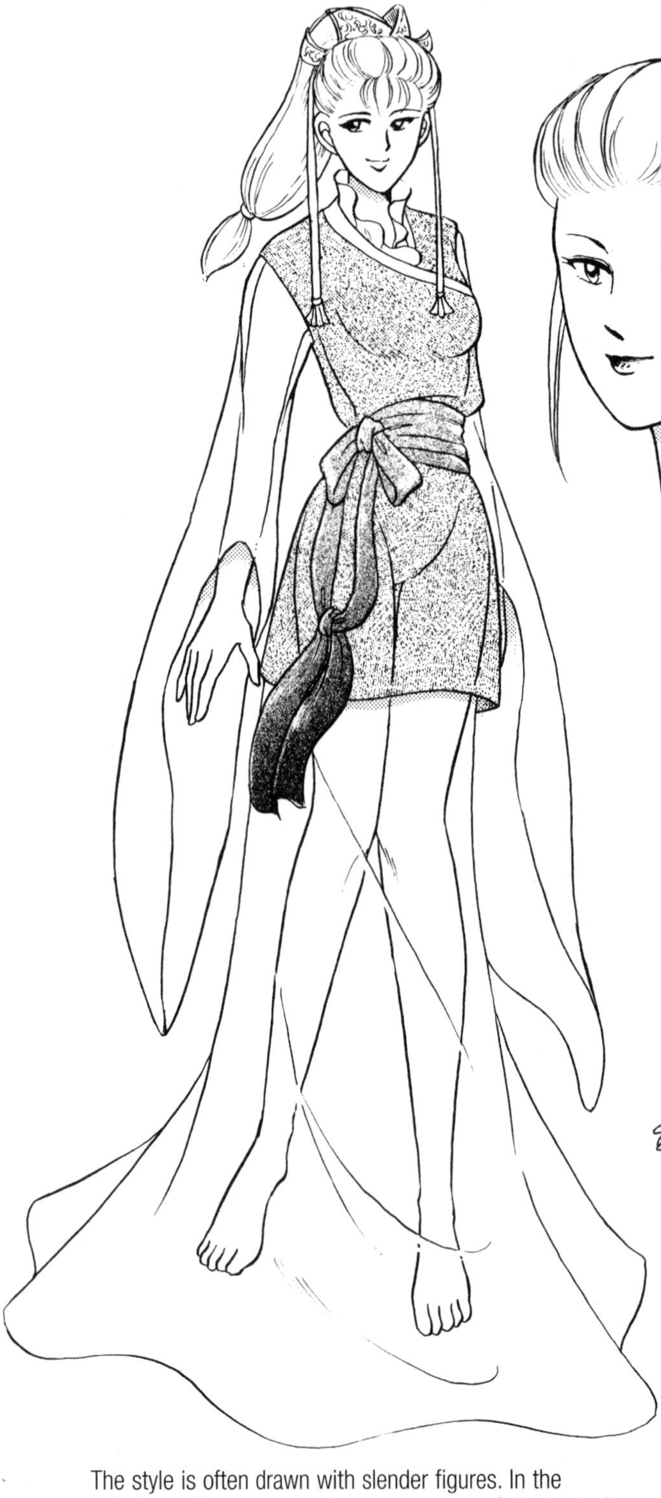

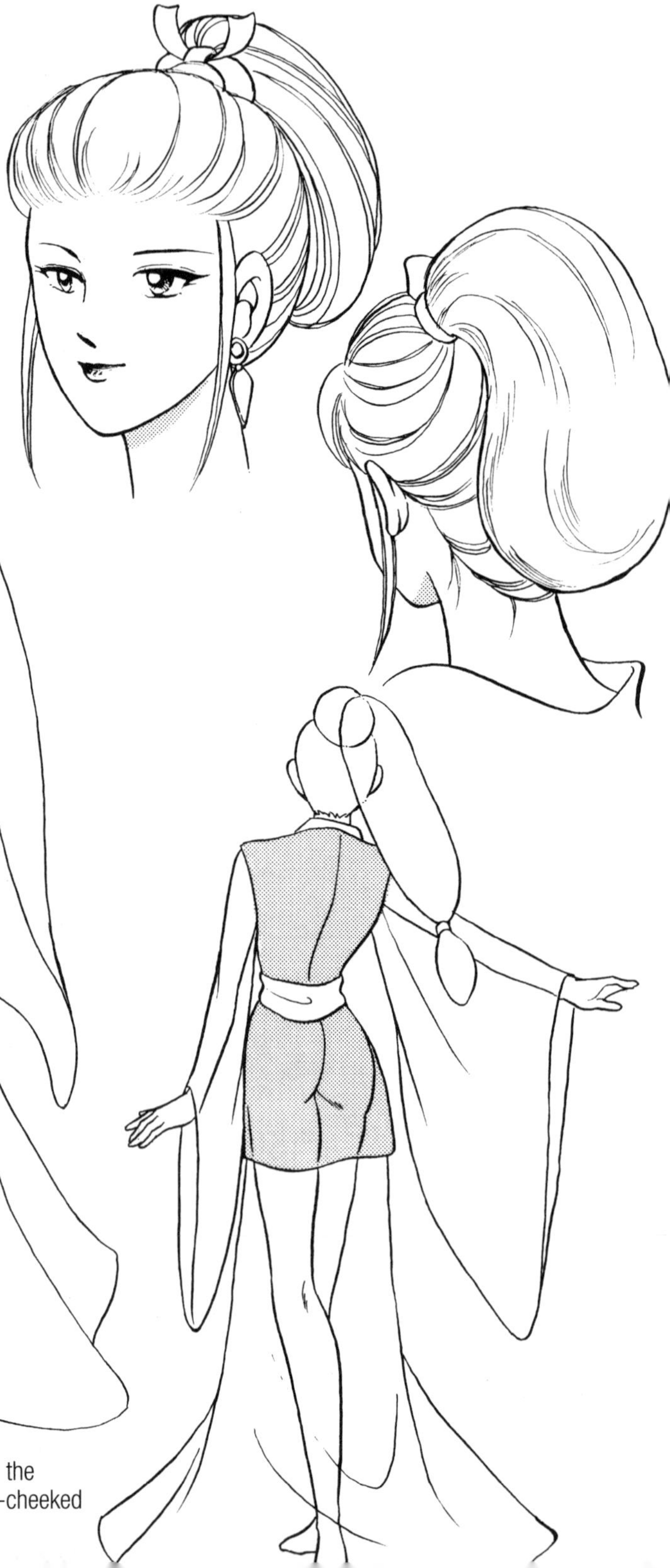

The style is often drawn with slender figures. In the paintings of the time, the faces were drawn full-cheeked and were a bit larger in proportion to the body.

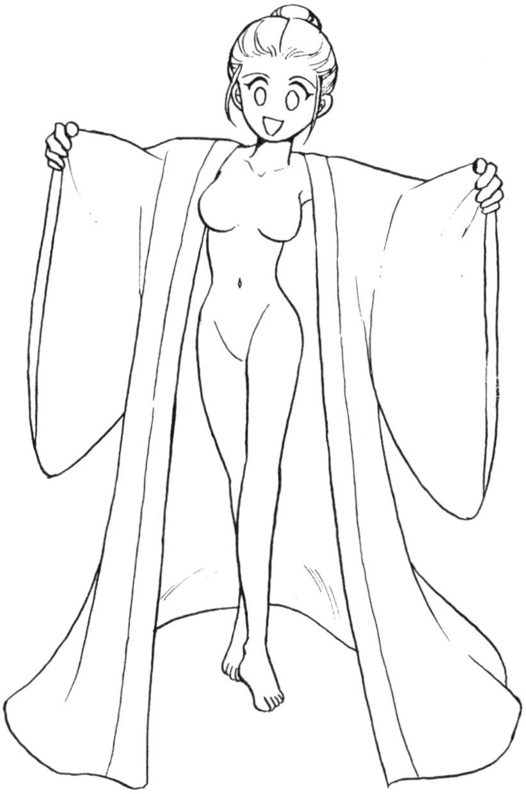

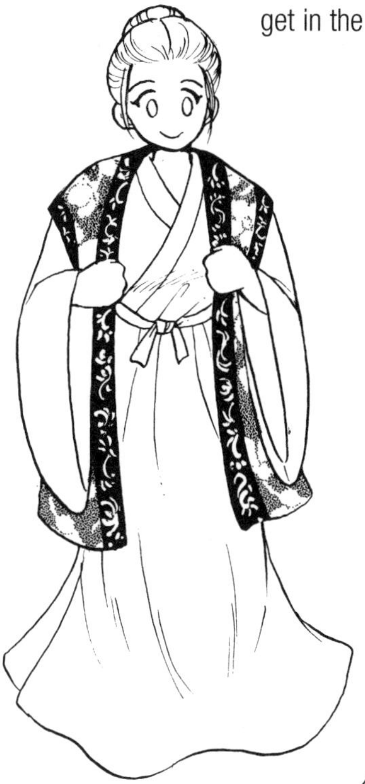

Tie the accessory belt since it tends to get in the way.

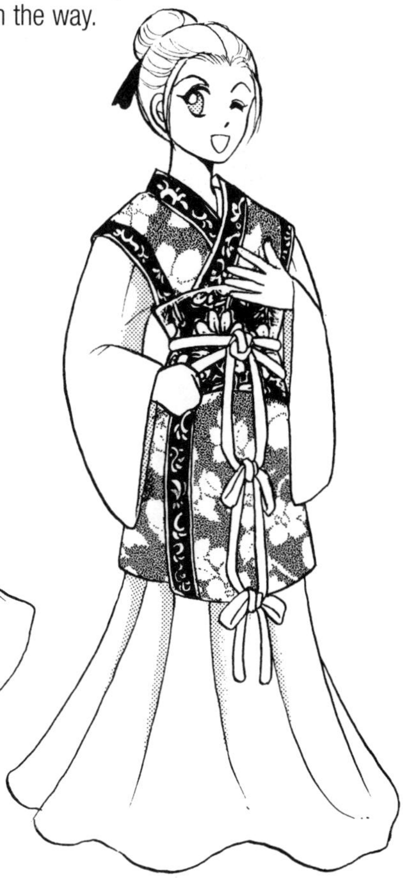

Make the colors in the lower garment light and the colors in the upper garment dark. Using patterns makes it look more authentic.

Male Attire

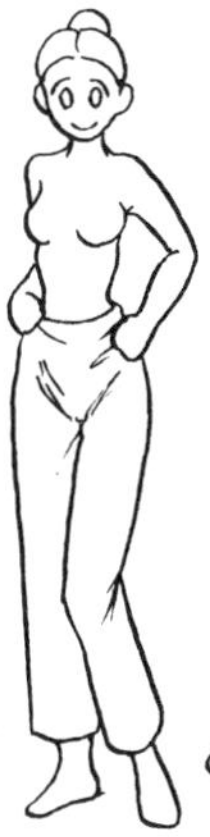

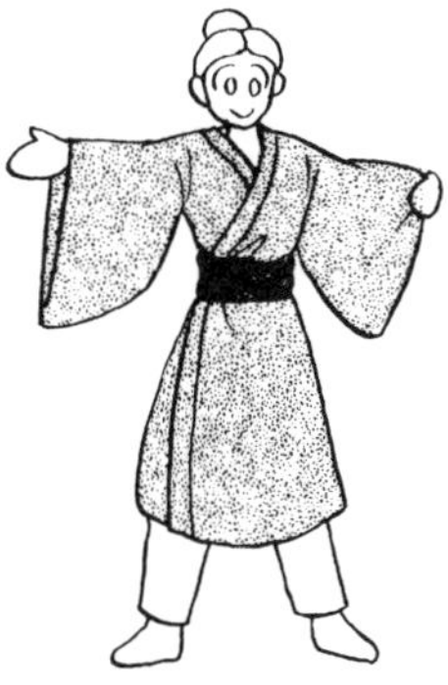

Add the jacket after putting on the undergarment for two-piece outfits.

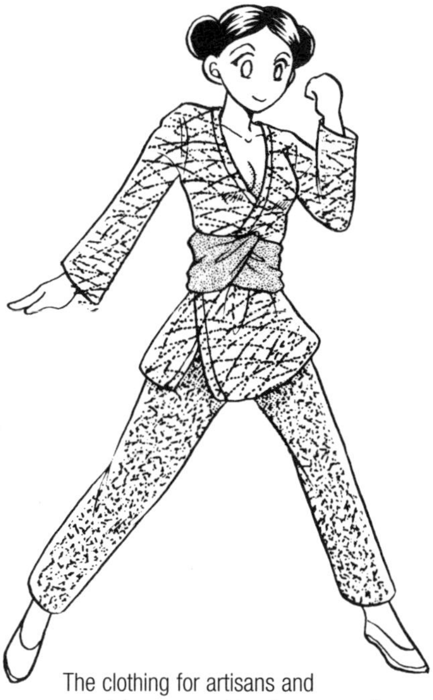

The clothing for artisans and entertainers resembles those worn for martial arts (i.e. Kempo).

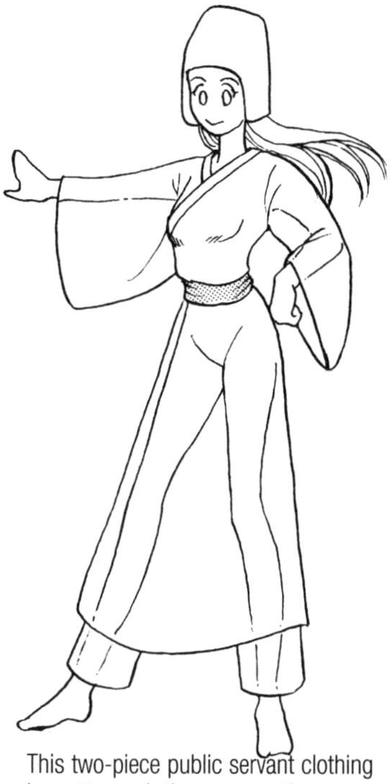

This two-piece public servant clothing is pretty much the same as those worn by men.

Heavenly Maidens, Unworldly Women and Flying Women

While the detailed differences and explanations vary from person to person, the key is to draw characters with a freely floating presence released from the curse of gravity.

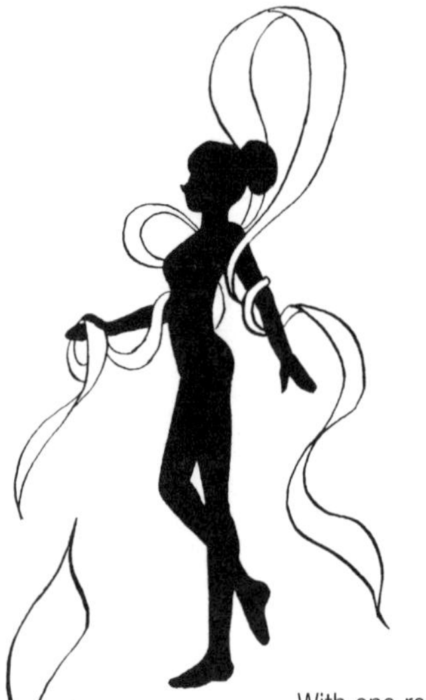

With one roll of cloth

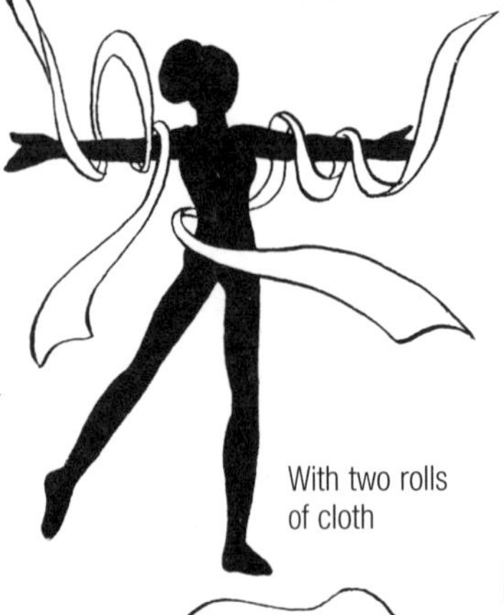

With two rolls of cloth

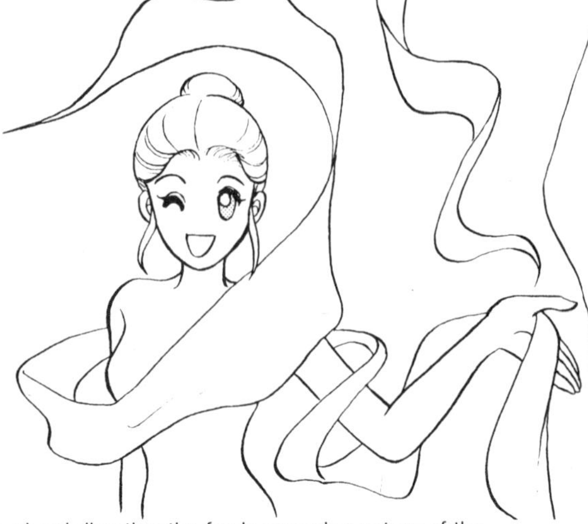

While visual directing the freely wrapping nature of the celestial raiment is important, the key is to express the change in the width of the cloth from the narrow parts to the wide areas.

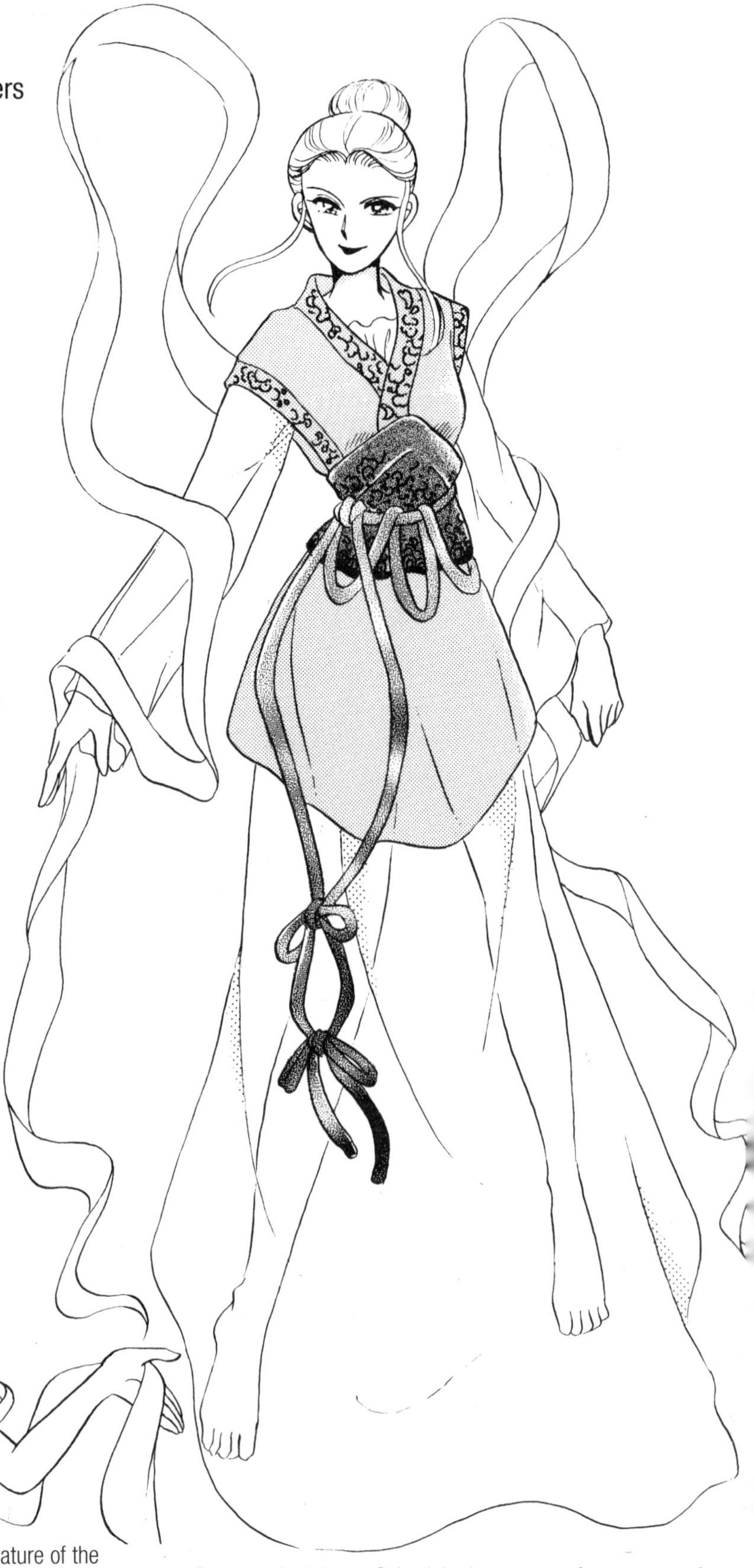

Since ancient times, Celestial raiments are often expressed with detailed, long cloths.

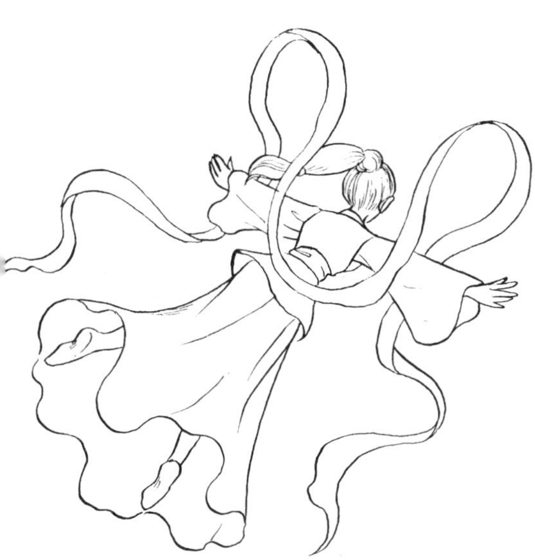

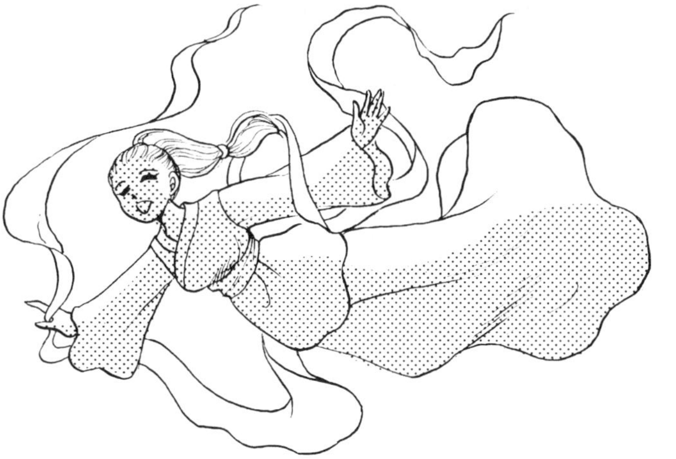

Visual Direction for Landing

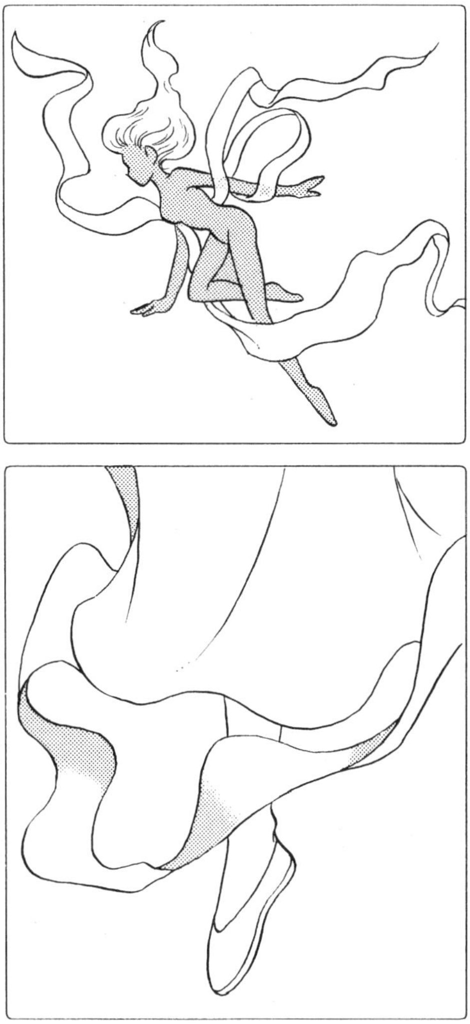

Drawing patterns along the collar instead of attaching tones distinguishes it from traditional Japanese clothing.

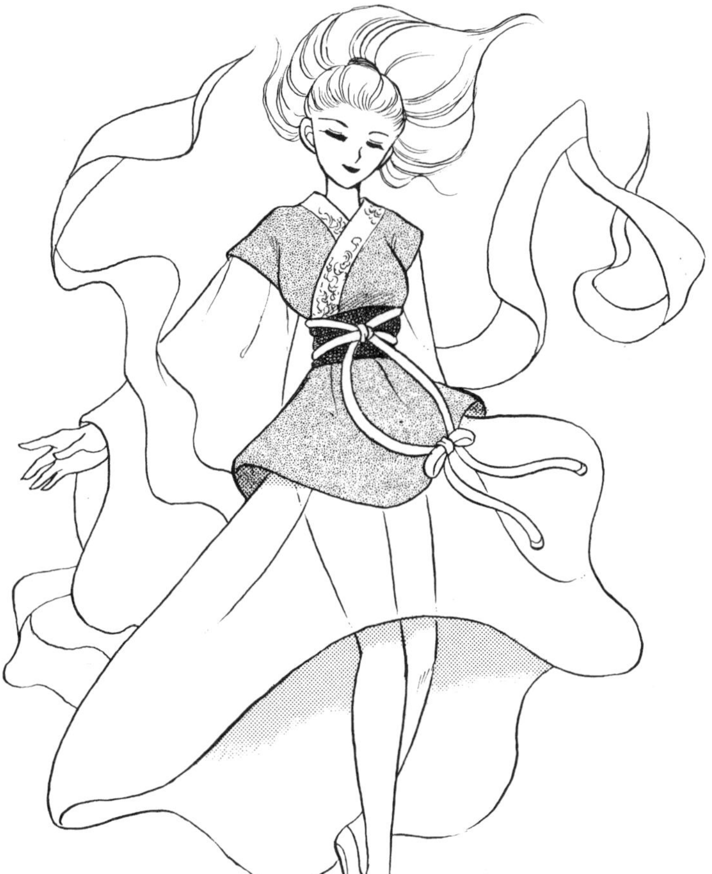

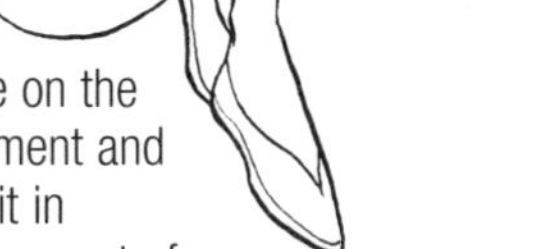

The motion comes to life on the page by making the garment and the hem fly as you see fit in accordance with the movement of the body.

Note the fluffy visual direction of the hem. The expression in the visual direction changes depending on whether the celestial raiment is controlling gravity or simply reflecting the heart of gravity itself.

Ancient Egyptian Bishoujo

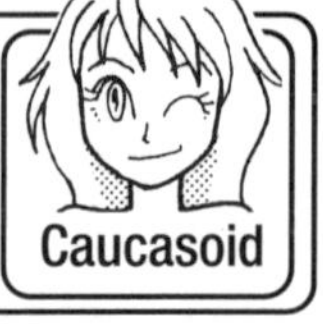

The contrast between the red-brown skin color and the white garment was said to be the aesthetics of the time. Three dynasties over 3,000 years gave birth to a variety of fashions.

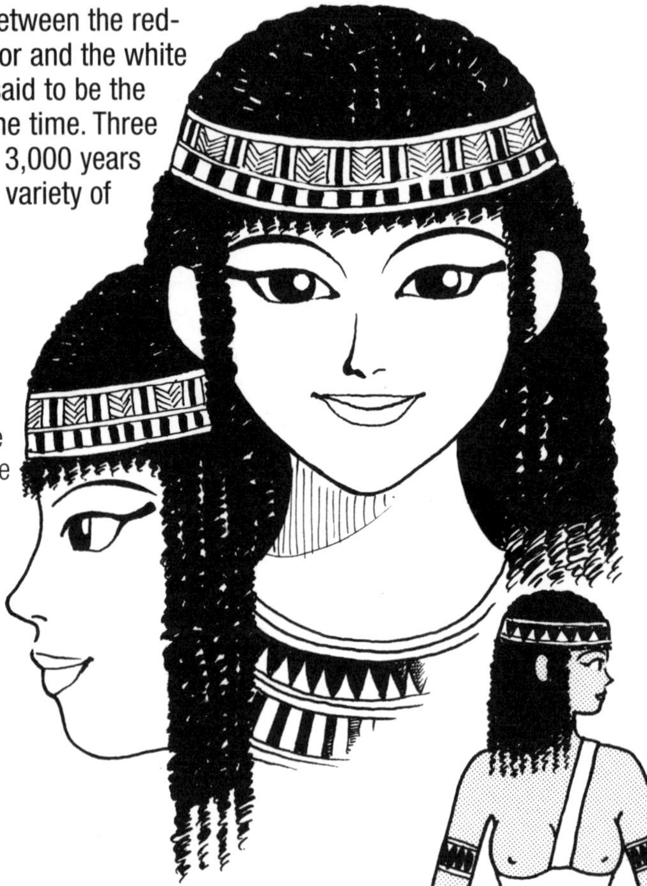

Egyptian Makeup
Extending the corner of the eye into one thick line brings the effect to life.

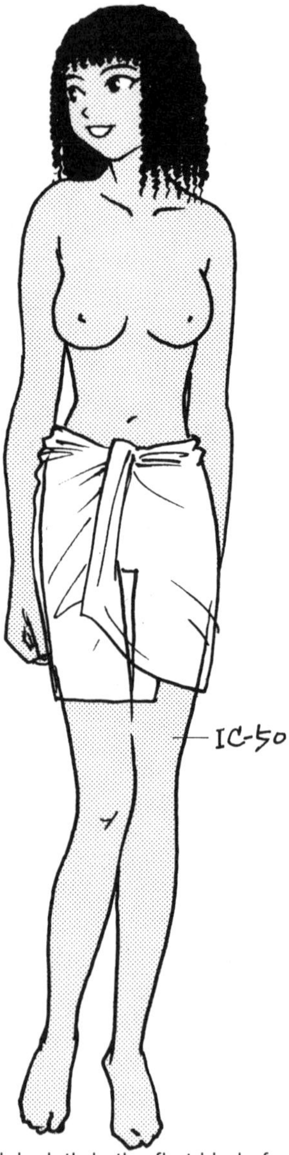

The loincloth is the first kind of fashion from the earliest time period. Both common men and women throughout the ages wore this style.

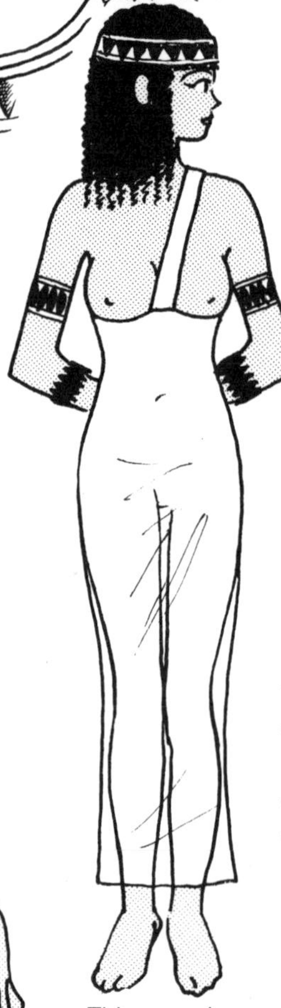

This one-piece outfit worn by servants comes with one or two straps.

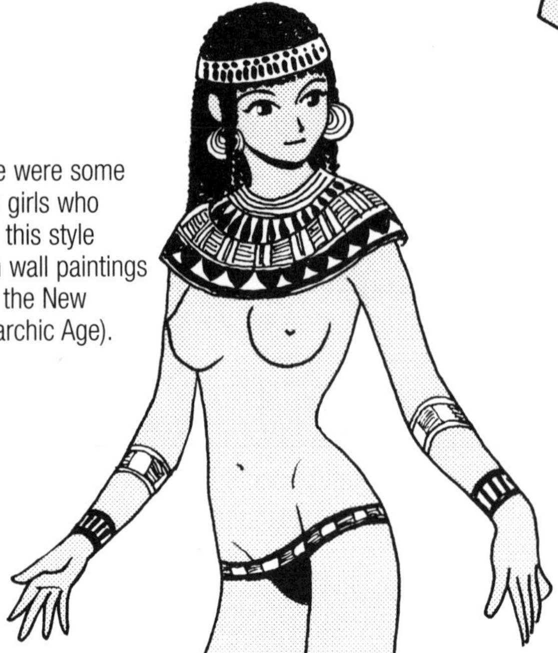

There were some slave girls who wore this style (from wall paintings from the New Monarchic Age).

Tunic One-Pieces

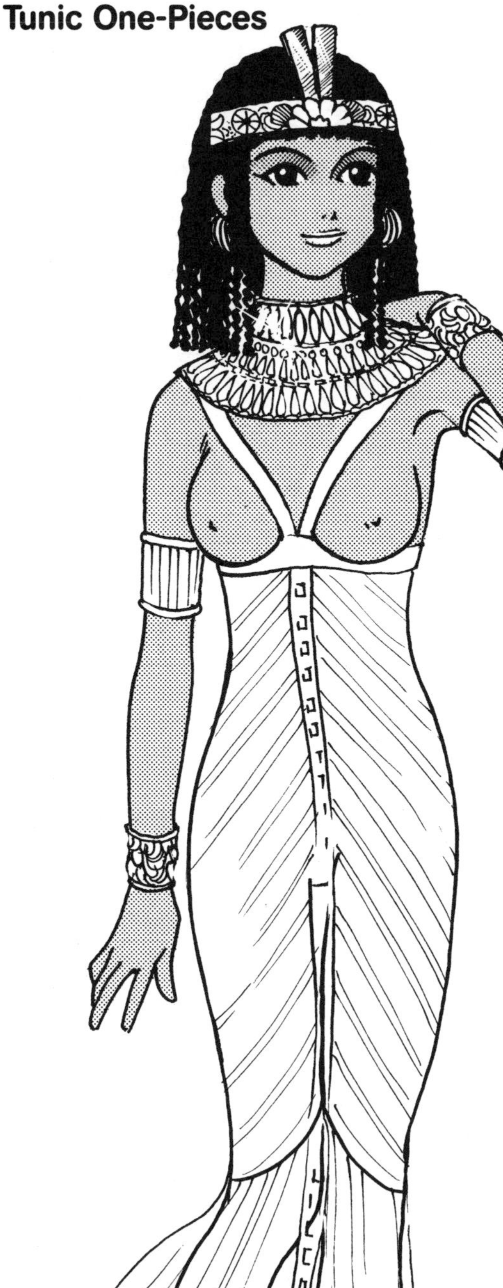

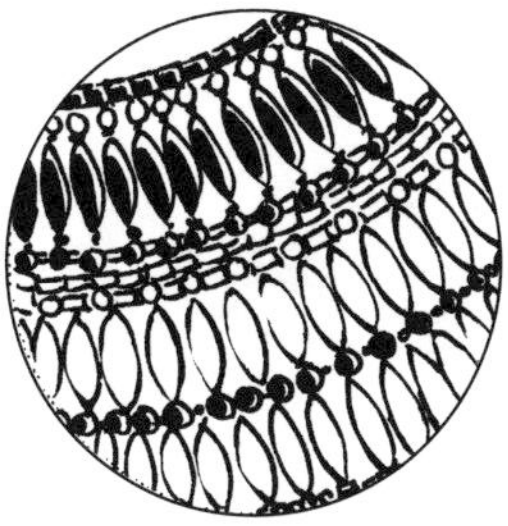

The ornamented collar is woven with jewels and beads.

Male Attire - Warrior Style

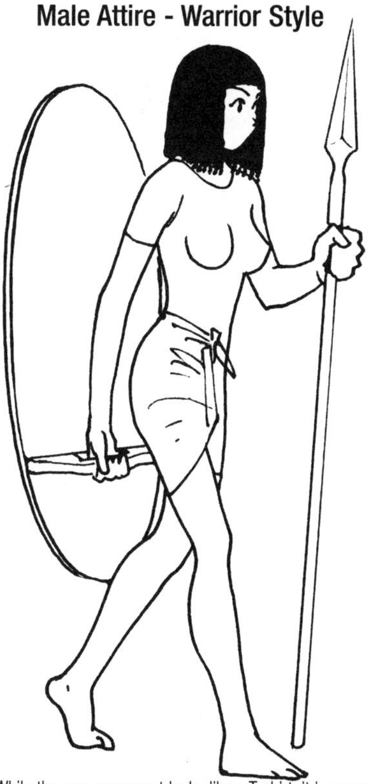

While the upper garment looks like a T-shirt, it is a poncho style robe. The bottom garment is a waist wrap.

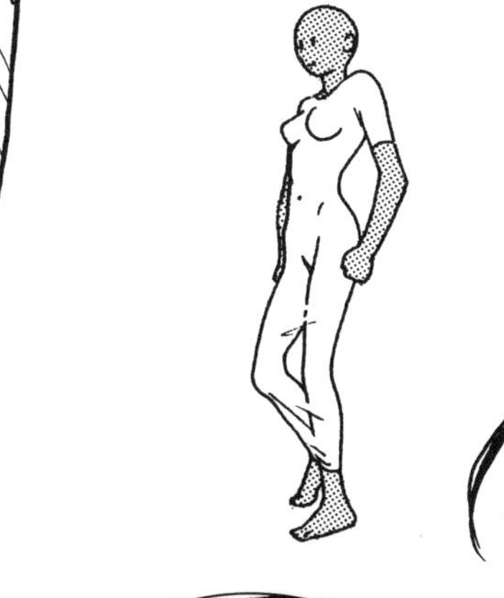

This is completely see-through one-piece made from thin hemp (New Monarchic Age).

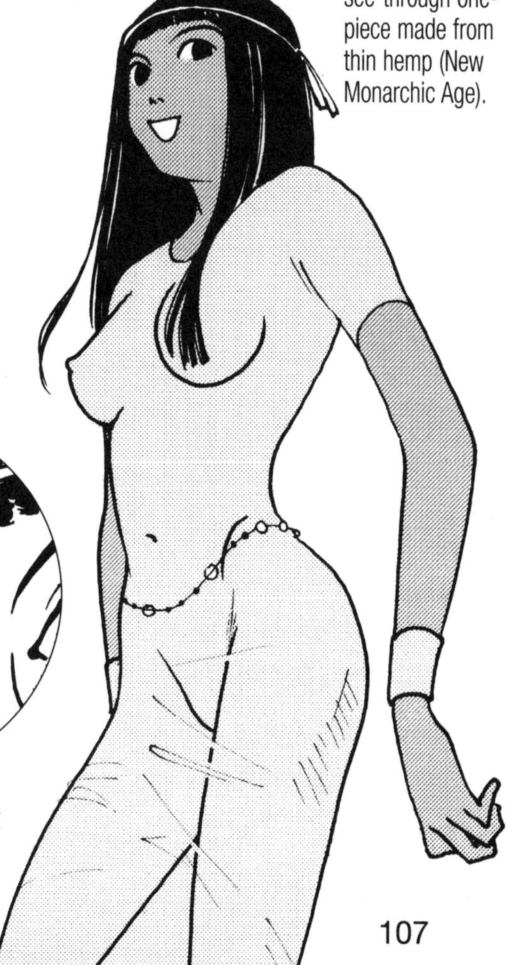

For the most part, the key trait is the hair being visible below the hairband.

Waist Wraps and Robes

Since there are no records on how the clothing was worn at the time, you have to use your imagination. It is believed that most girls of prominence were dressed by their slaves.

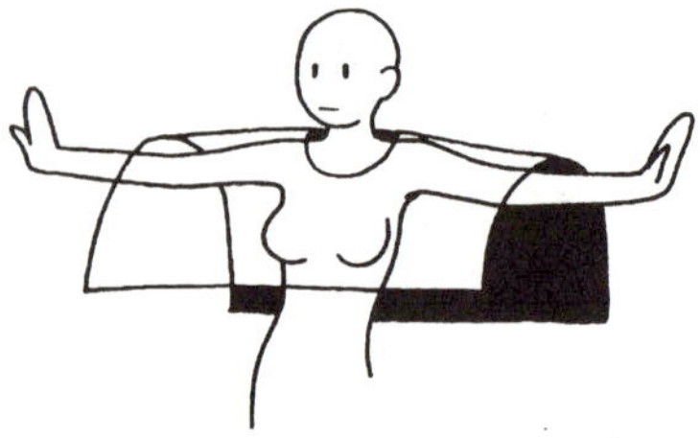

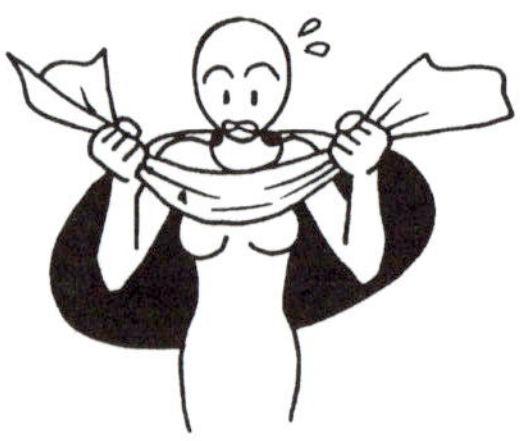

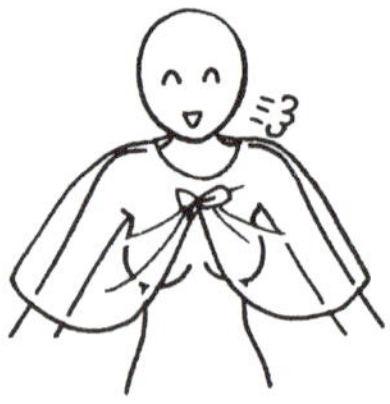

It was probably tied between the breasts.

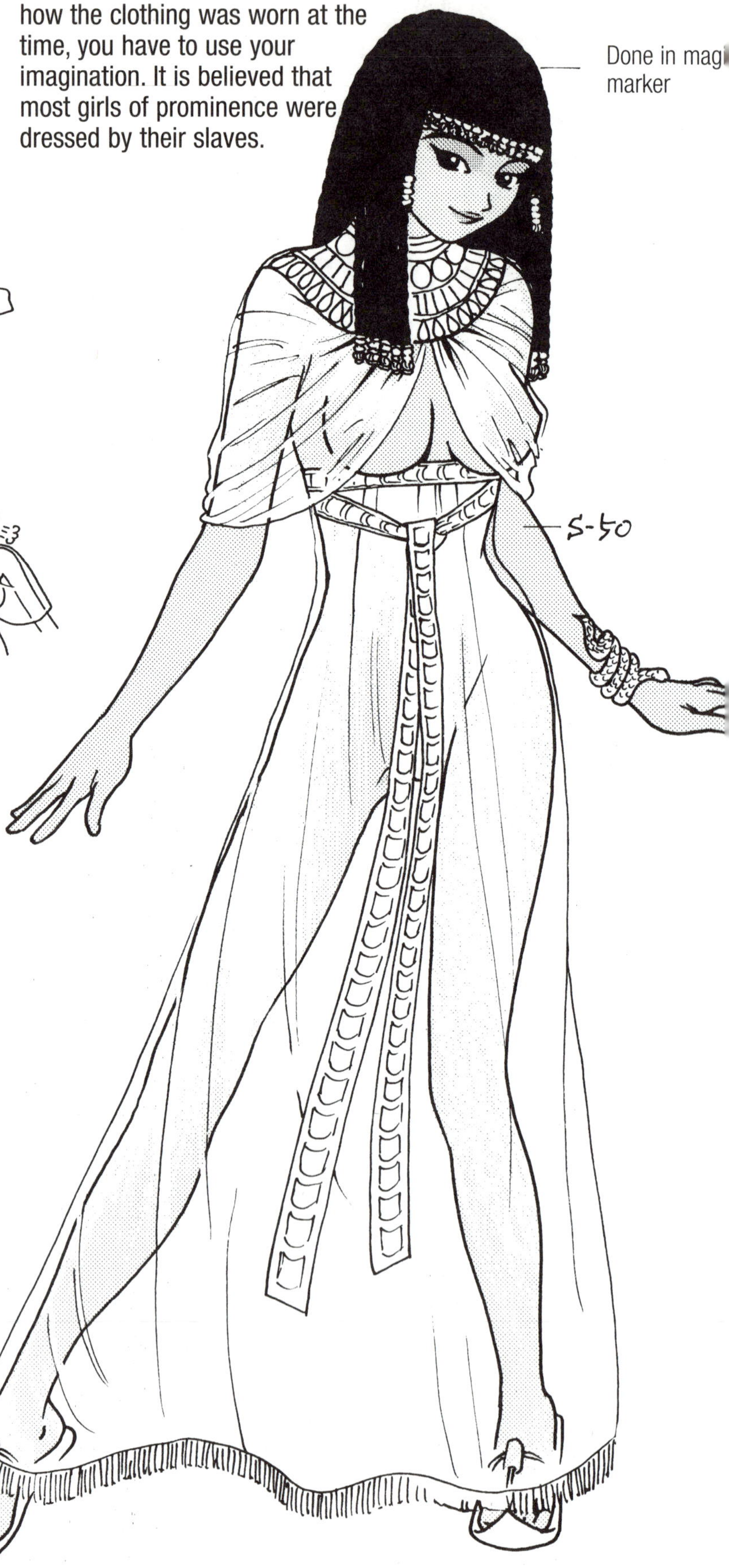

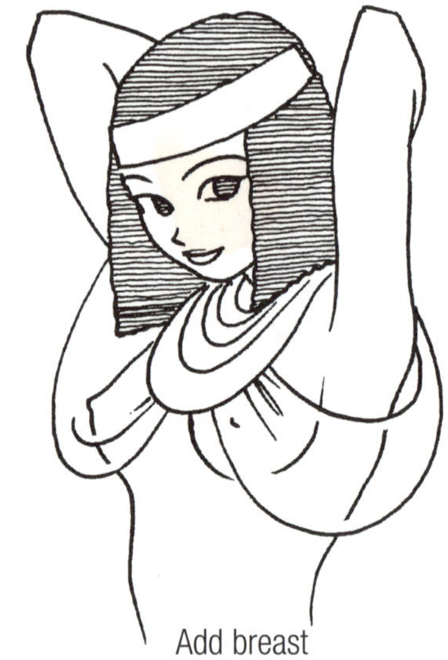

Add breast ornamentation.

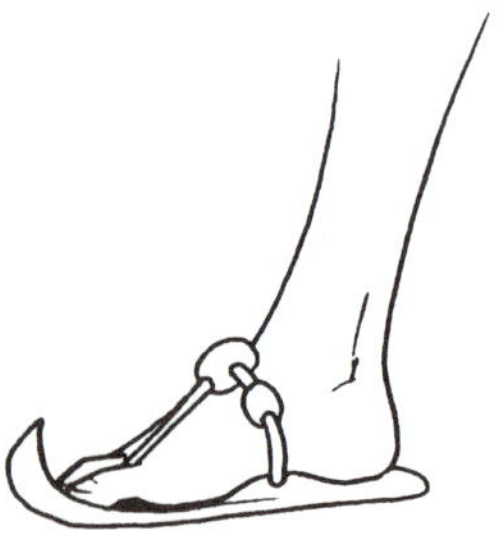

The tips of the shoes were curved up.

Male Attire

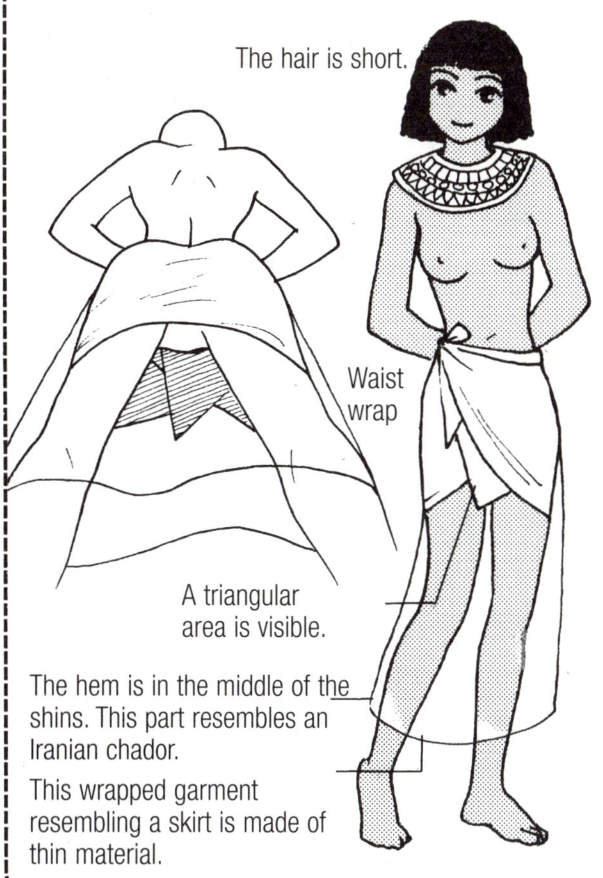

Variations

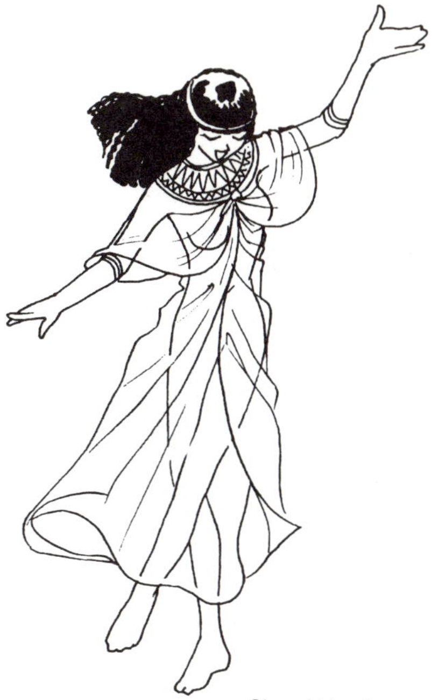

Shawl Version

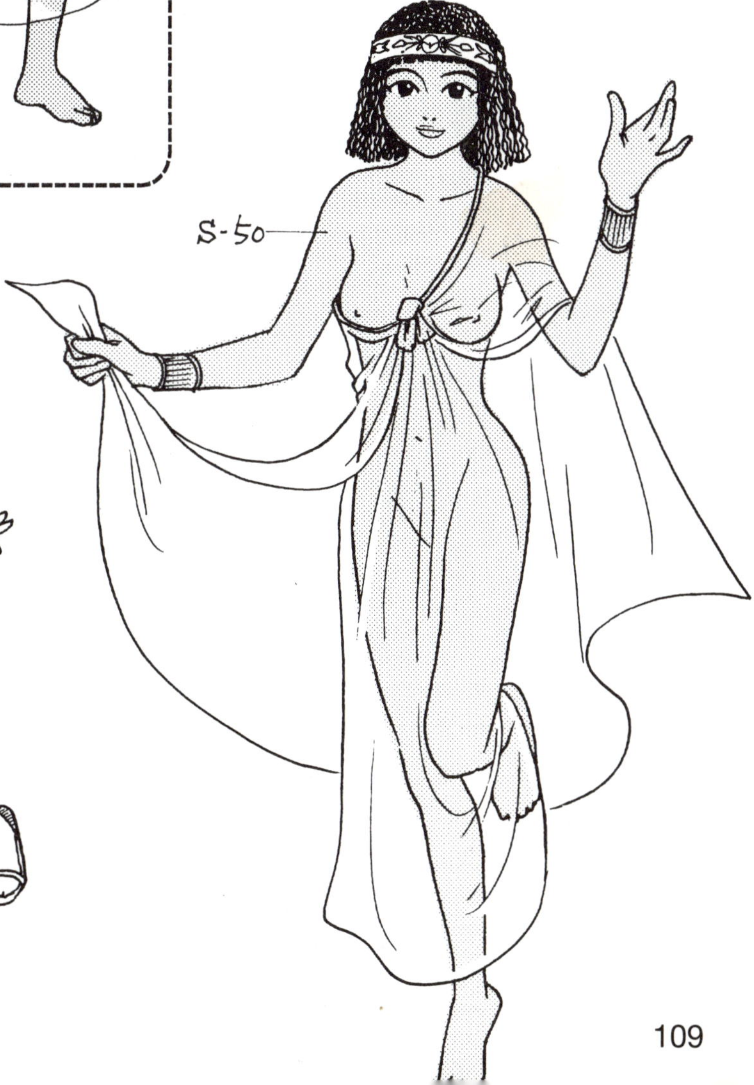

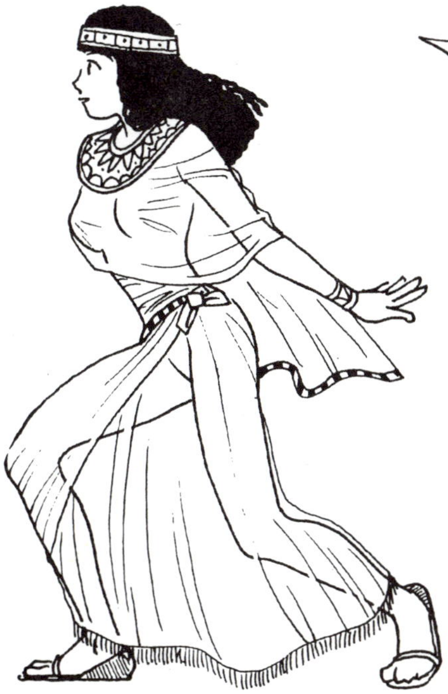

There was also a garment resembling an Indian sari (New Monarchic Age).

Ancient Japanese Bishoujo

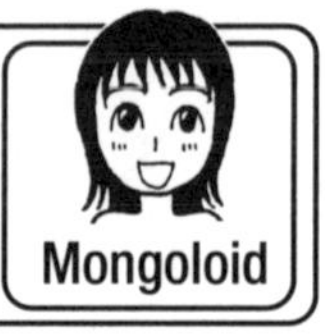

It is said that neighboring China and Korea probably influenced ancient Japanese fashion. The following are models of general style primarily derived from conjecture following a careful study of ancient ruins.

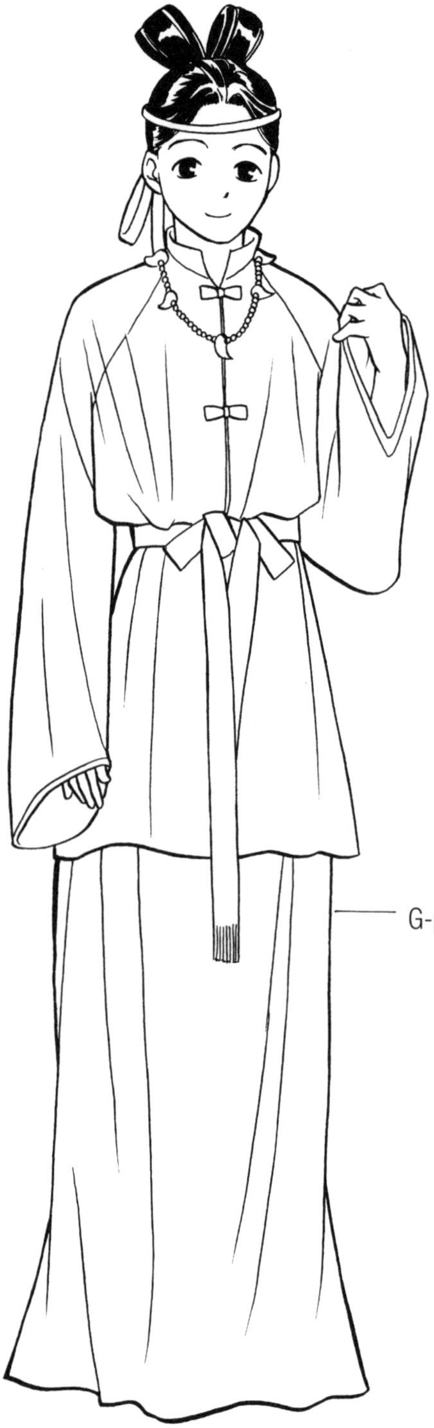

The 'kinumo' (silk) fashion of ancient times.

Steps to Creating the Hairstyle

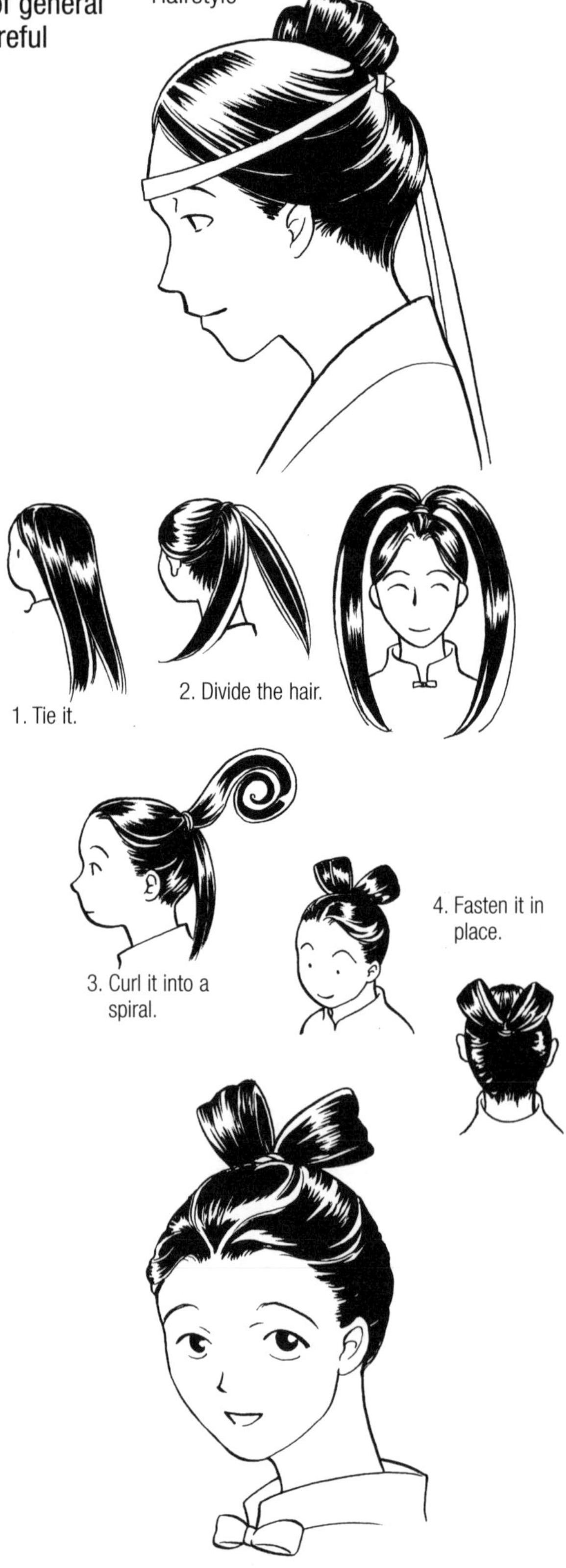

Male Attire

From conjecture based upon clay images and flat bell-like utensils, male fashion known as 'kinubakama' looked like the following. The garment being tied around the elbows and knees are the key trait.

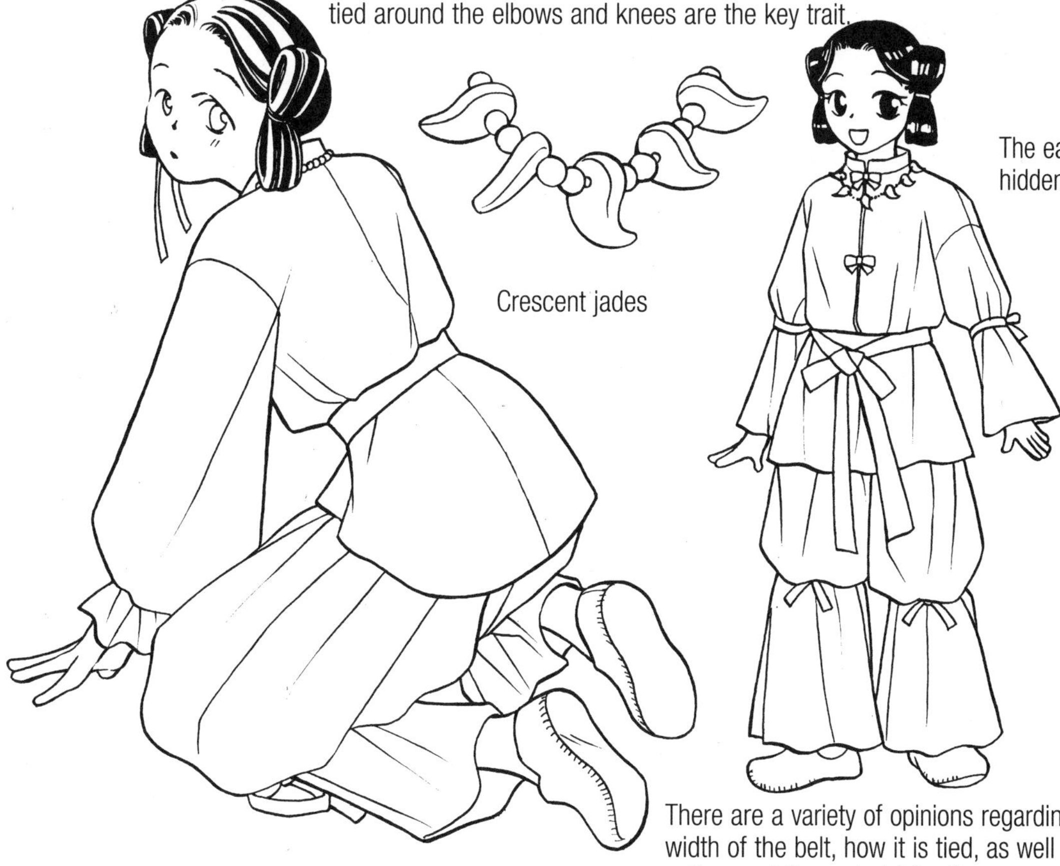

There are a variety of opinions regarding the width of the belt, how it is tied, as well as the softness of the material itself.

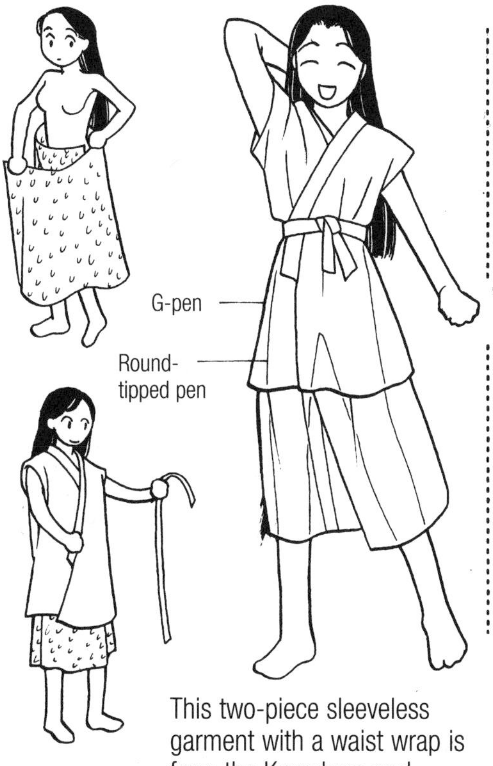

This two-piece sleeveless garment with a waist wrap is from the Kamakura and Muromachi Eras.

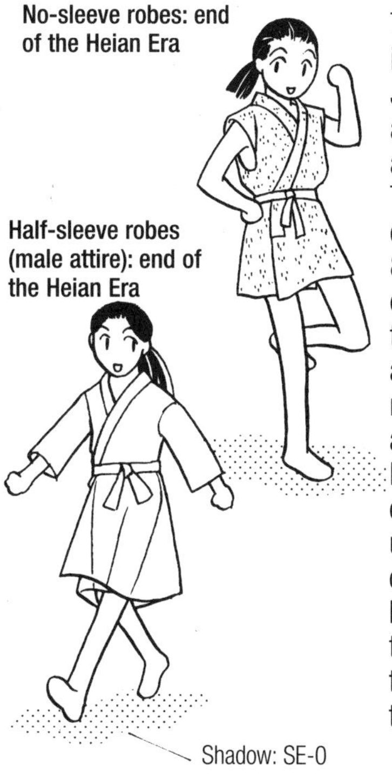

There is a wealth of information regarding Japanese fashion for aristocrats of the Nara and Heian periods. The first glimpse of commoners was in the 8th and 9th centuries of the Heian Era with the "no-sleeve" robe and the "half-sleeve" robe. The waist wraps are from the Muromachi Era (13th century). This style was upheld until the 18th century and the Edo Period. It is possible that commoners wore this style since ancient times.

Prehistoric Bishoujo

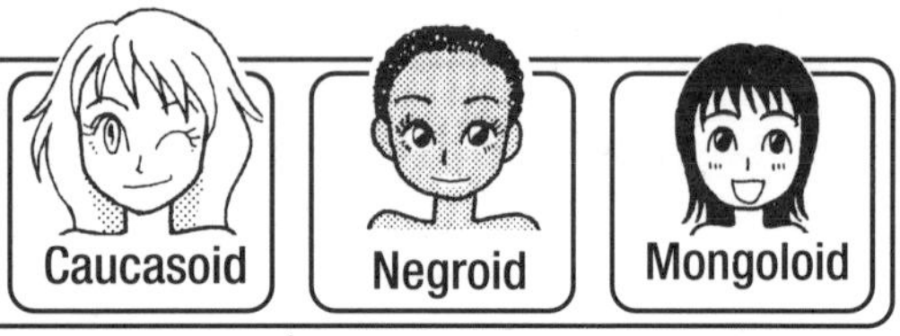

Based on the assumption that only plant and animal life existed at this time, we turn to the study of the expression of natural items.

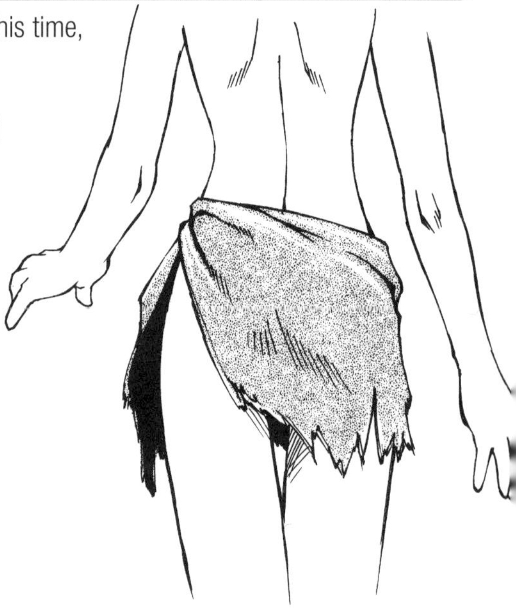

Mountain, Forest and Plain Environments (Warm Climates)

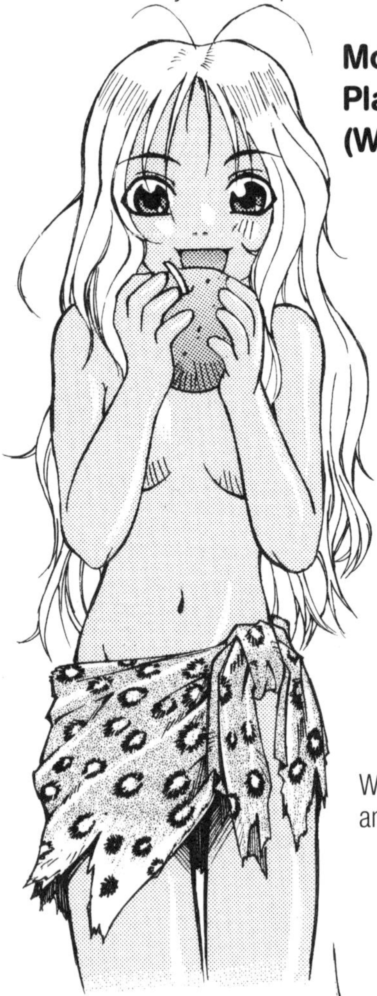

Wrapped item made of animal fur

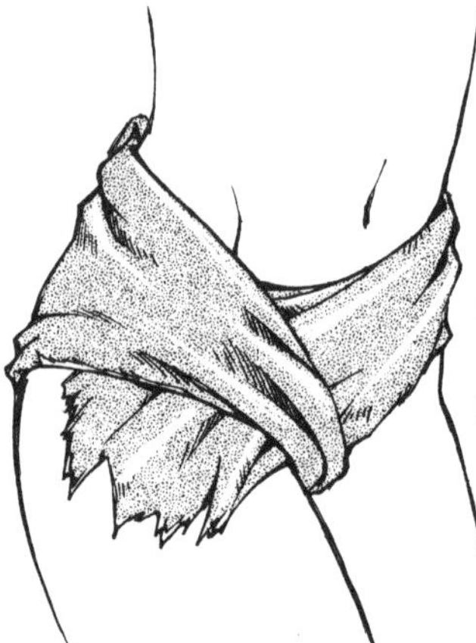

Loincloth made from animal skin

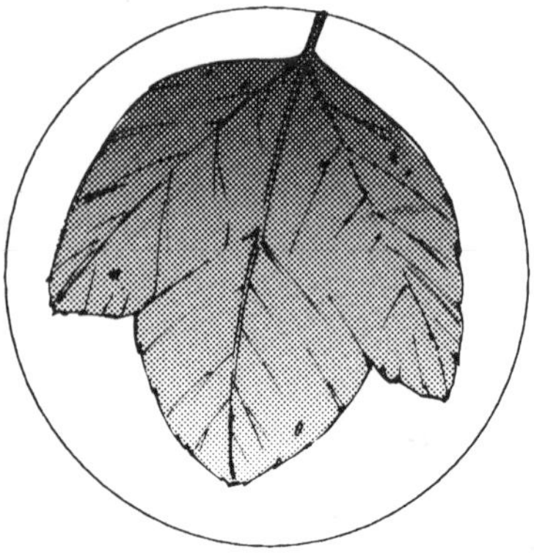

Fig tree leaf

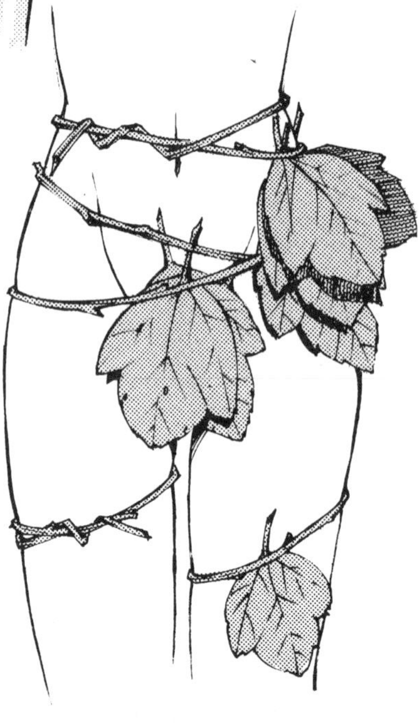

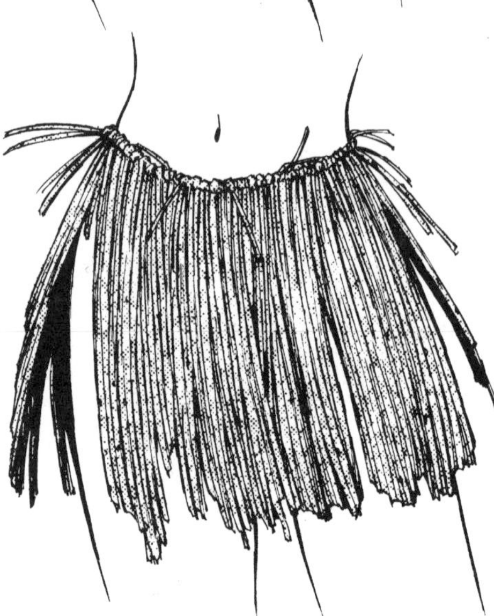

Waist wrap made of vines

Mountain, Forest and Plain Environments (Cold Climates)

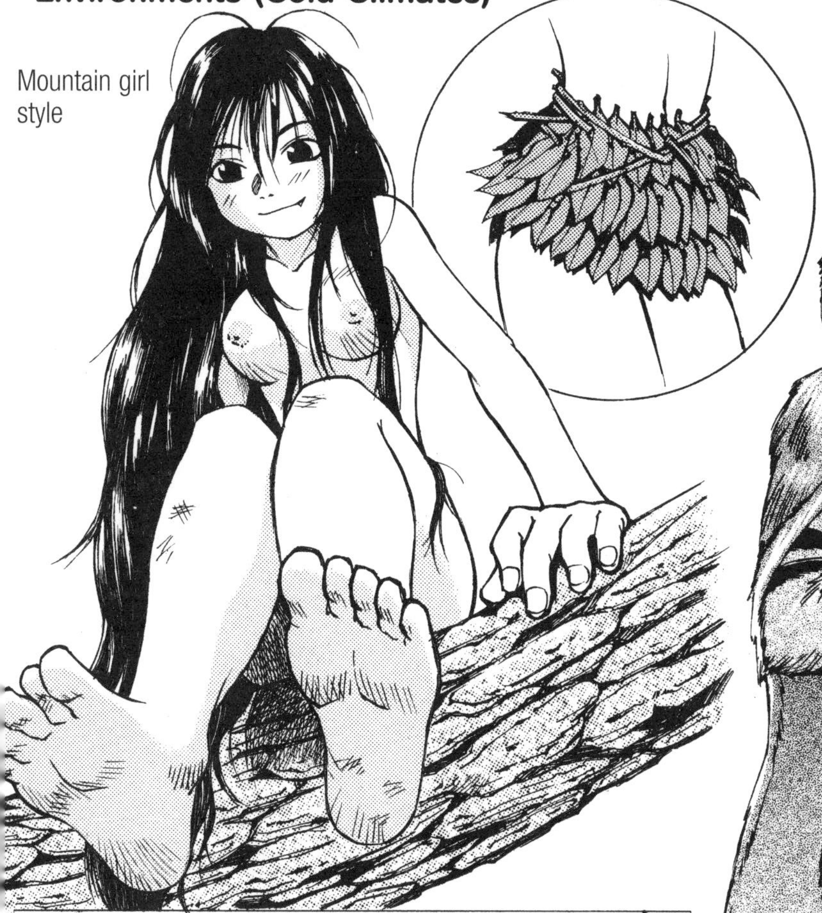

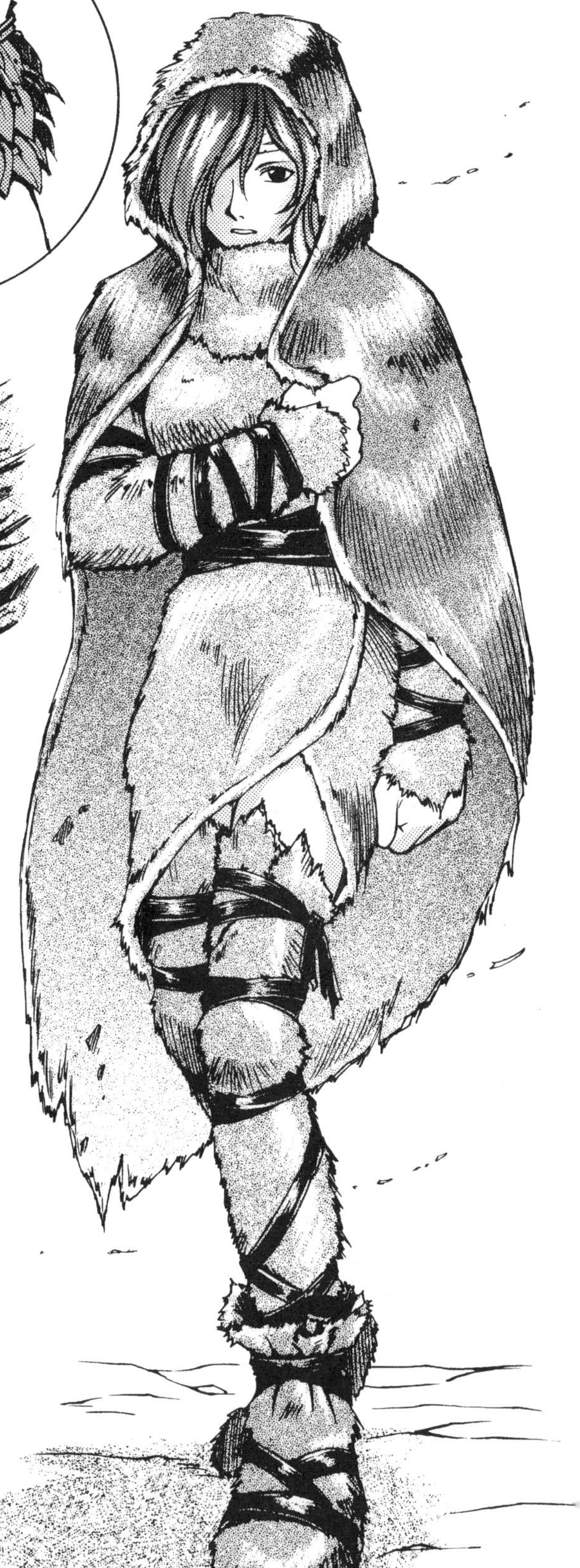

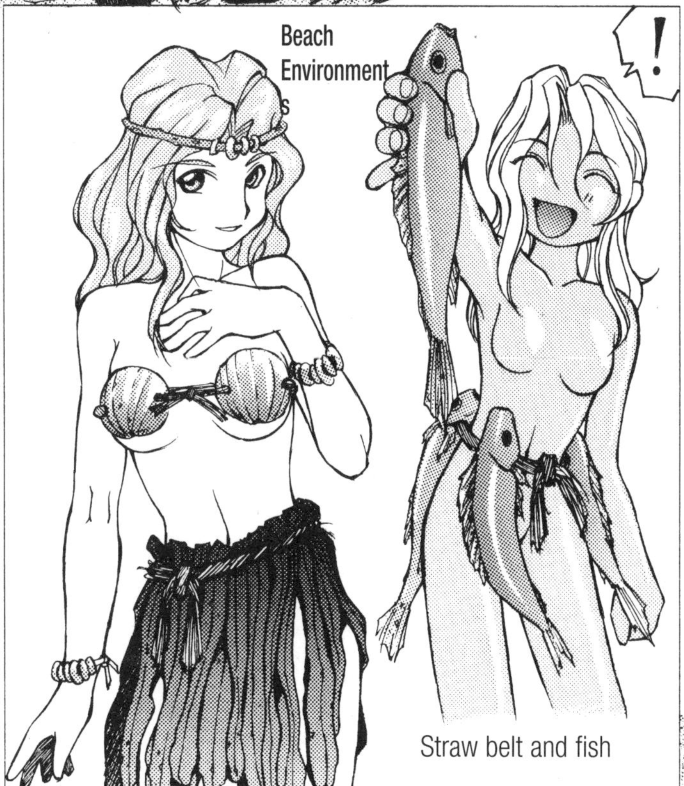

Bishoujo from the World Music Scenes
Rocker, Heavy Metal, and Punk

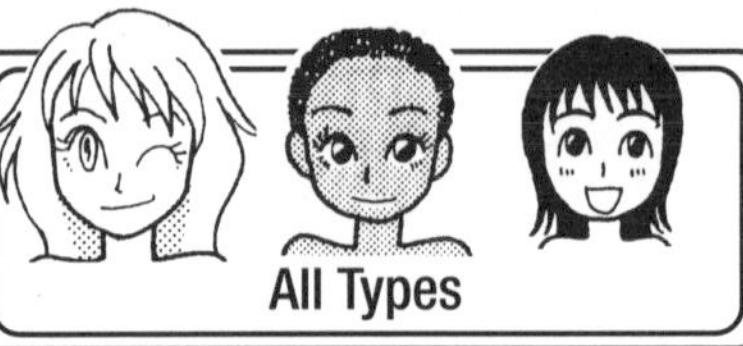

All Types

It is said the sports and music transcend national borders. Despite personal variations, there nevertheless is a distinct style in their attire.

Rocker Bishoujo

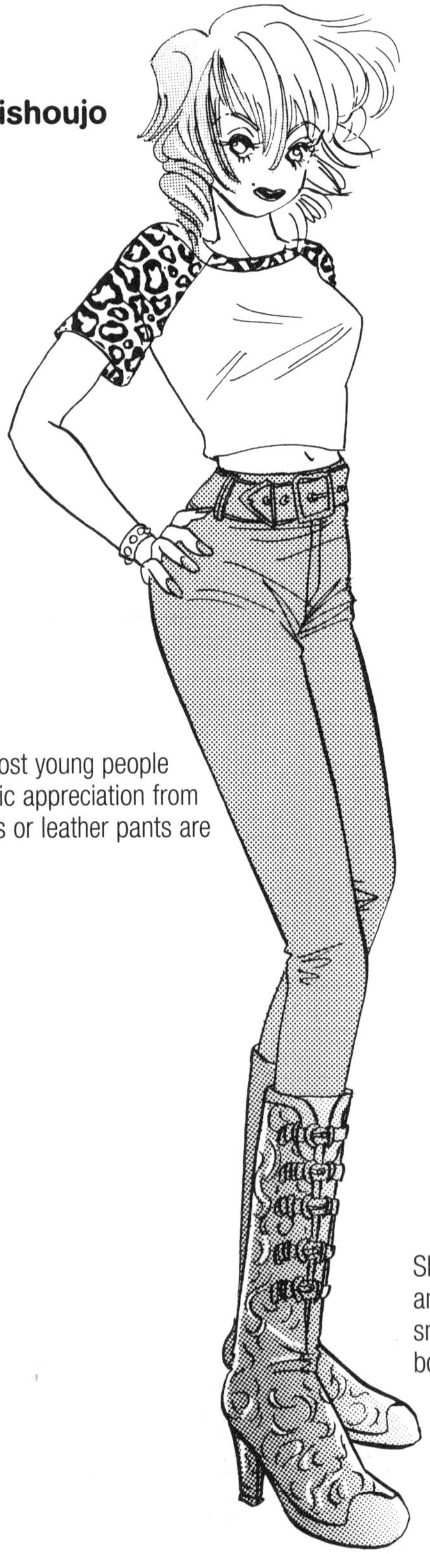

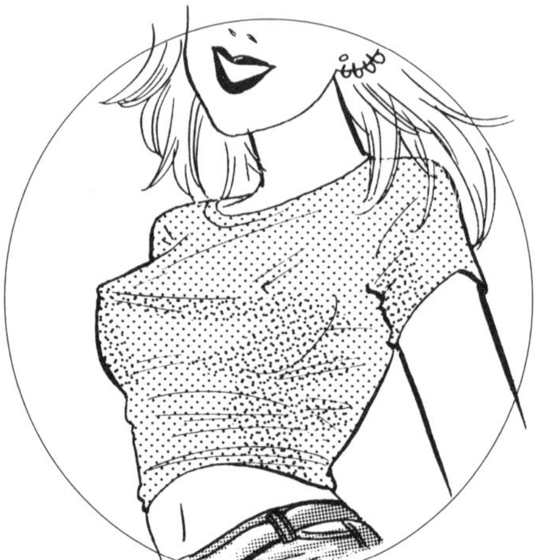

Tight T-shirts worn without bra.

A leather jacket is a standard item.

It is said that most young people begin their music appreciation from rock. Tight jeans or leather pants are often worn.

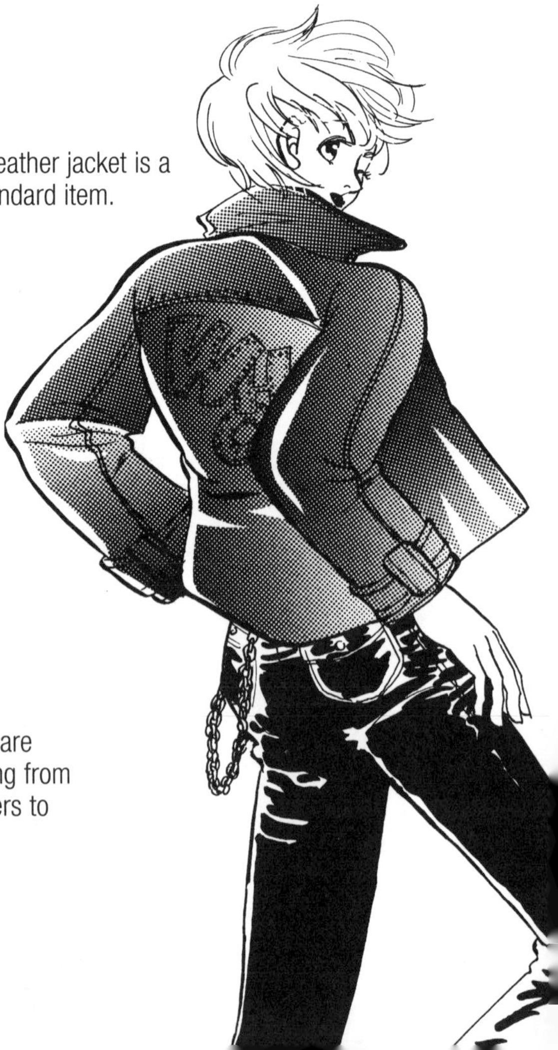

Shoes are anything from sneakers to boots.

Heavy Metal and Hard Rock Bishoujo

This leather jacket is an indispensable item for heavy metal fashion.

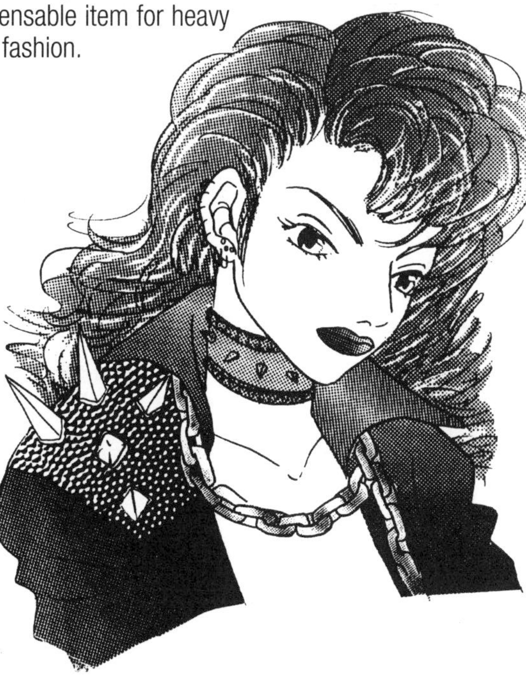

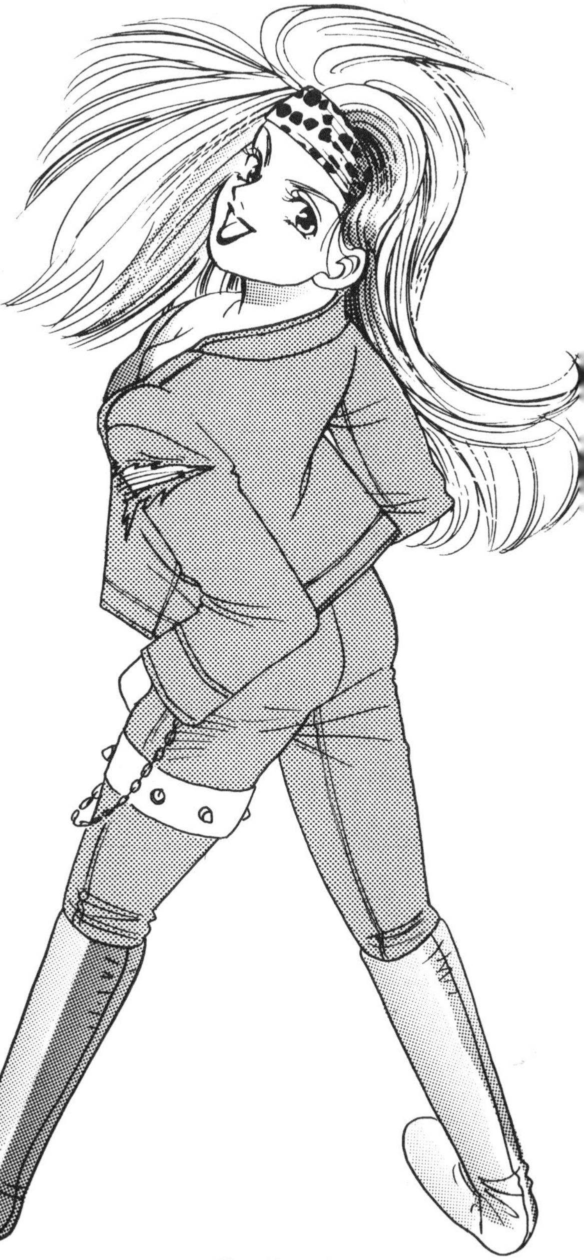

Small items like jutting studs, chains and skull badges lend an uncontrollable power to rock and often appear in the fashion.

Punk Bishoujo

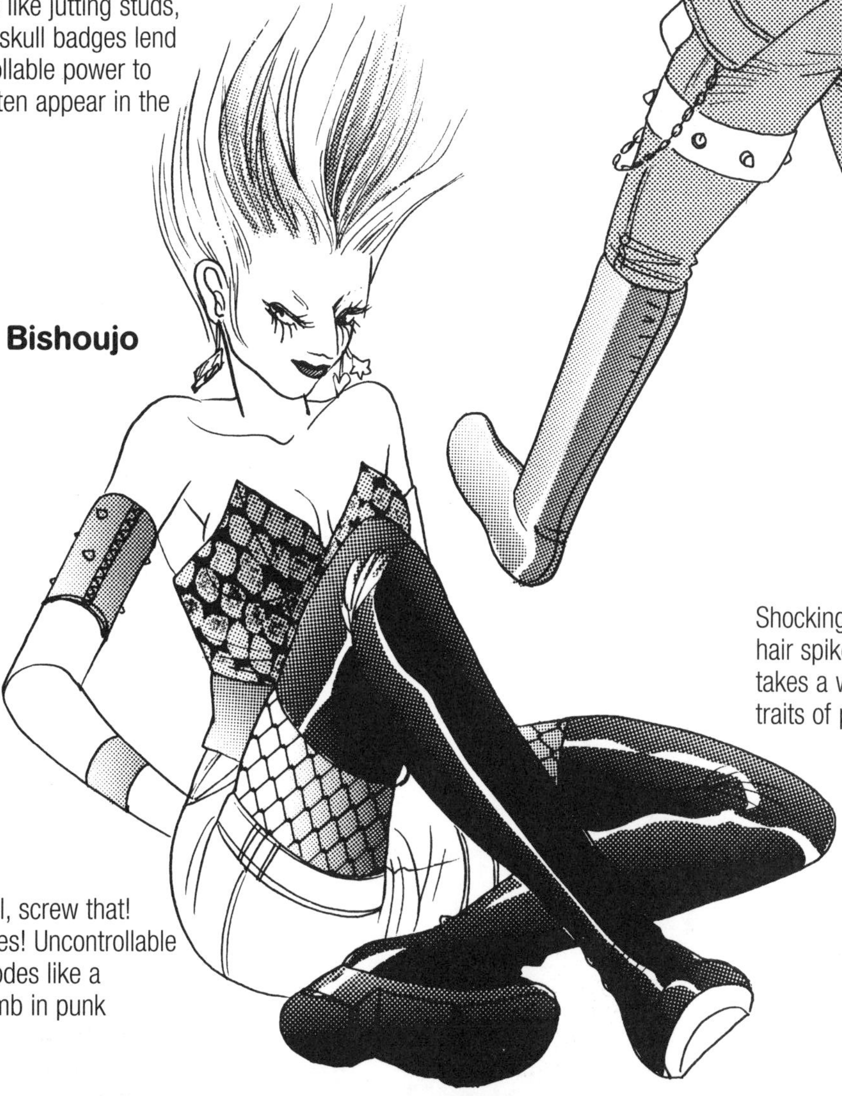

Shocking pink and blonde hair spiked with glycerin that takes a whole night to do are traits of punk bishoujo.

Heavy metal, screw that! Anarchy rules! Uncontrollable power explodes like a neutron bomb in punk fashion.

Running

The expression of costumes and characters goes beyond racial and national boundaries. Visually direct cuteness and fun with even the smallest, seemingly insignificant items.

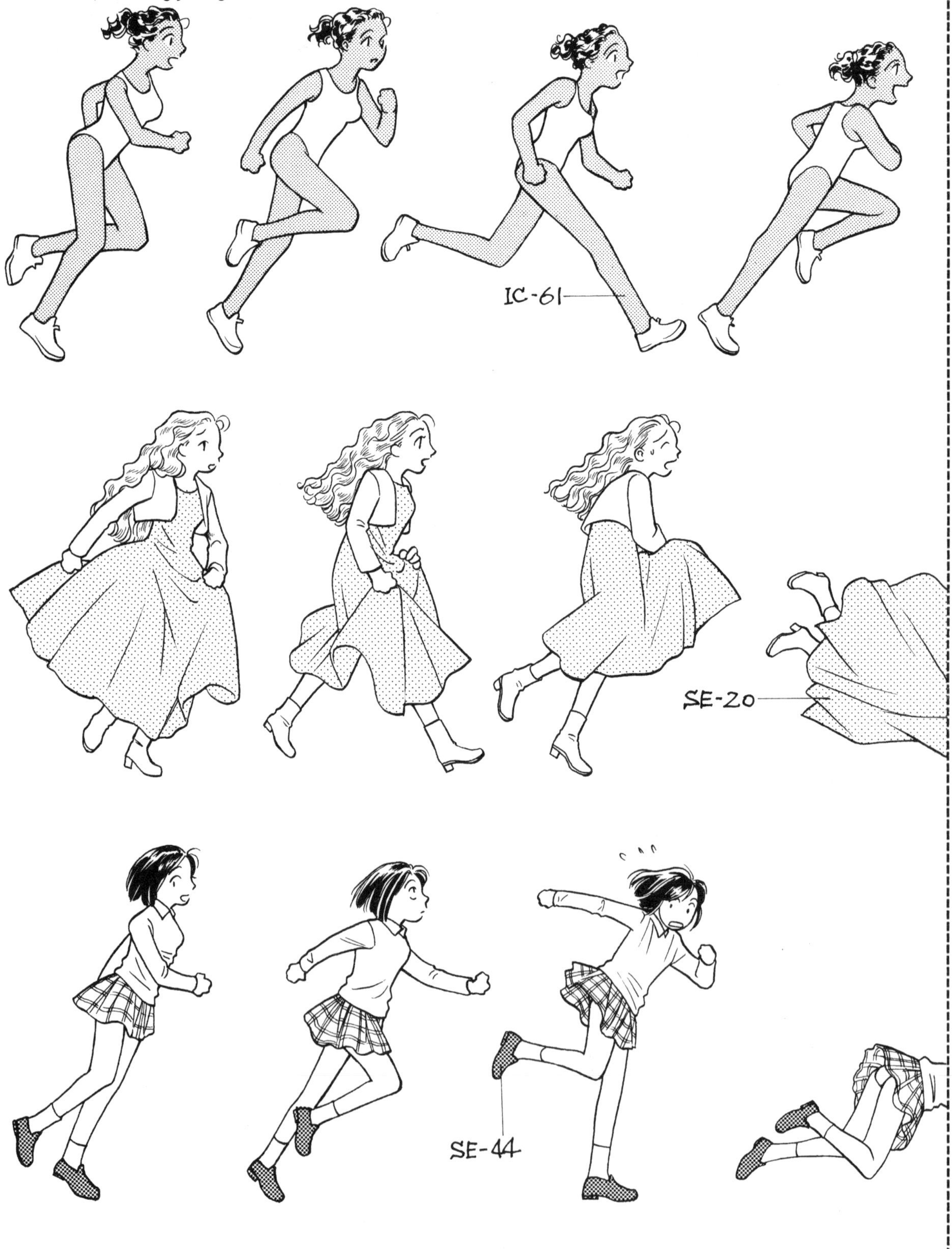

Chapter 4

Learn From the Masters
Manga Artist Case Study Techniques

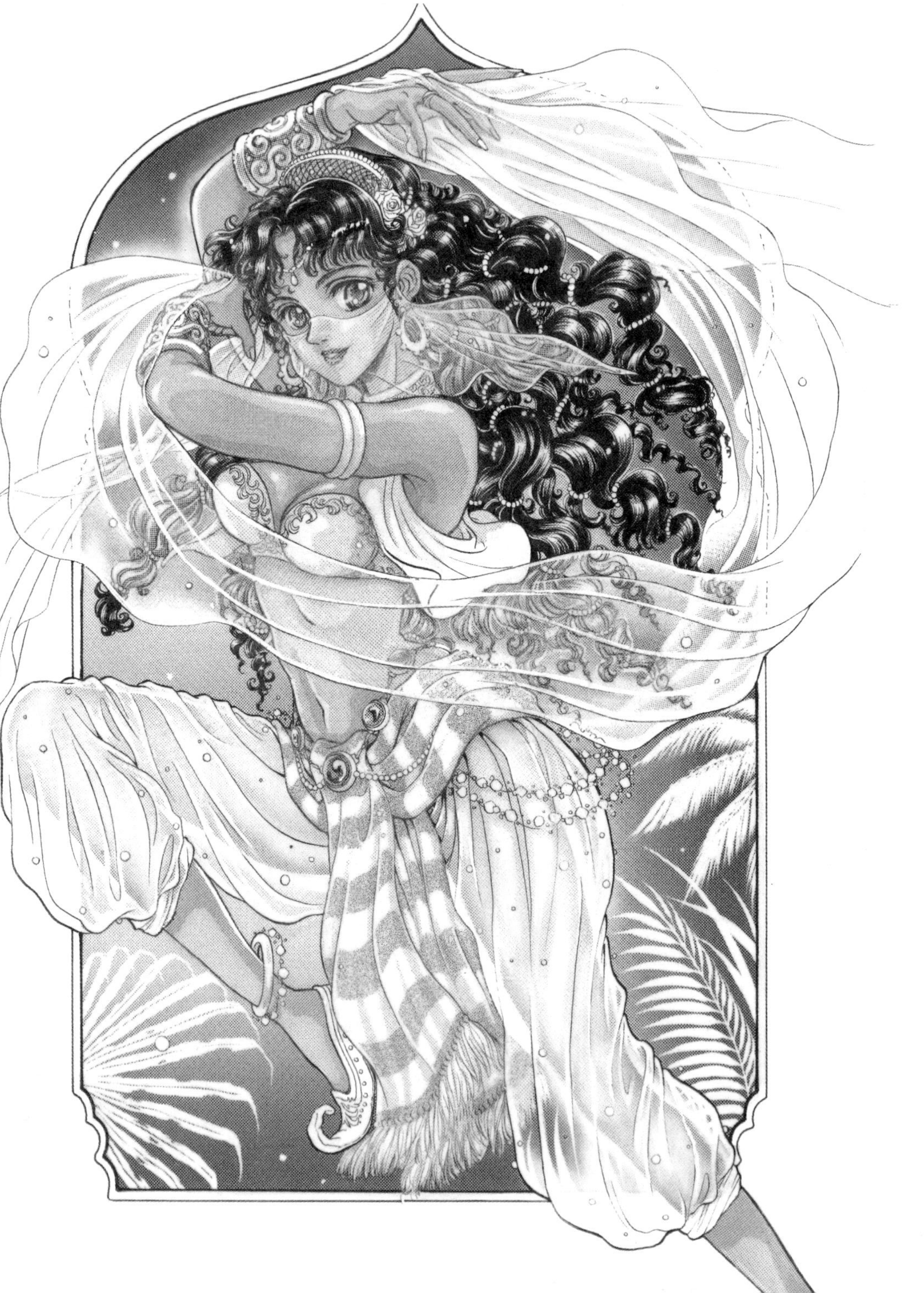

MYTHICAL MAIDEN

by Minoru Aki

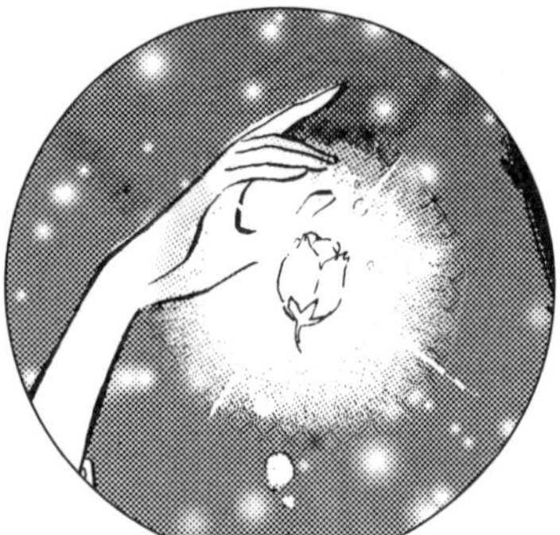

The tone of this etched item was gradated in a circular fashion. With the flower in the center, the slanted cross is drawn using white. This is a basic, yet, eternal technique. Notice how the shadow tone around her hand is also circular.

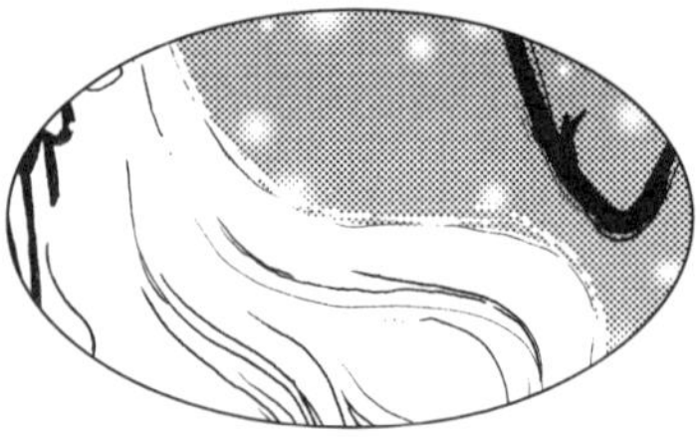

The line of the hair has been delicately drawn with white over the background tone. With dark, dreamy backgrounds such as this, not only does this effect convey fluttering motion of the hair; it serves to visually direct a mystic gleam.

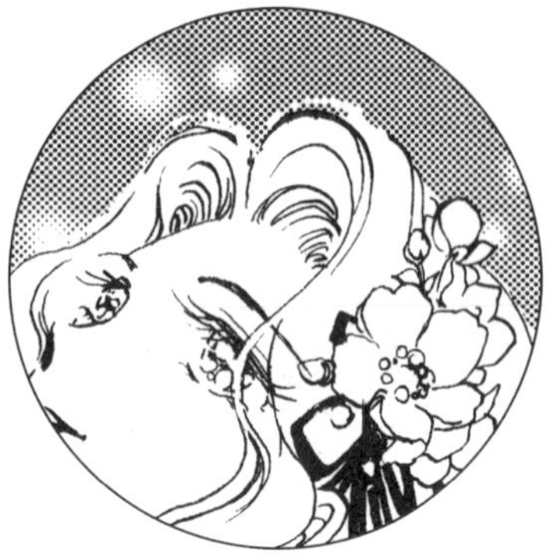

Additional areas to add white to the hair: 1) directly above the forehead, 2) along the curves and 3) along the line that covers the eye.

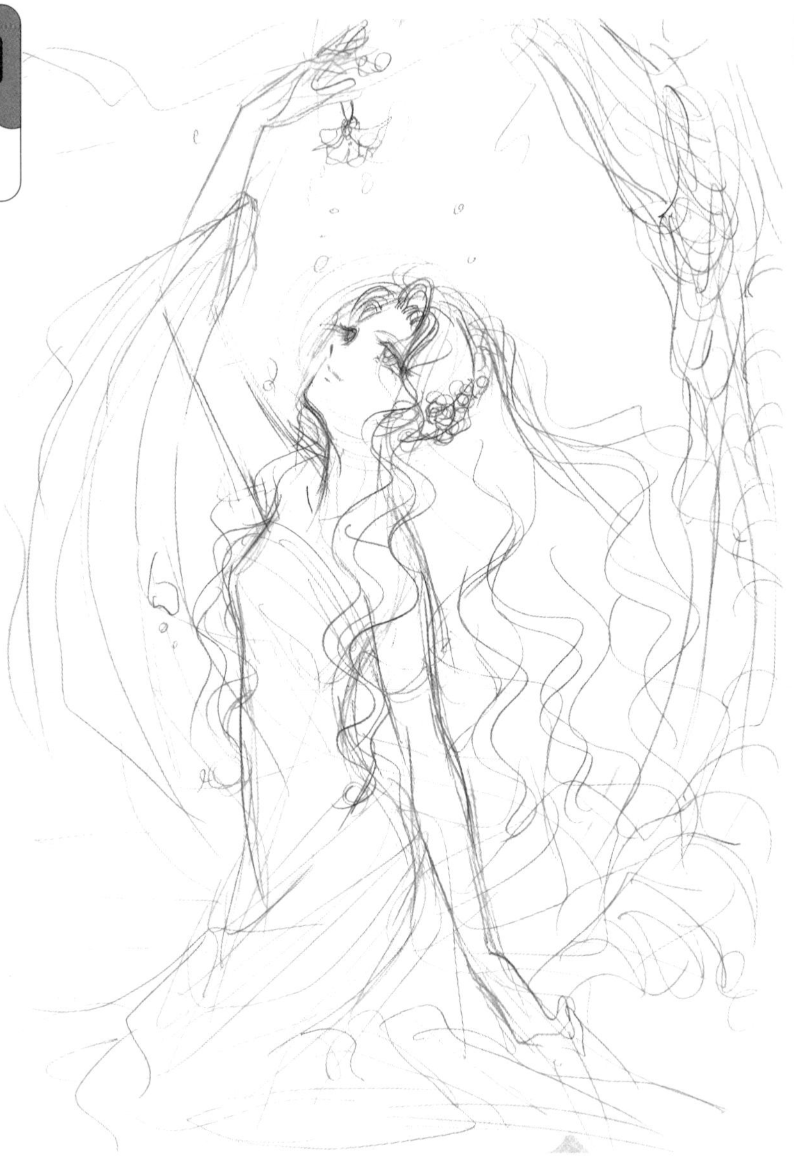

Caucasoid Type Characters Go Well With Mythical Maidens

Aside from the chest area, the wrinkles of the dress have been abbreviated as much as possible. By erasing the outline of the abdomen area here and there using white, the brilliance of the character and surrounding light are visually directed, bringing a sense of mystery onto the page. The long wrinkle lines stretched from the hip to the legs convey the comfort of the outfit while the short lines express its texture. Moreover, notice how the lines of the fine, wavy hair, the wrinkles in the dress and shawl are all drawn with different touches. The delicacy and softness of the hair and the feel of the fabric is brought about even without having to use tones.

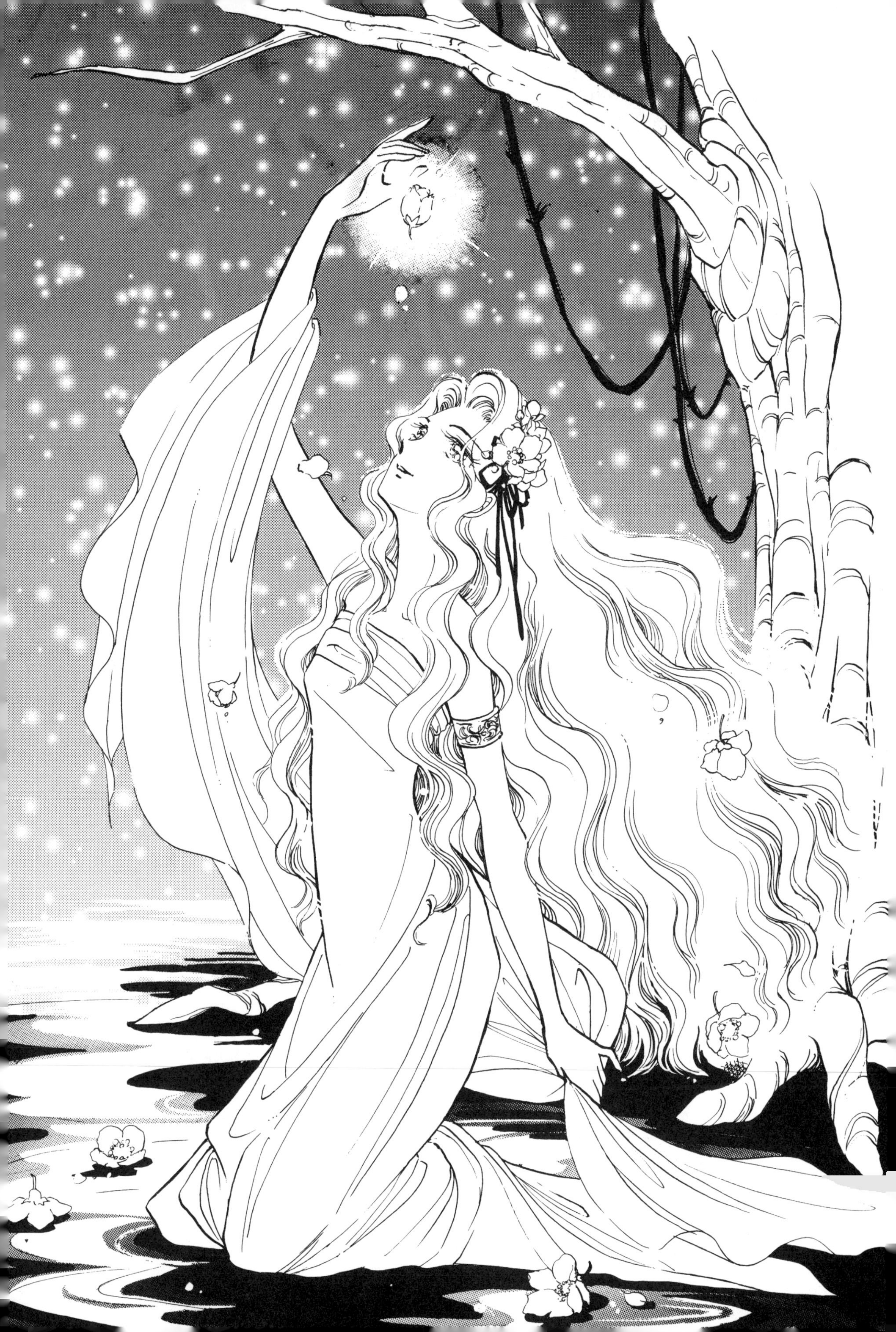

WILD SEXY

by Kimiko Morimoto

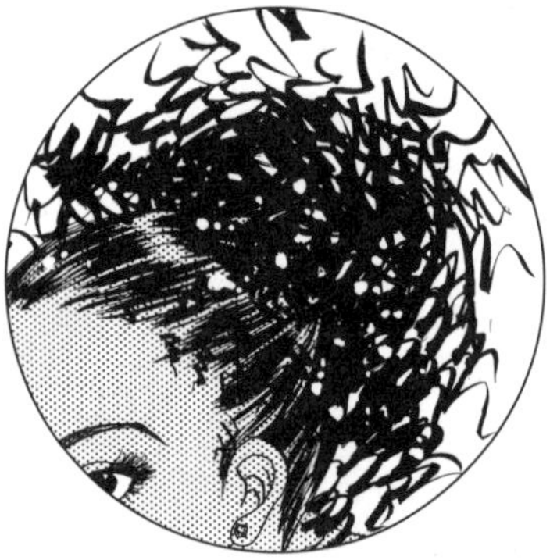

Vigorous lines express the hair being pulled back while rough lines are used for the bundled area. A brush pen was used for both. White was used for the spots in the hair and the feathers around the chest acting as an accent and contrast. While the technique is nonchalant, it is comes in very effective.

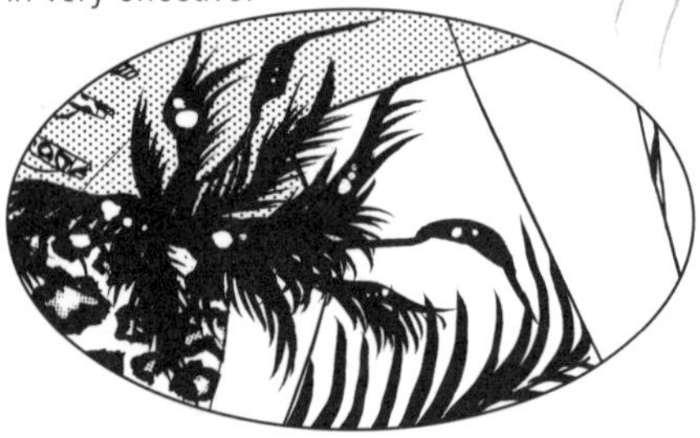

Each crow-feather, as seen in the illustration below, stems out from a single line.

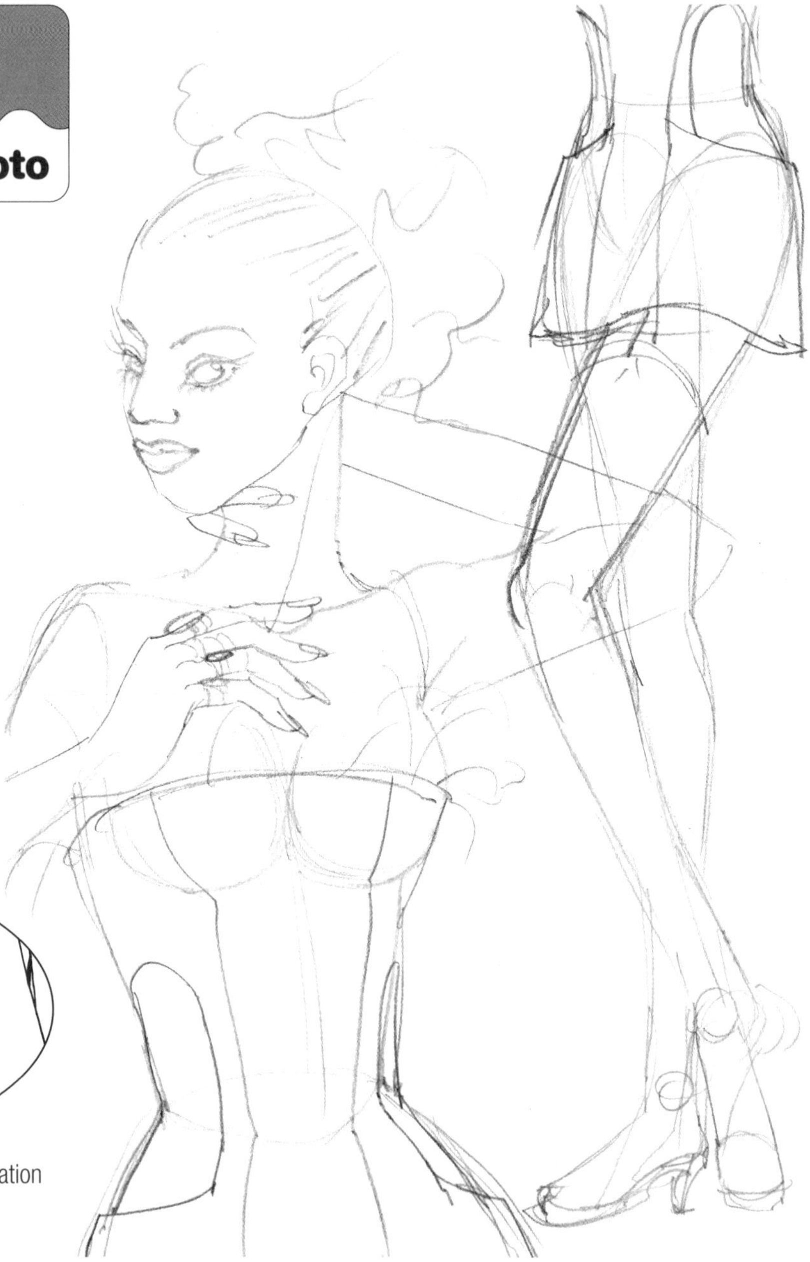

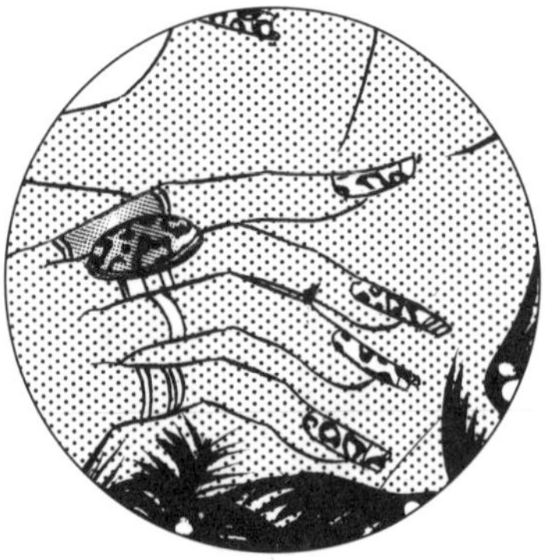

The boldly executed nail art based on the leopard pattern on the dress, combined with the matching large ring, express a wild, voguish nature

Nude Rough Sketches are the Key to Showy Fashion

Quite often in manga, the drawings are such that the clothing is indistinguishable from the character's body. It almost appears as if it is pasted on to the body. As in this illustration, the key to drawing clothing with openings around the waist and hip area is to clearly draw separate levels. By doing so, it brings out the presence of both the body and the clothing thereby leading to an impressionable character. While this may sound obvious, always keep in mind that the clothing is worn over the naked body. The figure should be drawn first followed by the clothing.

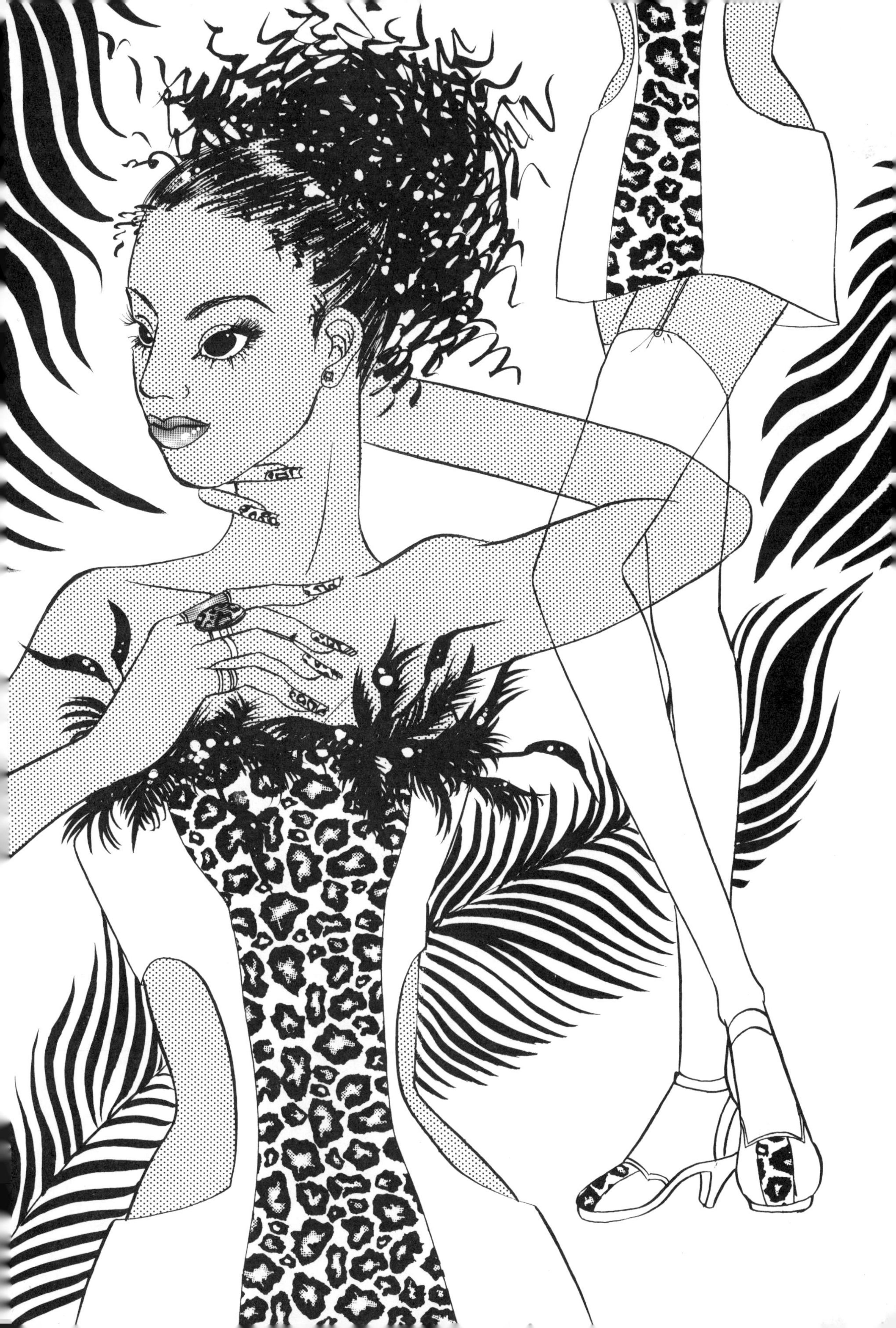

ELEGANT KNIGHT

by Yuu Fujio

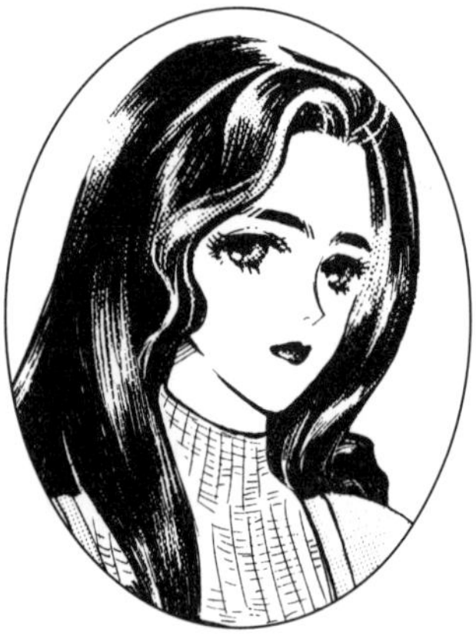

Note this brunette with gentle, wavy hair. Keeping in mind how the light strikes, carefully draw each strand of hair while incorporating light and shade to create volume. Bring out the charm by attaching a tone # 1, etching it here and there while also using white in places.

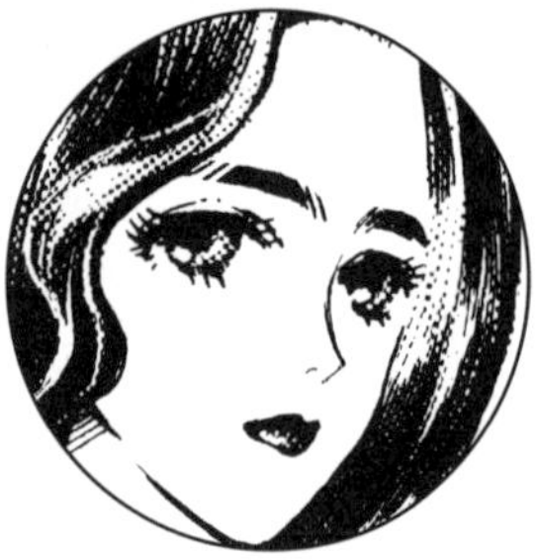

Neatly fill the upper lip using black. Add a gradation tone for the lower lip. By doing so, you can visually direct soft, sexy lips.

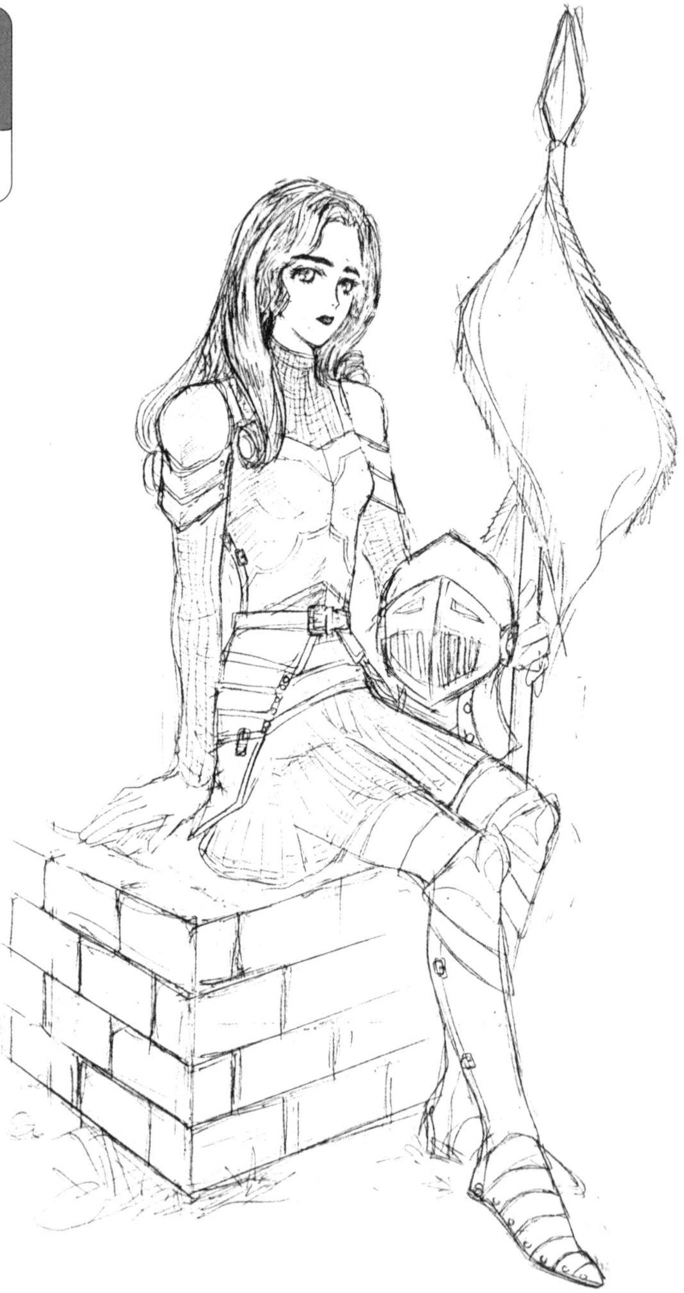

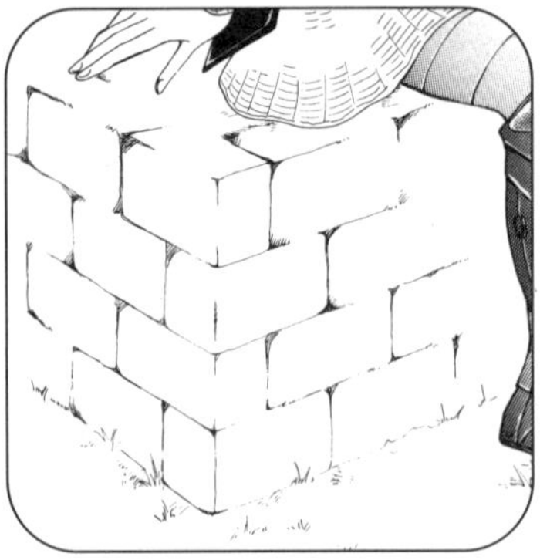

Notice how some areas of the bricks are abbreviated. By using these bricks as props drawn in the manner described, they serve to further bring the character into prominence.

Express the Delicate Physique with Small Torsos and Waists

Wide shoulders are symbols of authority and intimidation. Use this when you want the character to possess masculine traits such as a knight or a warrior. Put simply, women with wide shoulders such as models give a "cool" impression. In order to compensate for the rugged image possessed by the armor, the character must possess a delicate image in reverse. This is made possible by drawing the girl to have a thin torso. Since the armor is wrapped around her body and legs, it reflects the curved surfaces of her physique that brings out the delicate, feminine nature. Moreover, as the tone used for metallic expression is not too deep, it allows the armor to shine in an airy fashion thereby dramatically reducing the weighty image.

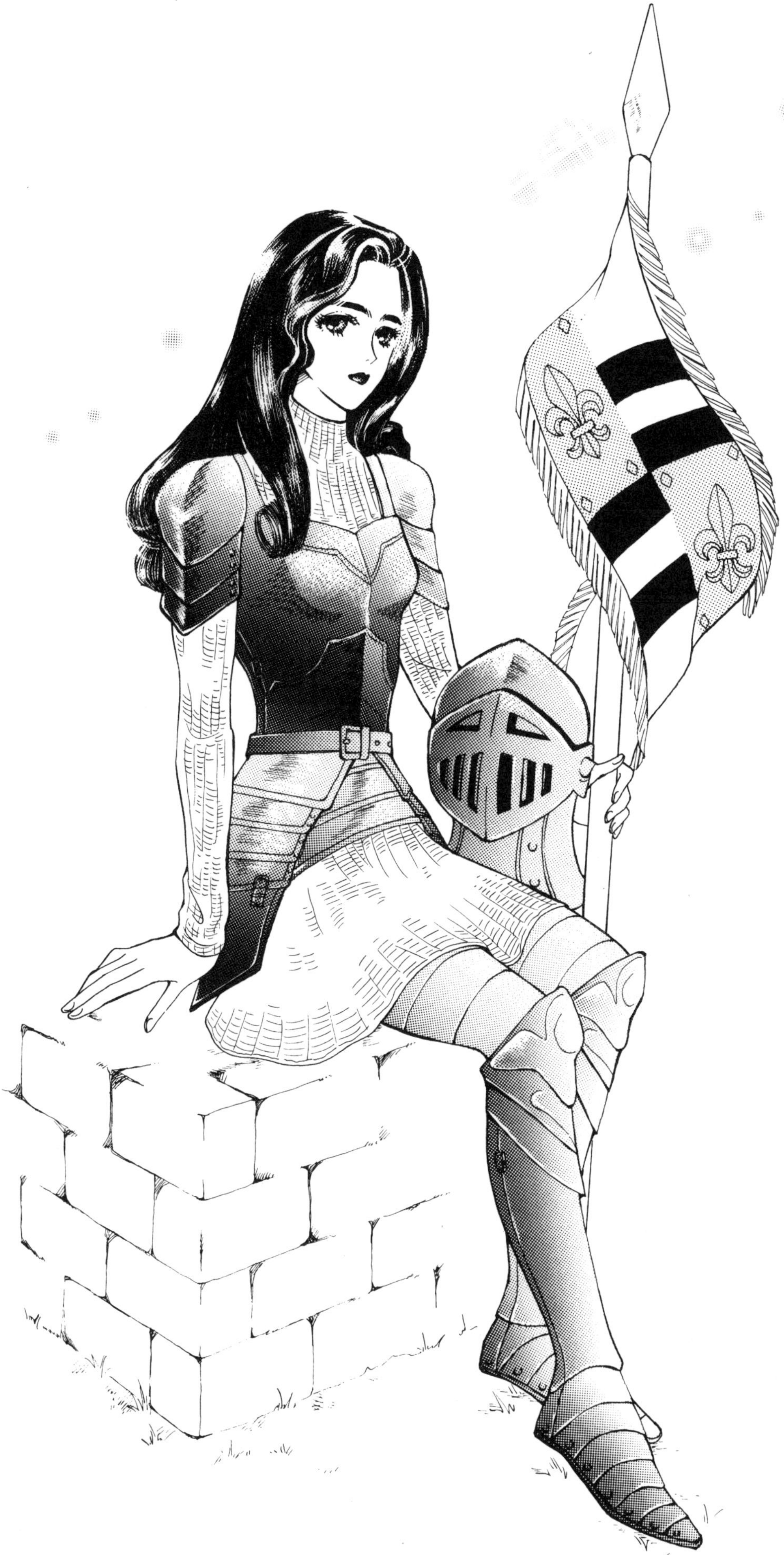

PIN-UP GIRL

Takashi Nakagawa

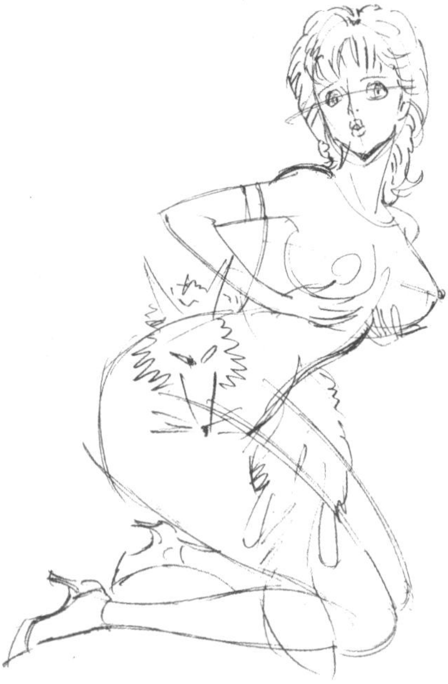

Simple lines capture the flow of the bodyline in this rough sketch. The key is to draw while visualizing the pose in its entirety.

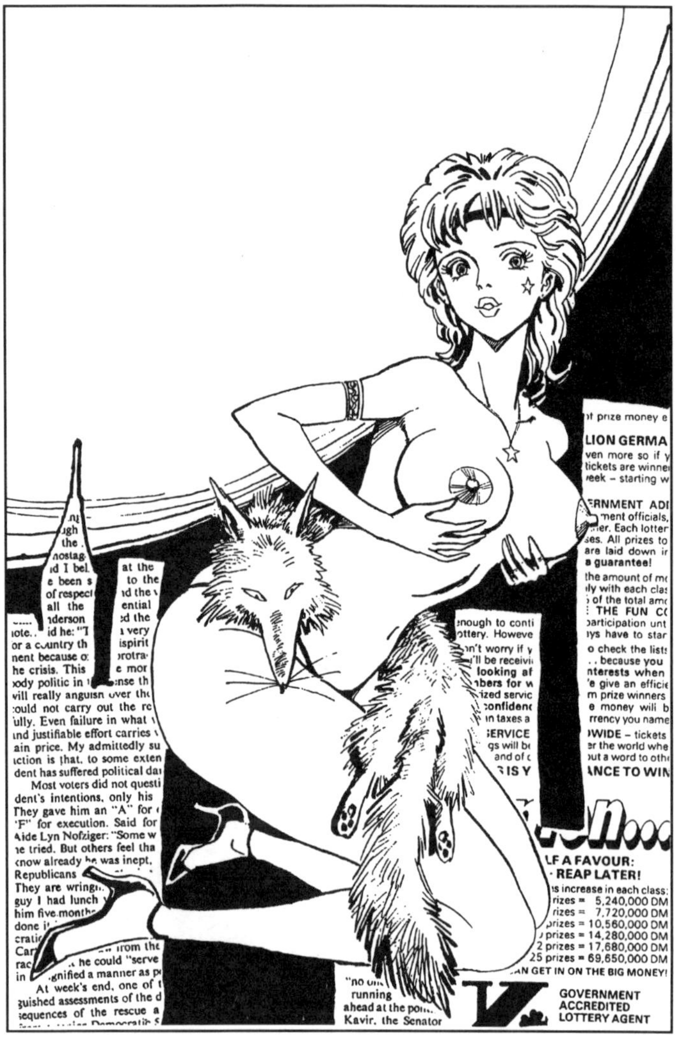

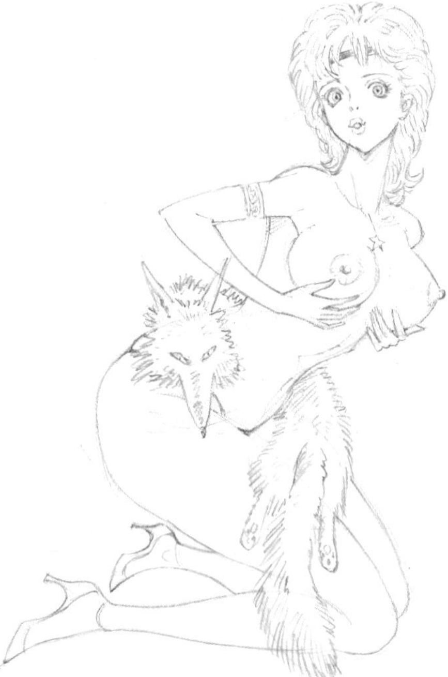

Finished outline

The Key to Drawing her Cheerful, Pop Expression is in the Eyes and Deformed Lips

Thick puckered lips can visually direct pop-looking girls. The pupils are relatively small in comparison to the wide-open eyes. Slightly widening the distance between the eyes gives an openhearted, cheerful image to the character. After expressing the basic three-dimensionality through the use of lines both thick and thin, strong and delicate, management techniques that can only be performed on a PC were then carried out.

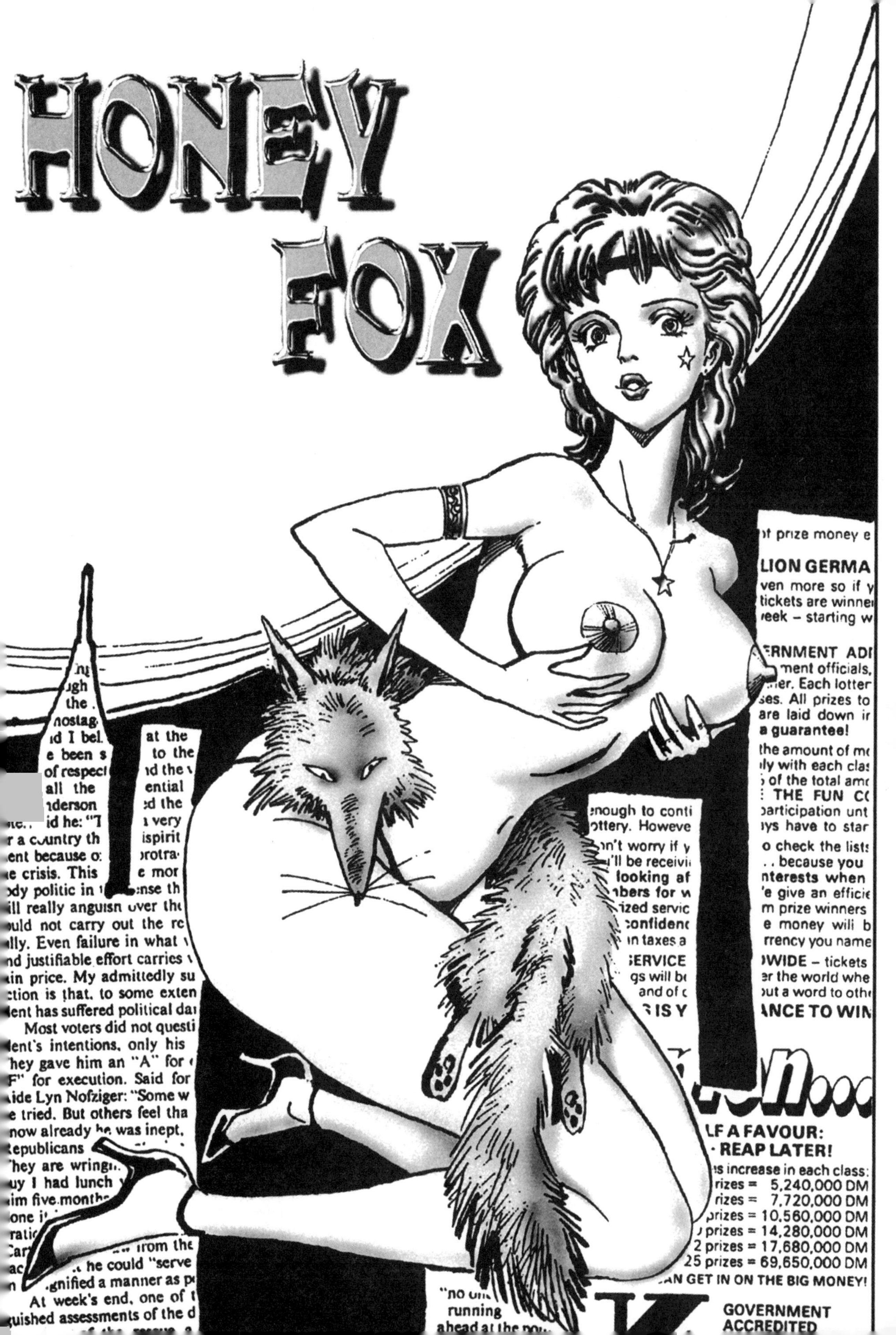
HONEY
FOX
LION GERMA
tickets are winne
a guarantee!
THE FUN C
Most voters did not questi
for execution. Said for
Lyn Nofziger: "Some w
LF A FAVOUR:
REAP LATER!
5,240,000 DM
7,720,000 DM
10,560,000 DM
14,280,000 DM
17,680,000 DM
69,650,000 DM
GET IN ON THE BIG MONEY!
GOVERNMENT
ACCREDITED

ARABIAN NIGHT

by Keiko Shiono

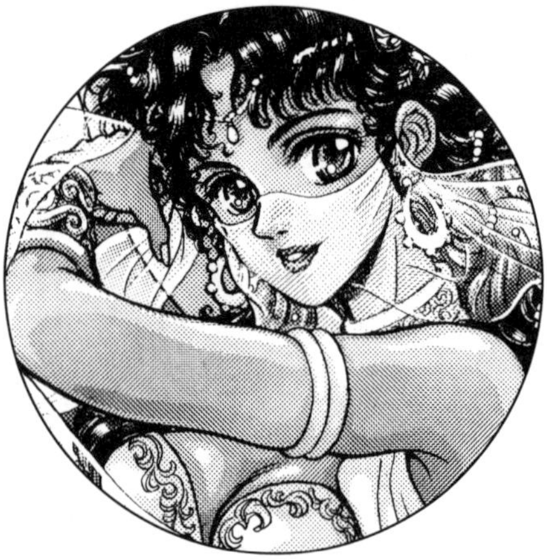

Layering three tones brings out the three-dimensionality of the arms and breasts. By cutting out the white sections where the light strikes, the quality of the roundness of the arms and lustrous skin can be expressed at the same time.

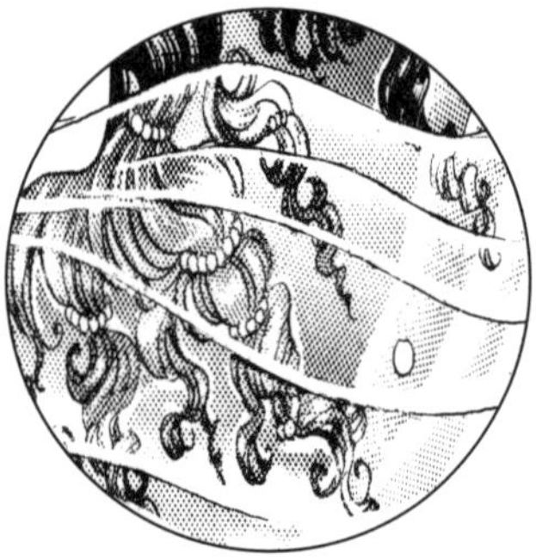

The parts of the hair behind the waving shawl were done using a thin gradation tone. Adding white along the lines of the wrinkles increased the feeling of transparency.

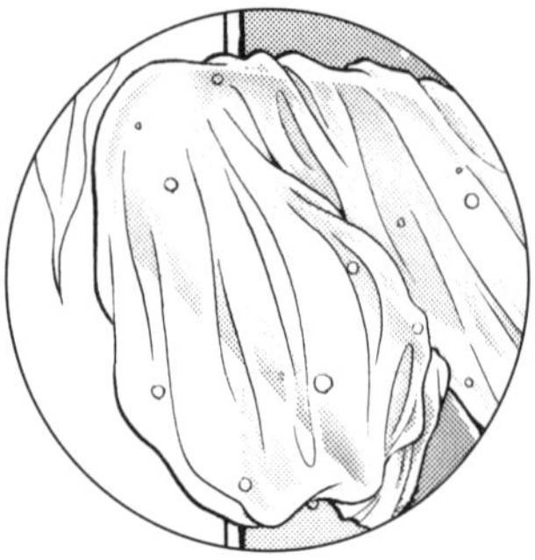

The artist chose to express the legs through the use of tones instead of actually drawing the outline. Gradation is on the lighter side. Heavier tones were attached on the outer areas while the middle areas were both whitened and gradated through the use of an eraser.

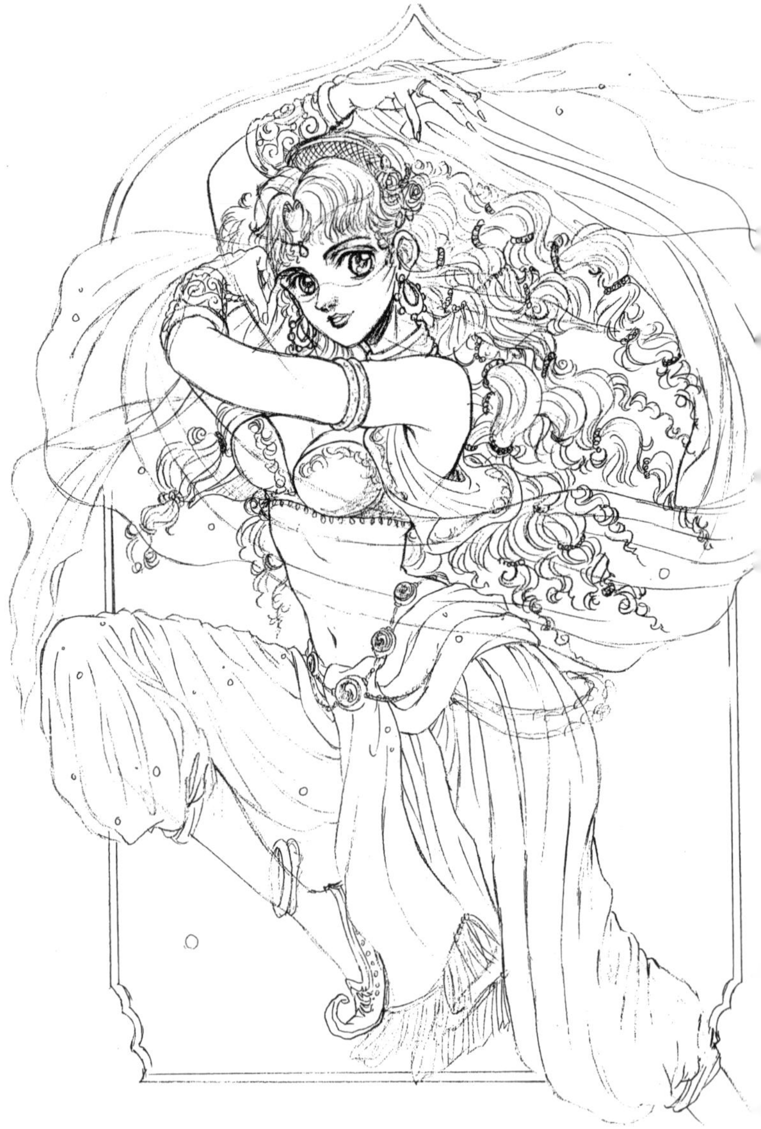

The Contrast of Laying Tones Brings Out Three-Dimensionality

Gorgeous hair can be visually directed by adding a glossy expression into each tuft of the wavy hair. The pearl trimmings drawn around the bundled points are also effective. Aside from the chest and arms, the rest of the body was done with two layered tones. Cut out white sections are always near all layered areas. In this way, the mid-range colors between light and dark are effectively expressed together with three-dimensionality. Also, by attaching tones along the lines of the curved surfaces in the pattern of the clothing wrapped around the waist, the swelling of the clothing is expressed. In addition, the silhouette of the plants in the background was done with gradation tones that have been technically etched into the shape of leaves. Compounded with the visual direction of the window frame drawn with Arabian architecture in mind, a sense of luxury and mystery are brought to life.

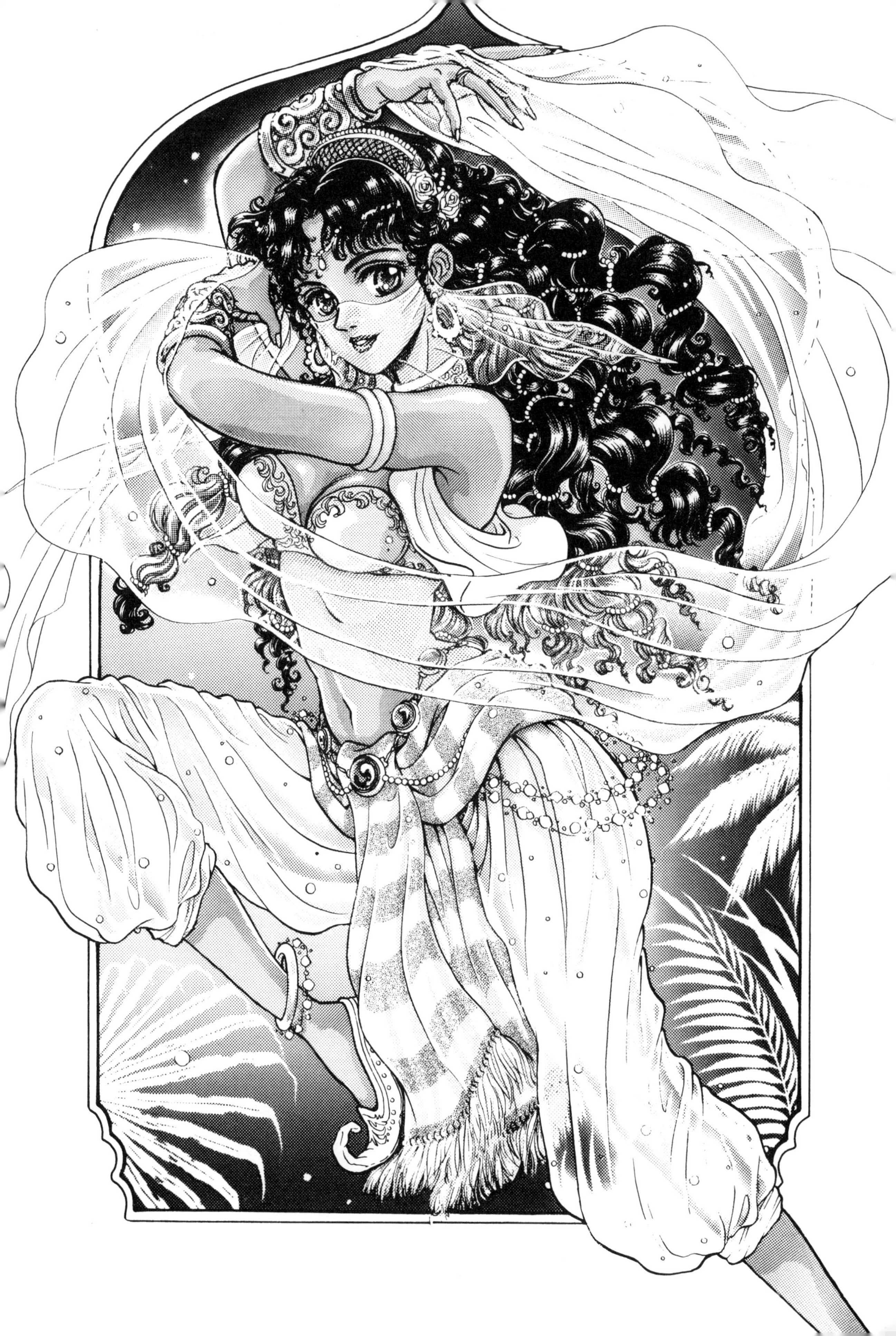